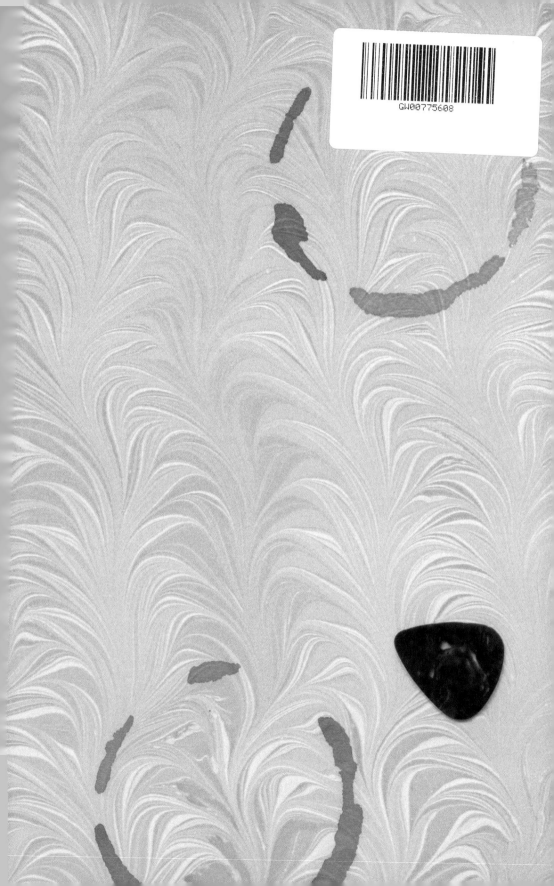

# Off the Pegg

*bespoke memories of a bass player*

by
Dave Pegg
*with*
Nigel Schofield

First published 2018
by Pegglets

Typeset in Abobe Garamond Pro
and Gill Sans.

ISBN 978-1-9996787-0-8

Off the Pegg
is dedicated to
Ava May
&
Austin Ocean
from Grandad

*May all your wishes be attainable*
*and all your dreams come true.*

# CONTENTS

# PREFACE

by

### Ralph McTell

*Few would believe it*
*If we told all we have seen*
(from *Clear Water* by Ralph McTell)

DAVE PEGG ("Peggy") and I first met when he was 19 and I was 22. It was at Digbeth Town Hall and he was in the resident band called the Ian Campbell Folk Group. I was a young soloist and although I remember playing there, I think Dave and I were too shy to get to know each other that evening.

I have always had a fascination for the bass both electric and upright and in 1971 I was lucky enough to hook up with Danny Thompson on double bass whilst still being aware of its electric cousin. The name I most frequently heard associated with that instrument among our contemporaries was that of Dave Pegg.

The first album I recorded with 'peggy-on-the-bass' was *Streets* for Reprise records and our bond of friendship was firmly established and water-tight from then on. So much so that his wife Christine became a little perplexed at the intensity and strength of our friendship and occasional risk-taking. Like me, Dave was married. His teenage sweetheart Christine and he had two children and were trying to raise them on the pittance produced by playing 'folk music'.

Nanna (my wife) and I also had two children and as young families we had a lot in common in so far as we were both raised by working class parents who had a certain dignity which in spite of low income, separation, bereavement or even poverty had a morality that was handed down to us along with respect for them and others. I don't know but I am willing to bet Dave went to Sunday School and whether or not we believe in anything today those ethics are still there in both of us which serves to be part of the cement in our outlook on life, it also added a great deal of excitement as we relished temporarily and permanently breaking a few rules later on.

I still call 'Peggy' Dave. I suppose mainly to underline our special relationship and probably I am the only one left to call him by his given name. The reason being that everyone Dave knows regards him as their best friend: this is both his gift and occasional burden. He manages to make everyone feel special and partly through necessity, partly through geniality the word networking could have been invented for him. He really does seem interested in even the vaguest peripherals to do with all aspects of music sound and presentation.

6

At the time of writing this I have still to read most of this book but knowing him like I do, it will probably emphasise the positive and play down the negative. It will concentrate on optimism rather than the darker days and experiences, also it will definitely be incredibly modest about his ability as a musician.

There have always been fiddles and the like in folk music especially in these islands but bass playing along with the addition of drums and electricity is what produced the new sound which we take for granted today. The fact that Dave can play complex fiddle melodies on this monster fret board is testimony to his dexterity alone but it is his harmonic interpretations, counterpoint, tone, rhythm and swing that provide the base fabric for all that is layered on top. He is also an excellent guitarist and mandolin player.

His tremendous bass playing was born out of Dave's deep love of rock and roll and respect for all good music. He is also very discerning, not so much in terms of genre but of the spirit and soul of music in general. I have grown to love our British and Irish traditional music and I love to hear old favourites but equally I am quite content to marvel at what Dave hears and plays in these familiar tunes.

As younger men our families spent several holidays together in my place in Cornwall where we drank copiously played until very late and took inordinate quantities of snuff (not the white stuff) which was enjoyed in excess by several of the old regulars at the local pub. We also have a treasured bit of footage of our kids all playing music in the garden and once we managed to get all ten of us from the beach in our old Citroen.

One year Dave had passed the audition to work in the band known as Jethro Tull. He devoted his whole holiday while the rest of us were playing on the beach etc laying on a narrow double bed in our back room with his earphones on and the bass lying across his body as he painstakingly learned all the tortuous time signatures and stops on the complex tunes that he would soon be playing out on the road. It's one of the tales herein, so I'll leave it to Dave to flesh out the details. True to form, he became Ian Anderson's friend too and spent fifteen years working with them which gave more security to his family than all the previous time in music.

Dave's first love has always been and continues to be FC. It has been a hard road to hoe but there has been a rich quality to the life of the band that few could equal and most would envy.

I love to play with Mr. Pegg and luckily for me I have albums to prove it and getting on stage at Cropredy is always a buzz for me.

Folk music seems to have a soft image but nothing could be further from the reality that this band has lived through. To my mind it makes most rock'n'rollers look like a bunch of weak posie chancers. As I have hinted there have been demons, angels, deaths and entrances, passion and pain that these once very young innovators had to navigate through. All lives are like that but in music it tends to be heavier or more underlined and perhaps it is because the songs are traditional and have no ego attached to them that individual egos occasionally wrestle for attention or because the new songs are not primarily written for commercial gain, they carry such a heart-rending honesty rooted in narrative that they actually mean something and are so powerful.

Through FC we glimpse a true, inspiring, dangerous and eventful journey where whirling stars, and fleeting sparks, illuminate their and our journey through music, darkness and humour, rooted to reality by the bass playing and humanity of my mate Dave.

# Prelude
## Folks, kids, grandchildren
### *On the fourteenth of May, at the dawn of the day*

It's six months on from September 2017, when Peggy and I spent the month recalling, reminiscing and recording the conversations that make up the majority of this book. That was in Brittany. Since then I've written up Peggy's narrative and dispatched the text to him for doublechecking. During a couple of weeks in Spain (on the first day of which Ralph McTell rang me to discuss his preface – strange to be wandering through the narrow alleys of a mountain-top pueblo blanco holding such a conversation: let me grab you by the ear and lead you through the streets of Monda…), I checked all my recordings lest something had been missed. One cut stood out – 30 minutes long – labelled "family, Steph, Matt".

Here's a transcription:

**Peggy:** Right. Where do you want to start today?

**Nigel:** Some more personal stuff, if that's OK. Steph and Matt have hardly been mentioned.

**Peggy:** Really? I thought we'd talked a fair bit about them?

**Nigel:** Yes, but not for the book. We haven't really recorded anything.

**Peggy:** We should. You're right! Do you fancy a coffee before we start?

**Nigel:** Does the sanglier eat truffles? Black, sugar.

Then follows the sound of the coffee machine injecting steam, shuffling of papers and a Breton voice calling through the open door. Peggy welcomes his visiting neighbour, introduces me, offers coffee and seamlessly slips in 'mon hôte' mode. The hard drive, like our bus, rolls on, capturing 29.5 minutes of side-mike conversation, noises off and distant birdsong. It then shuts down automatically and saves the result. Shortly afterwards we were in the car heading down to the coast for lunch.

As soon as I discovered the omission, I informed Peggy, who said that Ralph had mentioned that he should include some family stories, particularly about his younger life.

With a plan to meet up in Banbury on Bonny Black Hare Day (The 14th of May) to finalise details of the text and produce a final edit of this book, it was important to have this in place While we were working on the book, Peggy was making arrangements for a hip replacement operation. Old hippy gets new hip shocker! With the operation successfully completed and some recuperation prescribed, he was in the ideal position to plug the gap.

Getting my first guitar changed my life and I could never thank Albert and Beatrice, my folks, enough for the sacrifices they made on my behalf. Working-class Brummies who raised me in a council house in Tavistock Road , Acocks Green, they were teetotal, very Christian parents who encouraged me to go to Sunday School every week and to join the cubs and later the scouts. I really enjoyed the camaraderie as a member of Kestrel Patrol , Birmingham Pitmaston 178th group  and later went on to be a patrol leader!

Mom called my dad "Lal" and my earliest memories of dad were of him coming home from work as a carpenter at a factory named "Seats (Birmingham) Ltd.". They made wooden lavatory seats and from the residue wood they'd cut out made those wooden yacht table lamps that you can still sometimes find in carboot sales. My step-brother John also worked there and lost the end of a finger on one of the machines. Albert had remarried after John's mom passed away.

My first memories of John are when he came home on leave from the RAF: he had been to the fair and won some coconuts and asked me to choose one. I went for the biggest one and he went through several reasons why biggest is not always the best that I still remember to this day.

John had several jobs after the lavatory-seat factory. He moved to Cardiff to take over management of a Boyds' TV-rental shop in Splott (a placename that always tickles me). Despite its comic sound in English, the name is merely a contraction of the Welsh Y Sblot, which means 'surrounded by marsh'. That's exactly how the ancient village is described in its Domesday Book entry.

John was a huge Shirley Bassey fan and ironically got to meet her mother when he had to knock on her door to repossess the TV. This was due to late rental payments!

John went on to be a great pub manager and had some nice pubs as well as some dodgy ones. I suppose you could call him a "romantic". It was sometimes hard for us to keep up with his comings and goings. His kids, despite his marital excursions, all matured well and come to Cropredy every year. Jazz Stott, Ian and Honey Pegg's son, does a great job along with dad Ian building the site. My brother had a stroke last year and sadly never recovered: his ashes are scattered beneath Jonah's Oak. He had a good send off with his son Anthony and daughters Honey and Lorraine attending the service in Banbury. Pete Watkins "The Human Jukebox" and myself performed one of John's favourite songs. Pete who is a lovely singer had been kind enough to go to Banbury's Horton Hospital and sing to John during the last days of his life.

I miss my brother, despite his voting for Brexit!

My folks weren't well off. Mom worked at a sewing factory in Acocks Green village making pyjamas and night dresses on "piece work" rates. You were paid according to how many pairs you produced by the end of the day. She would also work at home on her Wilcox and Gibbs sewing machine and when she had the required number of garments put me in the seat behind her on her pushbike and cycled to the factory to hand them in and get paid. I can remember the noise in that building from thirty women all rattling away as fast as they could, making winceyette pyjamas. When I went to school mom would work there and I reckon that her early deafness problems were probably due to that noise. She was a great seamstress and made a lot of my clothes and even outfitted our band The Exception one time. More about that later!

Despite not being very well off my parents were keen travellers and camping allowed them to holiday away from Brum. Their early mode of transport was a tandem with me in the sidecar! I remember holidays in Barmouth, ("Brum-by-the-sea") as it was the nearest seaside resort and had loads of camping sites. A big brown army tent would be sent by train to be collected three or four days later from Barmouth station. Lal and Beattie would then pack a small green ridge tent and basic camping gear, strap me into the sidecar and off we would go. They would ask farmers en route if they could camp for the night: when, after a few days, they collected the big Army tent we would head for

Towyn and a proper campsite. The tandem did have the benefit of a little motor which would kick in on uphill stretches, but they must have been pretty knackered by the time they got to Wales.

The tandem came to a sticky end one Saturday afternoon outside Birmingham market when – with me in the sidecar – the wheels had caught in the tramlines and the tandem (and nearly the Pegg family) were wiped out! Dad eventually got an Austin van which he converted by fitting side windows and a double rear passenger seat.

Travelling on holiday by tandem imposes its own restriction – suitable roads, distance, energy levels: however, a car (albeit a van conversion) naturally means "magical mystery and your journey has only just begun." The Peggs travelled further afield, including a place where I spent several summers of my late teens running children's camps.

The van meant that we were able to have more holidays and being very religious the folks started taking me to Cliff College in Calver in the Peak District. This was the Methodist preacher training college and dad who was a lay preacher loved to meet, talk and attend the prayer meetings there. He befriended many young preachers and would take us to places like Southport and Rhyl to support them on their beach campaigns. Albert would play the accordion: he had a lovely singing voice and would be there spreading the word. I knew most of the hymns in the blue Sankey's Sacred Songs and Solos off by heart. My memory of this hymn-book only failed me once when Christine and I attended Matty Habberjam's wedding in the north of England along with Simon, Rob and Barbara Braviner and about twenty other people in the church. I didn't recognise any of the chosen hymns: none of the congregation was able to sing along. Just the vicar's voice and the organ were audible.

The days when Southport and Rhyl seemed like exotic faraway lands are well behind me now. Thanks are due to dad and mom for giving me the urge to travel and to a Fender bass guitar for the magic carpet which has allowed me to see most of the world at other people's expense!

We worked on this book in September 2017 in the *longere* in Lesteno where Peggy spends as much time as he can with Ellen, who's been his partner for the last dozen years. However, it was his childhood sweetheart who became his first wife and a key figure in the survival of Fairport and the development of Cropredy Festival after 1980.

My ex-wife Christine and I met at Grammar School and became lovers at the tender age of 15. When our daughter Stephanie heralded her arrival, we decided we would marry. I hasten to add that we did want to get married despite only being 19 years old. I was playing in the Uglys at the time.

Our wedding reception was held at Ray and Jean Pouncey's house in Sheldon. Jean is Christine's older sister. Roger Hill was the best man at Brum Registry Office and turned up ten minutes late driving the "Ugmobile", a blue Commer van that had previously belonged to the Moody Blues. The van was covered in girly lipstick graffiti and Roger was wearing a "British beer drinking team" T-shirt. Chrissy and I lived with my folks up until we moved to The Angel in Little Hadham to be with the Fairports.

That was right at the start of 1970; Peggy's first year as a Fairport was one so eventful it is the only year of his life to merit its own chapter herein.

My folks were great to us and babysat Steph whenever we asked. When Fairport went to the USA for a six week tour, Steph stayed with them. She really loved her grandad and vice versa. Life at The Angel was interesting to say the least for a three-year-old and Steph learned some interesting vocabulary from Mr. Swarbrick for sure. Steph was fascinated by Richard and spent lots of time hanging about by his door listening to him play his harmonium or guitar. She certainly had music thrust at her at an early age and, though she never became a musician herself, finished up after university working in Public Relations for Leister Dixon whose clients included Tina Turner, The Rolling Stones, Plant & Page, Steve Winwood, and many famous performers. I am sure she wasn't too phased by artistic temperament after her Fairport experiences over the years. Steph crops up throughout the Fairport story, though not in ways that might be obvious. The little girl running across the picture that fills the gatefold of *Full House*? That's Steph, taken in the "garden" behind The Angel. That's Steph. The young woman featured in the slide show Peggy made to accompany *The Hiring Fair*? That's Steph, photographed in the fields near Cropredy. Peggy's son Matt, a bass player like his Dad, had a more obvious role when he stepped into the breach after Peggy seriously injured his finger: he joined the band for their Spring Tour and played bass on some of the first tracks recorded for *Myths and Heroes*.

Which meant when we began to play those songs live, I had to learn his parts. And he's a bloody good bass player, which is why I decided not to replace what he'd done with overdubs on the record, which would have been possible.

Matthew Pegg was born in Sutton Coldfield on a day when I was playing at the Eastbourne Congress Theatre with Fairport. I remember driving back at top speed in our purple Ford Cortina to get to see him and his mom.

With a growing family and Fairport's experiment in communal living proving a disaster on several fronts, it was clear the Peggs needed to think about buying their own place. Dave the Bass became a first-time-buyer… except not as Dave the Bass.

The Fairports were doing OK and Christine reckoned that we could get a mortgage and buy our own place if I could convince the building society that I had a 'proper" job'. "Ask Island Records to give you a reference saying you work for them as a Midlands sales rep", she suggested. Dave Domleo, a lovely chap at Island, wrote me a glowing reference and confirmed my 'so-called' salary. All was going well at the lenders' Walsall office until the 'suit' saw my profession. "How cool you work for Island", says he: "I see so-and-so's in the charts this week at number 16. How's so-and-so doing?"

Of course, muggins here hadn't a clue whom he was talking about and just recommended buying the current Fairport release. Despite this I got the loan and we bought our first house for £3k in Elms Rd, Sutton Coldfield.

It was a first home, but after a couple of years, they were on the move, a change of location that would be life-changing for them and the village they moved to.

We moved to Cropredy when Swarb was living there and found a house in Chapel Row for us: it cost £7000. We sold Elms Road, borrowed a little more money and moved to the countryside! As usual, I was absent, away gigging on the day of the move and poor Chrissy got lost leading the removal lorry from Brum to Cropredy. The removal guys couldn't believe we were moving to this run-down cottage from our "done up" suburban house. Later, being "bought off" by Vertigo and given the sum of £7000 each not to make any more albums helped us renovate the cottage.

It was in Cropredy that both my kids attended the primary school, where Matt got his first interest in music. Rob Jenkins and his brother and Matt formed their first band Aggressive Hardware. Swarb and I had brought red T-shirts bearing this logo from a shop in America and I suspect the shirts shrank in the wash but fitted the boys perfectly. They were very punk in their approach and I remember one of their first compositions was called *Cropredy boys are we*.

Matt taught himself the bass and was heavily influenced by Mark King of Level 42. I couldn't and still can't play "slap" bass and Matt got really good at it. As he grew older, though, he began to appreciate music from the 60s and 70s and loved Procol Harum. Eventually he joined them and we spent a fab seven weeks touring America together – him with Gary Brooker and co, travelling by bus, and me, with the Tull chaps, on the plane. Matt is a wonderfully tasty player and has played on many sessions and tours with the likes of Rick Wakeman, Francis Dunnery, Tull, Fairport and the Procols.

Stephanie continued her PR work, joined the WOMAD organisation and moved to Wiltshire when she married my good friend Mat Davies. Mat lived in Barford St Michael and worked from time to time at our studio. A fine bassist and mando player, he played with PJ Wright in Little Johnny England. Sadly, their marriage didn't work out but did produce the lovely Ava May Davies. Steph got to travel worldwide with the WOMAD organisation and is now settled in South Oxon with her new partner Tim.

Matt Pegg's marriage also didn't last too long and he found a new partner Tammy and they have a son Austin Ocean. They live in Eastbourne – the very town I was playing the night Matt was born.

My grandkids are a couple of very talented youngsters. Ava is very arty and hopefully is doing a portrait of me to use in this book. She is very much into drama and wants to be an actress or a film director or work at the RSC. I am sure she will get to Uni and get to play the bass too! She is good on the uke already!

Austin has his own Go-Kart and with Matt driving their truck/camper to various meetings he is doing very well at it. Scares me of course when I remember his dad doing motocross with our mate Clive Warner. Austin also loves being in the Air Cadets and already at age 13 has had five flying lessons. He is determined to be an airline pilot and I am sure will make it. I hope he will also play the bass to keep the Pegg bass tradition going.

I'm happy to report both my kids are doing well and have great kids of their own. I am, of course, proud of all of them.

I owe a lot to Christine as she has always given them unconditional love. Due to my being on the road most of the time, it was down to Chrissy to raise them and be the village taxi service. It was hard being away from home a lot of the time but I always worried that the gigs would run out and so never turned down the chance to work. It took its toll but did allow Christine and I to help our kids out financially and get them on the property ladder at an early age. Now I'm 70 and I am hoping to cut down on touring and spend more time at our house in Brittany. Spring is just so gorgeous here and so is summer. Cropredy is Fairport's big event and we tend not to do other festivals in order to keep that special. This means that Ellen and I get a long summer break and can fit our mini-fest "Festeno" in at the end of June.

I have a little sailboat here which I am hoping to get more use out of once my hip replacement is fully functional. Matt has been working so hard for the past few months repainting our yacht in Eastbourne. Sadly, it had 'Osmosis' and needed a complete stripping down. He coppercoated the hull and she will soon be back in the water. I hope that I will get a chance to do some sailing with Matt and the grandkids next year. Matt is a great sailor unlike his dad – as Ava will confirm!

The world for us old guys seems to be a pretty horrid place to be in at this time. I often think and worry about my kids' and my grandkids' future and what makes me feel happy is when my kids tell me that they will "sort it". They are confident that they and their offspring will cope with all the shit that goes on in the world today. I really hope they do.

It's a great honour for me to be able to put some of my life on paper and to have it read by your good selves. I have tried not to slag anybody off or to upset anybody on these pages. There are many mates and stories that are not mentioned, but maybe there will be a volume 2.
Volume 2?
VOLUME 2!
No one told me about a volume 2.

As long as Nigel who really has worked so hard putting this together can tolerate hearing my monotonal voice relating memories of mostly happy times in order to translate them from Brummy tongue to Oxford English!

## CODA – Catheter: a late insertion
While we were working on this book, Peggy was experiencing problems with his hip and was scheduled for a hip replacement operation in March. By the time we came to finish the book, the operation had gone well and one particular old hippy had a nice new hippy.

My hip's behind me now. Not literally, of course, otherwise I'd be having words with my surgeon! However, it does put me in mind of a time a while back when I was having a prostrate problem.
Hard to imagine Peggy with a prostrate problem. It's the position he naturally assumes after a good night's drinking!

The problem was sorted quite quickly and isn't an issue any more. It did mean a visit to hospital, though. I got a letter saying "We are to inform you that tests proved positive for prostate cancer, but we are going to give you this new treatment" (called Bracy Therapy). It went on to explain that I would need to go to the hospital in Reading, where they would fit a small catheter. I was worried when I began reading the letter, the more I read the more worried I became. I would at least have preferred them to say, 'a large catheter', small reminded me of my manhood issues.

Anyhow, where there's a willy, there's a way and I made arrangements for the appointment.

It was rather embarrassing having it fitted. The nurse was lovely and very reassuring. I just lay there on the trolley and thought of Brittany. Not Spears, for those listening to the audio book version. Little Brittany (with the emphasis on the first word). After she had fitted it, I had to go to X-ray, so they could have a proper look. They wouldn't be the first people to see through me!

The kind nurse said, "Mr Pegg, would you like me to walk you down? It's about three hundred yards and you may experience some pain."

I told her I was fine, got off the trolley and said "Just one request: Don't leave me this way: I can't survive", which got a laugh out of her.

It's a story with a happy ending and my advice to any of you who has to have a catheter fitted is 'just go with the flow'.

# The Pegg Bass-Line
*A chronology*

I found a timeline of Peggy's career useful in putting this book together.
We thought you might too.
This indicates the periods when he was in bands: clearly some existed before (and sometimes after) he was a member.

| 1947 | Born – November 2, Acocks Green |
|------|----------------------------------|
| 1961 | THE TRESPASSERS |
| 1962 | DAVE AND THE EMERALDS |
|      | THE CRAWDADDIES |
| 1965 | ROY EVERETT'S BLUESHOUNDS |
| 1966 | JIMMY CLIFF BAND |
|      | THE UGLYS |
| 1967 | THE EXCEPTION |
|      | WAY OF LIFE |
|      | THE IAN CAMPBELL FOLK GROUP |
| 1969 | THE BEAST |
|      | FAIRPORT CONVENTION |
| 1980 | JETHRO TULL |
| 1983 | THE COCKTAIL COWBOYS |
| 1995 | |
| 1998 | THE DYLAN PROJECT |
| 2007 | with PJ WRIGHT |
|      | |
| 2011 | with ANTHONY JOHN CLARKE |
| 2018 | |

# Nigel Schofield
## Peggy's co-author
### *Wizard of the Wordy Game*

Nigel has been writing professionally since 1970, the year in which he first interviewed Dave Pegg, around a year after he first saw Fairport (when Ashley Hutchings was still their bass player) and Peggy himself (twice as a member of the Ian Campbell Folk Group and The – as yet unnamed – Beast).

Nigel was reading English and Classics at St John's, Oxford at the time. Following his graduation, and several years working as a teacher, he became Head of Music at Pennine Radio in Bradford. Since this was at the point where Peggy was first promoting Cropredy Festival (and later Fairport's Woodworm releases), Nigel was able to provide valuable airtime for the band whose career he had closely followed for a decade.

Through the eighties and nineties, they maintained contact as Nigel wrote reviews and articles for and about the band. As the new century dawned he made Fairport the subject of the third release in Free Reed Records' Revival Masters box set series: *Fairport UnConventional* was the first Fairport box set – later box sets in the series feature Richard Thompson, Ashley Hutchings, Dave Swarbrick and the first 25 years of Cropredy Festival. In 2007, Nigel and Peggy collaborated on the four CD career retrospective *A Box of Peggs*. A couple of years ago, Fairport invited him to put his extensive knowledge behind the creation of their autobiography *Fairport on Fairport*. He is Fairport's official historian.

Aside from his Fairport-based work, he has written for several national newspapers and various rock and folk magazines; currently he is editor of Tykes' News. Eight years ago, he set up the Follow The Fleece company which stages drama and music productions that he writes and directs, in Yorkshire.

Beyond music, Nigel's hobbies include writing, walking and cooking (though not at the same time). He lives in the World Heritage Village of Saltaire with his wife Christine, whom both Nigel and Peggy would like to thank for her tolerance and patience during the realisation of this and other projects.

# Introduction
## Bass-ic Instinct
### *Oh What A Time We Had*

**"This volume goes to II."**

For a long time now, Dave Pegg has been promising – or should that be threatening? – to write a book of memoirs: I used that word in its most proper and literal sense. Anyone who has spent even a small amount of time in Peggy's company cannot fail to be aware of the wealth of stories he has to share from his fifty-odd years as a professional musician: Peggy is a great observer with an eye for the unusual, amusing and amazing, as you are about to discover. Best known as Fairport Convention's bass player, he fulfilled the same role in Jethro Tull for fifteen years, with parallel careers in both legendary bands for over a decade, not to mention jointly running with his then-wife Chris, Fairport's Cropredy Festival. One of the most respected bass-players in the world, and quite probably the most liked, he has also managed to fit in countless recording sessions with a galaxy of music legends, almost all of whom you will encounter herein.

In fact, this session work predates joining Fairport in 1970 to the time when he was a mainstay of the Brumbeat scene.

Aside from his Birmingham session work, he was also a member of Jimmy Cliff's New Generation, The Uglys, The Exception, Way of Life, The Ian Campbell Folk Group and The Beast: it's a typically eclectic mix that embraces, pop, psychedelia, rock, reggae, traditional folk, proto-metal and a power trio. Among those he worked with (to find out more, read on, dear Reader) – Robert Plant, John Bonham, Cozy Powell, Dave Swarbrick, Ian Anderson, Gary Brooker, Clem Clempson and Steve Gibbons, who single-handedly brings the wheel full circle, not only was he the main man in The Uglys, he is also the man behind The Dylan Project, the other band with whom Peggy has played bass for the last eighteen years.

Can't this man ever be satisfied with being in one band at a time?

Of course not – he loves to play and never turns down the opportunity to do so. He's a bassoholic! Thank goodness he has finally found the time to write this long-promised, and much anticipated, book.

Nigel Schofield

It all began with a short email, a couple of days after Fairport's Cropredy Convention 2016 – the 37th for those who are counting...

To:
From: Dave Pegg
Subject: My Book                                                    19.8.2016

I've been promising myself for years to start writing a book but have always worried that no one would be interested in reading it, as I am no great wordsmith and am also lacking in the fame department. I do however have a wealth of stories and anecdotes gathered over fifty years of a life in music and the many colourful characters that I have been lucky enough to bump into.

Many of my chums have been saying I should get a book together: still being on 'the right side of the turf' I reckon that now's the time.

Not sure of a title at this time but *Feeling a little Peggish* I quite like.

Luckily, I have a good friend in Nigel Schofield who helped put my CD box set together and wrote the Fairport Convention book *Fairport by Fairport*. He has kindly offered to help by reading and editing my efforts.

I will be using the *Box of Pegg's* CD set to soundtrack various events: if you don't happen to own this rare item, you can download various tracks, should you wish.

I suppose then I should call it *A Book of Pegg's*.

I really hope you enjoy this and ta for your interest.

Cheers,

Peggy

The plan had been simple, I had an archive of existing interviews on which I could draw. We could bring more together whenever we met. In the meantime, Dave could write or record his recollections and I could then edit and organise them. It simply didn't happen. As an approach, it was bitty and impersonal. Peggy is also a man much in demand professionally and personally. Walk with him through Cropredy (the village or the Festival), stay at any of the places he's lived for more than a couple of hours or hang around after any Fairport gig, and one quickly becomes aware of how in demand he actually is. If this book were to happen, drastic action would be needed. We had to closet ourselves away, at least for a few hours a day, over a defined period of time.

After a few abortive attempts to make a proper start on the book (no lack of willingness but a mutual lack of opportunity), we settled down a year later in Peggy's Brittany home. I clicked the recorder and he explained his reasons for wanting to do this book:

The reason I wanted to do this book is that I've read lots of books by musicians – I have to say the best in my opinion is Keith Richards' which I just couldn't put down – and I've got so many funny stories and anecdotes about things that have happened to me in my so-called professional life that I wanted to find a way to get them all together. They are stories I wanted to share – and I know most people who'd want to read this are Fairport fans and perhaps Tull fans. Those are the bands I've focused on – though not exclusively, by any means.

I'm glad Nigel agreed to do it because he understands Brummy and can translate it into the English written word.

My father Albert wrote a book when he was getting on – he was 81 when he wrote it. I have to say he was my hero. He was a working-class chap from Birmingham and when it was suggested he should make a will, he said there was no point because he had nothing to leave anybody. This was after my mum died and he became very ill and ended up in intensive care.

It was my ex-wife Christine who said 'You have got something to leave – you've got your life story – your memories'. It was her that pushed him into writing it all down – which he did long-hand: she then got it all typed up by Steph and bound copies were produced. It's a wonderful book and when you read it, you realise that it recaptures a time you can't know about unless you were there... or someone who was there takes the time to share it with you. There's a copy in Birmingham City Library that can be taken out for reference – I am genuinely proud of that fact.

Reading it, you realise it's not the big events that make up a life... though they are significant milestones, if you like: it's the everyday things, the little details, the unique bits and pieces, the road between those milestones that are really the important bit.

It's been a pleasure to sit with Peggy as he took me along the roads that make up his life... journeys which cover the length and breadth of Britain and extend across the world – America, Europe, Australia – not to mention the Hungarian Odyssey that he once celebrated in one of his few songs.
It's also a journey in time, spanning two centuries, leaping back and forth like Dr Who's SatNav. Inevitably there were Tull tales and Fairport recollections, but it's about much more than the two great bands he's most associated with: herein, you'll find rock legends from every era, the forgotten heroes and the unforgettable superstars of Brumbeat, famous folkies, local characters from Sutton, Oxfordshire and Brittany, fifties rockers, the many bands of which he's been a member, policemen, parrots and passing strangers.
Or as he once memorably put it

> *Finished our food and got into the wagon*
> *To drive eighty miles and then do a show:*
> *Five hours later, we're still busy trucking*
> *Banging and bumping; don't know where to go*
>
> *Oh what a time we had down by the Danube!*
> *Eating our goulash and drinking our wine*
> *Listening to gypsy bands playing cimbaloms*
> *Everyone's happy and things are just fine*
> (*Hungarian Rhapsody* © D. Pegg 1972)

Most of this book is based on conversations in the autumn of 2017, when Peggy and I spent four weeks dredging his fathomless memory banks. As a result, the book takes the form of a conversation in which I supply context for Peggy's memories. In addition to those recent conversations, I have also drawn on interviews I've done with him over the years: the earliest was for a student magazine in 1970; since then I've interviewed him for radio shows, rock and folk magazines, several Fairport-related projects and the official biography *Fairport on Fairport*. I have also, occasionally, drawn on conversations I've had over the years with various musicians with whom Peggy has worked.
But essentially it is HIS book and should have on the cover in big comforting letters DP – Don't Panic Peggy

Chapter 1

# Just a rôle in your Brum
*Truth in the wood and the wire*

There are many strands to Dave Pegg's career. In fact, while his name means a great deal to a large number of people across the world, their immediate recognition response varies. To some, myself included, he is primarily the bass player with Fairport Convention; others think of him as a member of Jethro Tull; he may be the chap that made Cropredy Festival happen (and in recent years one of the key figures in the operation of Fairport's Cropredy Convention) or a go-to session player. There are very focused, hard-core fans of the many bands he has been part of who think of him in that context – The Ian Campbell Folk Group, The Dylan Project, The Uglys, The Richard Thompson Band and so on. To everyone who knows him, even remotely, he is Peggy.

Personally, I would describe him as a loyal, honest and reliable friend, a connoisseur of good food and drink, a knowledgeable music fan, a raconteur with thousands of stories to tell. Before we began work of this book, at Peggy's home in Brittany, he lent me the biographical memoir written by his dad after he had spent a couple of weeks in that delightful part of North-Western France. A brief excerpt about Peggy's first band seems a good starting point:

> *"I was talking one day about David and the group having difficulty finding a rehearsal room to Jim, when he suggested they use one of the classrooms. They could be used on Monday nights from eight until ten o'clock. One night as I was going to see if they had finished, I had a shock as one of the teachers, Ted Sanders, was standing listening at the door. He asked who they were and said he thought they were good. I told him and he said he had a son at the School of Music who played violin. His son wanted to go into this type of popular music but both the teacher and his wife had a job trying to convince him it would be a waste of talent...*
>
> *"It's spreading all over the world, I can't see any stopping place, that's a big stage to play on," I replied. My son had told his headmaster this when he was advised that pop music had no future. Little did I realise that this teacher's son, Ric, and David were to play together in Fairport Convention. In fact at the time of writing they still do, small world isn't it?"*

My Dad was proud of me and supportive of what I have achieved over the years with various bands. The Emeralds were the band I had at school. I went to Yardley Grammar School.

The school was famous for some of its ex-pupils, notably Ian Campbell whose group I would eventually join, I was with them just before I joined Fairport. Dave Swarbrick was in the group before me, though our time there didn't actually overlap.

Ian was a generation before me. One person there at the same time was Brian Hines or Denny Laine as he became known. He was in the fifth form when I was a fag in the first year. He was our hero because he was a bit of a rebel: he went against the grain of what you are supposed to do at Yardley Grammar School. He'd not wear his cap. Or he'd have the wrong colour trousers. Or even wear jeans. But he was so good at sport – gymnastics, football, rugby, whatever – that the school turned a blind eye. Of course, he went on to join The Moody Blues and later Paul McCartney's Wings.

There was Martin Jenkins as well: he was in the year above me. He's probably best known for playing in Whippersnapper with Swarb and Chris Leslie, but he was part of several influential folk bands in the early seventies. He had a Watkins Dominator amplifier – a triangular shaped futuristic bit of stage kit that he would never allow me to borrow! It had seventeen watts of output! Wow!!

Martin Jenkins played with Southern Comfort which Iain Matthews formed after he left Fairport in pre-Peggy 1969. He was later part of Hedgehog Pie and Dando Shaft, whose line-up included Kevin Dempsey, the fourth member of Whippersnapper. While they had no direct influence at the time, even at school Peggy had the Brummy double whammy of rock and folk that would shape his musical future. But there were influences and heroes from further afield too.

They say to achieve something you need opportunity and motivation. There was a school band – not an orchestra – a pop/rock group. That was quite adventurous for a school in those days. I was considered good enough to be part of that. That was how I got into music. That was the opportunity to play. So far as motivation goes...

For anyone of my generation, there were two figures who were massively important. The first was Bert Weedon, who was on Five O'Clock Club with his golden Hofner guitar. That was kids' TV programme, which was presented by glove puppets.

Ollie Beak and Fred Barker set the precedent of creating speaking glove characters for whom, in a reversal of the usual roles, the on-screen human presenter was merely a sidekick. Future generations would have Basil Brush, Gordon the Gopher and Roland Rat.

Ollie Beak was voiced by another influential figure – Wally Whyton who presented folk music on the radio and had been part of the skiffle movement. Like lots of the people we'll be talking about, he's appeared at the Cropredy Festival.

Bert Weedon made playing the guitar look so easy. I wanted a guitar early on in my life and he kind of convinced me I'd be able to play it. He had a book called *Play In A Day* which I think should be prosecuted under the Trades Descriptions Act. I bought it: it took me a month to be able to tune my guitar.

There was also Hank Marvin of The Shadows who wasn't just a great player, with a fabulous distinctive guitar sound you'd recognise anywhere, but looked ordinary: he wore glasses, a bit of a geek. And an inspiration to us all for that reason.

Talk to any British group member from the era when I started, they'd cite those two people as their big influences – Richard Thompson, Simon Nicol, Ashley Hutchings, Dave Gilmour and so on. The generation before us had Lonnie Donegan and skiffle and rock'n'roll of course: their influence created The Beatles, who shaped what we did with our first impetus to play. They've remained influential ever since, as I would say has Hank. Bert Weedon less so!

My Dad, Albert, bless him, spent a fiver on my first guitar from Woodruff's Music Shop opposite New Street Station in Birmingham. That was a lot of money in those days and we weren't exactly a well-off family. It changed my life, quite literally, though.

I know people think of me as a bass player, but I started out as a guitarist. I know my Dad thought that hard-earned five quid turned out to be a good investment in terms of providing a future for his son.

With my guitar and a lot of practice, and less help than I expected from Bert Weedon when I bought his bloody book, I ended up playing in the school band, which eventually became my first band, Dave and The Emeralds that my dad wrote about. The guitar was a Rosetti Lucky 7: it had been painted so the sides were black, and the front was white. It was an electric guitar with a pick up and everything, but the action was about a quarter of an inch high and it was agony to play: Bert didn't offer any advice or warning about that, though eventually, after three or four weeks, I realised you could lower the strings and it would become easier to play. I eventually mastered about three or four chords. That was enough, at least to be going on with.

There are no reviews of Dave and The Emeralds (though there is a recording – side 1, track 5 of *Box of Pegg's*). However, there is that surprising positive early accolade for a Dave Pegg group. Peggy's dad's book was not widely published but is available for reference in Birmingham public library, a fact about which Dave is rightly proud. Let's go back to Albert Pegg's story with which we started this chapter.

The person to whom he referred, sneaking a preview of my first band, was Mr Sanders, who was the English teacher and later headmaster. His positive – and I have to say unsolicited – comments were my first "review": I've had better since, but I've also had and (as we shall see) deserved a lot worse. He was seriously into all kinds of music and so my dad valued his opinion, He also told my dad that his son was a musician and that he was having violin lessons. No doubt as a budding pop star (at least in my own head) I'd have looked down on anyone studying something as dull as classical violin. No idea at the time that twenty or so years on young Richard Sanders would join the revived version of Fairport Convention that Simon, DM and I were putting together.

The amazing thing about Bert and Hank and all my heroes and influences is that through my career in music I got to meet them all. That was all through learning to play guitar and then bass and being lucky enough to be asked to join bands that played all over the world in all kinds of circumstances.

Joe Brown, who was another big influence (like Hank, partly because he seemed like such a normal bloke), has become a good friend. He's played at Cropredy a couple of times and has even been on a Fairport album... and in total contrast he's had a career that stretches from playing on British rock'n'roll TV shows in the fifties and touring as guitarist for people like Eddie Cochran to being the person who ended the wonderful memorial concert for George Harrison – you remember after all the legendary rock stars and hits and a huge band and Eric and Paul and Ringo and all that, he comes on solo with just his ukulele and sings *I'll See You In My Dreams* and it is amazing, just perfect. Makes me cry every time I watch it. He's moved to Cropredy now and so I see a fair bit of him and he's still one of my heroes, and he really is such an ordinary down-to-earth bloke.

While the many high and low profile strands of Peggy's career are obviously connected (and he certainly explores many of the "this-happened-because-this-was-happening" elements in subsequent chapters), most overlap and intersect. Things clash and coincide; men and mountains meet; parallel universes co-exit. His diary is a catalogue of contrasting commitments ("FC Wintour... Dylan Proj... FC acoustic... tour with AJC... Festèno... Cropredy" and so on). Most of this book is therefore not chronological, but, for the sake of clarity, let's start off that way.

Peggy's musical career began in the developing Birmingham rock scene while still at school and through the sixties he worked with or alongside almost all of the big names that came out of that city.

Having left school with two 'O' Level GCE passes in English and Art (both subjects at which I am really crap!), I went to work at the Royal Exchange Insurance office in Temple Street in Birmingham city centre. I was in the fire department on the third floor in an open office plan with about 40 people seated at desks arranged in groups of eight. My section had a great boss, Mr. Harrison.

One advantage of the office was that I had my own desk and a phone which allowed outside calls. The workload, in terms of what I was expected to do, was luckily next to nothing: once I had opened the post, sorted it and passed it back to the desk behind... who then passed it back to the desk behind them... who then passed it back to Mr. H, it would have been about 10.15 am. Perhaps an hour's worth of filing next: then I would have to pretend to be doing something for the rest of the day.

I utilised the time wisely by fixing up bookings for the Crawdaddies, the R'n'B band that I had joined.

The new employees sat at the two front desks: as you gained more knowledge, experience and, of course, age, you moved towards the back of the room eventually hopefully becoming a "section leader", like Mr. Harrison.

Naturally I didn't intend to be there that long, doing the 9 to 5 stretch.

I had to wear a suit and tie!

I wanted to be a pro musician.

Right now, I was a Crawdaddy.

The Crawdaddies were a semi-pro band, part of a developing Brum-beat scene which is often overlooked because of the way English music history has focused on Merseyside and London. Birmingham's semi-pro players would eventually turn professional and end up in bands like The Applejacks, The Moody Blues, The Move, Idle Race, Locomotive, The Rockin' Berries, Chicken Shack, Spencer Davis Group, Black Sabbath, Led Zeppelin, Judas Priest, Traffic, Wizzard, Medicine Head, Rainbow, Whitesnake, Wings, Steve Gibbons Band, ELP, ELO, Blind Faith and, of course, Fairport Convention.

Peggy played alongside members of many of these bands. Today he is known as one of the world's finest bass players: he started out, in this competitive environment, as a guitarist, part of the quartet of the blues-based beat group, The Crawdaddies.

The Crawdaddies were an R'n'B band. I was the lead guitarist. The name R'n'B has changed its meaning in recent years, of course: back then it meant rhythm and blues – the kind of music that came out of places like the Chess Studios in Chicago, which I was lucky enough to visit years later. Mick Heard was the rhythm guitarist; he'd played in some quite well-known Birmingham bands and was about five years older than the rest of us. Dave Peace played organ and bass: he worked at Rackham's Music Shop which was a good connection for the band in terms of hearing new releases and buying equipment at discount rates; his dad owned the van we drove around in. The drummer was a chap called Don Turner, who was a drayman at Ansell's Brewery in Aston; he was a great drummer but often at gigs he was pretty knackered because his job required him to get up at six in the morning to do deliveries and then he'd do an eleven hour shift; no doubt he was offered a free pint at every pub he delivered to – and it could be thirsty work shifting those barrels. It was certainly a lot more demanding as a day job than being a pen-pusher trying to look busy.

We gigged a lot for an amateur band – usually four or five nights a week.

We had an interesting start to our career by accepting a week's residency at an Irish club which was just off Hurst Street. Gigs ran Monday through Sunday starting at 9pm. We did five 45-minute sets in the upstairs club room. Downstairs was a really rough bar which all of us were scared to go into. The first night only two people came to the club; so, we took advantage of the time to learn and run through some new material.

Mr Peace had a Commer van and he kindly would collect his son Dave and myself from the gig, then drop me off in Acocks Green on his way back to Solihull where they lived. I would get to bed around 3 am  and had to get up at 7.30 am to catch the 31a bus to town (and go to my 'proper' job!).

Occasionally Bev Bevan would get on the same bus when it got to Stratford Road where he lived above a record shop that his parents owned.  Bev was one of my heroes as I would often go and see Denny Laine & The Diplomats. He was their drummer.

It hardly needs saying that gigging five or six hours a night and holding down a full-time job would take its toll. Peggy, ever the keen observer of the world around him, began to notice that in other ways his ideal career could represent a genuine danger to life and limb.

One Tuesday en route to work I noticed as we passed the Irish club that there was a man slumped on the pavement with his arms gripping the lamp post just outside the front door. After Tuesday night's gig as we were getting into the van, I saw the same guy emerging from the bar and then having a conversation with the lamp post. As the week progressed, he would be there every morning. By Friday he was still there – in a heap, asleep – at the bottom of the lamp post! There was something reassuring about someone who kept the same ridiculous hours as I did.

The attendances picked up as the week continued but there were some real dodgy characters and Brummy "mafia"-types in the audience, usually with expensively dressed women by their sides. One night during a break I was walking towards the gents' toilet when a bloke came out: I spotted that he hadn't done his flies up. Fortunately, only his shirt was exposed but I thought it best to point this out to him to save him any embarrassment. He picked me up with one hand around my neck and lifted me off the floor, while showing me a rather large fist with the other: then he said "It feckin' well better be, son, or you get this".  Luckily, my eyes hadn't failed me, and I was released without thanks but in one piece.

At lunchtime we had an hour off and I would often meet up with Christine and we would window-shop to look at all the great items on sale in Rackham's and plan our would-be house furnishings. Dreams are important: they give you something to aim for and keep you going, so long as they are realistic, and you don't get frustrated by them.

Each Thursday lunchtime, though, was reserved for The Fox in Hurst Street that did fantastic kidney rolls and great beer. Sometimes, we would leg it to The Greyhound where they did scrumpy cider for tenpence a pint. We would get about three pints down us then my mates, Dave Cliff, Max, John Woollams and me, would race back to work and spend most of the afternoon visiting the gents and sneaking a crafty smoke.

By Friday, I was absolutely exhausted and could barely stay awake at work. The adrenalin kicked in at the gig to keep me going, though.

Having a proper job had its advantages and I was now earning the princely sum of £28/12/- a month – that's £28.60 for younger readers.

The band was playing the usual Brum circuit. Places like the Bournbrook Hotel, Old Hill Plaza, The Adelphi West Bromwich, The Ritz Kings Heath and The Silver Beat Club which was in a cellar in Stephenson Place. We would also play at the Crazy E above Woodroffe's Music Shop in Navigation Street. This was formerly the Marquee Club, a major "mod" hangout. I saw some fantastic bands there including the Yardbirds with Jeff Beck playing a cream Fender Esquire. He was amazing: I went and bought a Telecaster on HP the next day from Ringway Music on the Smallbrook Ringway.

For anyone too young to remember – HP has nothing to do with Brown Sauce. It stood for Hire Purchase, whereby one would rent a household item (TV, washer, stereogram etc) or a luxury item like a musical instrument, paying a set amount weekly. At the end of a set period of time, when the value of the item had been covered, together with additional interest charges, it became yours, provided you didn't miss a payment.

The Tele's serial number was L39716: if any reader has it, I would love to see it again! I also had the iconic Vox AC30 with a treble boost – a superb combination.

The Crawdaddies would also do "all-nighters" at the Crazy E. Being bottom of the bill, we were the first and last band on. That meant an hour's set at 7.30 pm and the next one at 6.30 am. I loved it because the bands on in between our sets were always worth watching. Poor Don the drummer suffered, though, as, being a drayman, he would start work around 6am delivering beer: as was the tradition, he would have a free pint at every drop off. He'd be home about 4pm, throw his drums together for us to pick him up: he could often be spotted, nodding off behind the kit during the second set. When I was in The Crawdaddies I was still working at the Royal Exchange Insurance Offices in Temple Street. I didn't think at the time about turning professional and making my living from music. Looking back, I still wonder how I managed to gig so much and so late and still make it into work and give a convincing performance there.

I'd decided to leave the Royal Exchange having come to the obvious conclusion that insurance wasn't really my vocation in life. I wanted to become a professional musician because by this point I was probably playing about five times a week: not only was it exhausting catching the bus to be at work every morning but I was earning five times as much playing with these little semi-pro bands as I was in my "proper job".

I got to know a lot of musicians on the Birmingham scene – many of whom have become big stars over the years. Often, we'd share the bill with another local act.

One of those was a group called Roy Everett's Blueshounds. Roy was the lead singer. They were a fantastic band, one that I'd admired  long before I had to consider an invitation to join them.

I must have been getting better as a guitarist because at one of these "all-nighters" I was invited to join Roy Everett's Blueshounds who were on the same bill.  They kind of poached me from The Crawdaddies. This was a great band: Mike Burney playing superb saxophone and flute; Gordon Bache on organ; Henri Edouarde on bass; Frank Devine on drums. We played some great instrumentals – *Watermelon Man* in F, *Filthy McNasty* and *Night Train* in B flat, *Green Onions* in F. Roy would do Ray Charles songs and lots of blues and we even did *Ipanema* on occasions.

I joined them on May 6, 1965. They were a pro band, getting gigs all over the country. That meant I had to give up the day job. The results of a recent insurance exam helped the decision and with many well-wishes from the Royal Exchange Group,

I became a full-time professional "muso" after giving them a month's notice. Ironically, one thing that meant was that they would no longer insure my equipment as I was now a pro and more of a risk!

We got wind of a new night club opening in Aston High Street. The Elbow Room was to be a members-only club specialising in great music with a state of the art sound system and featuring well-known artists from the jazz/blues world. Don Carlos, one of the owners, had great taste in music and his "members only" policy meant that if he didn't like the look of the punters they wouldn't be allowed in.

Our agent Phil Myatt from Carlton Johns Entertainment (110, Wake Green Road) did an amazing job getting us a residency there: we were to play every night for the opening week, then Fridays and Saturdays whenever we were available; The Blueshounds were the first resident band at The Elbow Room,

Mike Burney, our saxophonist, played with the BBC Big Band and was much in demand as a session player. He knew a great many musicians: one night he turned up at the club with Brian "Creepy" Crawley, a jazz pianist. In one of our breaks, he dragged us all into the gents' toilet with "Creepy".

"Listen to this," says Mike.

Crawley then farted *God Save The Queen* with perfect phrasing and pitch. We were all on the floor in hysterics.

"He does requests too!"

We were sure he had some device down his pants but no – he was a real Le Petomane.

Don employed a great DJ, Erskine T, who was a black guy who worked at The Diskery in Hurst Street. This amazing record shop was where we would go to search the latest R'n'B and Motown discs: Erskine would play stuff at the Elbow Room that we'd all be down the Diskery purchasing the next day. I can remember when a new Beatles album came out standing in a queue there at 9am Thursday morning along with Steve Winwood, Jim Capaldi, Roy Wood, Jeff Lynne and many other Brum music mafia, trying to make sure we got what could well be the only copy in stock. You learned your repertoire from hard-to-find American discs, just like The Beatles and other Merseybeat bands had done in Liverpool, The Stones and The Pretty Things had done in London and The Animals and Van Morrison had done in Newcastle and Belfast. The Moody Blues, whose lead singer was Denny Laine, as he was now called, from my old school, got hold of a single by an unknown singer called Bessie Banks: they did a pretty straight copy of it, with added harmonies: that was *Go Now* and they haven't looked back since... even if Denny did leave not long after.

I was still living in Tavistock Road, Acocks Green, with my parents and my dad Albert would kindly drop me off in Aston and often have to pick me up again at 2am if I couldn't scrounge a lift. My dad was a saint, such a kind soul who would do anything to help out.

Phil, our agent, promoted gigs at the Carlton Ballroom in Erdington. This was re-named and became the famous Mothers Club. When Phil had a famous band playing there he would often bring them down to the Elbow after their show.

One Friday night, Graham Bond and Ginger Baker turned up and played with us for about an hour. Steve Winwood, who was very much a local hero, was always a very welcome surprise guest. The Small Faces came down: Nigel Pegrum the drummer and

Steve Marriott sat in with us. I handed Steve my guitar and he said, "I can only do one song on the guitar; I only know two chords!" They had the hit *Wotcha gonna do about it?* at the time and he had only been playing guitar for a few weeks. A great character and performer. Nigel went on to play with Steeleye Span.

I was well into blues and R'n'B. Fortunately, I had lots of opportunities to see the Spencer Davis Group who featured Steve Winwood on guitar, piano and Hammond as well as lead vocals. Steve was unbelievably talented for a 17 year-old and we became good friends: eventually, Fairport got the chance to open for his band Traffic on USA tours. Traffic was one band that I always wanted to play in. It's been great when Steve has played at Cropredy: it always takes me back to those Brum days.

Steve is not the only old mate from Peggy's Brumbeat days who has graced the Cropredy stage and even the Fairport line up, of course. One of Peggy's many parallel careers is his membership of The Dylan Project, alongside Steve Gibbons who looms large in the next phase of his Black Country saga.

But let's not get ahead of ourselves. Our hero has taken the momentous (and let's face it, risky) decision to burn his boats and go pro. Like so many members of unsigned bands throughout the years, he must have looked with a mixture of trepidation, admiration and anticipation as people he'd known in the same position found success and sang to him not from a local stage but from the TV on Top of the Pops on Thursday night.

His future associates were experiencing similar pop-hits envy: members of the original Fairport watched the other local band from Muswell Hill transform from The Ravens into The Kinks and take over the charts; Ian Anderson (not a flautist but a harmonica-playing blues guitarist at the time) saw The Yardbirds, Cream and Fleetwood Mac find chart potential in blues power. Peggy was still honoured without profit in his own town, while Stevie with The Spencer Davies Group, Denny with The Moody Blues and Bev with Roy in The Move became popstars.

We did all-nighters at Birmingham Town Hall. We'd be the first on – that would be around half-past-seven and we'd usually be the last on at half-six next morning. There was lots of great music between our two sets, of course – I saw John Mayall's Bluesbreakers there when Eric Clapton was still with them, right after they released the album where he's reading the Beano on the sleeve; Spencer Davis Group was local and they were already very good – Steve Winwood has always been a fantastic singer and musician; then there was Chris Farlowe and the Thunderbirds with Albert Lee who's always been one of my favourite guitarists. It was great for us because we'd be free to watch all these other bands: we'd do our set and then have nothing to worry about for nine or ten hours with all that great music going on.

The music scene was so vibrant in Birmingham that going pro seemed like the right thing to do. I remember thinking that if it didn't work out, I could always go back and get a job in a car factory or something. We're talking the early-to-mid sixties when it was easy to go out and find a job, unlike today.

It certainly became a decision that was necessary because The Blueshounds were such a hard-working band. We toured the length and breadth of the country, often travelling what in those days seemed enormous distances to do gigs. Remember this was all before the road system was improved and modernised and you had motorways to get you from A to B reasonably quickly and smoothly. Back then a lot of towns didn't even have bypasses. No satnavs of course. It was all down to following maps and watching signposts. You always allowed plenty of time to get to a gig because you'd no idea what you might encounter on the way. Very often we'd be at gigs far too early and have to find ways to kill time as we waited. I always say if you're serious about the music business, you'd got to learn to put up with the hours of travelling and hanging about in order to have your sixty minutes or whatever on the stage.

Of course, one thing you tried to do was get a residency somewhere. That was regular work and travelling became easier because you knew where the venue was.

We played the new clubs in London and were lucky enough to nab a Thursday night residency at the Marquee Club which was an amazing thing to have. We were support to The Steampacket which wasn't so much a group as a full package show with Rod Stewart, Long John Baldry, Julie Driscoll, Brian Auger, all before they were famous of course.

We played all the clubs that were in vogue, the places it was important for a band to be able to say they'd played.

We came to the attention of the George Webb Agency. They'd get us work that paid well. They also found us gigs further afield. We played the Club-A-Go-Go in Newcastle, which is the club The Animals came out of. We even turned down an offer of a residency at The Star Club in Hamburg, which Roy said NO to because he didn't feel they were offering enough money.

We entered the Melody Maker National Beat Group Competition and came second, being beaten by Amen Corner who got the recording contract that was part of the prize. Eventually, the Blueshounds morphed into the backing band for Jimmy Cliff.

To say the breadth of Peggy's musical involvement in the sixties is surprising would be a huge understatement. In the decade that eventually bought him to Fairport's door, he had played Shadows-inspired English pop to jazz and boogie. Perhaps his most surprising role, however, was as lead guitarist in Jimmy Cliff's backing band.

This was literally when Jimmy first came to the UK. He was already a star in Jamaica but here nobody had heard of him. In fact, hardly anyone in the UK had any idea of what reggae, or ska, or bluebeat as it was known at the time, was.

Jimmy had had a number of solo hits in Jamaica, including the "unofficial national anthem" *Miss Jamaica*. Chris Blackwell of Island Records (named in honour of Jimmy's home island) signed him, along with Toots and The Maytals. Initially, he played the rock circuit.

He too was represented by George Webb's Agency: George ran an agency which looked after the Spencer Davis Group and Millie... and bizarrely Hedgehopper's Anonymous. He himself was a respected jazz pianist.

Hedgehopper's Anonymous were a group, who according to their publicity were all serving members of the RAF: they were one-hit wonders with a fairly feeble protest song called *It's Good News Week*. However, the other two names on that list suggest the connection between West Indian music and Birmingham. Spencer Davis with a young Stevie Winwood on vocals and keyboards had emerged from the Birmingham scene in 1965 with *Gimme Some Lovin'*. Millie was the first artist to have a reggae hit in the UK – *My Boy Lollipop* remains a guaranteed floor filler to this day. Both were early signings to Island Records – a fact not easily identified since early Island recordings were released through Fontana at the time.

Spencer Davis always says it was him that played harmonica on *My Boy Lollipop*. I know Rod Stewart claimed he did it. It was certainly the Spencer Davis Group who recommended The Blueshounds to be Jimmy Cliff's backing group. The audition was attended by George Webb and Chris Blackwell from Island Records – he was Jimmy Cliff's UK manager. It was held at Cecil Sharp House, which, as I suspect most people know, is very much the home of English folk music... where people like Anne Briggs and The Watersons went to research songs, a young Sandy Denny too, I believe, and of course Ashley when he was researching *Liege & Lief* and lots of things afterwards.

For me, though, it was the place where my career and that of the first reggae superstar in Britain converged. He clearly liked us and the way we played. He told Chris Blackwell to sign us up. The next thing was some intense rehearsal time together.

Jimmy came up to Tavistock Road in Acocks Green to live with my parents for a week while we rehearsed. It was quite bizarre: he had the spare bedroom. My parents didn't drink and neither did Jimmy, unlike the backing band he'd engaged.

We were serious about the music and rehearsed every day at The Plaza, Old Hill, a venue owned by Mrs Reagan, who also owned The Ritz in King's Heath, The Cavern Club (the one in Birmingham that is) and at least one other venue.

I didn't drive at the time, so Graham Gallery would pick us up. Before that, Jimmy would be up early in the morning to go through his exercise regime – stretches and bends and push ups and running on the spot: he was very athletic on stage and it was important to him to stay fit. He used to come down the stairs on his hands.

On stage, he was visually amazing and a great singer, of course. But he was a total unknown at the time, at least in this country, so we ended up playing small venues to sometimes a handful of people. He wasn't playing reggae or ska or bluebeat or whatever it was called, at the time: instead his set consisted of covers of soul songs and old R'n'B numbers: he was a great soul singer. When I say I was in Jimmy's group, people think I'd be out of my comfort zone, but of course a lot of this was the same music that Birmingham bands played at the time.

In the first half of the sixties, London, Liverpool, Manchester, Birmingham and Newcastle were the great hubs of musical creativity. Each had its own style and influences. Newcastle's early rock music was influenced by the local folk scene and artists like Johnny Handle and because of that it was the first area of the UK where rock music felt the impact of Bob Dylan. Liverpool loved raw rock'n'roll and Motown. Manchester drew on the obscure street corner serenades of US harmony doowop groups. London was inevitably more cosmopolitan, but blues and Chicago R'n'B were the prime influence. Birmingham, however, drew its influences from southern R'n'B and soul, whose twin keynotes of funky southern guitarists (Steve Cropper et al) and gospel-inspired vocals are a signpost to the heavy rock that became the hallmark of the city's music in the late sixties and beyond (Zeppelin, Sabbath, Judas Priest, Deep Purple, Cozy Powell etc... even Slade!)

It was great working with Jimmy, even though it didn't last long. We used to drive around crammed in a red Bedford van with a Hammond organ in the back and Mike Burney's white Volkswagen Beetle. There were changes even in that time: Pete Hodges and Ayesha were brought in and we became Jimmy Cliff and The New Generation. Of course, eventually Chris Blackwell and Island allowed him to make the music that was more natural to him and he became an important reggae star and made the movie *The Harder They Come*. People who know Jimmy through his hits like *You Can Get It If You Really Want It* or *Wonderful World* or even his cover versions like Cat Stevens' *Wild World* or *I Can See Clearly Now* probably wouldn't recognise him from those days musically. It was still great music but not what he became known for.

Despite its title track which became his first internationally known song (it was included on his next two LPs, as well as three singles), Jimmy's debut *A Hard Road To Travel* also included versions of *Let's Dance* and *Whiter Shade of Pale*. The album was recorded in 1968, by which time Peggy had already moved on. Up to now, Peggy had been known as a lead guitarist – eagle-eyed readers of sleeve notes will know that he has returned to the instrument from time to time over the years on specific tracks. He was even lead guitarist on a celebration of the instrument recorded by Fairport's only other bass player, Ashley Hutchings. His switch to bass came in 1966.

The Uglys present a unique problem for any chronicler of Birmingham's beat scene. They never seemed to decide how to spell the name – variously they are referred to in reviews, articles, advertisements and record labels as The Uglys, The Ugly's, The Ugleys, The Uglys' and The Uglies. They'd adopted the name, if not a standardised spelling, in 1962, by which time the various band members had been playing together for four years. As was the case with so many amateur and semi-pro bands, the line-up was always flexible. The one constant, however, was Steve Gibbons.

I owe my career to Steve. I can't stress too much how important he was. I went for an audition with The Uglys as lead guitarist. I knew that even if I wasn't good enough as a guitarist I was at least ugly enough to be in the band. The Uglys were huge in The Midlands, but hadn't made it in the rest of the country. Strangely they'd made it to number 2 in Australia with a single called *Wake Up My Mind*.

The audition was at The Carlton Ballroom, which later became Mothers Club: The Uglys played there every week. Bands travelled from right across the country to play there – big name acts and bands that were just establishing themselves: Fairport famously played there of course on the night they had that terrible road accident on the way back to London.

There were a few guitarists at the audition, but when we saw Roger Hill turn up we knew he'd get the job because he was quite simply the best guitarist in Brum at the time. He wasn't limited to one style: he was a great jazz guitarist and that was his true passion, but he could turn his hands to anything from slow folk and country to fast rockers. He was phenomenal.

I still did the audition, though I knew I'd no chance. After I'd played, Steve Gibbons was really nice about it: he said something along the lines of "That was great, but Roger Hill's already said he wants to join us and that means there isn't a vacancy any more. He's much more experienced and he's been professional for five years."

I thought that was it. He must have liked me, though, because he told me that the bass player was about to leave, a chap called John Husthwaite (the audition had been to replace the guitarist, Bob Burnett). He said if I'd changed to bass, the gig was mine. I was honest about it and said I didn't possess a bass and I'd never played one. That didn't deter Steve, who proceeded to tell me that John was selling his, a 1962 Fender Precision. It was £80, a lot of money in those days. But I decided on the spot I'd have it – the bass guitar and the job in The Uglys. I was earning £7/12/- a week at Royal Insurance, so that bass was the equivalent of two and a half months' wages. If I'd thought twice, or even realistically, about the cost, buying an instrument I didn't even know if I could play, my whole musical career would have been different... that's assuming I'd have had one. So... let me say thanks to Steve for putting me on the spot back then: you changed my life, mate!

I thought it would be a struggle but actually I found it came naturally to me and I really enjoyed playing the bass. As someone who is, still, a guitarist, it's meant down the years I've got to play with a whole string of great guitarists, starting with Roger, but then there was Richard, Jerry, Simon, Dan, Maart, Martin Barre, PJ, Albert Lee, Ralph, John

Martyn as well as sessions and on stage. Best seat in the house to watch some people who really are legends. And to think I could have said no, or even packed up and left like some of the chaps did when they saw Roger Hill was in the running.

My style of bass playing is different because it evolved from being a lead guitarist. Even while I was with The Uglys, I gained a reputation quite quickly as someone who played bass differently: I started to get asked to do sessions, sometimes just demos but sometimes things that were going to be released, too.

I was never into the hi-tech stuff. I've always been what I'd described as a melodic bass player. I've never learned to slap, for example, unlike my son, Matt, who heard Level 42, discovered Mark King, and never looked back! That was all we heard in the house. He got really good. And I heard this day in and day out knowing it was something I'd never been able to do.

That's how I became a bass player. Everyone has moments that set their life on a new course. That was mine.

My style is best suited to accompanying singer songwriters, Luckily for me, from Steve Gibbons onwards, that's something I've been able to do all my life. So I became a bass player by accident fifty odd years ago and have been getting away with it ever since. Don't tell anybody, will you?

Musicians are fond of telling you about formative years, closeted away listening to ridiculously obscure musicians on even more obscure albums and absorbing their influence. Richard Thompson once invented a totally fictional highland musician whose music he said had shaped his. Otherwise, they observed the influence of the greats to an extent and depth impossible for mere mortals, be that Woody Guthrie or Robert Johnson, Billie Holliday or Buddy Holly, Harry Cox or Leadbelly. For generations after Peggy, that list would need to include The Beatles, The Stones and, of course, Fairport Convention. Peggy's take on such things is typically straightforward and (dare one suggest) probably more honest.

I'd join a band and learn what they played. If someone wanted me to play something specific, I'd borrow the record or get a tape. As far back as I can remember I was too busy playing to shut myself away listening for hours. I do listen to loads of music, and I'm lucky enough to have met and even played with lots of my heroes, but I listen for pleasure, always have and still do. If someone asks about musical influences, I can name people I admire, like McCartney and Rick Danko, but for me the real influences were the people I played alongside. You learn so much from playing with other musicians, especially skilled and talented musicians. It's important to do, even if the only thing you learn is how much you have to learn.

The second track on Dave Pegg's four CD Box Set is a version of Mark Knopfler's *Donegan's Gone* taken from Peggy's 2007 CD with P J Wright, *Galileo's Apology*. Ask most British musicians over a certain age who was their first big influence and they are likely to say Lonnie. Elvis, Eddie, Chuck, Buddy and the rest were important, but they were American. Even though most of his songs were American imports, Lonnie was ours. His music was raw-edged and emotional, and most importantly easy to play. He inspired thousands of young men to pick up a guitar, learn a couple of chords and form a skiffle group. If that reminds you of the advice on the front page of the first issue of a famous punk fanzine, then you have a flavour of the impact of Mr Donegan – from The Beatles to Led Zeppelin, Cliff to Van the Man, The Shadows to The Spinners, they all had their start in skiffle groups. Even Peggy's early career followed paths first trod by skifflers – Ian Campbell and Steve Gibbons had both fronted skiffle groups; Fairport Convention had been The Ethnic Shuffle Orchestra in a previous incarnation.

I was just a little too young to be part of skiffle, though of course I was aware of it and influenced indirectly by it. Some of the old Lonnie Donegan standards were things you had to know because at some point someone would ask you to play them.

You could say Lonnie was an influence, but not directly. He influenced the generation of musicians before me – The Beatles, The Stones, Alexis Korner, Jimmy Page as well as future folkies like Martin Carthy: even the Campbells, who were a really important folk group when I joined them – they had started out playing skiffle.

Skiffle, in case anyone is unfamiliar with the term, was a British phenomenon, a homespun basic sound modelled on the music of Leadbelly, Woody Guthrie and 1920s jug bands. British trad jazz bands used to include a skiffle set to give the rest of the band a break. Chris Barber included a skiffle break on an LP. The single taken from the LP, *Rock Island Line* sung by Lonnie Donegan, became skiffle's first hit. The skiffle craze in Britain ran parallel to the rise of rock'n'roll in the USA. Lonnie's *Rock Island Line* and Elvis' *That's All Right Mama* (two crucial debut singles) were recorded in the same week.

If you want to know more about skiffle, check out Billy Bragg's in-depth history of the music.

I was of course aware of Lonnie, of course. Lots of people involved with Fairport, like Gerry Conway, have worked with him. He was someone I had always wanted to put on at Cropredy. We'd had skiffle there over the years from various people, but never Lonnie himself.

We'd never been able to reach him directly, which is the way things tended to work when booking acts for Cropredy, because he always had agents. I prefer to speak musician to musician and explain why people would love playing there. They all do, from nervous young folkies playing their first big outdoor festival to an established star and bona fide legend like Petula Clark... playing her first outdoor festival aged 85.

One day, after I'd moved to Barford St Michael from where myself and my wife Chris were running Cropredy and Woodworm Records, before the web and all that new technology – when the fax machine was the pinnacle of communication and we had one of those – we got a fax from a new agency in Birmingham: I recognised the name because it was someone who was a singer in a Brum band when I was just starting out. There was a list of artists he represented and one of them was Lonnie Donegan. I decided to phone them up, putting on my best Birmingham accent to impress them.

A voice said "Hello, this is the Brian Yates Agency, how can I help you?" I explained who I was and that I was interested in booking Lonnie. "Oh, it's my dad who deals with that. He's on holiday". I asked him to get in touch when he got back and said I hoped he was having a nice time.

In the meantime, Lonnie got wind of the fact we were looking to book him, found my number and called me up. At the time, Martin Carthy was stopping at our house because we were planning a 60th birthday concert for him in Oxford. Martin answered.

"Is that Dave Pegg?"

"No, this is Martin, but Dave's here."

"Could you tell him it's Lonnie Donegan?"

"Lonnie! How are you?"

It was one of those moments. There was I watching two legends talking to each other on my phone. In my front room. I thought to myself, "I've done quite well for a lad from Acock's Green".

Anyhow, Martin passes me the phone: "It's Lonnie for you".

Lonnie said he'd heard we'd been trying to book him for Cropredy. He said "Don't deal with my agent. We can do a deal on the phone now. That'll be better for both of us." I could tell it was going to be one of those bundle of notes in a brown envelope jobs. I said, fair enough if that was how he wanted to do it. We agreed a fee that was about two grand less than the agency had said.

Lonnie said "Send me a fax, and could you send the money now?"

In those days no one even asked for deposits, never mind a full fee up front. I explained the festival wasn't till August and no money came in at all until we put tickets on sale. I agreed we could send some money in May.

Even that was a bit worrying. We weren't talking legally binding contracts: none of us was getting any younger... and it was a long time to August.

Lonnie understood and we came to an arrangement we were both happy about. He said just to send a fax with the dates of the first payment and an agreement to pay the rest in cash on the night, before he did the gig: that'd do as a contract.

That would have been fine but it wouldn't have stood up in court, which wasn't good for either of us really. I explained and said a verbal agreement or even a fax wasn't enough: it had to be hard copy. He said fine.

He took our address. I heard nothing for three or four weeks. Then the postman arrived with a bin liner containing something three foot high by two foot wide. I opened it up and it was half-inch thick cardboard with an agreement from Lonnie... literally a hard copy.

I wish I'd kept that huge contract. At the time it was just a great gag.

On the night, he was amazing. Great set of songs everyone knew, all his hits. Most years, there's a debate online about someone we've booked for Cropredy, a big name. People wonder how they're going to hold the audience for a full set. I don't suppose it occurs to them we've thought long and hard about that before booking them. On the night of course, it's an endless stream of songs people know and remember fondly, hit after hit: everyone sings along; people dance; everyone loves it; at the end everyone yells for more. Of course, that's exactly what happened with Lonnie, and, aside from the music, there was the bonus that he was also very funny on stage, a true entertainer.

I loved dealing with him. He was so old school and had a great sense of humour. Lonnie was great and it was an honour to get to know him.

I was so sad when we lost him not long after. When I heard Mark's song it meant a lot to me, and that's why PJ and I recorded it. It's a simple but fitting tribute.

Surprisingly, there were people who didn't hold him in such high esteem.

When he passed away, one of many tributes to him was the fact that the Musicians Union named a ward in the hospital attached to their nursing home after him – the Lonnie Donegan Room. Not long afterwards, Diz Disley, another of my heroes. was taken ill. Diz was a great guitarist – equally respected in both folk and jazz circles: a lot of people know him through *Rags Reels and Airs*, Dave Swarbrick's album with him and Martin Carthy: it became the bible for people wanting to learn folk violin and also for anyone wanting to know how to accompany traditional tunes on the guitar. If you talk to anyone on the folk or folk rock scene, they'll tell you how important that album was – whether it's one of the Fairporters, past or present... or someone like Phil Beer... or the new generation of folkies, people like the chaps in Bellowhead... or Kieran Algar who first played Cropredy after winning the BBC Young Musician of the Year. It's an album they've all listened to and gone back to. It's an iconic album. It's one of the best albums ever made.

There are lots of stories about Disley... and we'll get to them... but this was near the end of his life and he was taken into the MU nursing home. That's pretty ironic, because Diz never paid his Union dues – he avoided anything like that – car tax, insurance, income tax and so on were things that didn't exist in Diz's mind.

Diz used to tell a story about getting a tax demand, along with a detailed letter about how tax was calculated, where the money was spent and why it was important. He read it carefully and felt he should reply :"Dear Sirs, thank you for your letter which I read with interest. It is a fascinating and imaginative scheme but one which I have to say is not for me personally at the moment."

Diz was a monster guitar player and a huge character. It was him that nicknamed the double bass The Woodworm's Hilton, on the basis that if you were a woodworm and you were going to make a home a musical instrument, you might as well pick the biggest and the best. I used the name for our cottage in Cropredy : I just liked the joke. Of course, it ended up being a big part of the story in Fairport's later years because it provided the name of my recording studio and our record label; the Cropredy Festival was run out of the Woodworm Offices; musicians recording at my studio could stay at The Woodworms' Hilton, which was the cottage next to mine.

The Woodworm Years became the title of a retrospective album in 1991 which documented Fairport's first five years with the label. It remains one of the most essential and satisfying Fairport Convention compilations (and there have been a great many over the years) drawing together as it does perfectly chosen tracks from the first four reconvened Fairport albums as well as tracks from solo albums by Simon, Maart, Ric and Peggy. All the featured recordings were first released through Woodworm Records.

It's a tribute to Diz and the esteem in which he was held that many people, including Richard Thompson who was a significant contributor, helped him out fundwise when things got desperate for him near the end of his life. Part of that was making sure he was taken proper care of in the nursing home, because in his life he'd been notoriously neglectful of his personal needs.

When eventually, he was wheeled into what turned out to be his last place of residence, he was on the stretcher or trolley or whatever you like to call it (gurney for any American readers), he looked up and saw the sign that said he was being taken into The Lonnie Donegan Ward. He was pretty weak... but he managed to remark "Lonnie Donegan. Lonnie bloody Donegan. I fucking hate Lonnie Donegan".

Before we move on from prehistory, it's worth noting that Lonnie has other Fairport connections. 15 years before they defined British folk rock, he was recording rocky versions of traditional songs that delighted and offended the folk scene in equal measure. We tend to think of his repertoire as being American, but, like other skifflers, he would slip in an upbeat British ballad from time to time – check out his recording of Golden Vanity. He was also one of the first people to record Who Knows Where The Time Goes: his recording came out as a b-side in 1969, just a few months after Fairport's version. Sadly, it wasn't one of the songs he chose to include in his Cropredy set.

## Chapter 2
# Plants and roots
### *Horses' thunder in the valley below*

In 2017, Fairport Convention marked their half century with an album called *50:50@50*. Peggy had been part of the band for more the forty-seven of those years. Not only did the title reflect their fifty years before the mast (or should that be "before the Matty"?), it also reflected the two key aspects of their performance, being half live and half in-the-studio; it was also half new songs and half material which Fairport had recorded earlier. As they had done since their second album, in their touring set and, of course, during their epic Cropredy sets, Fairport invited guests to appear on the album. One of them was someone whose links with Peggy stretch beyond Fairport.

Robert Plant – doing *Jesus on the Mainline*. It's a recording we've always wanted to use and the 50th anniversary set seemed the perfect opportunity. The recording came about because we were doing Cropredy warm-up gigs at Banbury Mill. Robert was there because his girlfriend, Deborah Rose, was doing a spot at Cropredy and was taking part in the warm-ups.

As we were setting up, Robert said, "As I'm here why don't I do a couple of songs?" We thought that was a great idea. There was no time for rehearsals or anything like that, so we just went ahead– *Little Sister*, which we still have for possible future use, and *Jesus On The Mainline* which we put on *50:50*. Aside from Planty's singing, he plays some brilliant harmonica: he's an exceptional harmonica player. It's a recording that makes it obvious that Fairport are a great backing band – even with no rehearsal. (Course, some people would say we sound better when we don't rehearse).

Jacqui McShee's guest appearance on the CD serves as a reminder that Pentangle also formed fifty years ago: their first gig was on May 27, 1967, exactly the same day as Fairport's. Robert's 50th anniversary as a recording artist remained somewhat more low-key.

I don't know what officially the first release in the Robert Plant discography is, but I do know one of the first times he worked as a musician in a recording studio. I left The Uglys in 1966: shortly after that Roger Hill left too. We formed a group called The Exception with Alan Eastwood, who people will remember as Bugsy. We got a record contract with CBS (Some accounts, basing the fact that Robert had a solo deal with CBS in 1967 suggest it was he who recommended the group to the label). We were writing our own stuff by then – Bugsy was the writer in the group, really – and our first single was his song *The Eagle Flies On Friday*. Robert played tambourine on it.

That was in March 1967. Exactly half a century before the release of *50:50*.

After Exception split up, I was asked to join Way of Life, which was a band with two brothers, Reggie and Chris Jones: Reggie was the singer; Chris was the guitar player. Their drummer was John Bonham. The brothers had already been in some bands that were quite well known locally, in Birmingham, and had formed their own band and started to write songs.

Most of the repertoire was cover versions – standard R'n'B stuff, things by American rock bands, Cream stuff. John Bonham was already a great drummer and he was incredibly loud. That was a problem. Way of Life only did twenty-two gigs because we were just too loud. We'd get booked and play the first half, small clubs and pubs, four or five numbers in half an hour or so.

In the interval, the promoter would come up to us to ask us to turn it down because there'd been complaints from customers... or the people next door... or the place over the road. It wasn't that we had a big PA: only the vocal mikes went through it. The guitars and bass just used their own amps, which we didn't mike up. We could turn down the mikes and guitars of course, but we couldn't turn John down because he wasn't even coming through the PA. If we turned everything else down, he'd be all people would hear. It wasn't just how hard he hit the kit – though he did: talk to Dave Mattacks about the damage Bonham could do to a kit sometime! It was the way he tuned the drums and the way he had the kit set up. It was unusual in those days for drummers to spend ages setting up and tuning their kit, but John always did. Aficionados used to get there early to watch him do it!

Then there was his technique... the way he'd hit the drums. It produced this devastating sound.

We'd done some sessions at Ladbrook Sound in Birmingham – nothing to do with Way of Life. It was a little studio on the Bristol Road. Johnny Haines was the recording engineer and all he had were two Revoxes, linked together so it was possible to do overdubs and so on. It was all pretty basic, recording direct in stereo.

His facilities for limiting levels were non-existent. That meant he had endless problems when he was trying to record Bonzo: even with the faders pulled down as far as possible, it was bending the needles. At a result the drum sound was distorted on the tape and nothing like the noise that was being made in the studio. It was Johnnie in fact, who told Bonzo he was absolutely unrecordable.

Of course, with the right equipment and recording skills, you could record him. You can hear it on Zeppelin albums of course.

In fact, when John got his first gold album from sales of the first Led Zeppelin album, he had them make another one up for Johnny Haines. He went round to the studio and presented it to him. It was a really nice thing to do.

Anyhow, back to The Way of Life. One thing that was unusual about the band is that we never got rebooked. You know for any band, especially one starting out, being asked to come back to do another gig is a lot easier than having to hunt down every gig you play. Ideally, of course, someone will like you enough to offer you a permanent booking or a residency. If you're trying to get gigs and you start with a list of people you know don't want you back, it makes life even harder.

It's not that there was anything wrong with Way of Life. We were a good tight little band, in fact. It was just a question of volume level: we were too loud and that was that. I don't know whether anyone suggested asking Bonzo to play quieter, but it wouldn't have done any good. That's how he played and that's why he was such a great drummer...and it was a key aspect of making Zeppelin such a great band.

Nothing to do with volume, oddly enough, but the other memorable thing about

The Way of Life was the fact that John Bonham built the speaker cabinets for the band. You'd go to see Cream: Jack and Eric would have two 4x12 Marshall speakers each with a 200 watt Marshall amp on top. Then there was Ginger with his double bassdrum kit. It looked fantastic: you know, even before they played a note, before they walked on stage even, it looked great. Just seeing that kit in the stagelights was exciting.

After we'd seen them, Bonham said, "You've got to get bigger speakers." We didn't need them for the size of venues we were playing, but we knew they'd look good. The thing was we had no money and the band wasn't making money, really, for reasons I am sure you can imagine. As it happened I owned a Marshall 4x12 speaker cabinet and a bass amp, which would have been a Park or Laney – both of which were made by firms in Birmingham, by the way. The companies weren't well known then but they both went on to be successful: especially Laney, whose equipment I still use to this day.

That wasn't enough for Bonham. He said, "You need two 4x12 cabinets each. They need to match. And I'm going to make them for you." Our first question was "Fine. How you going to do that?"

At the time he was living in a caravan with his lovely wife Pat. This was in Astwood Bank, in the garden of his parents' general store and Post office. Space was at a premium. There wouldn't have been room to stand one of those speakers in it... never mind work on building it.

It turned out his dad also had a building supply firm. So he asked me to take round my Marshall cab and he'd build three more to match it. He then said, "I'll have them done for next week." My thoughts were "oh, yeah, sure, you will", but I didn't say anything. It's better not to in those circumstances.

I took round my 4x12 Marshall speaker cabinet round and left it with him. I went back next week. He hadn't exactly made one to match. I was now the proud owner of two matching speaker cabinets, hand-made by John Bonham, but not recognisable as Marshalls (or even one real and one fake Marshall): these cabinets were covered in orange leather and had lime green speaker cloth. They were incredible, but not necessarily in a good way. On top of which, only one actually worked. John asked if I had any spare speakers and, as I didn't (why would I?), I just told him to cannibalise the Marshall and put two speakers from it in each of his constructions. The twin speakers were basically cosmetic. Then he did the same thing for Chris Jones.

That's how The Way of Life achieved their striking stage presence. In all fairness, it did look phenomenal. It didn't sound any better. We were still too loud, though that had nothing to do with the speakers – people just assumed that because we had what looked like a lot of speaker power in stage.

The band looked incredible but sounded exactly The Way of Life had two weeks before, because essentially it was the same equipment.

Then one night we got booked at The Cedar Club, which was right in the centre of Birmingham. It was owned by the Fewtrell brothers. We were billing ourselves as Birmingham's Best Band, which was quite a claim given the bands that were from Birmingham at the time and the very small number of gigs that we'd actually played. The gig went really well. There were lots of Birmingham musicians in, including a drummer called Mac Powell, known to everyone as Mac the Mouth; he was full on and very opinionated – he knew everything about everybody (or at least gave that impression); he knew how good or bad every band was (in his opinion). He was a self-acclaimed expert.

After the gig, Mac came up to me and said "That was great, Peggy, fantastic. It sounded wonderful. Mind you, how could it sound anything but fantastic when you've got all that gear?" Don't know how word got round but suddenly people seemed to take less notice of his opinions.

It can get complicated trying to trace who was in which bands in those days. Lots of people were semi-pro and had to fit gigging around other commitments: as a result, there was quite a lot of depping and standing in. Sometimes someone would leave a band and because they had bookings, someone else would stand in. Half a century later, it's hard to remember who was in what band when... or even whether you were in them yourself, sometimes. If I'd known I was going to have to remember all these years on, I'd probably have drunk less beer at the time.

Bonzo – John Bonham – was a great good mate, though: we hit it off as friends as well as fellow musicians. His sister Debra played Cropredy a few years ago with her band.

A couple of years later Melody Maker's POSTBAG page included a letter from "Dave Pegg, Sutton Coldfield".

> IT'S NICE to see young musicians from Birmingham gaining national recognition. Led Zeppelin's Robert Plant's incredible voice and John Bonham's percussion have really been brought out to the full by the brilliant playing of Jimmy Page and John Paul Jones.

Led Zeppelin had grown out of The Yardbirds. Like Fairport, The Yardbirds were one of those bands that served as a kind of finishing school for great musicians, who left to pursue remarkable careers. For Fairport, the list includes Richard Thompson, Sandy Denny, Iain Matthews, Ashley Hutchings; The Yardbirds had Eric Clapton, Jeff Beck and Jimmy Page, brought in originally as bass player, but moving on to lead guitar.

When lead singer Keith Relf left to form Renaissance, Jimmy found himself in the position of having gigs to fulfil and no band to do it with. Briefly envisioning a New Yardbirds, he recruited John Paul Jones.

Jimmy Page is one of the great session players of all time. Back in the sixties, it was quite common for musicians not to play on their own records. Someone might be good enough to play on stage but perhaps not on disc, where you tend to get more close scrutiny. Or maybe you just want a virtuoso player. I think Jimmy's on records by The Kinks, Them, The Stones... all uncredited of course. He probably features on more hits than any other artist in the sixties.

A glance at the Sessions section of Jimmy's website (www.jimmypage.com) proves this... and turns up some surprises. We might expect his name to be linked with pop-rock with great lead guitar parts, but the huge list includes Kathy Kirby's Secret Love, Shout!, It's Not Unusual, Tobacco Road and Walk Tall. Among the more obscure items is Jack O'Diamonds by Ben Carruthers and The Deep, which Fairport covered on their first album. There's also Al Stewart's LP Love Chronicles where Jimmy is credited alongside two other guitarists, Marvyn Prestwick and Simon Breckenridge (noms de strum of Mssrs Thompson and Nicol). There's even an obscure B side by Mike Heron of The Incredible String Band, where Jimmy's fellow musicians are Dave Mattacks and Dave Pegg.

Session work was important back then. You didn't make anything from records unless they sold really well and you had a good deal that made sure you got the money when they did. Gigging was expensive because of travel, equipment and accommodation: if you were in a group, as I was as a bass player, you got a share of what was usually not a very impressive fee. I was lucky to be in bands that got quite a lot of work, but you weren't guaranteed work every week. Sessions, though, were always available. They paid quite well and were pretty hassle free so long as you were a competent player. You might be playing uncredited for some band or providing bass for a duo who didn't have one. There was other session work as well – TV themes and adverts, incidental music and so on. It may not have been inspirational or fire up your creative responses, but it added to your bank balance nicely and put food on the table.

I did lots of sessions, as did other members of Fairport. DM and I became a kind of go-to ready-made rhythm section. Richard and Simon also got a lot of work outside Fairport or whichever bit of their career was happening at the time. Of course, it doesn't always mean that you were in the studio at the same time as the other musicians on the track. I was one of several people on the Mike Heron sessions, which became his solo album and the track which didn't make it on to the LP. (Another track features Peggy and DM with Elton John and Gordon Huntley from Matthews Southern Comfort.) I don't think I was in the studio at the same time as Jimmy. That might have been the album that Rose Simpson bought my McCartney bass for! I finally got round to replacing it this year.

In the early seventies, Dave Mattacks and myself were getting a lot of session work in London at various studios. We'd just done a few gigs and DM had been staying in a hotel up in Sutton Coldfield where I was living. We had to catch a train to go to London to do some sessions: I picked him up at the hotel – the plan was to drive to the station and then my wife Christine would drive the car back to where we lived while we 'continued our onward journey' as they used to say in those days.

I'm driving along the Aston Expressway, which is a dual carriageway that changes into single carriageway with traffic in both directions. I'm not speeding but about ten cars ahead of me I see a bus pull out across the line of moving traffic. I sense there's going to be an accident because there simply was no reason for the bus suddenly to block the lane. There's a line of traffic and somewhere in that line someone's going to miss the emergency stop.

The inevitable happens. Not a serious accident fortunately. What the Americans call a fender bender.

Three or four cars ahead the crunch happens. I'm aware of what's coming, and I stop in time, leaving a gap between me and the car in front. I turn to DM and Chris and say, "Hold tight. Keep your seatbelt fastened", because even though I've stopped I know there's a good chance a car behind may not. We could get rear-ended, as they used to say. I've no sooner said it than we feel the crunch at the back. This shunts us forward so that now we bump into the car in front. I check with DM and Chris that they are ok, then get out to inspect the damage.

Fortunately, it's not significant. There's hardly any damage at all to my car... nothing that would be worth repairing. The car in front has a broken rearlight.

I apologise and say it's not my fault. I explain exactly what happened. The chap in front seems fine about it.

It was an elderly couple and, even though the bump was the fault of the chap behind who ran into me, I had a train to catch and wanted to be able to move on as soon as possible – missing the session would cost me and DM far more than paying for the repair to his rear light. So, I accepted responsibility and said if he was happy I'd pay for the damage. No need to get insurance companies involved, and all that. Bear in mind I was a 21-year-old musician who was very aware of what could happen to his insurance premiums.

I then checked the car behind. The couple were still in the car with their windows wound up. I was worried they were ok. They hadn't been fully concentrating on the road and accepted their mistake. I explained the situation.

Off I went to New Street Station, quite happy everything was amicably sorted out and we would make the session on time.

Two weeks later I get a letter from Aston Police station saying I've been reported for an accident on such and such a day, asking me to attend the police station. Of course, I went along as requested, thinking they would ask me to be a witness or whatever. Turns out it was not a matter of being involved in an accident but being accused of causing it. I went into the station with Christine. We were taken into a room where they confirmed we'd been involved in the accident and asked whether I'd make a statement regarding what had happened. Of course, I was happy to "assist with their enquiries", and wrote down about going for the train, the bus swerving, stopping clear of the car in front, the jolt from behind, what everyone had said, and so on.

The officer looked at it and said, "You're not going to sign that, are you?"

I said I was because, so far as I remembered, that was exactly what happened.

He told me it was "a pack of lies" and what's more I'd be "committing perjury" if I put my name to it.

Things had obviously taken a more serious turn than I expected.

He then pointed out that he had statements from occupants of four other vehicles, all of whom agreed that I had caused the accident. He advised me, "in my own best interests" to redo the statement and admit to it.

Naturally, I told him I couldn't redo the statement, because that is what happened and to put my name to anything else would be lying. That was what happened.

He clearly didn't believe me and told me I was about to be charged with dangerous driving. To which he now added charges of not reporting an accident and leaving the scene without giving a statement. I tried to explain about catching the train and the people involved all agreeing with me leaving. He just looked at me coldly and asked, "Have you reported this incident to your insurance company?"

I hadn't, of course. All I'd done was, through no fault of my own, broken a guy's rear light, which I'd agreed to pay for. My car had suffered no damage and the car behind had driven into me while I was stationary. I explained that, being a musician, I made every effort to keep my insurance bill as low as possible.

The word "musician" didn't help. If anything, it seemed to confirm his worst fears. His immediate reaction was to reiterate the charges in detail, confirm that I was about to be charged and recommend that I plead guilty. I'd end up being responsible for paying for the damage to all the vehicles, including those ahead of me which had run into the bus and were write offs.

The whole thing was turning into some kind of nightmare.

There was also the fact I hadn't reported it to the insurance company at the time. That could well mean, he reassured me, that they might decline to honour my claim.

It took me a second to realise what he meant by that and at the same moment came the realisation that not only was it a nightmare, it was also a financial disaster.

I again protested my innocence, but he was having none of it. "Do what you like, mate, but you'll be done for it and you'll lose the case. There's too many witnesses against you."

As it happened, my brother-in-law was a barrister's clerk in Birmingham Law Courts. One of his jobs was providing reportage of the proceedings to silks and so on. His name was Ray and the only thing I could think of was to ring him and explain everything that had happened.

His advice was to go see a specialist defence lawyer who dealt with driving offences. He gave me the name of the best in Brum. Ray knew him personally and said I could use his name when I got in touch. He added "It sounds bad, but if anyone can get you off, he can." That was not quite the kind of reassurance I was looking for.

I went to him and explained the whole situation in detail. His advice was simple "Plead guilty. I can't guarantee that I could get you off. It would cost a lot to hire me to represent you and you might just be throwing that money away, Dave." It really annoyed me that he called me Dave, after a slap in the face like that.

For some reason, perhaps to see what I could afford, he asked what I did for a living. I told him I was a musician and explained that was why I'd tried to avoid getting the insurance company involved. As I said it, I realised, taken the wrong way, that made me sound even more guilty. I was starting to get desperate. I told him it would cost me my house, which I paid £3,000 for less than a year earlier. Totalling the damage, it came to a couple of thousand pounds which I simply didn't have. I was beginning to feel anger at having to sell something I had worked hard for to pay for something I hadn't done.

The guy wanted to help, but he knew he couldn't be sure of getting me off.

Then suddenly he asked a very odd question, "You say you're a musician. You're not the Dave who played with the Ian Campbell Folk Group in the sixties?" I said I was, though since then I'd joined Fairport Convention: "I was their double bass player."

"I knew I'd seen you before. I used to go to the Jug O'Punch".

"I was there every Thursday night for over a year."

His attitude changed. I tried to explain how desperate my situation was, but he stopped me and said "Just sit there a minute. I need to go make a phonecall."

I had no idea who he was ringing or what was being said. In many ways, I didn't want to know. Ten minutes later, he came back and said "Dave, the case against you has been dropped."

I was gobsmacked and for once in my life lost for words.

He explained, "It's like this: the guy who's prosecuting for the police is someone I know. He owes me a few favours. I just rang him and explained the situation. He understood and asked me to tell you to forget all about it and get on with your life."

Obviously, it was a fantastic relief. Afterwards, it made me think about British justice. I was totally innocent, but that counted for nothing. The fact I'd been in a folk group, however, got me off.

Setting aside Peggy's Kafka-esque memories of being a session man and returning to those two New Yardbirds in search of the rest of a band, we find JP and JPJ, having been unable to secure the vocal services of Terry Reid, heading North to Birmingham, fortunately without accident, to hear Robert Plant, who was currently singing with a group called Hobbstweedle. They asked him to join on the spot. After a few days rehearsing at Jimmy's home in Pangbourne, he plucked up courage to recommend his mate John Bonham to fill the drummer's seat.

John was currently touring with Tim Rose and had been offered permanent jobs with both Joe

PLANTS AND ROOTS

Cocker, who instead recruited future Fairport drummer Bruce Rowland, and Chris Farlowe. He took the job with The New Yardbirds on the basis of already being mates with Planty. By the time the new four-piece made their debut, they had been renamed by Keith Moon Led Zeppelin (the a was dropped from the first word to avoid the risk of mispronunciation). Their first gig was at Surrey University on October 15, 1968, though for contractual reasons they played a handful of subsequent gigs as The New Yardbirds.

Led Zep became famous really quickly. It was great to see two Brummy mates finding success playing the kind of heavy blues-based music that was typical of the Birmingham scene. Typically, as all that was happening, I was about to put rock music behind me and join the Campbells, a move which, as I just explained, later proved useful in ways I could never have guessed.

There wasn't much common ground for them and Zeppelin, but after I joined Fairport our paths frequently crossed.

In August 1970, Led Zeppelin (Peggy always clearly pronounces that middle E) were, like Fairport, on their second US tour of the year. Despite having gigs in the first half of August cancelled because of John Paul Jones' father being ill, it was, as one might expect, a somewhat grander affair than Fairport's, startng in the North East and zigzagging across the country throughout the rest of August. By the start of September, they were going through California, after which they had a couple of days' concerts outside mainland America. The last California date was at The Forum, Inglewood on September 4.
Fairport were also in LA, recording a potential live album during their week's residency at The Troubadour.

The Troubadour was an all-night kind of gig, certainly into the small hours. So very often people who'd been playing locally would come along after their gig. Normally they'd stand by the bar or take a seat at one of the tables and word would go round the band – "Look, there's so and so". Sometimes we'd ask them to join us for a couple of songs; sometimes they'd ask to sit in: mostly, having just played a gig themselves they were happy to sit back and relax and enjoy what we were doing.

On the night Led Zeppelin played nearby, they heard that we were playing The Troubadour and, after their show, decided to come down and see us. All of them. Back in 1970, The Zeppelin were at the height of their fame and this in itself was a big deal. I recall the other Fairports were quite shocked to discovered their bass player was mates with two members of the biggest band in the world.

They came in and were given a good table. Up on stage you could sense the change in atmosphere in the audience. I had a definite feeling that more eyes were focused on the guys sitting at that table than us chaps on stage.

They didn't sit in the audience long. They were still buzzing from their own gig. Bonzo – John Bonham – was first; he simply took over DM's drumkit, which I don't think Mr Mattacks would have been too pleased about. Simon handed his electric guitar to Jimmy Page: I'm not sure, but I think he carried on playing acoustic. Simon's guitar was an old Gibson but it had a wound third string which made it hard for Jimmy to play in his normal style, bending the notes. John Paul Jones played one of my basses. Robert Plant sang. Swarb was on fiddle and, for someone who was supposed to be a folkie, he was having the time of his life.

I got the beers in.

Basically, they did the whole of the Fairport set, though not, of course, the Fairport setlist. They played half a dozen numbers, with a fair amount of jamming and extended solos as you might imagine. I think they did *Hey Joe*, a couple of early Elvis songs, certainly no Fairport material, a long version of *Morning Dew* and I don't think any Led Zep songs, though I may be wrong about that.

**The obvious question arising from this, given the presence of the Island mobile and John Wood is whether any of this was recorded.**

I honestly wouldn't know. If it was, I never got to hear any of it. The machines were all outside, set up to record our set. That costs money so opportunities are never wasted. No one knew Zeppelin were going to be there, let alone join us for the set. I don't know what you'd do then…keep it rolling it case you get something? Turn it off to save tape? Maybe John just realised what was happening and knew there was no way we'd ever get permission to release it. Knowing John Wood, I can't believe he wouldn't have recorded it: that's what he was there to do, after all. The mystery remains…the same.

I knew their manager Peter Grant and he was notorious for taking control of any Zeppelin media – partly because it was so valuable: if there was a tape of the night, I am sure he wouldn't have left without it. He was not the sort of man you refused!

After the gig, no one felt like calling it a night. Everyone, on stage and off, knew it had been the kind of night you remember for a very long time. It's fair to say, however, that even by the end of the set, many details were blurring in a haze of consumed alcohol.

Probably more than anybody, I was grateful they didn't just finish the set and leave.

I had time to catch up with my old mate John Bonham. Our careers had kept us both busy and it was ages since we had seen each other. The only place still open after we finished was another rock club somewhere on Sunset Strip. We headed off there. In fact, it hadn't actually opened: it didn't get its license till next day. The owner had been getting things ready for the opening night and had popped into the Troubadour for a break. He saw what was going down and basically invited all the musicians down to his place afterwards. I know Planty went and John Paul Jones and Bonzo: I went; I don't think any of the other Fairports did. When we got to the club there were about a dozen people there already, including Aynsley Dunbar. Savoy Brown were there because they were the band booked to open the club next day.

Aside from being a music venue, the place also had a superb new pool table. Bonzo was a really good player and couldn't resist having a game. The guy gave us all free drinks on the house and everyone was starting to get really stuck in: I don't think he was used to the drinking habits of British musicians! Eventually, he asked us to cool it and explained because his liquor licence didn't start till midnight tomorrow he could be in serious trouble and basically loose his license before he'd even opened, which would be some kind of record, even for LA.

We just carried on drinking and eventually he became a bit insistent. Eventually, he said "It's 2am: the lights are on. The place should be shut even if we had a license. And it's getting noisy. You know, someone could call the cops and I'd be, like, totally screwed." Not his exact words but you get the gist.

Bonzo stepped in and struck a deal on the pretence of pacifying the situation: basically, he offered to play the guy a game of pool; everyone else would just watch quietly; if the guy won, we'd all leave; if Bonzo won, we got another drink. He agreed and the first game took place: inevitably because he was such a good player, Bonzo won and we all got another drink.

They played another game. Same story. We get another round of drinks. Eventually it's after three. The guy's getting worried. He's turning lights out; people are turning them back on. The only way he can keep us quiet is by playing pool, because that's become important to us as a free drink is at stake.

At just at half-four in the morning, a guy shouts "Everybody out! Use the back door. I just heard a police car and he'll obviously have seen the lights." The cop car's doing a U turn as we speak. The owner kills all the lights.

Everybody dives out the back door… except me and Bonzo, who somehow end up on the stage which has been carefully set up for Savoy Brown the next night. Bonzo points to the big speaker stack on one side of the stage, Marshall 4x12s, and tells me to get down behind that, while he hides behind the other.

I can't tell you what happened next, whether the police arrive or not, because once I'm there I just pass out as does Bonzo on the other side of the stage.

The next thing I know is it's next day. I won't say next morning because that could be an exaggeration of how much I actually knew at that stage. The sun's streaming through the window. I'm trying to remember if anything I recall from last night actually happened. I have no idea where I am. Then I spot the breathing heap of John Bonham on the other side of the stage. It's gone 10.00 am.

I wake him up. By now I've started to panic a bit. He says, "Don't worry. My limo will be outside." I presume he's confused. Sure, the limo that brought him to The Troubadour would have waited. It probably would have moved with him when he went to this club. But that was hours ago.

Each member of the Zeppelin had his own limo and driver. Fairport shared a van. That tells you something, doesn't it?

Apparently, his driver had strict instructions never to leave him anywhere but to wait till he's ready to go. Terrible job, I know. Nevertheless, we stagger out into the blinding LA sunshine – not the best weather after a serious night's drinking – and sure enough, there is the limo with the driver all smart and ready to take us wherever we need to be. I can only assume he'd eventually just given up and spent the night sleeping in the car: maybe the LA police are just so used to the sight of limos they never checked it out.

It was at this point, Bonzo realized he has to fly out to Hawaii that night for the rehearsals for a big gig.

**Led Zeppelin were due in Honolulu to play two nights at the Neil S Blaisdell Arena on the 5 and 6 of September. Both gigs had sold out weeks ago.**

I say, "You're ok. It's only just after ten. We've got plenty of time. Just go back to the hotel and collect your stuff and go over to the airport." I was sure his driver would be aware of all the details of the arrangement.

That seemed to do the trick because the next thing is, he's inviting me to meet him for a drink later as he'd got some time to kill. We fix that up.

The driver then drops me off at The Tropicana, which is a notorious hotel on Santa Monica Avenue. All kinds of people have stayed there. It had seen better days but was quite notorious. We'd picked it, as a lot of bands did, because it was less than a mile from The Troubadour where we were playing. I think Tom Waits was staying there at the time as a permanent resident.

Meanwhile, Bonzo's driver took him to The Riot House where Zeppelin always used to stay.

Located on Sunset Boulevard, the hotel had opened in 1963, named after Gene Autrey who part owned it. In 1967, it had been taken over and renamed by Hyatt: rock stars gave it its punning (but far from inappropriate) nickname. It's the (alleged) location of several legendary rock events – both Keith Richards and Keith Moon have dropped TVs from upper-floor windows; Lemmy wrote *Motorhead* while sitting on Roy Wood's balcony; Spinal Tap's end of tour party was filmed there. Elton John and his entourage had occupied a couple of floors in a spectacular manner in August 1970, immediately before Led Zepp's arrival. They themselves occupied at least three floors (which in a couple of years would have escalated to six). During one of their stays, John Bonham famously rode a motorcycle around the expensively carpeted corridors (an incident pastiched by Stanley Kubrick in *The Shining*). Meanwhile, back at The Tropicana, Peggy was enjoying somewhat less luxurious surroundings.

I stagger to my room, fall on the bed and am instantly asleep still wearing the clothes I've worn on stage the previous night.

There I remain till around 3.30 when the phone goes. It's Bonzo. "Are we going for that drink? I have a plane to catch at 7.30". For some reason, the increased accuracy of his flight information filled me with confidence that he knew what he was doing.

He stressed he only had a couple of hours and suggested we meet at Barney's Beanery which is no more than 500 metres from The Tropicana: it was quick and convenient for me, as I didn't have a driver to take me there, and it would be handy to get back to The Troubadour later. Bonzo's trusty limo would get him there, and later to the airport.

I'm hung over and barely awake. Bonzo asks me to remind him to go for his flight, which is now somehow at 8.30. I've already decided to be careful and pace myself because I have to play two shows at The Troubadour that night. I am aware that there's a live album being made and nothing from last night's session is going to be usable in the context of a Fairport LP. It's just a farewell drink... or two. Everything's back under control.

The best laid plans, as they say...

I walk along to Barney's. Bonzo arrives almost as I do.

We have a few beers. Then we have a few margaritas. Then Janis Joplin comes in and she's all over Bonzo, which he doesn't exactly object to. She joins the party and more drinks are being ordered. Everybody's ordering drinks faster than anyone can drink them.

Janis, who would be found dead in her hotel room exactly a month later, was in LA working on her new album, eventually released posthumously as *Pearl*.

Eventually, I say to Bonzo, "John, it's six o'clock. I need to think about going to The Troubadour and you need to get to the airport." John, of course, has a fair amount of booze inside him and Janis wrapped round outside him. He's in no rush to go anywhere. He tells me he'll be fine and his limo, as always, is waiting outside.

Eventually, Anthea Joseph, a lovely lady who works for Joe Boyd's Witchseason management company, arrives to make sure I get to the gig. Well, actually to drag me out. She gets me out of the place and Bonzo comes with us. I need to change so we stop by The Tropicana, As we pass the swimming pool, which is right in front of the main building, Bonzo pushes me in.

There's loads of people sitting around including Andy Warhol and his entourage, none of whom are likely to find the antics of a duo of drunken Brummies particularly amusing. I'm fully clothed. I climb out, strip down to my Y-fronts and start to chase him around the pool. He somehow manages to strip to his underpants as he's running and leaps into the pool. I dive him after him. Now we're chasing each other in the water. Eventually, we climb out. Two girls then appear with big towels and say we can borrow them. The girls come back to my chalet, where they open literally a carrier-bag full of grass.

While all this has been going on, Anthea, bless her, has gathered up my discarded clothes and headed back to The Troubadour, I can only assume with hindsight, to make contingency plans.

The girls start spliffing up. I still can't recall what happens next. I do know that Anthea, bless her, arrives at 8.00 pm to make sure I am suitably dressed and escort me to the gig. Which is where I go – leaving Bonzo in my room, with two girls, a large bag of grass, a plane to catch and presumably a limo driver still dutifully waiting outside. His clothes, meanwhile, the only clothes he's got, are strewn where he dropped them around the pool.

At the gig, I have what feels like gallons of coffee poured down me so I'm in a fit state to go on stage and play two sets which are, lest we forget, being recorded.

I discover there's been another problem, also Bonzo-related. Of course, we'd all enjoyed playing with Led Zeppelin the night before, but DM's drum kit had been assaulted. The drumheads were peppered from John Bonham's ferocious battery. He'd been hitting the drums so hard that it looked like someone had fired a machine gun at it. DM is a man who takes great pride in and care of his kit. I'm told that when he saw what had happened his reaction was less than calm. Before the gig could start that night, they'd had to go out and buy him a new set of drumheads.

It could have been much worse, except DM is a huge Bonham fan: John Bonham was a huge fan of DM as well. It was a kind of mutual admiration society. Totally different styles of drumming, of course. It was great watching Feast of Fiddles at Cropredy when they did the Zeppelin number *Kashmir*. I watched DM, who was clearly loving it. I wondered whether he was remembering the night Bonzo trashed his kit.

But I digress... back to sunny LA in 1970.

We have to sort ourselves out... especially as I am so late... and make sure tonight's performance justifies the cost of the recording truck outside.

By the time we hit the opening number, *Walk Awhile*, I'm fine, except I've totally forgotten about Bonzo.

It was part way through the second set – so that would be around 11.30 – when the sound guy relays a message that there's a very urgent phonecall for Mr Pegg from Mr Bonham. Unprofessional as it might seem, I put down my bass and made my way to the nearest phone.

It was Bonzo's familiar voice: "I don't know what's happened Peggy but I'm still at The Tropicana: I've missed the plane; I've got no clothes; my money's missing."

It's obvious what's happened. Too many distractions in my room. His clothes, with his wallet in the pocket, were left beside the pool and someone's helped themselves. Presumably his limo's still out there waiting, but now he's sobered up he doesn't fancy parading to it in his Y-fronts and getting arrested for indecent exposure the minute he steps into the street. In any case, where would the limo take him: he can't go back to his hotel because the band will have been checked out hours ago and his bags, clothes and money will by now be in Honolulu, which is, of course, where he should be.

I explain I'm in the middle of a set and will get back to him as soon as I can.

In the end we have to bail him out. Anthea Joseph had to buy him a ticket next morning. We manage to kit him out in some of our clothes: I lend him a pair of jeans. Eventually, he gets to Honolulu, but I have a feeling that the Zeppelin and particularly their manager Peter Grant, not a tolerant man at the best of times, are not going to be exactly grateful for the help we've given him, rather they are going to blame me for making him late and possibly causing him to miss a rehearsal. After all when he should have been at the airport, he was at our hotel, in my room, doing…well, let's leave that to your imagination!

Peter Grant is going to be on my case. I'll be scared to open my front door in case I'm faced with some kind of Zeppelin hitman. The man was legendary and rumours about him were shared on a don't-need-to-know basis.

Certainly, if Peter Grant had taken charge of the tape of the Fairport-Zeppelin gig it wouldn't have been a good time to ask him about it.

Because I spent most of the set listening rather than playing – John Paul Jones was on bass – I know the two bands together – Led Convention or should that be Fairport Zeppelin – sounded great. As I said, I'd never heard the tape, but I'd love to.

The rest of the tapes gathered dust until Fairport left Island, at which point they decided to take them out and put together a live album.

Which brings us back to the question, when they were going through all those old tapes from September 1970 to find the tracks they were going to include, was there a reel missing or did they find a reel with Planty on vocals, Swarb on fiddle, Richard and Jimmy on guitars etc?

It's forty-seven years on and I still don't know. But then, I'm only the bass player.

**This encounter took place nine months into Peggy's time with Fairport. Nine years on, Led Zep figured large in what seemed at the time to be the band's last hurrah.**

Things had pretty much reached the end of the line so far as Fairport were concerned. It was 1979: we'd been dropped by our record label, despite being contracted for five more albums; our fan base seemed to be getting smaller; Swarb had been given strict medical advice to stop playing amplified music; the kind of venues we used to play had gradually disappeared; punk had happened and we definitely fitted into the kind of act regarded as dinosaurs; folk music, and anything akin to it, was again out of fashion for a time, unless you happened to be Billy Bragg or The Pogues. It was as if someone was trying to tell us something.

We decided to call it a day. The plan was simple: a farewell tour on which we'd go back and play some of the music we were remembered best for. I ended up playing some songs that are rightly regarded as Fairport classics for the very first time.

A couple of gigs would be recorded so that we could release a souvenir album, though we had no record company to put it out at the time. We'd wind up in Cropredy, where Swarb and I still lived and play a farewell event there: it's been described as the first Cropredy, a small festival. The truth is it was an outdoor gig that started mid after-noon and lasted into the evening. That was on August 4, 1979. I'm sure we'll count it as the first one and celebrate *Forty Cropredyyears* in 2019.

Led Zeppelin heard about it and asked if we'd like to be special guests at their Knebworth appearance as a way of going out with a bang. It seemed a wonderful idea. Then they told us the date: August 4 – the date of our Cropredy gig – or the week after, by which point Fairport would be a dead parrot, "we are no more, we have ceased to be".

It was too good to miss, so we agreed so long as we could go on early.

It was a huge crowd and the biggest PA most of us had ever seen. I was convinced we were going to die the death, but they loved us and demanded an encore. We'd finished early because, having partaken of various substances earlier, certain members of the group upped the tempo of the tunes somewhat. The set should have lasted just over an hour: 45 minutes in we were on the last song. We were asked to give the crowd another twenty minutes, so I think we just jammed some dance tunes at them.

There's a story that you were provided with a helicopter to get you to the Cropredy gig.

That's an urban myth, which is what you call a lie when everyone starts to believe it. I think one of us, probably me, said it to someone in jest, pretending to be all rock'n'roll. The rumour spread. It was a rusty old white van that took us to Cropredy. It struggled to get out of the Knebworth site too, battling against crowds of latecomers moving in the opposite direction. We resisted the temptation to mow them down for missing us.

We didn't get to see Led Zep, of course, either on or off stage. By the time they arrived we were playing what we believed to be our last ever UK set at Cropredy.

Aside from Peggy's personal friendship with Led Zep members, the Fairport-Zeppelin connection has rolled down the years. Famously, Sandy Denny became the only person apart from Robert Plant to sing on a Led Zep album when she supplied guest duet vocals on *Battle of Evermore*. A performance of that song with Kristina Donahue was the climax of a Fairport tribute to Sandy in 2008, just one of several surprise appearances Planty has made over the years at the Festival

Robert's a keen supporter of Cropredy: most years, he pops along at some point – he'll be backstage chatting to people, or at the bar, or, if there's someone he wants to see particularly he'll just go into the crowd and stand and watch. This year (2017) he came to see Petula Clark!

Of course, the years people remember are the ones where he gets up on stage and sings with Fairport. That's happened a surprising number of times: you've got to be proud of the fact that someone of the stature of Planty, because let's admit it he is a Rock God, is prepared to come along to Cropredy and sing with the Fairports. That's not to put down all the other people who've come along to sing with us: I'm not going to go through them all, because I'd hate to leave anybody out and there have been so many. But as we're talking about Robert, over the years he's sung all kinds of stuff with us, not just heavy rock – Elvis, blues, Dylan, rock'n'roll: one year we did a Zeppelin set in our set, half an hour or so; Maart in particular was over the moon to be doing it – I can still see the look of bliss on his face as he played the opening riff of *Whole Lotta Love*.

2008 was the twentieth anniversary of Sandy Denny's death. By way of tribute, Fairport planned a sequence of her songs, each performed by different female singer. The occasion was, unusually, clearly previewed in the programme. Backed by a band made up of Fairport members past and present, with minimal fuss, each singer took her place. The audience had no idea who would come on next or which song she would choose to sing. We heard

*Fotheringay* – Vikki Clayton

*Farewell Farewell* – Julie Fowliss

*It'll take a long time* – Chris While

*John the Gun* – Kellie While

*Who knows where the time goes?* - Chris & Kellie

Then Kristina Donahue came up to the mike. We wondered which song she could possibly choose to follow that. Chris's mandolin and Simon's acoustic guitar began the unmistakable intro, as Robert Plant walked up to the other vocal mike. We were about to hear the song that featured on the Sandy recording that was owned by more people than any other. Her guest appearance on Led Zep IV.

When Robert did *Evermore* with Kristina it was a unique performance. We'd run through it with Chris Leslie doing the vocals and the only time we did it with Robert was on the night. Chris is actually very good at emulating the styles of other singers – when Roger Hodgson from Supertramp sang with us at Cropredy we hadn't had the opportunity to play with him and all the rehearsals were with Chris singing his parts.

That's another thing about Feast of Fiddles doing *Kashmir* – listen to Chris's vocals: they are perfect and yet it's not at all what people expect him to do.

That was the only song Robert performed that night. After it finished, there was an explosion of applause, as everyone but he left the stage. He shared a few words in tribute, then, as the screen displayed a beautiful portrait of Sandy and the sound of *Quiet Joys of Brotherhood* flowed from the speakers, he turned and like everyone else in that packed, rain-drenched field, he stood looking up at the image, lost in thought. As the song finished, he bowed, slightly, not to us but to Sandy, and walked off stage without looking back.

the magic runes are writ in gold
to bring the balance back
bring it back.

## Chapter 3

# Taking The Bullring by the horns
### *Since we're in good company*

In 1967, Peggy was briefly in Way of Life. Famously loud and uncompromising, the band found its place in rock history because it was there that John Bonham first made an impression (on his audience as well as his drumheads).

The Way of Life didn't last long as far as I was concerned. I'd been doing a lot of session work with The Ian Campbell Folk Group. They'd made an album of contemporary songs for which they needed a more up to date sound: I was hired as session electric bass player.

The LP was called *The Circle Game*, on which the engineer was Gus Dudgeon. They used London session men on it, but Ian asked me to play bass guitar on it. It was a big achievement to be asked to go to London and play on such an important album.

Swarb left the Campbells to work with Martin Carthy and they were having a bit of a rethink. So, Ian offered me a regular wage to play with them – that was every Thursday at the Jug o'Punch, concerts, tours, TV and radio work, recording in the future. It was too good an offer to turn down. Of course, it meant switching from electric to upright bass, which is a very different instrument. It seemed like the price of joining a new band that offered a hope of a steady income was learning a different instrument again.

The double bass wasn't my instrument but they'd still asked me to join. I appreciated the compliment and the challenge. It led to one of the biggest mistakes of my life, I traded in my 1962 Fender Stratocaster for a Czechoslovakian double bass from Ringway Music in Birmingham. Today the guitar would be worth around £20,000. The bass would be worth a lot less, even if it still existed.

Anyhow, I took the bass home and found I could play the open strings – not particularly well, of course, as it was an entirely new technique to me – and I could play fairly accurately up to about the fifth fret. In fact, the most advanced position I ever got in my year and a bit with The Campbells was the seventh fret – the note of D, probably a bit out of tune and with very sore fingers.

None of that mattered. I was now a double bass player... with The Ian Campbell Folk Group who were paying me £25 a week – a regular income. It was, you know, a proper job in music, full time. That was important because Christine and I were married with a young daughter; we were looking for some kind of security, which a band that does not get return bookings can't really provide, no matter how good they are and how great their speakers look.

That's how I moved into folk music. Bonzo meantime went through a number of bands, and even more drumheads. Eventually, he became the drummer for Band of Joy.

He met Robert Plant. I joined the group Swarb had just left. Both important figures in our respective futures.

The Campbells tours were quite extensive, nothing like when a rock band said it was doing a tour which might be three or four gigs. That was the way we worked in England – three or four clubs, a Town Hall, a concert and so on, that would be the extent of a UK tour. But we went to Europe a lot: we did dates in Germany, Holland, Scandinavia. We had a residency at a cellar club in Aarhus in Denmark. It was folk music, but it was exciting – a long way from low-paid gigs in smoke-filled cellars, which is what a lot of the folk scene seemed like to me as an outsider. Not that it was all like that...

Folk had made inroads into the mainstream too and there were regular folk based shows on the TV – Hootenanny, The Julie Felix Show, The Spinners TV series.

Of course, The Spinners were the pop end of folk. There was supposed to be big rivalry between them and the Campbells, because they'd started off in the same place (a concept EP for Topic Records was the first release for both groups) and then gone in different directions. I never got into all that, partly because I knew nothing about it. I was very new to the whole folk scene. In the world I came from, you heard a good song and you nicked it, if you could get away with it: my old school hero Brian had become Denny Lane and had a huge hit with *Go Now*, a pretty close copy of a record by an American lady called Bessie Banks. Ruined her career apparently. That's the way it went. On the folk scene, you acknowledged your sources carefully and with respect. If you found a good song, woe betide anyone else who started playing it. That sort of ended when folk-rock arrived when Fairport and Steeleye took songs and made them their own – the rock approach, though Fairport still tended to give a nod to our sources, like pointing out we got *Hexhamshire Lass* off Bob Davenport.

The Spinners stuck to more well-known folk songs, the sort of things most people could sing along with. The Campbells were more purist and had a much bigger repertoire, partly because of their Scottish heritage. Like most people who are into pop or rock, I'd tended to be quite dismissive of folk music. Through the Campbells I learned about the great wealth of music in the folk tradition – amazing tunes, great songs – which would be useful when I joined Fairport of course.

The truth is when I joined Fairport, despite what people might think, I wasn't really a folkie. I was a recent convert and had actually stopped playing folk.

Musically, The Campbells was a departure for me. Obviously, they didn't need electric guitar or bass, though I had played electric bass on the sessions for their album of contemporary songs. I had to get an upright bass and basically learn how to play it. They'd had two fantastic musicians in the group – Dave Swarbrick and John Dunkerley – and when you play with people like that all the time, it ups everybody's game. Musically, they were very strong.

They didn't replace Swarb, so although I came in to the group after he left, it was part of a change of direction. After John died, they brought in Andy Smith who was a great banjo player but from the bluegrass tradition, which added another dimension to the group. That's one of the great things about The Campbells, as a group they were developing and evolving all the time, branching out, trying new things, very aware of what was going on in the current music scene, definitely not stuck in the past.

The Campbells albums drew on a vast range of British tradition – their native Scottish songs, industrial songs from the North East, English folk song and ballads:

they were also one of the first British groups to include what today is called World Music and to feature the work of the new generation of contemporary songwriters. They own the distinction of being the first act to take a Bob Dylan song into the UK charts.

Ian and his sister Lorna were well-establishd figures on the folk scene. They came from a Scottish musical family with roots in the tradition: both their parents were singers. Ian was also a respected songwriter. The one thing that set them apart from most folkies was that Ian had his finger on the pulse of what was happening currently. He was really au fait with what was going on in America... The Byrds and the early elements of folk-rock... people like Tom Rush, whom Ian brought over to play in England, Joni Mitchell, Tim Hardin, Randy Newman and so on... the singer-songwriters...

The Campbells gigged a lot. They travelled in style. No group van with no rear seats or heating for them. The double bass would be put on the roof of their Jaguar and off we'd go to gigs – not only all over this country but in Europe as well – recording sessions, radio and TV appearances. I loved being in The Campbells and really got into what they were doing, despite my background being in rock music of various kinds. It opened my mind to the music's possibilities... and of course, it prepared me in various ways for becoming a member of Fairport, whom I joined after I left the Campbells.

I started playing the mandolin with them... it wasn't an instrument I'd played before, but unlike the violin, it's a fairly easy instrument to play – not to play well like, say, Chris Leslie. I listened to their old recordings, on which Dave Swarbrick was featured, of course: he played mandolin as well as fiddle and I just thought I could help continue that element of their sound. But I was never their mandolin player: I was their bass player who happened to play mandolin sometimes. I was a mandolin owner.

I sort of learned to play both double bass and mandolin as a member of The Campbells. I also learned to drink large amounts of whisky. By the time I left I could do one of those three things really well.

The club they ran at the Jug O'Punch was also fantastic. It was every Thursday night and they'd get around 400 people in and some great guests…so through that I saw most of the best folk acts act the time. Joni Mitchell played there; Paul Simon played there. Bert Jansch and John Renbourn one night. Martin Carthy and Swarb of course; Swarb would join his old group for a couple of numbers usually. The *Full House* line up of Fairport even played there – that was my first album with them, since leaving the Campbells. I've been back and played with them a couple of times since... they've done Cropredy; Ian sang at both my fiftieth and sixtieth birthday concerts.

As a member of The Campbells, I found myself being asked to be a session player on folk recordings.

I played bass on *Farewell to Steam* which was an LP of railway songs by Don Bilston. Aside from Don the only players on that album are myself and Andy Smith. Unfortunately, we didn't get a credit on the sleeve, which is a shame because it's an album I'm really proud to have been part of. It was a great album and still is. I still have my original copy, in one of those protective plastic sleeves. I gather it's very rare and quite valuable these days, though I'd never sell it.

It had *The Fireman's Song* on it which became something of a standard, one of those songs that's almost like a folk song because a lot of people sing it without knowing who wrote it.

Aside from playing on Don's original recording of the song (BoP1:10), Peggy also played on

The Campbell's recording of it in 1969 (on which Dave Swarbrick was a guest musician). It's been a staple of Phil Beer's solo set for years. Pete Coe and The Dartington Morris Men are among the many who have recorded versions of it.

Andy Smith, the Campbell's second banjo player, also appeared on an obscure Fairport Convention recording. *Fiddlestix* was a high-speed virtuoso tune set performed by the Fairport *Nine* line up. The only contemporary release is on the *Fairport Live* LP. However, a studio recording, released as a single in Australia, was also made.

I'm really pleased the studio version of *Fiddlestix* is one of the things on the latest Fairport box, especially as Andy played banjo on it. I think Dave Peacock (from Chas and Dave) had a go at it with us as well. I do remember the session though. It had been decided we'd do it with an orchestral fiddle section. They all turned up and were expecting a nice easy pop session. Then they looked at the score, which is millions of notes going at a hundred miles an hour, you could see them thinking "What the hell's this?" Swarb tried conducting to make them play faster because they weren't keeping up with the pace of the track. Arms all over the place, getting increasingly frustrated, Swarb persisted until they finally were able to do what he expected of them.

Swarb himself is just superb on that track, one of the best things he ever did (and that's saying a lot), absolute virtuoso fiddle playing. If you ever get anyone asking why Swarb was the best, just play them that track. It's a really great track. I'm glad the raw Fairport version, before the overdubs, has turned up. In fact, we used it as the intro for this year's set at Cropredy. We had to do something to mark the fiftieth anniversary. We didn't want just a slide show, so it was visually much more inventive and to accompany it was this absolute gem of a Fairport track that people hadn't heard before but was the perfect representation of what the band is all about.

I joined The Campbells on October 20, 1968, so, although they were important in my career, I wasn't a member very long. The album that I'm on was made before I joined. It was their last LP for Transatlantic. My time with them was much more about gigging than making records, which set a pattern for how things would be with Fairport. I did make one more record with The Campbells. As it turned out, Swarb played as a guest on that album. It was recorded for Music for Pleasure which was the first budget price label in Britain. There's been cheap labels before, like Embassy that you bought in Woolworths and included terrible cover versions of songs. Music for Pleasure was different because it put out decent quality records by people you'd heard of. Most were reissues of albums that had been out and been deleted, usually with a couple of tracks removed. Some of them were specially recorded. Ours was one of those. It had a ridiculous clumsy title [*Ian Campbell and The Ian Campbell Folk Group with Dave Swarbrick*] and I think of it as a live album, because we went into the studio for one day (Friday April 11, 1969) and cut an album just playing the songs we knew. In a way, it was a session just like the first Campbells' LP I played on: it's a shame we didn't make what you could called a "proper" Campbells' LP while I was with the group – one that reflected the new directions they were moving in.

When people trace the history of a musician, particularly in the sixties, they like to see a simple line where you resign from one band and join another. Things might over-lap – for me the obvious time when that happened was when I was in both Tull and the Fairports, but that wasn't the only time. You might leave a band and not be certain what you're going to do next. You could end up working with different people, trying things out and then eventually something works out. It's complicated, as those amazing Family Trees that Pete Frame used to do made clear.

There's a few things worth mentioning that happened between The Uglys and Fairport, apart from The Campbells.

1967 – The year of the Summer of Love, *Sgt Pepper,* emerging new bands from London and America's West Coast, often with bizarre and confusing names (Fairport Convention, for example). Peggy left The Uglys and joined a band formed by Roger Hill, also a recent Uglys departee. They were The Exception, whose third member was drummer Alan Eastwood.

He was known to everybody as Bugsy and was a singer-songwriter, which is quite unusual for a drummer: he was a very good one too. He was also a great vibraphone player.

The Cream were getting big. You could argue they were the band that created British rock: Eric, Jack and Ginger who were all amazing players: Eric had been in The Yardbirds and The Bluesbreakers; Jack and Ginger had played with Graham Bond. So, their music was a mix of pop, blues and jazz. They played everything from short songs aimed at the pop charts to massive blues jams that could go on for half an hour. They drew on a vast blues repertoire, but also wrote their own songs, classic psychedelic pop. They also looked great on and off stage. In short, they had it all – hits singles, huge selling LPs, rock credibility, talent. As a result, a lot of trios sprung up, up and down the country, often comprising of three musicians who weren't as good as they thought they were. If you look at some of the four-piece bands from that era, what you see is an instrumental trio modelled on Cream with a lead singer. Free, Led Zeppelin, Queen – still pretty much that for that Clapton, Bruce and Baker invented.

Roger Hill and I had both left The Uglys and decided if we formed a rock trio we'd become rich and famous too. The Exception were a power trio.

I was in the group for a few months. We did gigs locally and some TV in Europe. There were a couple of singles and a record deal with CBS. That sounds quite impressive, but I'd already "been there/done that" with The Uglys. Hadn't "bought the T-shirt" because merchandising hadn't really been invented.

My mum was a great seamstress and made all our stage outfits. We had green, gold and silver shiny tops and thought we looked great. We were quite into the image of the band and Bugsy in particular, who was our front man despite being the drummer, always looked good.

Rock bands seemed to spring up every week in Britain's major cities. Birmingham, with its vibrant music scene, had plenty of venues for new bands to play at, as the groups who had played there in the early sixties moved on to find fame and chart success. Where once one might have seen The Move or The magnificent Moodies or The Spencer Davis Group in small local clubs, they now played the concert halls and cinemas which were the largest and most prestigious venues the country had to offer. New bands, often formed by people who'd missed the boat on the first wave of Brumbeat stardom, were quick to form to fill those empty stages. Bands like The Idle Race with Jeff Lynne, The Farmer brothers in The Virus who became Blackfoot Sue, Ambrose Slade (formed to fill a gap when The N'Betweens secured a year long residency at The Star Club in Hamburg) and even a kind of supergroup that came about after the fourth line-up of The Uglys fell apart – Balls, whose members included Steve Gibbons, Richard Tandy (later of ELO), Denny Laine, Trevor Burton (from The Move), Dave Morgan, Alan White (later with Yes) and Jackie Lomax (who signed to Apple Records and was produced by George Harrison): Steve, a couple of hits and a curious rebranding as a punk/ New Wave act, will reappear in our story around 1998.

Thirty years before that, like any professional musician, Peggy was on the hunt for the band that would bring him fame and fortune... or at least a decent weekly wage.

He briefly considered joining Band of Joy, before Robert Plant became a member, and then Way of Life with John Bonham.

They were both loud rock bands, of which there were a lot in Brum at the time. Saying I was a member is a bit deceptive because in a way it was a "blink and you'd miss me" sort of thing. To be fair, I was sticking in my comfort zone, playing the kind of music I knew, usually with mates. It's not usually a good career move, even if I seem to have got away with it for my entire career.

To be fair, the key career changes in Peggy's musical odyssey have involved going into unfamiliar territory with people he didn't know but befriended as rapidly as he mastered the music. When he joined Way of Life, though, he was teaming up with a great mate John Bonham, who would shortly become one of the most famous drummers in the world. They had a social life outside their musical career – holiday snaps and memories of Bonzo's parties and partying attest to this. He'd decided to form a new heavy band after leaving The Senators, whose only single *She's a Mod* is now regarded as a collectible classic of the genre.

The Way of Life didn't last long as far as I was concerned. We rehearsed a lot, which was fun, and played a few gigs, without getting invited back, sometimes even for the second half. Fun though it was, it was a dead end. Another!

When I joined Fairport, despite what people might think, I wasn't really a folkie.

Musically, The Campbells had been a departure for me. Obviously, they didn't need electric guitar or bass, though I had played electric bass on the sessions for their album of contemporary songs. I had to get an upright bass and basically learn how to play it.

An unexpected spin-off from joining The Campbells was that he found himself much more in demand as a session player by the many folk acts on the Birmingham scene. Aside from a lot of demo recordings by people hunting elusive deals with major labels, he recorded for albums by folk acts like Harvey Andrews, The Ludlows and Phil Pickett whose career arc became as tangential as fellow Sutton Coldfield lad Peggy – he was part of Sailor and wrote *Karma Chameleon*.

One of the sessions I ended up doing, while I was in The Campbells, was with a trio called The Crown Folk, who made an LP for the BBC called *Folk In Worship*. Another was Don Bilston's album.

It's natural that people assume I went from The Campbells to Fairport and that because Swarb was in both he was instrumental in that. That simplifies things. I know there's a myth that Fairport were unsure about whether to hire me because they didn't want another folkie in the band, but I don't believe it was ever considered in those terms. In fact, though I knew Swarb, he didn't play a significant part in me getting the Fairport gig. It's a bit like people assuming Ric got the gig with Fairport because he'd played with Simon and DM in The Albion Band.

I'd already decided to leave The Campbells when I heard that Fairport were looking for a bass player. In the meantime – we're talking about late summer to winter of 1969 – I'd formed a group called The Beast with Cozy Powell on drums and Dave Clempson on guitar. It was a great trio, loud and again in the style of Cream, who'd broken up the year before. We rehearsed for two weeks solid, every day. We got a set together. But we never did a gig anywhere. You're going to have to take my word for how good we were.

One hates to disagree but billed simply as a trio, Peggy, Clem and Cozy did at least one gig - for Trinity and All Saints College in Leeds. It was at the New Bakerloo on September 19th, a Friday. My diary says "Tight, Cream-like, a bit too loud for the size of venue. Bass player claimed to be from the Ian Campbell Group!". Three weeks later I went up to Oxford, where, a year later, I met Peggy face to face for the first time.

Clem got offered a job with Colosseum and Cozy was asked to join Jeff Beck's group. That left me in a trio of one. It's very hard to get a gig as a solo bass player. So, aside from playing in The Campbells, I continued to do session work. Aside from the bit of extra cash it brought it, session work was also good for making contacts and keeping an ear to the ground about any gigs going – I suppose we should call it "networking" these days.

So, in the latter part of 1969 (as Sound Techniques studio filled first with the sound of Jethro Tull recording *This Was* and then Fairport creating *Liege & Lief*) Peggy's session work included demo sessions for Tony Cox, Harvey Andrew's first LP and more work with Phil Pickett. There were rehearsals with Terry Reid, who had recently turned down a gig as lead singer with the new band that Jimmy Page was putting together. From that rehearsal, Peggy went to a gig at Leicester de Montford Hall, where Terry played support to Savoy Brown and Jethro Tull, whom Peggy saw for the first time – the date was October 23, 1969.

The simple fact was if you were a musician in Birmingham and not part of a band that had taken off like The Moody Blues or The Move, the only way to survive as a professional rock musician was to go to London and join a band. So that's what I tried to do.

I auditioned for The Foundations. Failed.

I auditioned for Aynsley Dunbar's Retaliation. Failed.

I auditioned for Spooky Tooth. Failed.

Finally, I was told that Ashley Hutchings had decided to leave Fairport and they were looking for a bass player. I went and auditioned. Apparently, they liked me.

Peggy joined Fairport straight after Christmas. However, he agreed to overlap his membership of the UK's first folk-rock group with his departure from its most high profile folk group. Peggy remained a hard working member of The Campbells: his diary for December 1969, reflects this – the weekly gig at the Jug O'Punch; Lancaster University sharing the bill with Magna Carta; Bradford University with The Strawbs (the second time I saw him on stage); a five day tour of Scotland; staff parties for The Goodyear Tyre Company and The Wellcome Research Lab; folk clubs in Stratford, Coventry, Hyde and Reading. That was just December. On Wednesday December 31st, The Ian Campbell Group staged a special Hogmanay concert at Digbeth Civic Hall. They headlined: also on the bill were Bob Davenport, Diz Dizley and "The Purple Flange"

I suppose you'd call them a rock and roll revival band. Very much a one-off. It was me, Brian Clark and Andy Smith from The Campbells, Harvey Andrews on vocals and Cozy Powell on drums. It was a fun thing to do, like when Ralph and Richard, me and DM formed the GPs, or Captain Coco who were an all-star ceilidh band we put together for early Cropredies.

Four days before that, the day after Boxing Day, Peggy began his new full-time job at his first rehearsal with Fairport Convention. Within two weeks he was out with the band playing live.

Ironically at the first gig I did with Fairport, which was in Swiss Cottage, Clem Clempson turned up and afterwards asked if I'd be interested in joining Colosseum. A couple of days later, Albert Lee got in touch to tell me Heads Hands and Feet were looking for a bass player if I was interested, but of course it was too late to consider either of those options.

The question is often asked about how Fairport manage to attract such an impressive array of acts and guests to Cropredy. The first answer had to be that it is a much-loved festival, where artists and audience appreciate its friendly atmosphere and laid-back ambiance. It's only when you look closely as the acts that have played there alongside (and especially on stage with) Fairport that you realise how many have a link to Peggy. There are those who knew him from the mid-sixties rock scene. There are those who know him through his bass playing on their albums. There are those who recorded at his Woodworm Studios. There's an astonishing list of folkies he first met when he was in The Campbells.

We gigged a lot – concerts, festivals, radio and TV. Naturally, you bumped into all kinds of people. It was around that time I first got to know Ralph McTell and we've been mates ever since. I wasn't a folkie, so hadn't heard of a lot of them before, but some, especially the American visitors, were already big enough to have registered in the boozy brain of a brummie bass player.

Among the people The Campbells played with during Peggy's time in the band: Paul Brady, Alex Cambell, Martin Carthy, Bob Davenport, Sandy Denny, Diz Dizley, Robin & Barry Dransfield, Jacqui & Bridie, Nic Jones, Christy Moore, Leon Rosselson, Al Stewart, The Strawbs, Red Sullivan, Cyril Tawney, and Hedy West.

It was a great opportunity to meet all those people and to hear them play. Most of them were at The Jug O'Punch. There were a lot more and you know how it is with folk music, I often wonder whom I heard doing a floor spot, either with The Campbells or when I played a club with someone else, who was just a local singer but went on to become famous later. I think it was Allan Taylor once told me he'd done a floor spot when we played a club in Yorkshire.

Over time, I began to realise I wasn't getting any better as a double bass player and I felt that was unlikely to change. Nobody complained, and everyone seemed happy with me, but in myself I felt frustrated. I decided to go back to playing rock music.

There was no falling out and I remained friends with everyone in the group. I have played with them on various occasions since.

The most high-profile gig of his time with the Campbells was July 3, 1969, as part of the Pop Proms lasting a week at The Royal Albert Hall. Over seven days, for between five bob and £1/5/- a night, you could see Led Zeppelin, Fleetwood Mac, Chicken Shack, Chuck Berry, The Who, Amen Corner, The Equals and Pentangle. The Campbells appeared on Thursday, folk night, alongside Young Tradition, Carthy & Swarbrick and The Dubliners: the previous night saw a change to the advertised programme – The Incredible String Band and Family were due to share the bill with Fairport Convention, who were unable to appear because of their recent motorway accident. John Peel dedicated the evening to them with the wish that "despite their recent tragedy they would find the strength to carry on."

I still hadn't seen Fairport at that stage. I didn't own a Fairport record. I had heard their music on the radio. Everyone in music was shocked by the news of Fairport's accident. We all admired how they found the strength to carry on. Because Swarb joined – he'd been in The Campbells just before me and was already a legend on the folk scene, Fairport caught my attention. Not with a view to joining them, of course. When that happened it was as much a shock to me as everyone else. Whenever someone does something new in music, I like to check it out. I don't mean things that are wildly experimental – but something like The Band's first two albums which are from roughly the period we're talking about. They were new, different. Most important – for me – was the fact that they were so well played, great musicians playing together. The same was true of Fairport: we're so used to the combining of traditional folk and rock music now that it's easy to forget what an innovation it was. Or how much it put the cat among the pigeons with the folkies!

Did I plan joining Fairport as a long-term career move?

It's impossible to say. All the other bands I'd worked with were Birmingham-based, so from that point of view it was a big decision, an upheaval. I was still young, but I had a family to support and I was looking for security. Up to then, like most musicians, I'd been in bands that weren't commercially massively successful – aside from The Campbells – and I'd moved on when something else caught my attention. It would be unfair to the people I played with to say I got bored, but I was in the habit of moving on.

I suppose when I joined Fairport I at least subconsciously expected that to happen. That was at the end of 1969. I'm still their bass player. That's a long time to get away with it. Lots of years to have been doing the same job – not just in music, in any field of work. Certainly more *Matty Groves'* than you'd thing it would take to get bored with! In case you're wondering, I never have.

I didn't move on to Fairport because I'd been in The Campbells: I wasn't a folkie that went electric, but when I joined I had a knowledge of folk music that I wouldn't have had otherwise. They had a huge repertoire and because they weren't releasing a new album, they had a free range over the old stuff. It was like a crash course in essential British folk music.

## Here's to you, Neil Cutts

The last song in many a Campbells' set was a singalong bit of fun that would resurface two decades later on a Fairport CD.

*The Five Seasons* released in December 1990 is not a record that many fans would cite as their favourite Fairport album. Its songs, even its one trad arr song *Claudy Banks*, are not ones to which the band returns in live sets, even at Cropredy. There is, however, one which deserves a mention in this context.

*The Card Song* was recorded by The Ian Campbell Folk Group on *New Impressions*, the album made between the departure of Swarb and the arrival of Peggy. Ian first came across the song as a drinking game during his national service. It was probably 18th century in origin (well enough known to be the subject of a parody in an early edition of Punch). It had been collected by Frank Kitson and recorded by Ewan MacColl (as Ian made clear in his original track notes).

The Chorus

*Here's to you [INSERT NAME]*
*Here's to you, with all my heart!*
*We'll have another glass, my boys,*
*At least, before we part:*
*Here's to you [INSERT NAME]*

was what was called a 'nomination refrain' in which the singer added the name of someone in the room who then had to sing the next verse and chorus. (Because of the standardised Ewan and Ian versions the name Tom Brown is often sung throughout.)

The verse simply lists playing cards in order of trumping superiority with an improvised rhyming second line. Should the nominated singer fluff the sequence of fail to come up with a rhyming line, they pay the forfeit of either taking another drink or buying a round. The more you drank, the harder it became to remember where you were in the countdown of cards; therefore the more drink was taken... you can guess the rest.

In Fairport's version the nominations feature a catalogue of friends of the band...

They're all people who appear somewhere in this book... Doug Lake, Jonah Jones, Ralph May (which is Mr McTell's real name), Dave Glass, Tom Lynch and Neil Cutts. It's a silly song, pretty boring to sing and probably even worse to have to listen to. I don't recall us singing it much on stage. It was a nice way to acknowledge a few mates and it filled a slot on a record at a time when we were a bit short on stuff. I think there's quite a lot of instrumentals on that CD.

One of the most distinctive features of the performance field at Cropredy is the huge bar which juts out as a triangular wedge on the right side of the field. Like many of the standard aspects of Cropredy, its location and shape have changed over the years until it has reached an unvarying optimum. Its shape gives it an extended bar area, large enough to be seen from the air by anyone in the many planes that traverse the field in the course of the three days. Its sales output is enormous: over three days, bold Cropedeers have been known to consume more beer than at the week-long National Real Ale Festival. Over the years a number of annual Fairport beers have been created for the occasion.

Appropriately the origins of this Cropredy institution lie somewhere between *Gottle O'Geer* and *Tipplers' Tales*.

It was when the Fairport line-up was myself, Swarb, Simon and Bruce... not the farewell tour but in one of those tours promoting *Bonny Bunch of Roses*, I think... that we first heard about the White Bear in Masham. It's a bit off the beaten track in a lovely part of Yorkshire and I have to say it turned out to be one of the finest pubs in Yorkshire. Martin Satterthwaite, who was a promo man for Island Records, had been laid off by the record company. We decided we'd employ him as a driver. We felt a fair bit of sympathy at the time, because we'd just been through a similar experience. Fortunately, we'd been signed up for seven albums by Phonogram on their prog rock label Vertigo, so we'd landed on our feet... or so we thought. Anyhow, we were in a position to offer Martin a job which was a good thing to be able to do because he was a great bloke and had been supportive of the Fairports.

Our tour took us to Yorkshire and Simon suggested we went to The White Bear: he said, "it's a lovely pub, beautiful part of Yorkshire, great atmosphere and a lovely pint of Theakston's". The last part clinched the deal in my mind and I suspect Simon Nicol's as well. So off we went travelling through the Yorkshire Dales.

Detours to good pubs and recommended eateries have become part of the Fairport tour ethos. When they used to play Bradford, it somehow always seemed to coincide with the annual curry festival and often one of the band's rare days off. Now when the band play Leeds, Wakefield or Huddersfield, the next day usually includes a detour to the Kashmir. On a tour with Anthony John Clarke, Peggy once called to ask if I'd like to meet up as he'd be having curry at the Kash in Morley Street. Thinking I might have missed a gig I asked where they'd played last night – "Hull, a great gig": ah, then they must be playing near me tonight? "No, we're up in Teeside". One hardly needs a satnav to realise this detour, which incidentally crosses the A1, the A1(M) and the M1, describes a geographic wedge worthy of the relative groundspace of the Cropredy bar!

Martin was driving Swarb, Simon and myself. Bruce was with Birgitte whom he'd married after she split with Swarb (again) and they were travelling separately by car. The idea was a lovely pub lunch, a pint or two and then on to out next gig which was on the West Coast – Blackpool I think: I don't believe we played Southport on this occasion, as we usually do.

The pub was every bit as great as Simon had promised, beautiful beer – Old Peculiar and Theakston's bitter. The only problem was that they didn't do food. Swarb was quite upset about that as he was fond of his grub and at the time more into smoking than drinking. Simon and I were well content because we could just get as much Theakston's as possible down us in the time available.

We knew it'd take maybe two-and-a-half hours to drive to Blackpool. We'd arranged to meet Bruce there for the soundcheck. It could be a leisurely lunch.

Anyhow, as two o'clock approached we were told we'd have to drink up because the pub was closing. We were well settled in by now and didn't fancy moving for a while at least. I said to Simon that perhaps if he had a word with the landlord, explained we were a band, maybe he'd let us stay a bit longer or at least recommend somewhere else, perhaps somewhere we could get lunch, as Swarb was making it clear he was getting hungry.

The landlord had changed since last time Simon was there and he didn't know the new one. It turned out to be Neil Cutts who ran the pub with his wife Leslie: Neil will be a name familiar to many Fairport fans and if it doesn't ring a bell, this explains who he was and why Fairport and its fans continue to hold him in great affection.

Neil told us he was big mates with Lindisfarne and of course he'd heard of Fairport Convention. He apologised for not being able to serve us another drink because he and his wife had been invited to a Licensed Victuallers' lunch: because of work commitments and the fact they were spread over a fair distance, local landlords have very few opportunities to get together and it was important he didn't miss it.

All the publicans in the area got together and it was a big posh lunch which was held on a Sunday when mostly they were able to shut their pubs for the afternoon. Chances of the recommendation of an alternative local watering hole vanished with those words.

The lunch was in Skipton, which is only about ten miles away.
In fact, it's thirty-five miles away and in the wrong direction for anyone bound for Blackpool.

Neil said we were welcome to join them. It seemed a good idea, not least because food was involved and it would keep Swarb happy. Not only did the idea of lunch make Swarb happy, he also told us he was born in Skipton.
Actually he was born in New Malden: his family took the high road to Linton, near Grassington, when he was still very young and he grew up there. Skipton would certainly have been familiar to him.

Neil closed up the pub and we set off for Skipton with the Fairports driven by Martin following him in our car. It was only two o'clock and we knew we had plenty of time. The lunch, as you might expect, was fantastic: roast beef and all the trimmings; the company was great; the dark cloud lifted from Swarb's mood and he started praising the wonders of Theakston's Old Peculiar. In fact, he was having such a good time that, even though Martin was pointing out that the hour was getting late, as it tends to when you're enjoying a lavish meal, he announced he was just going to fetch his fiddle and play them a few tunes. Which is what he promptly did. It was an unexpected treat and Swarb played particularly well. He went down a storm. Naturally, he decided to play them a few more. Martin's looking anxiously at his watch but we're having a great time and are by now quite refreshed. We assure him it will be fine.

Eventually proceedings draw to a close and people start to head back to open up their pubs for the evening. We go back via the White Bear where Neil announces he's going to have a lie down but if we want to have another pint, just help ourselves. We didn't need to be asked twice. He gives us all Theakston's T-shirts and hats as a souvenir of the day and we promise to wear them at that night's gig.

By now Martin is really starting to panic. We're passing the point where we're going to get to the gig in Blackpool in time for the soundcheck and now he's worried whether we're even going to make the start of the gig. It's part of his job to get us to the gig on time and he decides to get insistent. Despite the attraction of a serve-yourself free bar and our by-now over-refreshed state, he finally convinces us.

We arrive at the gig at about ten to eight to be confronted by Bruce Rowland and the promoter standing outside – a queue of punters has already formed: they have a very worried look on their faces and we can see them checking their watches. As we tumbled out of the van, our welcome was somewhat less than warm.

It was a good gig, despite all that. We were used to playing in a refreshed state. I suspect the audience wondered why we appeared to be sponsored by a brewery that had nothing to do with the venue, though.

Every time we were in Yorkshire, or, to be honest, any neighbouring county of Yorkshire, or if we were on our way to Scotland, we managed to detour for a visit to The White Bear. Over the next couple of years Neil and the band became good friends.

We were also became mates with the Theakston family. Simon Theakston eventually decided, as the pub had developed a reputation for putting on great music, that he'd sponsor a festival there. They put Jethro Tull on (this was when I was playing bass with them) and Swarb and Simon were put on as support.

Swarb and Simon were among many acts who appeared at The White Bear in their own right. In 1982, Neil Cutts was behind the release of their first album as a duo, a live recording, originally made for the BBC, of an appearance there. *Live At The White Bear* was the first release on White Bear Records (WBR 001) and featured duo versions of several songs from Fairport's repertoire including *The Widow of Westmoreland's Daughter*, *Fiddlestix*, and *Three Drunken Maidens*. A kind of official bootleg, it was sold over (or should that be under?) the counter at the pub. Eventually it was reissued by Woodworm along with the studio album the duo made there two years later under the title *Close To The White Bear*.

We started having Theakston's do all the beer at Cropredy. They'd bring a big tanker down. All the bar staff were from Masham, all mates of Neil's who'd worked for him at some point. They were a great team and perfect for the general vibe at Cropredy. Lots of Fairport fans got to know them well and think of them, like Leon's vegetarian food stall, as very much part of the whole festival experience.

These days we sell Wadworth's beer, from Devizes (in glasses of different sizes), the staff that serve it and run the bar are still, after all these years, from Masham. People often remark how good the Cropredy bar is and the reason for that is down to them, their attitude, their experience and the fact they are such a great team. The Neil Cutts Crew.

Sadly, Neil is no longer with us. He died a few years ago and his passing touched far more people than he realized. He was able to attend one last Cropredy before he died, though he was far too frail to be working by then: I am really glad he was able to do that because he got to hear the cheers he received when his name was mentioned from the stage.

Neil wanted his links with Fairport to be remembered. He even requested in his will that the inscription on his tombstone should read "Meet On The Ledge" which is a lovely permanent tribute to our connection. Christine, myself, Simon and Chris Leslie all went up to Masham for the funeral. It was, as you can imagine, a big event because he was so well known and such a loved man. The church was full and people had to stand at the back and in the porchway: there were even people outside who simply couldn't be fitted in. The coffin was brought on the dray belonging to Theakston's, pulled by shire horses.

As often happens, the gravestone wasn't ready in time for the actual burial, but in the service it was explained that there would be another service three weeks later for the installation of the gravestone and the congregation were told what the inscription would say. Simon, Chris and myself played *Meet On The Ledge*. It's a song that's asked for a lot at funerals – as is *Who Knows Where The Time Goes* – and Simon in particular has played it at a lot of funerals of friends of the band in recent years.

It was a sad affair, really moving and the song is hard to play on such occasions. *Meet On The Ledge* is an amazingly powerful song especially when you consider it was written by Richard when he was eighteen.

Everyone knows it as Fairport's anthem today and it is powerful in so many contexts – whether it's at the end of a gig on tour or at a small funeral gathering or with 20,000 people joining in when it's the last song played at Cropredy each year.

Anyhow, because of work commitments, we couldn't go back to Masham for the placing of the gravestone but we heard about what happened. Words were spoken at the graveside to the large number of people gathered for its installation. Someone explained about the inscription for anyone who didn't know the details of the Fairport connection. I don't know if there'd been some confusions about Masons and stonemasons but as everyone raised their pints of Theakston's and the covering was raised to unveil the stone, everyone saw the inscription "Meet At The Lodge".

Although *Meet On The Ledge* first appeared on *What We Did On Our Holidays* at the start of 1969, by the time I joined Fairport at the end of that year, the band had stopped playing it. It might surprise some people that we didn't play it throughout the seventies – though I know other acts did. I've played it enough times since to make up for that, though.

We eventually revived it when we knew that the tour we were doing would be our last – or so we thought as the time. We deliberately put together a setlist that included not only our current repertoire but songs that people associated with the Fairports. That was where I first really realised what a powerful song it is. It's an anthem and playing it to those long-term Fairport fans who'd stuck with the band and come out to see us for what they assumed would be the last time I realised how powerful those apparently simple words are.

The so-called Farewell tour, partially documented on the *Farewell Farewell* LP subsequently reissued on CD under the title *Adieu Adieu* (neither of those songs is on the actual album), unwittingly set the pattern for Cropredy setlists which, outside the big anniversary years, tends to feature the current album and the touring setlist enhanced by songs from the whole extent of the band's half decade. It was John 'Jonah' Jones – another of the nominees in Fairport's *Card Song* – who defined *The Ledge* as the absolute and ultimate Fairport encore when, after it had been played as the closing song (not a position it naturally held on the Farewell tour or at early Cropredys), he greeted demands for more with the words, "That's it. That's the last song. You cannot follow that. We simply cannot follow that."

Chapter 4

# The More We Walk Together
*When FC met Peggy (a Brumcom)*

When Peggy joined Fairport, the band had just gone through a traumatic year of triumph and tragedy.

It was the best of times, it was the worst of times. It was a year of discovery: it was a year of loss. They had everything before them: they had nothing before them.

Over the past twelve months, they had released three albums. They began the year with the expectation that *Meet On The Ledge* would be their first hit single, but later ended up on Top of the Pops performing their only hit, a classroom French version of a Dylan song that had been a hit for Manfred Mann. Their distinctive twin lead vocal approach changed when Iain Matthews quit the band and was not replaced.

They toured Britain extensively but their planned US debut (and indeed almost the band's future) was cancelled after a major accident on the M1 claimed the life of their drummer and left the rest of the band hospitalised with mental and physical scars that last to this day.

They began the year as an underground group playing clubs and College halls. They ended as a band, known to a huge audience, that could attract a who's who of folk and rock to a sell out gig at The Royal Festival Hall.

They released songs that half-century on still define the band – *Fotheringay, Genesis Hall, Who Knows Where The Time Goes, Matty Groves...* Yet no sooner were they added to the repertoire than they were dropped from the set as the band moved on to fresh fields and genres new. They (literally) invented British Folk-Rock.

Released at the end of an astonishing year, *Liege & Lief* was like nothing we had heard before. Though it divided opinions, its significance was beyond dispute. Today it features in lists of all-time great albums of both rock and folk: BBC Radio 2 listeners voted it "the most influential folk album of all time."

Yet, even before it was in shops, came the news that first Sandy Denny and then Ashley Hutchings had decided to leave. At a stroke, they'd lost their lead singer and founder.

I joined Fairport as their new bass player, not as Ashley's replacement. Playing bass was only part of what he did with Fairport. I felt confident about my skills on bass. I think what concerned us more, initially, was the decision not to replace Sandy. Though both Simon and Richard had done the occasional song on stage, only Sandy had sung lead on their last two LPs. She was a key part of the Fairport sound. We were a band without a lead singer.

Fairport played only five concerts in which they featured the music from *Liege & Lief.* Peggy attended the last of them. It was the last time the classic line-up of Denny, Thompson, Nicol, Swarbrick, Hutchings and Mattacks performed live in public (aside from a brief appearance on Danish TV). The date was November 2, 1969.

It was a coincidence. I'd no idea that I'd join the band in just over a month.

It was at Mother's, which I used to go to when it was The Carlton Club. A lot of great bands from outside Birmingham came to play there and I could get in because it was run by the same agent who looked after The Uglys.

It was my 22nd birthday and I'd decided to give myself the night off. [He'd spent most of the day at Zella Studios, Birmingham, playing bass on tracks for The Couriers' new LP] Like everyone, I'd heard of Fairport. I can't remember whether I saw them on Top of the Pops – it's one of those things that's talked about so much, you convince yourself you've seen it. Like everyone in a group that's travelled up and down the country in a shaky old van, the news of the accident gave me second thoughts. I was married with a young kid and I suddenly realised I was working in a dangerous job.

Wherever Swarb went, he left a trail of tales, a mix of fact and legend, in his wake. I'd followed him in The Campbells and, naturally, he was talked about a lot. We'd met when he'd come back to Brum to play with Martin Carthy. There was a Campbells album on Music for Pleasure that we both played on. Of course, his decision to break up his successful duo with Martin Carthy and start playing rock music was much debated in folk circles. Carthy/Swarbrick splitting was almost as traumatic as The Beatles' break up.

I was interested to see what Swarb was up to. He was a highly respected traditional folk musician and now he was part of an underground electric rock band. This was only three years after all the fuss when Dylan went electric.

The Campbells had been the first act to take a Dylan song into the charts – their version of *The Times They Are A-Changing*. Years later Ian told me how personally disappointed he was when Bob went electric. Dylan played Birmingham Odeon on May 12, 1966: he spent the day with Steve and Muff Winwood who took him to visit a haunted farmhouse in Solihull. It was the final leg of the so-called "Judas" tour – first half acoustic, second half loud and electric with the band. The Campbells went to the gig but left when they discovered how loud the second half was. According to Ian Campbell and Beryl Marriott (though Swarb himself challenged their recollection), Swarb stayed and enjoyed it.

Swarb joining a rock band (and bear in mind that, *A Sailor's Life* nothwithstanding, Fairport had not publicly become the pioneers of folk-rock when he joined) was tantamount to a betrayal by one of their own.

I was interested in discovering what Swarb was up to in what I thought of at the time as his new band. The fact that it was a rock band didn't worry me, of course. I might be a member of The Campbells, playing folk music for a living, but I'd spent years playing rock and would go back to rock music before I joined Fairport. Folk and rock. I had a foot in both camps, which proved useful playing bass with Fairport, of course.

Leaving aside the mental image of Peggy as The Colossus of Brum... The Mother's gig was a significant one for Fairport. It marked their return to the club at which they'd played before the journey back to London when a crash on the highway threw their van to a field. The band was still caught up in the mental aftermath, quite fragile, yet still taking the bold step of playing a full set of music unlike anything anyone had done before. It would be unfamiliar territory even to their long-standing fans. Everything they had done previously was swept away: they didn't even play their hit single. Instead, the audience at Mother's heard a set made up of the songs on *Liege & Lief*. The final session for the LP at Sound Techniques had taken place the day before: they recorded *Sir Patrick Spens*, the third song in the set that night, which didn't make the album but was revived for their first LP with Peggy.

I was blown away by Fairport that night, how good they all were as musicians. A lot of people still regard that later 1969 line-up as the classic Fairport and I can see why – Sandy on vocals, Richard and Swarb playing lead, Simon, DM and Ashley as the rhythm section; the music, combining really old traditional songs with rock, was adventurous and innovative and exciting.

It was Sandy's last gig with Fairport (unless one counts an appearance on Danish TV that she literally had to be manhandled to attend). At least for now.

Of course, Sandy is always associated with Fairport. Even in the nineties, fans in America would ask why she wasn't with us. People also often assume she must have played at Cropredy. She died in April 1978, so both those things would have been impossible. By the time I joined she'd already left and the band had decided she was literally irreplaceable. Eventually she rejoined, of course, so I got to play with her in Fairport. I already knew her by then, because I played on her solo albums.

Peggy's lyrical bass lines grace several tracks on *Like An Old Fashioned Waltz*, the album Sandy made shortly before rejoining Fairport.

For me, session work took off properly after I joined Fairport. Joe Boyd was the in-house producer for his own company Witchseason. Fairport were just one of the acts he managed. He handled people like John Martyn, Sandy and Fotheringay, The Incredible String Band. Richard and Linda Thompson (after he left Fairport), and Nick Drake. Because DM and I had a wide experience of lots of styles of music – and because we were both reliable musicians – we ended up doing a lot of session work, not just for Joe's acts, but for hundreds of people. People do know I played on LPs by the acts I just mentioned because my name's there as bass player. There were lots more where it wasn't, including some big hits of the time. Sometimes you'd go in and do three tracks in a couple of hours and later you'd recognise something you'd played on because it was on the radio. There were a lot of us supplementing our income with that kind of journeywork – Pat Donaldson and Gerry Conway were another in-demand bass and drums combo (for younger readers, in the unlikely event there are any, that's not the same as drum'n'bass!)

In December 1969, Peggy received a phonecall to say that Ashley Hutchings had decided to leave Fairport and they were urgently looking for a bass player.

When the chance to join the band came, despite being disappointed by not getting a job with some other acts, I was really pleased because in all honesty Fairport were exactly where I was at musically. It was compatible with the way I played the bass.

I'd been given a recording of *Liege & Lief* which I learned for the audition. That was what I played the first time I played with them. Essentially it was the songs I'd heard them play at Mother's six weeks earlier. It goes without saying they must have liked what I did because I got the gig.

Simon Nicol recalls being amazed that Peggy could not only play the bass parts that Ashley invented but that he could play them better than their only begetter.

By the time I joined, a lot of that stuff had been dropped and our first rehearsal was the songs that became *Full House*. We did keep a couple of *Liege & Lief* songs in the set for a time – *The Deserter* and *Tam Lin* – but they didn't last long, a couple of months at most: *Matty Groves*, of course, has never been out of the setlist!

Nowadays, The Fairports always like to dip into the back catalogue and add some older songs to the winter tour set. For more than twenty years now, we've had a policy of looking for classic material that we can revive. I love the response when an audience hears something they weren't expecting. We're kind of unique among bands with a long history in that there are no "greatest hits" that people are expecting to hear. You know the kind of thing – it happens at Cropredy – there's a singer or a band and you know there's going to be a sense of disappointment if they don't play a particular song. Like, you'd always hope Procol Harum would do *Whiter Shade of Pale*. This year (2017) we had the Trevor Horn band, so I suppose everyone was expecting *Video Killed The Radio Star*, but the great thing was every song in the set was a classic and they were all things he, or someone in the band, had been involved with – you forget how many classic records he produced. Then there was Petula Clark, too: *Downtown* began as a bit of a running joke, when Antony John Clarke, who was the compere this year, mentioned it from the stage on Thursday. By the end of the weekend, it was almost an unofficial anthem!

Including a song we haven't played for a long time makes for a nice surprise. It's not just a nostalgia thing: we certainly don't aim to recreate the earlier recording. I believe older fans are interested to see how the current line up of Fairport would tackle that older material. That was the idea behind the *By Popular Request* CD we did a few years ago. Of course, younger fans might hear those songs for the first time. *Liege & Lief* is probably the album we've gone back to most: we've probably resurrected every song on the album with the new line up at some point.

With the exception of *Come All Ye*, a calling on song written to introduce the LP, the concept behind it and the new Fairport configuration, there are recordings of all the *Liege & Lief* songs by the current Fairport line-up.

It's "the one before I joined", of course. Technically, it was just out when I became a Fairport, but it wasn't an album that we went out promoting. That's the thing about the Fairport back catalogue, especially since we started holding our annual get-togethers at Cropredy: it's a resource – a vast store of songs that are primarily Fairport's. No matter how many people cover *Who Knows Where The Time Goes*, for example – and there have been a lot of different versions – it will always remain a Sandy song and a Fairport song. It's a legacy and by the time I joined, just over three years after the band was formed, it was already part of a treasure trove of songs I inherited.

*Liege & Lief*, though, was the first stuff I ever saw Fairport play live, the one time I got to see them before I joined the band. There's been a couple of times when they've (sic) done it at Cropredy – including this year – when I could almost become a member of the Fairport audience rather than the band for an hour or so.

We've always brought out older material at Cropredy of course, though often when we did something from *Liege & Lief* it was a year when Ashley was able to play with the band. There's probably some of those classic Fairport songs that I'd never played until we decided to put them into the winter tour set.

In 2007, after *Liege & Lief* was voted the most influential folk album of all time by BBC Radio 2 listeners, we reassembled the original line up from the LP with Chris While taking on Sandy's vocals on Friday night at Cropredy. It was a significant moment: Fairport hadn't played the album live since 1969 and then only a small number of gigs. As you reminded me at the time, they'd never played the album in sequence.

Because I wasn't involved in that, since I wasn't in the group at the time, I was able to go out into the field and just watch Fairport as a punter. I remarked to you at time, because we were standing together, that it was like being back on my birthday in 1969.

It hit me how much of a turning point in my life that was. Without it, most of this book wouldn't exist.

After the accident in 1969 which almost put an end to Fairport, they'd played very few gigs before the band fell apart and Peggy joined. Their return to the stage – introducing audiences who knew them well to music they had never heard before – was on September 20, 1969 at one of their favourite haunts, Van Dyke's in Plymouth: the night after I saw Peggy in Leeds with The (as yet unnamed) Beast. On September 24, the day after recording a session for John Peel, they introduced their new music to a packed audience that included many of the biggest names in folk music at The Royal Festival Hall. Next came Fairfield Halls in Croydon and Dunstable Civic Hall on October 10 and 14 (nights on which Peggy played with The Campbells in Birmingham and Warminster). From October 16 to November 1, they were at Sound Techniques recording the album. The day after that was the day Peggy saw them at Mothers. The next time they appeared on stage, Peggy was in the band.

That night I saw the Fairports for the first time, I wished that I could play in a band like that. Be careful what you wish for!

A few days later I got a call from Dave Swarbrick to ask if I would audition for the band as Ashley had decided to leave. I couldn't believe it and immediately went out and bought a Fairport LP and started swotting in case the audition was really going to happen. We were living with my parents at the time in Falcon Lodge, Sutton Coldfield and I borrowed my Dad's Blue Austin A35 van to drive to London with my gear. I had to leave very early as there was a problem with the steering and it was much easier to turn left than right. (This was in the final months of the pre-MOT, "ten year test"). Not knowing London that well I purchased an A to Z and noted down the last bit of the city route in a list of ever-decreasing left turns. Stressful indeed but it distracted me and helped alleviate any fears I had about doing the audition. Apparently, the chaps were worried that coming from the Ian Campbell Folk Group, I would be wearing an arran sweater and be a die-hard folkie and therefore not the right man for the job. The audition went well, though, and the rhythm section of DM and Simon and the interplay between Richard and Swarb was amazing. You can't believe how happy I was to be invited to join them.

Peggy's first rehearsal with Fairport Convention was on December 27, 1969. He had taken the decision to join a band which on the one hand had a huge reputation and released three critically acclaimed LPs in one year but on the other hadn't actually played a gig in its current form (crucially lacking what in those days was called "a chick lead singer"!).

Having experienced the benefits and working and living together at Farley Chamberlayne (when they worked on Liege & Lief), Fairport decided to repeat the experiment. They ended up taking a lease on an out-of-the-way 'deconsecrated pub'.

Before Fairport went back on the road, they'd spent weeks at Farley Chamberlayne, sharing a big house and working on the music. Those were days when bands liked to "get it together in the country" as they say. I think everyone got a lot out of the experience and when I joined, there was talk about finding a place where all five members, our wives, girlfriends, roadies, dogs, kids and whatever could co-habit. I wasn't particularly taken by the idea, but I knew the value of members of a band being close together: most bands in the sixties were local to start with, including all the ones I played with regularly in Birmingham and Fairport in North London. At the time, Fairport's members were pretty scattered – Simon, Richard and DM were in various parts of London, I was in Sutton and Swarb was 250 miles away in remote Haverfordwest.

It was Swarb who found the place: apparently, he took it on without even seeing it. It was a big contrast to the mansion at Farley Chamberlayne, The Angel was an abandoned pub in Little Hadham that was scarcely fit for human habitation when we all moved in. It was also, as we were later to discover, located on a particularly dangerous road junction.

So in January 1970, Christine and Stephanie, our two-year-old daughter, and myself moved into The Angel, Little Hadham near Bishops Stortford, Hertfordshire. We were allocated two and a half rooms up the main stairs next on the right after Richard Thompson's room and the TV room. We placed Steph's cot in the smallest room and set about making the limited space into our new home.

I decided to hang my mandolin up on the wall using the 'Birmingham screwdriver' method. I marked a cross on the wall and taking a nail and a large hammer proceeded to knock the nail into place. After a few gentle taps a hole appeared – admittedly somewhat larger than the one I had planned. In fact, it was large enough to put my head through and as I peered through my latest DIY disaster I realised I was looking into Dave Swarbrick's bedroom and even though it was only 3pm, he was already in bed with Birgitte, his Danish second wife. They were involved in an exercise that I certainly hadn't witnessed people doing up to that point. Swarb's head turned my way and he asked, "What the fuck are you doing, Peggy?"

"Hanging up me mandolin", I replied.

"I didn't know you played the mando" says he.

"I don't" says me.

"Well you bleedin' well do, now" says he...

The next day he taught me how to play *Flatback Caper*!

The time spent learning the intricacies of *Liege & Lief* served little purpose beyond Peggy's interview. The band moved on, as it had many times before and would repeatedly in the future, dropping current repertoire and replacing it with new material – *Full House* tracks, including the instrumental *Flatback Caper*. To the pressures of joining a new band and moving house, Peggy had some clear deadlines – his debut tour with Fairport started at the end of January and took in some of their old haunts (Van Dyke's, Mother's) and some of the country's most prestigious venues (Manchester Free Trade Hall, Liverpool Philharmonic, Colston Hall Bristol); before the tour finished, on February 24th, 1970, they were booked in to Sound Techniques to start recording their next LP, there was radio work booked and, of course, their first trip to the USA.

It was quite a thing at first. None of us was sure how we'd go down. I was replacing Ashley who was the man who formed Fairport, the group's leader. People were used to a female lead singer: now there were no females in the band and no lead singer either. Fairport had released three LPs in 1969 which were popular and had sold quite well; we were playing nothing from two of them and hardly any of the other.

Those early gigs weren't exactly a tour, more a series of individual concerts, so we'd often return to The Angel afterwards. We just piled in the van and the roadie – Robin Gee, known to all as "The Mighty Glydd" under which name he appears in Angel Delight – who'd had a chance to have a sleep, drove us all back to the same place. Then it was a matter of falling out of the van and into bed.

In Spring came Fairport's American debut – a West-East tour that began at the end of April and ended six weeks later. Fairport's first trip to play in America in 1969 had been cancelled in the wake of their motorway accident: it would have seen them unveiling their vision of

English folk rock with the audience at the 1969 Newport Folk Festival. They would have shared the bill with 42 other acts which included Carl Perkins, Joni Mitchell, Van Morrison, Pete Seeger, The Weavers, James Taylor, Arlo Guthrie and Buffy Sainte-Marie; also on the bill were some of the acts whose songs Fairport covered in their set – Muddy Waters, Johnny Cash and The Everly Brothers; British contemporaries, Pentangle also appeared.

Fairport's tragic M1 accident in May put paid to those plans.

By the time the Festival took place on July 20, they were ensconced in Farley Chamberlayne creating *Liege & Lief*.

By the time Fairport Convention made their US debut – on April 30 1970 – the band that appeared was unrecognisable from the one that had been booked to play Newport. Of that line up, only Simon and Richard remained; instead of a band with a male/female vocal lead, the line up was entirely male; the lead instrument was now electric fiddle as much as guitar. the American covers repertoire was now determinedly British and largely traditional; Peggy have been their bass player for four months. Rather than an East Coast festival, they found themselves making their debut in West Coast rock clubs. The music press ran it as a headline story, making sure to stress that for some of their first dates they would be playing alongside Crosby Stills Nash and Young.

We played the Fillmore West in San Francisco: four nights on the same bill as Jethro Tull, which was probably the first time I met the band, though even then they had a very different approach to Fairport, much more structured serious musicianship and far less generally having a good time. I had that impression at the time and it would be confirmed at first hand a decade later.

Then we did a week at The Troubadour in Los Angeles, which was the gig that really established our reputation in more ways than one. The story about us drinking more at the bar than we were paid has passed into legend.

We did a free outdoor concert at UCLA and then travelled across the country, ending up in New York in mid June, not the best time of year to be there in terms of the weather - Detroit, Cincinnati, Chicago, Washington DC, ending up at the Fillmore East in New York where Traffic were the headline act and Mott the Hoople were also on the bill.

One gig at the University of Chicago was broadcast by the student radio station and shows how Fairport's set was still heavily influenced by *Liege & Lief*:

Walk Awhile,
Lark in the Morning
The Deserter
Dirty Linen
Sloth
Flatback Caper
Tam Lin
Sir Patrick Spens
General Taylor/Mason's Apron

We came back to England and had a very busy schedule playing gigs and festivals – there was the disaster at Krumlin and our local festival in Little Hadham, which went much better. We went back to America in August, where we played the Philadelphia Folk Festival then the Fillmore East and then the Fillmore West. With Savoy Brown as I recall. Then we had another season at The Troubadour

They got back from The States on June 14. Within the week, they were back to playing gigs across the UK – everything from small clubs to large festivals like Bath on June 27th. A month after that they were on stage at the London Palladium. In between came a trip to Germany and Holland where they topped the bill at the National Pop Festival in Rotterdam. Peggy's abiding memory of the trip is certainly non-musical.

Swarb's romances were legendary. He and Birgitte split up for the first time while we were still living at The Angel. Obviously, when five couples are sharing a house, things like that make for uncomfortable situations all round.

Luckily, we had some dates in Germany. We went to Heathrow, and Swarb was excited. "Hamburg Peggy. We'll be straight down the Jumpingstrasse" (which was his name for the Reiperbaun). We were on our way into the gents and I was explaining that I was a married man and had no intention of joining him on this expedition, when he reaches the urinal, unzips himself and goes "Oh, fuck! Spotty Dog".

I guessed what the problem was... but had no idea what he meant by Spotty Dog. It turned out the previous week, he'd picked up a woman when we did a gig at Cambridge University, which was not far from Little Hadham, and had brought her back to The Angel. Like many of Swarb's conquests and encounters, he remembered her by the nickname he'd given her. I never found out who she really was or why she was called Spotty Dog. However, the effect of her encounter with Swarb was apparent.

Naturally naughty nocturnal adventures in Hamburg were abandoned.

Fairport's next album, named *Angel Delight* in honour of the pub where they had spent 1970 together would include a song called *Sickness and Diseases*.

Tours and one-off gigs in Europe, the UK and America kept Fairport busy in 1970. In all they played 125 gigs, several of which required multiple sets: they did ten sessions for BBC radio as well as a further 25 for overseas broadcasters. But in July, they played a gig that was remarkably easy to get to and probably served as an unconscious and certainly low-key model for the approach later taken at Cropredy.

We'd become part of the village life. We were their tame long haired hippies. In July, we agreed to play the village fete. *Full House* had just been released. The papers reported about 1000 people turned up to see us. The gig was in a field opposite the village pub that hadn't closed down, The Nag's Head, where we had already become familiar faces. There were sideshows, a procession (which we missed because we were setting up) and competitions: I entered the shapely ankle competition and won a pair of socks, which were presented to me by Judith Chalmers – a true career highlight.

Wherever Fairport have been based – Cropredy, Little Hadham and, I'm told, before that in Muswell Hill (before my time, y'know) – we've always tried to be part of the community. Luckily, we've always been accepted. That's why people in the village think of us as "the local band" and not some well-established, world-famous rock act (hope you can tell I am saying that with my tongue in my cheek). They therefore have no qualms about asking us to play – often for free – at some local fundraiser. In fact, during the Wintour in 2018 we've got a gig in Cropredy to raise money for the local school because it needs a music room and is short of equipment.

The local police in Little Hadham asked us to do a gig for their charity.

The week after the Policemen's Benefit they were once more aboard a plane across the Atlantic, this time for a fortnight which saw them traversing the country East-West.

Joe Boyd had put the tour together. Because of his background and having worked for Elektra and at Newport before he came to Britain, he knew so many people, lots of contacts, people that knew and trusted him. He knew all the big names on the folk scene over there. He also got us a great tour manager – a chap called Walter Gundy. He'd worked with loads of big names, including The Loving Spoonful, who were another band that Fairport admired.

It was a great experience, though sometimes didn't go quite as smoothly as it should.

For example, we got off the plane in New York and went straight to the Chelsea Hotel, which was famous even then for the people who had lived there and indeed those who were still living there... writers, artists, musicians, poets. The rooms had already been sorted... or should have been: when we got there, we found that everyone had been allocated a room apart from Anthea Joseph and Christine and myself. They set up a makeshift room in the basement, with three beds – we had to share: so that's where I spent the first three nights. Ah the glamour of the rock'n'roll life on the road.

We had a good tour, though we played mainly weekends, Fridays, Saturdays, Sundays, when you could pull the biggest crowds normally. The rest of the week we'd either be driving enormous distances across the USA, which becomes a bit of a slog after you've done it a few times, but that first time, you get such a buzz. You see signs to places that are legendary through songs or films or whatever; you pass buildings that are everyday but also iconic – roadside diners, old farmsteads, that kind of thing. We knew – or at least Walter knew – how long the journey between gigs would take, so we had time to hang around, get to know places a bit. It wasn't one of those do-a-gig / pack-up / move-on / play-the-same-gig-in-a-different-place-next-day things. It was an adventure in the course of which we got to play music, make friends, even get paid occasionally. It was like The Fairports starring in their very own road movie.

As part of the schedule, Joe had fixed us up with some free concerts, university gigs in the afternoon mostly, as a way of getting our name and our music known to what was our biggest potential audience over there. Years later, people would turn up at gigs in the States saying they'd first seen us as one of those free gigs and they'd followed the band ever since. Things don't work like that anymore, but it was a great way to get yourself known. We'd play somewhere like UCLA; maybe a thousand would people would turn up and just sit on the lawn and listen to the music.

**If you go down in Flood's, it'll be your fault.**
We were in a big University town near Detroit, Ann Arbor, and the way things worked out we were there from Monday through to Saturday, which is when we were due to play. We were staying in quite a posh hotel – certainly posh by Fairport standards. We had a daily allowance – spending money if your like – of ten dollars a day for each person involved in the tour. It sounds like a pittance, but both my wife Christine and myself lived off that quite comfortably. Breakfast was something like $1.50: it was enough to feed two people; so that's what we did, bought one breakfast and fed two people. Nobody seemed to mind you doing that in those days.

There was a place called Mr Flood's in Ann Arbor. It was a bar. We were in town all week, so we went in there Tuesday night to check it out. It was quite expensive: as I recall we could afford one beer each. But they had bottled Bass, English beer. Simon, who was always good at such things, struck a deal with the owner. He explained we were a band from England, in town for the week, with nothing to do; how would he feel about us coming along and playing, maybe next night. Although the owner liked the idea, he said he couldn't afford to pay us. We were hardly likely to draw in customers to make it worth his while to do so. Simon, as planned, said, "Just give us free beer when we're playing and that'll be fine." That seemed like a fair deal.

The guy then asked what kind of music it was. Simon just said "It's folk-rock". That meant nothing to him, so he decided we'd have to audition. Quite rightly, Simon assumed we wouldn't be prepared to audition for an unpaid gig. So he just went back, on his own, with his guitar and auditioned on our behalf. He got us the gig... and the free beer.

We went in next night... all five Fairports on a tiny little stage. We had a great time; the audience seemed to like us; we got free beer. Some people asked when they could see us again, so we plugged the free Saturday gig on the university campus. At the end, the owner grabbed us and asked if we'd be up for playing the next night, which was Thursday. We said, "yeah, fine". He went straight on stage and announced it. Next night the place was heaving: word had got round and it was packed. Bar takings were clearly going through the roof. The owner had a huge smile locked onto his face all night. He asked us back on Friday and we said yes... with the same free beer arrangement. Come Friday and Dave Mattacks has decided he doesn't want to come. He's never been a big drinker, so really he's working hard and not getting much out of the deal. He also pointed out the bar was raking it in and we weren't seeing any of that. Simon and I were just keen to get as much free Bass down us as we could. That night, Robin Gee played DM's snare drum: Dave's very particular about taking care of his kit and he went absolutely spare about it afterwards.

Next day – afternoon – as planned we played on the campus. We drew a much bigger crowd, not only students but also a lot of familiar faces from Mr Flood's.

On that same tour we were booked to play the Philadelphia Folk Festival. In those days, folk events could be quite specific and there was a risk you might not fit. Like, in Britain, there were clubs that were entirely traditional and didn't want people to sing composed songs and especially not their own composed songs. We knew American folk festivals could be quite purist and so we were quite nervous about how well we'd go down. Like most American folk festivals, it was a dry gig – no alcohol allowed: that might have been something to do with being granted the permit to hold the event, I don't know, but the rule was strictly enforced.

It was a fantastic line-up. I know Doc Watson and his son Merle were there, because I was excited about being able to see them in the flesh as it were.

Fairport played on the Sunday between 5.00 and 6.30 – straight after the "Bawdy Song Workshop". The festival line up also included Mississippi Fred McDowell with Bonnie Raitt, John Hartford, Kate McGarrigle, Dave van Ronk, Rambling Jack Elliott, John Denver, Tom Paxton and Ralph Stanley with The Clinch Mountain Boys.

Because of Joe Boyd and Walter Gundy's contacts, in the course of that tour, or perhaps calling it "that road trip with occasional stops to play music" would be more accurate, we got to meet some incredible people. We visited the home of Bill Keith the banjo player; we got invited to Linda Ronstadt's house and as a result she became quite a good friend of the band.

When we stayed at The Tropicana in Los Angeles we'd eat in the restaurant next door, Dukes, because they had special rates for residents. We weren't huge drinkers at the time but our reputation for enjoying the odd can of whatever went before us. Our first time in Los Angeles, on that tour, one of the reps from A&M, who released our stuff in the States, Bob Garcia, threw a big barbecue for us. He lived up in one of the valleys. I remember us all being impressed with his fridge! I think it was Swarb who spotted it and called us in "Come and look at the size of this!" We couldn't resist the temptation to open the door and when we did we discovered it was full of cans of Fosters lager. The choice was a mistake because we've stolen the idea of "loving a tinny of Fosters" from the Barry McKenzie strip cartoon and of course the Americans understandably missed the reference. They'd assumed it was literally us. You know sometimes you've created a reputation and now you have to live up to it... We did our best until the intake of gas and alcohol began to compete in our digestive systems. Fairport has always been home to some world champion farters – a fridge full of Fosters reinforced our farting fame.

The main thing about LA, though, were the nights we played at The Troubadour. We'd played there at the start of the year, but now word had got round and we were a happening band. You'd look into the audience and it was full of famous faces – not there because they'd come to see us particularly but because it's where they hung out. Linda Ronstadt was there most nights and would get up and sing with us: Simon found her presence on stage particularly distracting – she was gorgeous with a voice like an angel and very short skirt, after all – and she played up to that, never missing a note in the process: Simon was still the young kid in the group, 19 years old, and so the rest of us were most amused by his discomfiture. On a couple of nights, Odetta got up... and she was a powerful woman: she dominated any stage and when she sang, her voice was so powerful she could override the band without a mike!

This stint included the night, long passed into rock legend, when Led Zeppelin turned up. They shared the bill with Rick Nelson, a fifties child star who'd become one of the biggest acts in rock'n'roll's highschool era. Like many American pop stars of the early sixties, his career has been curtailed by the arrival of The Beatles and then the first wave of singer-songwriters, whose music he loved and included on the album he'd record at The Troudbadour a year earlier. I interviewed him shortly before his death in 1985 and he recalled playing alongside Fairport with obvious pleasure.

*I was looking for a new direction and not really finding it. I was singing Dylan, Phil Ochs and Eric Anderson but in a way that was still something of a throwback. Then... there were these guys whose music was based around stuff that was older than America, real roots music, proper folk. We had folk music in America, but it was played with reverence, like handling a museum piece. Fairport played loud rock and they really went for it, as you say. They made it relevant and they didn't seem to give a damn what people thought.*

*It struck me then, if I could do what they did, just find roots that went deeper than Elvis, maybe I could find a direction for myself. I did and I have Fairport Convention to thank for it.*

The bass player in Rick's band was similarly impressed, particularly by Peggy (*"The guy was using the bass guitar like a lead instrument, playing jigs. He blew me away. I realised the potential of my instrument."*). Following the Troubadour gigs, he quit Rick Nelson's band to form a backing band for Linda Ronstadt (*"Seeing what she did with Fairport gave me an idea of what a band could do behind her."*). His name was Randy Meisner: among the musicians he recruited were Bernie Leadon, Glen Frey and Don Henley. A year exactly after drawing inspiration from watching Fairport at the Troubadour, they became The Eagles.

Fortunately, we have more than memories as a record of those nights at The Troubadour. The

Island Mobile was outside, recording each set. Various individual tracks have been released over the years and just after Fairport were told their contract was not being renewed, Island decided to unearth the tapes and put together an album recorded seven years earlier.

I don't think we even reviewed the tapes at the time. As soon as we got back from America we had a huge tour of the UK. In any case, back then it would have been down to Island to produce a live album, picking the tracks and so on. Because they'd recorded several nights they had several versions of songs to choose from as well as one-off performances. Richard left the band three months after the Troubadour recordings. Like Sandy, we felt he was irreplaceable: so we didn't. Of course, at a stroke, that removed the band's lead guitarist, joint lead vocalist, and songwriter. The decision not to replace him put a lot of pressure on Simon, demands which being Simon he naturally rose to satisfy. Meanwhile we had to think about putting out an album that represented the new four-man Fairport and out of that came *Angel Delight*, of course.

For some reason Island decided not to release the live album. Over the years there have been a few great Fairport live recordings that were supposed to be released and then weren't. There are some great recordings of us with Sandy on vocals, also recorded at The Troubadour, which were done just after the Australian gigs that became the *Live Convention* LP. The performances on them are better, but by the time we'd played LA, we were so strapped for money that we couldn't afford to pay for the tapes so we could use them. A lot of the stuff has come out since in various forms and there are some great performances to be discovered – things I am genuinely proud of being part of.

As for The Troubadour recordings, Island just sat on them. I think odd tracks escaped on compilations and so – there's one on the RT retrospective double LP. They finally decided to release an album of them after they decided not to continue our contract and our new record label was about to bring out our latest LP. So far as I am aware no one in the band had any say about what went on the finished LP, though it has some great, classic Fairport stuff on it.

Because I was so involved in the business side of Fairport from 1980 onwards, people expect me to know what went on with that aspect of the band before then. The truth is, I wasn't involved at all. So, I genuinely have no idea. I was just the bass player: my job was to arrive on time, know the music and play it to the best of my ability.

Live at The Troubadour both delights and disappoints. Its eight tracks focus on the band's instrumental prowess – three medleys and a mighty eleven-minute version of *Sloth*. Each side ends oddly too: side one closes with the song removed at the last minute from *Full House*, *Poor Will and The Jolly Hangman* in a dubbed and doctored studio version; side two ends with a throwaway version of *Yellow Bird*. When Joe Boyd reissued the album (retitling *House Full*), he removed both those tracks and one other, and replaced them with three excellent live recordings, including *Staines Morris* and *Battle of The Somme*, two numbers otherwise unavailable by Fairport. When the Troubadour recordings came out on CD, all the live tracks from both vinyl releases were included.

It's a great album, but as I say, none of the Fairports was involved beyond playing on the night.

That's still true today. While a band, like Fairport, may have control over its new releases, very often older material is no longer under their control. People come up to you at gigs and sometimes it's embarrassing because you simply don't know about everything that's coming out these days. It's common practice for small record labels to lease old albums to other companies once the initial sales have died off – say after a couple of years. There's all kinds of reasons for that, which I don't need to go into. That new company can, of course, repackage, recompile, anthologise or whatever so long as they hold the lease. Quite often the artists have no idea what's happening. Sometimes that label will sublease again to someone else.

Sometimes the first time you're aware of an album is when somebody turns up with it for you to sign. You look at it and think "What's this?". Is it a bootleg, for example... because, yes, even Fairport get bootlegged: Tull much more so.

When it's awkward is when someone complains about a reissue because it's simply not your fault: they're maybe been tricked by packaging or a changed title or the wrong picture on the sleeve – and of course there's CDs that look like studio albums but are compilations of live recordings. You told me about an album of early Fairport songs with a picture of the line up with Sandy and Iain on the sleeve where all the recordings were live from Cropredy.

It's something by and large beyond our control. All we can do is not sell that reissued material on the merch stand.

That having been said, though The Troubadour album came out without any band involvement and pissed us off a bit at the time, I think everyone in The Fairports at the time is really glad those recordings are available because they capture one of the greatest Fairport line ups in absolutely top form.

It was fantastic. We were playing to and sometimes with people who we really admired but had never been more than names on record sleeves. It was exciting to be in America, in fact to have travelled across America and seen so much of it. Those first tours of the USA, the five lads together, all mates, all excited and intent on having a good time, it was wonderful, and it still makes me feel good to think back to it.

A month after returning from America, Fairport began a massive UK tour which began on October 7 at The Royal Albert Hall and ended two days after playing Ian Campbell's Jug O'Punch club in mid-December. On November 9, half way through the tour, I got my second chance to see them live, when they played Oxford Town Hall. Hoping to grab an interview, I blagged my way into the soundcheck. DM was scurrying about doing clearly precise and hugely important things with his drumkit. Swarb made some excuse about needing to be somewhere else. Simon and Richard, I was told, had spotted a nearby guitar shop (Russell Acott's, probably) and disappeared thence. Which left me the option of interviewing "the new boy". Out of archive interest, here is the result of the very first interview I did with Dave Pegg.

*Fairport Convention went through a lot of changes last year.*

DP: I'm probably the wrong person to ask about that. I joined at the start of this year. So all that stuff had already happened.

*When you joined, the group had just released Liege & Lief which was hailed as the first folk-rock LP. Did you have much time to learn all that material?*

DP: I learned the songs on that record for my audition. We're not playing those songs with the new line-up. Mainly it's things on our latest record *Full House* because that's the album made by the current Fairport Convention line-up. Richard Thompson and Dave Swarbrick have been writing a lot of songs together and we'll be playing some of those tonight, too – things that aren't on the record because they wrote them after it was finished.

*You come from a folk background because like Dave Swarbrick you were a member of The Ian Campbell Group before you joined Fairport Convention.*

DP: That's true except Swarb and I weren't in the Campbells at the same time. I didn't leave the Campbells to join Fairport. Last year I was working with a rock trio. Mostly, I've played with rock bands in Birmingham. When Ian offered me a job it was regular work with a good wage, so naturally I accepted.

One thing about being in Fairport Convention is that it brings together those two things... rock and folk. We're playing folk-songs and traditional tunes, or songs written by the band in a folk style, but we play them as rock songs.

*You've toured America with Fairport Convention this year. Was that the first time you've been there?*

DP: Yes. We toured earlier in the year and then went back for a second tour which included Philadelphia Folk Festival, which was good because I got to meet some of my heroes. Tours in America aren't like here because you tend to spend a few days in a place, instead of playing a different town every night. Instead of travelling all the time, you can get to know places. We were able to spend time in New York, Los Angeles and Boston, which was all pretty cool.

*Your new LP Full House is out and it might be a shock to fans of the group who are used to hearing a female singer.*

DP: That's because we're all men. There's nobody in the group you'd called the singer, though four of us do sing on the LP. It's something of a radical approach. We're putting together new material all the time, so you'll hear a lot of things you haven't heard before tonight. A lot of those will be on the album we're planning to make next year.

*No doubt I'll find out tonight, but I wonder who it is singing on the LP?*

DP: On the first track, Simon, Swarb, Richard and myself take a verse each. It's a Richard song called *Walk Awhile*. It's a great opening number and it gets over the idea that no one in the band is the lead singer.

We're all big fans of The Band, who were Bob Dylan's backing group. They have a similar approach because if you listen to their LPs, each of then sings on different tracks. They're better singers than us, of course – better than me, at any rate.

*Does the fact that Full House has several songs written by members of the group mean you're not carrying on with electric folk?*

DP: We're still doing traditional songs. Richard is writing a lot of great stuff with Swarb and it really fits in with what we want to do. So, from now on, it will be a mix of the two. I can't imagine Fairport Convention not playing traditional tunes and songs. It's something of our trademark now.

*A shout from the mixing desk told us Dave ("Call me Peggy") Pegg was needed on stage for a soundcheck. He left, suggesting we meet up next time they're playing in my area. I hope we do.*

Fairport, then as now, were a great festival act. They'd been in at the start, and their pre-Pegg days had seen them playing several free festivals in London (on one occasion sharing the bill with Jefferson Airplane): they closed the very first, 1968, Isle of White Festival, playing till 5.30 am on a day which had included Plastic Penny, Aynsley Dunbar's Retalliation, Smile, Blonde on Blonde, The Move, Arthur Brown, Tyrannosaurus Rex, The Pretty Things and Jefferson Airplane. As jazz, blues and folk festivals rebranded themselves in order to include crowd-pulling underground bands. Fairport, whose albums before Peggy joined, included pop, rock, psychedelia, blues, original songs, traditional songs, material from upcoming singer-songwriters, obscure Dylan songs and extended guitar jams could fit almost any bill.

I think Fairport have always been musically open-minded despite everyone thinking of us as a folk-rock or even just a folk band. Certainly most of what we play is folk-influenced, but I think it's years since we last recorded an actual traditional song that the band hadn't done before.

The same is true of Cropredy. I know a lot of people think of it as a folk festival and of course we always have folk musicians there. One thing I'm really proud of is the fact we give a slot every year to the BBC Young Folk Musicians of the Year: it gives many of them their first chance to play on a big stage in front of thousands of people. Over the years, I'd say most of the big names in folk and folk-rock have played there, but so have bands that have nothing to do with folk. We aim for a conscious mix of music that might take in classic pop, reggae, rock, country. We're lucky that some of the biggest names in music actually want to come and play there: sometimes we're definitely punching above our weight when you consider the size of the festival – which is a maximum of 20,000 people – and the calibre of acts who appear.

I often find myself out in the field watching some artist I'm really pleased we've been able to book, thinking "Bloody hell, they're supporting us", which is usually rapidly followed by the rather more scary "Christ, we have to follow that?"

I have to say our audience is pretty supportive too. It's not a specifically Fairport audience, though obviously real Fairport fans want to be there and there are those who have never missed a year in all the time it's been going. They are very open minded and will accept what look like quite sudden lurches in style. Sometimes it's the acts you find it hard to image that go down best. The Pierce Brothers, whom no one had heard of when we booked them for 2016, went down a storm, for example; so much so, that we took the unusual step of having them back, by popular demand, the following year.

Back when I joined Fairport, we played a lot of festivals, in an era when a festival would expose you to a lot of different music. I wasn't that precisely aware of Fairport's music before I joined, so I've had the pleasure over the years of going back and discovering it. *Unhalfbricking* is one of my all-time favourite albums. I'd attended a lot of festivals before I joined, but as a participant it was with The Campbells who tended to play dedicated folk festivals.

### Loud and boisterous blew the wind

In the wake of Woodstock and the next Isle of White Festival, 1970 became the era of the festival – Fairport played ten on this side of the Atlantic in the course of the year. Some of those events stand out as great moments for the band – an appearance at Maidstone Fiesta that became a cinema film directed by Tony Palmer; Bath Festival of Blues and Progressive Rock, where their performance was included on a highly prized bootleg; Philadelphia Folk Festival, which in 1997 selected their set for release on a limited-edition CD as an all-time highlight to mark its fortieth anniversary.

But of all the 1970 musical gatherings, the most remarkable was The Yorkshire Folk and Blues Festival, held on August 14-16 in the moorland near Barkisland, the height of summer. No one had reckoned, however, that this was the height of summer in the pre-M62 wilds of the Yorkshire Pennines. The name Krumlin is whispered among rock fans with the same aura of dread as First World War veterans uttered the word Somme!

The advertised line-up was astonishing. The programme (which cost 3/-) listed almost sixty acts and promised "last minute surprises". One might assume the latter included big names, last minute additions, unscheduled guests – rather than inadequate facilities, an inaccessible site (some acts couldn't actually make it along the narrow moorland roads), insufficient staff, angry fans who had unwittingly bought pirate tickets via Melody Maker and were refused entry, over twenty hospitalised cases of exposure and weather conditions that were little short of apocalyptic.

So instead of Pink Floyd, The Who and Ginger Baker's Airforce, fans were treated to torrential rain, hail, plummeting temperatures and winds so high they destroyed everything apart from the main stage. Fairport Convention were booked to appear on the Saturday, along with Fotheringay, Pentangle, Ralph McTell, The Johnsons, Manfred Mann, Amazing Blondel and Alan Price. So chaotic was the event that even today no one can say who actually played and which bands failed to turn up at all. Fairport were one of those acts that definitely made it to the stage before the whole thing was abandoned as an unmitigated disaster: the band feature in some of the very few photos that showed performers on stage.

Add to the acts already mentioned Zoot Money, Georgie Fame, Yes, The Humblebums, Juicy Lucy, Atomic Rooster, Mungo Jerry and Taste and you have a festival line up to die for. The problem is, a lot of the audience very nearly did. For Fairport, it all began in the golden warmth of a Hertfordshire dawn...

We were all living together at The Angel. I was the only driver in Fairport at the time. No one else had passed their driving test. Robin Gee was our roadie – that's what we called them at the time though maybe it's no longer politically correct – and part of his job was driving the white Transit van with our gear and the band to wherever we were due to play. It wasn't an ideal way to travel, so sometimes I'd go separately in my car, especially if it was a long way.

We'd been booked to play at "a festival in Yorkshire". That was as much as we knew really. We'd been given the address, which didn't really mean much. We just knew Yorkshire was a long way... beyond the end of the M1 as it then was... and the place we were going to looked rather small on the map when we eventually found it. Still, the thought of the Yorkshire Moors in the August sunshine had its own special appeal (I'm very aware you're from that part of the world, Nigel, so I'm choosing my words very carefully at this point).

We left our home in the quiet village of Little Hadham to head to the wilds of the North. We made jokes about it, which we came to regret. My wife Christine and I set off in our blue Ford Anglia and at the same time, Robin with Swarb, Simon, Richard and DM left in the Transit. It was a very early start, around dawn as I recall, which would have been really early because this was mid-summer. It was a long drive and not an easy one – you tend to forget what it was like travelling round Britain in those days before the motorways.

By two o'clock, we found ourselves on a small moorland road – drystone walls, remote farm buildings, villages you'd miss if you blinked: there was certainly no sign of anything resembling a rock festival, not even signs to suggest which way to go. Even more worrying was the fact we seemed to have been driving for ages and hadn't seen another vehicle.

Suddenly, in the distance, appearing and disappearing as the road dipped and twisted, we saw a white van approaching us. My first thought was finding somewhere wide enough for us to pass. Then as it came close, we realised it was Robin Gee and the rest of the band... coming in the opposite direction: not a good sign. If we'd come one way and not seen the supposed festival and they'd done the same thing from the other end of the valley, one might safely assume something had gone wrong.

We asked, "Are we going the wrong way?"

He replied, "Don't ask me: we can't find the venue."

Venue was how he put it, I still remember – a term which no way applied to the large scrubby field that, as it turned out, we were looking for.

We stuck together after that and more by luck than clear directions, we eventually found the festival site... or field as I should call it. The weather was becoming inclement to say the least: it was windy, the clouds were low (or maybe we were just nearer to them, which is how it felt), so it was drizzly and everything you touched felt soaked, you could feel it getting colder and there were occasional sudden blasts of rain. Perfect for a remake of *Wuthering Heights* – not so good for a three-day outdoor music event.

Anyhow, we found our way to what I'll call backstage, which meant little more than literally not-in-front-of-the-stage. Ostensibly we were due on after Pentangle; however, for some reason, they'd decided they wanted to go on after us. I've no idea what the problem was: we weren't bothered when we went on. In fact, looking at the state of affairs, the sooner we could get our set over with and find our way to the hotel we'd booked for the night, the better, so far as I was concerned.

Normally, it's great to be at a festival: you get chance to meet up with friends; you can hear bands you don't normally get chance to hear; you might even bump into one of your heroes. This was not that kind of thing: you could see the situation going from bad to worse. Not the acts... and especially not the fans who deserved a medal for endurance in the face of adversity... but generally the organisation of the whole thing and the weather which would have been appalling in November, and this was August.

Anthea Joseph, who was representing Joe Boyd's agency, was there to collect the money on behalf of the acts he represented. That included us: I think we were being paid around three hundred quid for the gig. She discovered there were problems: the two guys running it didn't have the money – there'd been problems with people turning up with forged tickets; the walk-up on the day – people arriving without tickets and paying on the gate – was virtually nil because of the weather; advance tickets hadn't sold well because people had bought them from illegitimate sources. It was a mess. There were lots of rumours going round and I have to be careful what I say, even now – but I know those three things were definitely true.

Anthea, along with everyone else there to represent bands or the acts themselves if no one was there for them, was basically trying to get money up-front by saying that unless an act was paid, they wouldn't go on. That's never a good negotiating position because, as anybody in a band will tell you, if you're advertised and don't play, everyone's going to blame you, whatever the reasons behind it.

Jo Lustig, who as you know was pretty much an old school manager, was there on behalf of Pentangle. Then there were lots of folkie-types who were trying to collect money on their own behalf. We felt sorry for them. In fact Swarb and I knew a lot of them from our days on the folk scene, but when it comes to getting paid and the cash is limited, it's every man for himself.

It was billed as a Folk and Blues festival. In addition to the big name, crowd pulling acts, blues bands and main-stage folk acts like Fairport, there was also a giant marquee which had hosted an all-night folk concert the previous evening once The Pretty Things finished on the main stage. The extensive list of local and national folk acts playing the all-nighter (and in some cases the main stage over the next couple of days) included Dave Burland, Tony Capstick, Diz Disley, Mike Harding, Hamish Imlach, Marie Little, Christy Moore, Johnny Silvo, Roger Sutcliffe and Martyn Wyndham-Read.

I remember bumping into Diz Disley, bless him, and Johnny Silvo. We were all herded into this big Folk Tent which was now designated The Artist's Bar and waited until we found out if our representatives had got enough money to allow us to go on stage.

This all sounds rough, but that was the way it was. A lot of people were trying to do things for the first time in those days – artists, organisers, crew, managers: no one had written a handy guide about how to go about these things. People made mistakes. We were all learning. Back in 1970, you often made sure you always got your money before you went on. If you didn't, chances are you wouldn't get paid and there was not a lot you could do about it.

While all this was going on, the weather was getting worse and worse and worse – really really bad. Apocalyptic. We were OK: the so-called Artists' Bar was big and didn't leak much, but for people out in the field – people who'd paid good money for three days of music – it was getting increasingly awful: that was obvious anytime you took a step outside the tent, as I was shortly about to discover.

These days, of course, you can easily buy good outdoor gear that's cheap and keep warm and dry. Back then, nobody could afford that kind of gear; it was specialist kit. People were trying to shelter under umbrellas that the wind was ripping apart or lying in sleeping bags that weren't waterproof or wrapping themselves in plastic sheeting. Not a good situation.

Aside from us, various folkies and folk-rockers, there were all kinds of people in that tent – Elton and Bernie Taupin; The Move, who weren't booked but had turned up because they're heard that other acts couldn't get through – Brummies of course – Roy Wood, Bev Bevan, Jeff Lynne who I think had joined quite recently. We were in the Artists' Bar, just drinking because there was nothing else to do – and that includes Richard Thompson who at the time did drink. And so it continued until we were told it was OK for us to go on.

I've no idea what was happening on the stage at this point, because by now all you could hear above the noise of increasingly refreshed musicians was the rain hammering on the roof of the tent and dripping through in more and more places. The bar now had several interesting water features and was becoming muddy with leaking rain, spilled beer and used beer expended by those not prepared to brave the weather and go to the distant "facilities".

Eventually, much later in the evening, quite a while after we were due to play, Anthea came up to us and said, "I've got the money: you can go on now." To be honest, I think we'd all assumed it wasn't going to happen and had tried to make the best of a bad situation. But there it was: time to go and play for these poor people huddled together in conditions you wouldn't send a sheep out in.

We were in a state of some alcoholic disarray, but we picked up our instruments and headed for the steps to the stage.

Dave Harper – who'd previously worked for The Fairports as a kind of tour manager/assistant – had somehow got the job as stage manager at Krumlin and he blocked our way, telling us he wasn't letting us on stage. We tried to explain – we'd had an awful journey, waited for ages, suffered the weather and finally got our money. He then said, "That's fine for you: we haven't been paid. So nobody goes on until the crew get their money."

That meant another delay. We trudged back to the bar. And what else was there to do but carry on drinking? I'm surprised the audience hadn't rioted yet.

It was during this delay that Nature called and I managed by accident to acquire a reputation as something of a hard case. I left the Artists' Bar and went in search of the nearest Gent's. This happened to be down a long slope which, as a result of the rain and the number of people going up and down, had become rather treacherous; I set off and started to slide so that suddenly I found I was running faster than I could control my speed. As I reached the toilet, two guys were coming out and I knocked them over. I tried to explain and say I was sorry, but one of the blokes said "You will be sorry when I stand up." I tried to make peace and help him up but he slipped and fell down again. There am I with these two huge aggressive Yorkshire blokes at my feet as Roy Wood and Bev Bevan come rather more steadily down the slope to the loo. Roy says, "Bloody hell, Peggy, what're doing, taking on these two?" They'd obviously misjudged the whole scene and thought I had floored these two blokes who quite frankly could have made mincemeat of me. By the time I next went to Birmingham, I discovered my reputation as a bruiser and person not to be messed with had gone up enormously.

None of this helped me when eventually we got on stage, of course. By the time the stage crew had sorted out their differences with the people running the festival, the majority of the Fairports, with the exception of Dave Mattacks who tended to be more sensible than the rest of us, had passed the point where going on stage was necessarily a good idea. On a scale of sober, Richard would have been a close second, which, as it turns out, was a good thing.

Prior to this, Dave Swarbrick, also taken short, had impressed the journalists who were in a pit right by the edge of the stage by going under the stage, sticking his chopper through a gap in the canvas and pissing on them. He said he was just desperate to go to the loo and lost his sense of direction.

The audience had been kept waiting a ridiculously long time. Half of them were dying of exposure. What little infrastructure the festival had had was falling apart around them. They didn't have things like food concessions, of course. I think there was a fish-and-chip wagon, someone doing hot dogs, an ice-cream truck but not much else: by this point, I think they'd given in and shut up shop anyway. Things that people had brought with them were soaked. It was truly awful for them.

A review in International Times catches the mood – It was the worst organized festival ever. It was a piece of moorland. About 25,000 kids turned up, but the weather turned almost immediately from mild grey clouds to grey rain, hail, sleet and rain, blue rain and thunderstorms. This went on for the entirety of the festival so there was this incredibly damp and miserable audience in the downpour in this rather cold and bleak up-land where trees don't grow.

There was a full-on tempest by now and all the audience had to protect themselves were plastic bags.

On top of which, word had come through that the roads were now blocked. No one seemed to have considered how these narrow country roads that in those days probably saw half a dozen cars and a tractor in a day were going to cope with hundreds of people arriving. No one had thought to arrange special bus services or anything like that. Whether there was anything happening on stage or not, no matter how much the wind blew and the rain fell, no matter how hungry they got, these people were stuck. They were in need of rescue: what they got were five very over-refreshed folk-rockers.

To be fair, Dave Mattacks was still reasonably sober, which meant we were at least in time when we played. Richard, who was also still in a compos-mentis state of mind, rapidly realised that Simon's rhythm guitar playing was not, shall we say, up to its usual high standard. He wasn't so much out of tune as being beyond the point where you could tell whether he was playing the same song as everyone else. Richard went to the back of the stage and simply unplugged Simon's guitar from his amp: it says a lot for Simon's state of mind that he didn't notice and carried on playing anyway. He didn't notice, either, when Robin Gee, who was on the sound-desk, turned his vocal mike down and eventually off. Simon may have been on stage, but he was inaudible.

I was wearing a pair of white Levi jeans and I was pleased that I made it to the stage without getting mud on them. That feeling of self-satisfaction vanished when part way through the set I shat myself, on stage. It sobered me up. That was when I noticed that the bass was a bit loud: at the time we were playing through quite large stage speakers and at some point, I must have turned mine up a bit too much. That was when I realised that to turn it down I would need to turn my back on the audience, thereby revealing my predicament. So the bass stayed loud at the back while the white jeans – size 32" waist, 32" leg – got brown in the same place. To the audience, everything looked fine: on stage, those Fairports sober enough to notice knew something was wrong, as did any other musicians who had come into the side stage area to see the band: one of them, I know, was Elton John because there is a photo from the wings of Elton and me in the background on stage in my white jeans: worth looking closely at the look on our faces is all I'll say.

From the front though, so far as the audience was concerned, everything was fine. And so it remained, thanks to a careful exit from the stage, until the time came for me to leave the carpark and drive to the Selby Fork Hotel. This is a good hour away: if you're in the state that I was, that's a very long hour. I'd thought we'd be OK: Christine could drive, get us out of the carpark and on our way: I hadn't thought she'd been enjoying herself as much as we had, plus she'd had the time we were on stage to carry on drinking at the bar. She was in as bad a state as I was – at least so far as being inebriate is concerned: obviously she didn't have my other issue to contend with!

Somehow, I managed to get my Ford Anglia out of the carpark, which was, like everywhere else, a sea of mud by now. I got out of the festival site and onto a proper road where I successfully followed Robin Gee driving the white Transit to the hotel.

Christine very kindly dealt with the by now very unpleasant task of cutting me out of my much-less-than-white jeans. At last I was able to get into the shower, get clean and feel altogether much much better. Discovering the hotel had a swimming pool, I decided to go for a swim. This turned out to be a good thing because Roger Spencer was there doing incredible diving tricks into the pool (Roger was the drummer with The Idle Race, one of Birmingham's better bands: they had a singer/guitarist called Jeff Lynne who had just left the group to join The Move and would soon form The Electric Light Orchestra with Roy Wood).

Roger stayed with The Idle Race until 1971 when a major reshuffle changed the personnel with the exception of bass player Greg Masters and brought into the band a key figure through Peggy's career – Steve Gibbons.

Roger had a particular trick called The Porpoise. He always waited till he had a bit of a crowd watching: then he would do a low dive, hitting the water at such an angle that the force of the contact pulled down his trunks exposing him bum. It wasn't particularly offensive and because it required a bit of expert diving was usually appreciated by people watching... so long as they were guys in bands or their wives. Other people seemed to find it inappropriate for some reason. There you go: no accounting for taste!

Roger eventually moved on from music and became a great comedian.

Afterwards lots of stories have emerged about Krumlin... and it's hard to say which are true. I know very few of the bands who were supposed to play did: I don't think anyone played on the Sunday at all. Someone told me it was officially declared a disaster so emergency services could be called in to rescue people: because we left early, I've no idea how the people attending got home – or even whether they did. A story about the organisers says that one of them wandered away so depressed he drowned himself; another says they were picked up wandering on the moors in a confused state clutching a carrier bag full of money. All I can say is, in my first year of Fairport, which was memorable for so many reasons, that was one of the more memorable moments: I was there; I played on stage; I was around at the birth of all the subsequent legends.

One Krumlin legend which certainly isn't true is that one of the organisers was future TV star Jeremy Beadle. This rumour did, however, have a basis for its existence. The following year, still a shop owner in Wigan, Beadle organised the Bickershaw Festival. (The original mistake seems to have originated with someone who didn't know Barkisland from his Bickershaw.) Another potentially great line up (Grateful Dead, Kinks, Captain Beefheart, Country Joe among them) at an event beset by mud and mayhem. Ticket sales were a fiasco as security people took tickets and resold them to people arriving without advance booking. The festival site was prone to flooding; naturally it rained, but what made matters worse was when the deep pool, used by one of the non-musical turns (a high diver), was emptied in front of the main stage. Game for a bath, perhaps?

Over the years, I've attended a lot of festivals – lots where Fairport or Tull or earlier the Campbells were appearing of course, but also festivals where I just went along to enjoy the entertainment. I've been at some of the very best and some of the very worst, like Krumlin. There's so much that can go wrong, but not if you plan carefully: and, of course, you have to have a contingency in case things go wrong despite your planning. It's no good, for example, looking at the date and assuming the weather will be good without thinking "but what if it isn't?".

When we developed Cropredy, which was a long steady process that brought us to where we are today, we looked at the things we knew worked well at festivals and tried to use that as a model and we looked at all the things that we'd seen go wrong and tried to avoid that.

A lot of people think running a festival is about booking the right acts... and of course it is. But even that isn't simple: you have to have the right mix of acts – right for your audience and right for the event. This year at Cropredy we had Petula Clark who's 80-odd making her outdoor festival debut and then Richard Thompson who's part of the fabric of Cropredy really, solo and then with me, Simon, DM and Christine Collister. On paper that shouldn't work for all kinds of reasons: but we knew it would and it did. It wasn't just good, it was also memorable.

But you can put on the best acts in the world and if you don't get everything else right, you can have a disaster on your hands. If things go wrong, it's not only bad for the people who are there, but word gets round and soon nobody wants to come: so many of those seventies festivals went under because of that.

It's the details – have you got good food on sale at sensible prices (because two things festival goers hate are feeling hungry and feeling ripped off); is there a decent well-stocked bar; do you have plenty of convenient, clean toilets; what happens if it rains? And equally what do you do if it's dangerously sunny. That's all part of the joy of English weather.

When it was obvious more people were starting to come to Cropredy... before the Farewell Fairport Cropredy in '79, I remembered Krumlin and being lost on those York-shire moorland roads. Everyone who's been to our Festival knows it's down some narrow country lanes. Right from the start, we always sent out detailed directions – rail and bus as well as road – to anyone who bought tickets. We made sure there was clear sign-posting to the event from as far away as was practical. We've even persuaded the village to have a temporary one-way system that prevented routes becoming blocked.

Stuff like that doesn't just happen. Somebody had to make it happen. That was down to Christine Pegg and then Gareth Williams, without whom... (as they say). When it works perfectly, festival-goers aren't even aware of it. All they have to think about is the reason they're there – to watch the music.

Alongside the festivals that have, for better or worse, passed into legend, Fairport also played some that are less remembered – The Maidstone Gala, where they had to contend with a dog show and a helicopter display team, is remembered because their set was filmed for cinema release and shown as support to *Pink Floyd: Live at Pompeii;* free afternoon gigs as they made their way across America in May and June; and the two festivals on their doorstep.

After we'd done the Little Hadham village fete, we were asked by the local police if we'd do a benefit gig for them at the end of August. The date they wanted was just before we went back to America and we were free. So we said yes, because it always pays to keep on the right side of the law. This was just after some of the biggest names in music were getting busted – The Beatles and The Stones and so on. Luckily for us, the local constabulary regarded us more as a scruffy local band than a commune of drug smoking hippies who had descended on their quiet village. "The next door hairies" as we said in *Angel Delight*.

Giving the more nefarious and less salubrious habits of certain members of the band, not to mention the copious alcohol consumption of its bass player [hey, I told you not to mention that], we might seem an odd choice to represent Her Majesty's constabulary. It was local, so travel wasn't an issue and of course we were glad to donate our services. I think the expression "you scratch my back..." might have been bandied around in the common rooms of The Angel.

Having checked that the block of dark material in Swarb's violin case was rosin and not resin, off we went to entertain the police and their supporters. It's a pity we didn't do old songs then – *Genesis Hall* – "my father he rides with your sheriffs". Still, we had plenty of criminal activity in some of the songs we did.

Word somehow got round and about 4,000 people turned up. The local paper reported that they'd travelled from all over the country. I don't think they'd travelled all that way to see the Police Dog Display Team – good though they were. It was the first time I became really aware of Fairport's pulling power and the dedication of its fans.

The local press reported that the event raised "in excess of £500 and everyone concerned voted the event an unqualified success." Next came a fortnight gigging in America, over two months solid gigging on a UK tour and an impressive series of sessions for Radio 1. As they celebrated the joint anniversaries of Peggy's first year as a Fairport and a year of communal living at The Angel, change was in the air. On January 24, 1971, the day before they were due to depart for five days gigging in Holland, Peggy wrote starkly in his journal "Ritchie Quits Band."

I'd had a great year as a Fairport, been to places I never dreamed I'd play, done things I'd never even imagined. When Richard said he was leaving, I thought "That's it." His guitar playing was one of the reasons people came to see the band, some would say the main reason back then. He was our in-house songwriter. In a way that was the problem, because he was writing things that he wanted to write but didn't really fit in with what Fairport were about. I can't say which songs because Richard knew they weren't right for us, so didn't even submit them for consideration: I suppose they included songs that ended up on his first LP and *Bright Lights*. I think he gave songs to other people to record too – Iain Matthews and Marc Ellington and so on.

There was nothing unamicable. He carried on living at The Angel, writing songs, going off to do sessions: planning his future, I suppose, though Richard, like God and Steve Ashley, moves in mysterious ways.

Simon Nicol has summed the era up. "Richard carried on as normal in every respect except getting in the van and going to gigs with us – he paid his share of the cornflakes and became the gig fairy: we'd head to play somewhere and when we came back, he'd have tidied the house and done the washing up."

Fairport have always been a "keep calm and carry on" kind of band. We always had a full diary and we always needed to gig to earn money. That's always been both the band's weakness and its strength. So when Richard left, we didn't cancel the next set of gigs – which started next day in Leiden, in the south of Holland, near The Hague. So, on our way there we planned what we were going to do as a four piece, without a lead guitarist. We doled out Richard's songs – Simon drew the short straw because he got *Matty Groves* and he's been singing it ever since.

We probably put in more fiddle tunes to replace stuff we had to drop, because they were easy and everybody liked them.

Fairport seems to have had an unspoken policy of not replacing key members who left. I came in when Ashley left, because they had to have a bass player – but that's what I was then, the bass player: I didn't take on any of Ashley's other functions within the band… though oddly I did years later. I could, however, drive, which Ashley has never done.

But Iain left and no one replaced him; Sandy left and no one replaced her; Richard left and we carried on as a four piece. Even years later, when Swarb decided he was no longer part of Fairport, we made *Gladys' Leap* without a fiddle player in the band, which was a pretty radical move.

So Richard left. Me, Si, Swarb and DM carried on. After the short Dutch tour we had a string of University and rock club gigs, some radio sessions and tours of Ireland and Scotland. We were a busy band.

As it turned out this was the most stable line up of Fairport to date. It was the first time exactly the same band made two albums. It wasn't to last, however. By end of the year, Simon – the last original member from the group that made its debut five years earlier – had decided it was time for him to go. Before that, however came an event which dramatically marked the end of an era. It was February 20, 1971 and the band had just returned from one of those rock club gigs – on the south coast – at The Big Apple, Brighton.

All living under one roof made things easy. We all set off from one place and there was only one return destination. Usually we'd unwind on the way back. It would have been about a hundred miles back from Brighton... probably took three hours. Basically, when you get home all you want to do is dump your instrument somewhere safe and collapse into bed, hopefully without disturbing the wife. Which is what we all did that night.

Swarb was in the downstairs room, which had been Simon's until Swarb bought an antique four poster bed that was too big to fit anywhere but there.

The Angel stood at the foot of a steep hill. It was on the route to Harwich. A Dutch lorry-driver who was trying to make the ferry fell asleep at the wheel and the truck ploughed straight into the front of The Angel. The whole place shook and there was a lot of noise... then dust as the chimney collapsed. We thought there'd been an earthquake!

We went down to see what had happened and when we looked through the door of Swarb's room you could see devastation – bricks everywhere, the crushed cab of the lorry, the road beyond. Swarb himself was sitting up in his expensive bed, not a mark on him... and not a fragment of rubble on the bed. Talk about a charmed life.

We were all lucky – Richard's room was hanging in the air above this carnage. Simon, if he had still been in the room, would have been right next to the wall where the lorry hit. If the lorry had been full it could well have demolished the whole place. If it had been carrying something flammable... that doesn't bear thinking about.

Being part of the community really paid us back that night, the village rallied round, fed us, made us cups of tea, the butcher opened up and turned up with bacon and sausage. Of course, the place was even more uninhabitable than it had been previously. We all had to find somewhere else to stay. We also had a gig that night (at The Greyhound in Croydon) which we didn't cancel.

It was as if the clock had unwound – the era at whose heart sits *Liege & Lief* and Peggy joining Fairport begins and ends with a serious road accident. The first began the journey to Farley Chamberlayne and communal life; the second destroyed their communal abode and left Fairport Convention homeless.

The song *Angel Delight* which was the title track of our next LP is a homage to Fairport in 1970. The accident is in the middle of the song – end of the story so far.

> *There's a hole in the wall*
> *Where the lorry came in*
> *Let's split*

# Chapter 5

# Time for them to go
*I have no thought of leaving*

Logically, for Peggy to have been a key member of so many bands, he had to leave almost the same number. (Currently, he's a member of Fairport, The Dylan Project and a duo with Anthony John Clarke).

I've been lucky in that (so far as I can remember) I've never actually been sacked from a band: to be honest there was a time when I sailed pretty close to the wind with Fairport, but they're mates and are both understanding and supportive. I think each time I left a band it was because another opportunity came up that was too good to miss. Every band I've been in has understood that and wished me well as I moved on. Of course, they might just have been hiding the fact they were glad to get rid of me.

I've remained friends with all of them... that is to say, we've never actually had fall-outs. Famously there were issues with Swarb but that was long after he left Fairport and nothing to do with the time he was in the band. I've played with most of them since I left – The Campbells a few months after leaving and off and on over the years; most of the members have passed away now, but Lorna is still in touch; Jethro Tull had me back for sessions and things like *The Christmas Album*, I'm still on good terms with Ian and Martin Barre is very much a mate; Steve Gibbons is one of the most important figures in my career, he understood when I left The Uglys to form The Exception and fifty years on we still play together regularly in The Dylan Project; it's always great when I get chance to play with Richard Thompson, like we did at Cropredy this year.

So even though I left bands behind, I didn't leave the people in those bands.

I suppose you could say that approach applies to Fairport – you've written yourself about how virtually every ex-member of the band has at some point rejoined them on stage at Cropredy. For the fiftieth celebration we were able to have the original recorded line-up play together for the first time in half a century – with DM standing in for the late Martin Lamble. There was another time we recreated the *Liege & Lief* line up – the wonderful Chris While sang Sandy's part: that was great for me, because that was the first Fairport line-up I ever saw and all those years on I could walk out into the field and be a member of an audience watching them again. Fairport has never been my band in the sense I felt I owned it or had some exclusive right to it: it's my band in the way someone might call a Football Club they support, my team.

The other thing about Fairport – and some people forget this about us – is that we're a band that people have left and rejoined quite outside the Cropredy reunions. Sandy had just left when I joined but she came back in the mid-seventies and some of my fondest memories are of that *Rising for the Moon* line-up – that and *Unhalfbricking* are my two favourite Fairport albums still, along with *Nine* and *Jewel In The Crown*. I say that as a Fairport fan. I didn't know much about the band or its music before I joined. I saw them once. I didn't own any of their records. What I've heard of them would have been on the radio, John Peel's show probably. They were a London band. I was more interested in Birmingham bands, because most had at least one of my mates in it – I even knew The Applejacks. There was so much going on in Brum that you didn't need anything else to occupy your attention. The other thing was, I kept in touch with the Brum scene because that's where I thought my job opportunities were. I'd hear of someone looking for a bass player – for a session, to replace someone who'd quit or to help form a new band. Whenever possible, I put my name forward. Ironic then that it was the London band I hadn't followed that I ended up joining. I've been a Fairport first and foremost since 1970, even when I was in another band: there have been occasions when I've needed a bit of time out and missed on gigs, a tour or some of the recording sessions for an album, but I've never left and rejoined. Which is what we were talking about. Sorry... I got distracted!

Dave Mattacks – DM – has almost made a habit of quitting and rejoining Fairport – I think it was three times in total: he's a regular guest at Cropredy and it was great this year to watch him and Gerry drumming together. Then there's Simon, the last original member to leave the band: at the time, he seemed so cheesed off with it all that it was hard to imagine him coming back, but a few years later he did, first as producer and then rapidly as full-time member and lead singer: it was a bit like Sandy, you can't be on the fringes of Fairport long before being sucked back in. Ask Chris Leslie... or Gerry... or even someone like Ralph or Richard.

It was Richard who said we were like the Hotel California: you can check out any time you like but you can never leave. He also said, "I left Fairport Convention at the end of 1970 and I've been playing with them ever since."

Of course, as Nigel once pointed out, that time that Simon took out from the band means I am the longest serving member of Fairport Convention. Now the band's been running for fifty years and I've been the bass player for all but two and a half of them, I doubt it's a record that's going to be challenged any time soon. Things like that tell you a lot about The Fairports.

Other opportunities have come up over the years. but Fairport were very much where I was at musically. What they were doing was totally compatible with the way I play the bass.

Without Peggy and his wife Chris, it's fair to say Fairport would not have survived beyond the early eighties. Through Cropredy, an increasing tour schedule and eventually fresh album releases, the moribund band became a going concern. Even as Fairport re-established itself as a going concern, Peggy was heavily involved with Jethro Tull. After a decade and a half, it became too much. Something had to give.

Fairport had grown stronger and stronger as a band. We'd effectively relaunched with the release of *Gladys' Leap*. The tours, a steady stream of albums and Cropredy, of course, established us as a strong force. In effect I had two careers going – one as the bass player with Tull and the other with all the Fairport-related stuff which included playing bass, but also myself and Chris were handling all the band's affairs from our home in Barford St Michael. That's not just Cropredy, which has far more facets to it than people realise, but also answering correspondence, arranging tours in the UK and overseas, sorting out royalties, putting together publicity, programmes and merchandise. On top of that there was the running of Woodworm Studios. It was a lot of stuff.

In 1993, Fairport were strong with a great line-up that included Ric and Maart. I was organising Cropredy with Christine which had become a year-round job, which is something I think a lot of people don't realise: a festival doesn't just happen – as soon as the festival finishes you start looking for acts for next year. There's always requests from well-known acts and piles of tapes or CDs from less well-known bands: I try to listen to them all and at least discuss whether we can book someone. There's all the logistics from things like making sure the fields are available and booked to arranging the stage, lights and sound, to providing toilets... it's literally a calendar of events that lead up to making those three days happen.

Then there was the band's publicity, organising the winter tour which was getting longer every year: instead of just looking for places to play, venues were approaching us: again, you have to organise that carefully so you don't end up schlepping up and down the country every night. You don't want gigs too close together either. You don't want fans in a particular part of the country to feel they've missed out. I was also running the record label and the studio.

It sounds like madness when you go through it all. It was in a way. Then, as an aside, you add "Oh, and I was a full-time member of Jethro Tull who were huge at the time." That alone would be what people would regard as a full-time job. 'Money for nothing and chicks for free'? No chance – no time!

It was obviously all too much. It was a lot of pressure working with both bands. Ian Anderson was very understanding and as the demands of Fairport grew, he planned Tull's commitments around them, which, given the profile of the two bands, was incredibly considerate.

I still have the wallchart for my commitments for the year leading up to leaving Tull. It's a sort of silent warning about what can happen. I was playing music on about 320 days in the year either onstage or in the studio. That doesn't leave much space for all the other stuff or indeed days off. Something had to give and I decided to resign as Jethro Tull's bass player. Financially, I suppose it might seem a bit illogical, but all Tull would have to do if I left was find a new bass player; it would have been a very different situation if I'd left Fairport. I've no idea whether things would have fallen apart if I'd left: it seems a bit immodest to assume so.

Fairport biographies have tended to conflate or reinvent stories about Peggy's joining Fairport. His own audition story has certainly, by his own admission, grown in the telling. One version has him joining the band "on Dave Swarbrick's recommendation as they had worked together in The Campbells": this is clearly unlikely to be the case as they weren't in The Ian Campbell Folk Group at the same time. A variation on this suggests other band members were reluctant to bring another folkie into the group: Simon Nicol doubts the band were even aware of Peggy's recent folk background but had certainly heard of the rock groups he'd played with – "Peggy came along to the audition like any other bass player: we played songs from Liege & Lief and he played along; not only did play the parts better than anyone else, he played them better than Ashley who invented them. There was no contest." No big debate either: no, 'we'll let you know': Swarb, Richard and Simon huddled in a corner like entrepreneurs considering a surprisingly generous offer on Dragon's Den. "He got the job there and then. Dave Pegg was Fairport Convention's new bass player. The best decision the band ever made."

Most accounts of Fairport's history or Peggy's career have him shifting directly from The Ian Campbell Folk Group at a New Year's Eve concert to rehearsing with Fairport at The Angel next day. It certainly wasn't that simple.

I decided to leave The Campbells even though I loved being and playing with them and I really enjoyed their music. It was that old cliché really – a change in musical direction. Not "musical differences", you know, they were musical and I was different. I didn't figure I was getting any better on the double bass and it really didn't look like I would improve. I wanted to return to the bass guitar, an instrument I felt more at home with and really loved... I still do: I enjoy playing the guitar and the mandolin (though it's harder since I cut a tendon in my finger a couple of years ago) but I love the bass. I wanted to try something new or at least go back to playing rhythm & blues or rock music, as we had begun to call it.

You've got to remember that bands like The Beatles and The Stones and The Kinks and so on were all thought of as pop groups. Even when their music moved on and became complex and sophisticated. Pop was what my generation started out playing. There was a blues influence early on but even very bluesy things like *House of The Rising Sun* were thought of as pop music. The big thing was to have a hit – even the people we think of as purely rock acts today – Pink Floyd, Hendrix, Cream, even Tull and so on – were focused on getting a song in the charts. It was Zeppelin who broke that mould. There's that verse in *Angel Delight* – which is a few years after this of course but it's still relevant – that says we "peer through the haze watching Top of the Pops and smile": we'd watch it on a Thursday night if we didn't have a gig and have a good laugh when one of our mates was on. Of course, Fairport had done Top of the Pops once: ironically, we ended up playing two songs from *Angel Delight* on TotP's album slot, if you remember that: in a way the joke was on us.

Anyhow, back to leaving The Campbells.

Because of Cream and Hendrix and a few other bands who were around at the time there was a buzz about three-piece bands playing loud hard rock – power trios as they came to be known. Dave (Clem) Clempson and Cozy Powell were wanting to form a trio and asked if I'd like to join on bass. Working with a superb guitarist and a great drummer, both from the Midlands: I could hardly refuse. We called ourselves The Beast – rehearsed a lot for about ten days, had a great time, sounded wonderful and never did a gig. Cozy went off to join Jeff Beck's group and Clem joined Colosseum. So I didn't leave the group: the group left me. Clem said there could be a chance for me to join Colosseum but the kind of jazz-blues-rock fusion they were playing didn't appeal to me at the time.

It was all very amicable. I just went off and started auditioning for various London-based bands, like The Foundations and Aynsley's Dunbar's Retaliation – I suppose subconsciously I'd realised it was time to break the Brum-based mould. Eventually, of course, I ended up travelling down for an audition with Fairport, who, to go back to what I said earlier, were very much considered a rock act – very credible, musically adventurous and inventive. Because they'd just done *Liege & Lief*, which was the album I had to learn for the audition, even though we never played a lot of the songs from it at the time: that was folk-rock... a totally new thing; of course, purely by chance it brought together those extremes of music which I'd played during the sixties. I felt very at home straight away... and instantly made some great mates, friends for a lifetime.

With Fairport, of course, the leavings I experienced were different: it was other people leaving the band while Dave Swarbrick and myself tried to hold the whole thing together. I got to work with some amazing players and singers and again have remained friends with all of them.

Richard was the first to leave – though he continued to live at the band's communal home at The Angel.

# Chapter 6

# Angels over Oxfordshire
*An everyday story of country folkies*

Fairport's time at Little Hadham was about to come to a sudden, unexpected end. After the triumphs of 1970, Peggy was about to face a challenging 1971

Actually, you could say that about most years in Fairport, certainly until the mid-eighties and even after that they're been quite a few intense periods. 1971, though, was up there with some of the most earth-shattering. We became spectacularly homeless. We went from a five piece to a four piece until at the end of the year there was only me and Swarb left. And then there were two. If it had been an Agatha Christie, Whodunnit, one of us would have been the murderer!

The crucial folk-rock foundation of Fairport Convention sits between two brackets, both of which were fatal road accidents: the first was the crash on the M1 which indirectly changed the course of Peggy's life because it ultimately led to his joining the band; the second was the lorry's collision with the front wall of The Angel, which terminated their tenure and ultimately led Peggy to establishing a new base which directly changed the course of his life.

After the crash, the four current members went their separate ways to find somewhere to live. Peggy returned to Sutton Coldfield. They paid tribute to their former communal home with their next release *Angel Delight*. Expensively packaged, with attached photos of the band, the album's gatefold sleeve included an excerpt from a forthcoming biography.

Robin Gee was our road manager. There was no biography and the excerpt was just a kind of in-joke. *Full House*'s sleeve had those surreal notes as a kind of mediæval sports report that Richard wrote as well as a lot bits and pieces designed to make fans and friends who knew us well laugh. *Angel Delight* was like that in many ways. The title was a tribute to our pub in Little Hadham but also that instant pudding that Birds used to sell. Not The Byrds, by the way – the custard company. I don't think Roger McGuinn would have considered The Byrds' *Instant Whip* a good LP title.

It's hardly likely that anyone in the band realised at the time, but Birds' launch of their popular desert coincided exactly with Fairport's very first gig in May, 1967.

## Friends may come and friends may go

1971 began with a traumatic change for Fairport. On January 24, Peggy noted in his diary: "Ritchie quits band." A simple but significant statement.

When people have left Fairport, it's usually been amicable. That was particularly true of Richard, who continued to occupy his room at The Angel until the crash that forced us all out. It's just his career was heading in a different direction. We'd be piling into the van to do a gig somewhere or head off on another tour, he'd be going to a gig, solo or playing with Linda (they did a lot of folk clubs playing acoustic), or he'd be off playing guitar on a session (he did loads of session work, often uncredited) or just writing songs. In terms of direction, The Fairports were still focused largely on electric folk while Richard was a singer-songwriter. We didn't have any kind of fall out. We remained friends. He just knew which direction he wanted things to go and it wasn't the same way as Fairport were heading.

He's stayed mates with us and has been a guest at Cropredy more than anyone else over the years. When he was looking to put a band together – either to gig or to record – he often turned to Fairport. I was lucky enough to get to play with him whenever Fairport commitments allowed. The last time was the second half of his set at Cropredy in 2017: as it always is, it was a total joy to be on stage playing alongside him.

The word often used to describe Richard was irreplaceable: we took that literally and didn't replace him.

## The racecourse has taken my Angel away

Richard continued living at The Angel for as long as the rest of us. He was still there when the lorry ploughed into the front of the building, though he wasn't at home on that particular night.

Although the crash was traumatic – the poor driver lost his life and we were all there to see it – and disruptive, we still carried on with our schedule of gigs. Fairport have always been essentially a live band. That's how we earn our living. If we don't gig, we don't get paid. If you acquire a reputation for cancelling gigs, no matter how valid the reason is, it can do serious damage to your viability as a working act. Fairport never made much from our albums: they sold OK but never in massive quantities. If you look at the gold discs in my dining room (note to potential burglars – they're only copies, the genuine ones are in a bank vault in Zurich!), you'll see they're mainly for Tull releases. There's one Fairport disc and that's for accumulated sales during our time with Island Records.

We carried on gigging, but the crash meant we had lost our permanent base where we all lived together. More importantly, we had all lost our home. Finding somewhere to live was a priority. I moved back to my parents in Sutton for a while.

Four of us were still in the band, of course, but Richard who had remained very much in the Fairport family now had a lot less reason to be in contact. He and Simon are old friends, of course, going back beyond Fairport and naturally they maintained contact.

He was big loss. He was already a legend as a lead guitarist: we were all aware some people came to Fairport gigs just to see Richard play. He took quite a lot of lead vocals too. His confidence and skill as a lead singer had really grown. It's easy to forget that he made *Henry the Human Fly* which was a solo album with him singing all the songs, before he started recording with Linda. He was also our songwriter. I know he worked with Swarb and when he was in the band songs were co-credited, but really it was Richard who did the lion's share and Swarb who came up with tunes and arrangements.

I know Richard has said that he felt the stuff he wanted to write didn't really fit in with Fairport, but we've covered quite a few of the songs from the early part of his solo career. I suppose as a writer, he felt the fact we were still doing a fair bit of traditional stuff gave his songs less opportunity.

Because both Richard and Sandy had been in Fairport we have a great legacy of songs. We tended to overlook most of it through the seventies, which was odd, really. I suppose the current project or the writers currently in the band meant we didn't go back to it.

I know we decided that, like Sandy, Richard was irreplaceable. So we didn't replace him. That did leave a gap and it put a lot of pressure on Simon to fill it. In the course of that year he got tired of being referred to in the press as "the last original member of Fairport Convention."

Although he'd left, there were a couple of RT songs on our next LP which was *Angel Delight*.
Like *Full House*, which alluded both to a powerful poker hand and the over-occupancy of The Angel, *Angel Delight* refers both to their recently near-demolished home as well as the popular Birds' instant treat.

*Angel Delight* is one of many songs written about Fairport, like Chris' *Our Bus Rolls On* on the last CD. We each wrote bits about each other and then made our comments fit together to make the song. By the time we made the album, Fairport was a four piece – Simon, Swarb, DM and me – but, even though he isn't credited, I'm sure Richard joined in writing that one at some stage; who wrote what and whether anything Richard wrote made it into the finished song I couldn't say. It's an odd song in a way: if you listen to it, it's about us all living at The Angel. I know we wrote bits of it there. Yet it also refers to the lorry incident and so part of it must have been written later.
A review of an appearance shortly after the accident refers specifically to the song, suggesting it was brought to a performance level pretty quickly.

One of the reasons I end up with so many stories to tell is that I always think the best way to cope with anything difficult is to try to see the funny side of it. My "greatest hit" – which I know is one of your favourite Fairport songs – came about like that. Since we've mentioned songs about Fairport, let's get it out of the way now. This is the story behind *Hungarian Rhapsody*.

## Oh what a time we had Down by The Danube

Eventually we got rid of the white Transit van that had taken us up and down the country, most notably to Krumlin. We bought a Mercedes which is the rather better vehicle: that was what took us to Hungary. We may even have bought it so as not to get caught out in an unreliable vehicle in Eastern Europe. I must say it was our pride and joy. It had a three-seater front seat, sliding doors, four aircraft seats in the back, lots of space for all our instruments and equipment.

It was a tour by the *Angel Delight* line-up – Simon, Swarb, DM and me – organised by the British Arts Council and whatever Society is its equivalent in Hungary as some kind of cultural exchange. So, a Hungarian band – probably traditional folk musicians – came to the UK to play a few dates; the Hungarians got us.

It was fantastic, not least because it was a tour without the pressure of worrying whether we would sell tickets and put bums on seats each night. We also knew that the audience would have no expectations about what we'd play. No one would be going "Where's Richard?".

We arrived in Budapest, which is a fabulous city: we met the band that was going to be touring with us, who were called Tolsvag & Trio. Oddly enough, they were a five piece band: all really good players. Bela Tolsvag, who was the lead singer with the group, spoke fluent English which made things so much easier for us. Unfortunately, their agent or manager or whoever tended to treat them like second class citizens. Whereas we stayed in proper hotels, they were dumped in grubby digs. It seemed unfair and disrespectful, but we discovered there were many strange divides in society which we hadn't expected under Communism.

We were paid £10 a day for each day we were in Hungary: that's £70 a week. In England we were earning on average £30 a week. So it was good money to start with. We were also aware that it would be worth more relatively because the cost of living was so much lower in Hungary. The problem was, there really wasn't anything to spend your money on and what there was, was really, really cheap. For example, the local red wine, Egri Bikavér, which I mention by name in *Hungarian Rhapsody* was the equivalent of five shillings a bottle: we could have bought forty bottles a day each. Except we didn't need to, because in many places we went they were keen to feed us and ply us with booze anyway.

If we decided to go out to eat, the most expensive full meal you could find in a good restaurant cost about two pounds. The payment was in local forints, which you weren't allowed to bring out of the country or convert back into sterling. The Fairport chaps have seldom been in a position of not knowing what to do with their money: usually, we had to worry what to do without money; but we were flush on that tour. It was like being in The Beatles!

I recounted some of the things that happened on the Hungarian tour in the song, so take a listen if you want to hear about that. It was on the *Rosie* album and is also on my box set and a couple of compilations. But there was a lot more: it was a real adventure. The Fairports were based in Budapest in a hotel called the Bora Schillig. It was a very plush hotel which had a great gypsy band that played their every night. I mention them in the chorus of the song – great violinist, wonderful double bass player, zimbalom player (that's in the song too: it's a traditional Hungarian instrument, a bit like a zither, you play it with small hammers), clarinettist. We went to listen to them whenever we could.

We were now at the stage where we could employ other people, apart from Robin Gee our road manager, to help us out when we were on the road. Dave Harper, who you might remember stopped The Fairports going on stage at Krumlin, was now employed by Fairport to set our gear up.

Roberta Nicol – Simon's first wife – came on tour with us to Hungary: she was a bit picky about what food she would eat. Basically, she wanted to know what was in everything. That was difficult because in a lot of places we ate, nobody spoke English. When he could Bela would come along to the restaurant to translate the menu for us. So he'd run through things generally for the rest of us and then go into detail for Roberta's benefit.

It took Dave Harper and myself a couple of days to realise that we could order the most expensive thing on the menu and it still made only a small dent in the money we were being given on a daily basis. Don't forget this is money we had to spend. We couldn't see any point in going through a half hour discussion, translating everything, then having it retranslated because you've forgotten what it was by the time you get to the end of the list. We'd just point to the most expensive item – on the basis that if it cost most, it was likely to be good – and order that: as a result, our food usually arrived while everyone else was still deciding what they were going to have. It was usually half a pig or something like that. We ate incredibly well.

One night, we went out of Budapest to play a gig. It was quite a journey and felt really out in the wilds. We arrived and Dave had set everything up efficiently, as usual. We did the soundcheck and were then taken to the hotel next door to the theatre to order food. Bela was with us – though not the rest of his band who had to fend for themselves and find somewhere to eat, probably somewhere where the food was a lot cheaper, though given the prices that was hard to imagine – but Bela was allowed to come with us because he was acting as our translator. He's doing his usual thing of going through the menu, explaining each item to Bert Nicol and everyone else. Everyone apart from me and Dave, because we've just ordered the most expensive item as soon as we arrived – me because it was easier and Dave because he had to eat quickly and then get back into the theatre to take care of our gear. People are still deciding and debating, discussing whether a particular dish might have nuts in it or whatever when my food arrives. By the time we'd been there half an hour, everyone had got served, apart from Dave Harper, who by this point is looking at his watch and starting to get worried. He's calling out "I ordered first: where's mine?" I offer him mine – my half a pig or whatever it was that night – but he refuses saying it's the principle of the thing. He gets increasingly angry and refuses any offers that might sort things out. Eventually he disappears. I decide there's nothing we can do. The only thing is to finish my meal and go back to the theatre in the hopes he's simply given up and gone there to set the gear up.

Outside the theatre I was accosted by a man who spoke really good English. He asked if I was David Peggy from the Fairport Conversions and said he was a good friend of the opening band – Bela's group: he offered to let me sit beside him through their set and he would translate all the songs for me.

We end up sitting on the balcony to watch the first half. An uncomfortable situation is not made any easier by the presence of two armed guards with big guns by the entrance on either side of the stage. The band comes on and starts the first song. I'd no idea what it was about but the guy beside me starts to translate. I am somewhat distracted, though, because halfway through the song Dave Harper appears on stage, banging a tambourine. He then goes and stands by Bela and tries to join in. Bela's doing his best to ignore him, but it's clearly not easy. He starts to look worried: so do the rest of the band. Dave is not happy, being ignored; he wanders off stage, only to return with his tambourine but without his trousers. He wanders right across the stage, left to right, with his bits hanging out. There are young girls in the audience and they are screaming. It's pandemonium. I look over at the guard and I just think 'He's going to be shot and I can't do anything to stop it.' If one of the guards had turned round – because their job was to keep an eye on the audience not the stage – and seen him that would have been it. Somehow, he makes it to the other side of the stage and disappears.

I excuse myself to my new Hungarian friend and head backstage to find Dave and try to work out what on earth is going on. I can't find him at all. The rest of the band arrives, having finally finished their meal. Robin Gee immediately asks "Where's Harper? The stuff's not set up!" As best I can, I explain what happened ending by suggesting that if he's lucky he'll be on his way to the salt mines by now.

Robin had to set the gear up, which he regarded as very much beneath him in his new managerial role. You can tell the rage against Dave is building within him by the second. Eventually, it was time for The Fairports to go on, which I must say was a relief: short of Dave deciding to do another surprise appearance, it was no longer our problem for an hour or so.

We finish the set, do our encore and as we come off Robin Gee greets us with the news that there is still no sign of Dave Harper, who should of course be available to dismantle the gear and load it into the van. I go to Bela to see whether he might have any idea where he'd be. His best guess is the police station or even prison by now: he seems to think it's not a good idea to get personally involved if he is.

He was missing. End of story. Whatever's happened, he's brought it on himself. Robin and the Fairports set about derigging our gear and taking it out to the new Mercedes van.

Eventually, everything's loaded, we all climb in and are about to set off, when I notice a strange moaning sound, a really weird noise. We get out to investigate, and there's Dave under the van. He's decided it's the best place to hide and he's right by the wheel with his head literally pressed against the tyre tread. It's a good thing we hadn't set off because we would have driven straight over him.

Clearly, even if he didn't get any food, he knew where the booze was. He'd set about drinking, not a good idea on an empty stomach.

We drag him into the van, in the front seat between Robin who's driving and me. Robin's reading him the riot act, telling him he's fired, saying he'll be on the first plane home in the morning: Dave, meanwhile, is oblivious to all this because he's comatose, just propped up in the seat moaning horribly. Robin is driving quite aggressively, banging the gears, into reverse, then first gear, onto the main road where Dave suddenly announces "I wanna be sick". Robin tries to pull over; before we stop, I slide open the door and pull Dave across me; his head is hanging out of the door with me holding his collar, so he doesn't fall out head first. Then Robin brakes suddenly, the door slides shut and Dave's head is trapped. It's like the guillotine or something.

Anyhow, he does what he has to. We drag him back in. He passes out. We drive two or three hours to Budapest. At the hotel, we carry him up to his room and just dump him there. Robin calls a group meeting for the morning and to him it's a foregone conclusion that Dave will be fired.

It's 3am at least but amazingly we all make it downstairs next morning in time to have late breakfast. Everyone except Dave that is. Robin takes over and effectively starts the meeting over our toast and croissants. To him it's simple – Dave's behaviour was inexcusable; he simply has to go, the sooner the better; we'll manage and in fact we'll be better off without him. This upset me because, despite everything, Dave was a mate and I'd watched the situation which had led up to the previous night's events. Luckily Swarb supported me, pointing out that everyone has off days and suggesting we give him another chance. Robin was having none of it.

Then we said, "Have you not noticed that he's somewhat bigger than us? What if he doesn't want to go home?" Robin, however, stands firm, determined to fire him.

Eventually, Dave wanders in, still rather in a daze, with the most enormous bruise down the side of his neck where the sliding door hit him, but clearly without any recollection of how he got it. Robin immediately stands up and tells him to go and pack because he's fired and he's going home.

Dave walks over to him, grabs him by the collar, lifts him off the floor so their faces are level and says in a voice still slurred from the previous night's alcohol: "Ah don't fink so, Robin: do you?" before letting him drop to the floor.

From that position, Robin just says, "Oh, all right, Dave, let's have another think about it."

Wonderful to witness a bit of constructive employment negotiation.

Fairport has always been a very sociable group as I've said. When you're on tour, being forced together in often very confined spaces for sometimes lengthy periods of time does put a lot of pressure on relationships within the group. Nowadays, when the van rolls into a town, we often take the opportunity to go our separate ways for a while, stretch our heads as well as our legs.

It didn't used to be like that. You'd heard the stories of The Beatles on tour, getting cabin fever, seeing nothing but stages, hotel rooms and the insides of cars and aeroplanes. Turning up in strange cities day after day, often with not a lot of time to spare, it could get like that with the Fairports. The band was once famous for its changes of line up – it became almost a joke in the music press – and there were lots of reasons why various people left at different times. I should say, the current line up, with only a couple of changes has been the same for over thirty years so I wish people would let that whole Fairport Confusion thing go.

Through the seventies, I'd say every tour saw someone say they were going to leave the band; usually they came back after a day or so; sometimes they left permanently.

On that Hungarian tour, it was Swarb's turn. At one point he told us he'd decided he was going to leave the band. He walked out and went, as he put it, "in search of 'real people'". He disappeared for three hours.

Peggy's account of the tour, in his song *Hungarian Rhapsody* would have to wait a couple of albums before finally being unleashed on the public, by which point it was hard for fans to figure out which of Fairport's many recent line ups the song referred to. Meanwhile, in June 1971, a new album which in many ways celebrated Peggy's first year in the band was released. The album and its title track took their name from their former home, *Angel Delight*.

*Angel Delight* was a very jokey song. Everyone wrote a bit of it. I think even Richard may have chipped in despite no longer being in the band, because he still lived there. Received wisdom is that we each wrote a verse about someone else, but I think we all came up with ideas about everyone including ourselves. Then we just strung the best bits together. We finished it off with a verse about the crash, which was added just before recorded it, I think.

After *Come All Ye*, *Angel Delight* established a personal subgenre of songs from within the band about the band, often identifying individual members. The most recent example (at the time of writing) is Chris Leslie's *Our Bus Rolls On*... The cover shot caused some further Fairport confusion.

The picture on the front was taken at some abandoned old building. From the minute the album came out, rumours started that it was the wreckage of The Angel. It wasn't: The Angel was a pretty run down place, but it was never that bad.

*Journeyman's Grace* was on that, which was the last song Richard wrote for the Fairports before he left: he played it with us a few times and there are recordings of it with the five-piece Fairport – live and a Peel session as well, I think.

*Bridge over the River Ash* was an instrumental with everyone playing fiddles and DM on bass. We began playing that when Richard was still with us. The Ash was the river that ran through Little Hadham, right by The Angel. If you stepped out of the front door and turned right, you'd reach the bridge in a couple of hundred yards. Although we called it that on the album, on stage we renamed it for whatever the local river was where we were playing – Thames, Avon, Aire, Tyne or whatever: most British towns were built on some kind of river. At Cropredy, it became *Bridge over the River Cherwell*.

As so often happens in the story of Fairport, the album contained an unwitting glimpse of their future. The opening song is a heroic ballad celebrating The Duke of Marlborough. He was John Churchill, a Royalist whose career spanned the 17th and early 18th centuries. He was the leading military commander of the era. For his services to the crown he was made Lord Marlborough in 1682, when he was 31: subsequent military triumphs led to his elevation to Earl and finally Duke. His reward for his greatest triumph, the victories in the War of Spanish Succession was a stately home gifted by a grateful nation and named after his ultimate triumph: Blenheim Palace is the only palace in Britain that is neither a royal residence nor the dwelling for an archbishopric. It is in Woodstock, Oxfordshire, less than twenty miles due south of Cropredy. That's actually less than a third of the distance from Yasgur's Farm to Woodstock NY: imagine if Fairport in 1980 had decided to co-op the name!

After the accident, which demolished the Angel, Swarb and Birgitta and all their possessions moved to Cropredy into a lovely little cottage. Like most of the places he's chosen to live, in terms of public transport it was a truly bad choice, a nightmare for a non-driver. There wasn't a regular bus services and the railway station had closed down sometime in the fifties. Because it was remote, because then as now you had to travel down narrow Oxfordshire lanes to get to it, it didn't appeal to commuters, so houses were comparatively cheap.

He was the first of the Fairports to move to the village which is now, of course, so much associated with the band.

I moved in to a smaller house opposite Swarb's thatched cottage. It was right next door to the Methodist Chapel which was also near the village post office – that was handy when we started doing mail-outs for Cropredy Festival.

Simon moved to Chipping Norton. Sandy and Trevor lived in Byfield. Cropredy became Fairport's base by default and it's figured in the group's life story more than people perhaps realise.

Today, I think everyone recognises The Brasenose. For years, it was "that pub on *Fairport Nine*" to most fans. To us it was one of our locals and the place where the rest of the band stayed when we were rehearsing, which we used to do in the Village Hall that was at the other end of Chapel Lane from where Swarb and I both lived.

*Angel Delight*, which was released in June 1971, earned them an appearance on Top of the Pops on July 14 (playing *Hens March* and the title track): it became the highest charting LP of their career. They appeared at Glastonbury Festival that year. They toured Britain and Scandinavia in July and August. In September they played in Germany, Austria and Holland before returning to the studio to record *Babbacombe Lee*. They spent October on a US tour that took them from Syracuse, NY to San Francisco and LA. November and December were spent touring the UK with an elaborate show to promote the John Lee LP .

After *Babbacombe Lee*, Simon decided to leave and Fairport became just me, Swarb and DM. DM had other commitments too, so it felt like Swarb and me keeping the band going some of the time.

Simon's departure was very sad. He was the last surviving original member of

Fairport, of course: I think most people know the band was named after his family home, but this is a good place to mention it just in case. We were touring America with Traffic.

Simon was a big part of *Babbacombe Lee*: aside from his performances and writing for it, he'd also been in charge of production working with John Wood. It wasn't an easy album to produce, either, because it left you no flexibility – all the songs had to go on and they had to be in a particular order: there's really only a handful of albums in the history of rock to which that applies.

Towards the end of the tour, the test pressings arrived and we had our first chance to hear the album as a whole as well as the individual mixes. Simon, being Simon, had been meticulous about it. But there was something Swarb didn't like – it was probably some insignificant niggle; or perhaps he was in a bad mood. Anyhow Swarb, being Swarb, had to make a thing of it – *Babbacombe Lee* being his pet project and all.

Simon took the hump and said "That's it: I'm off."

Simon, to be fair, offers a different slant –

Simon Nicol : "Half way through the tour of the USA with Traffic, I was half-way through playing *Sloth*, yet again. I suddenly felt like I wasn't in the band anymore. I was a moment of standing back from myself. I actually felt 'I'm not in Fairport any more: why am I doing this?'"

In his typically humorous track note to the version of *Sloth* on *The Airing Cupboard Tapes*, Dave Mattacks identifies that performance.

"Of the 137,422 performance of 'Sloth', sadly only 28,156 have been recorded for posterity. Back at the hotel after this San Antonio gig, Simon calmly announced his intention of leaving the group"

The date was October 22, 1971.

Simon didn't walk out on us: he stayed to the end of the tour and then agreed to do the UK tour we had lined up to promote *Babbacombe Lee*. He didn't leave us in the lurch in any sense. He gave us chance to decide what to do next...

Again, as with Sandy and Richard, someone had left the band whom it was impossible to replace. Equally a trio of fiddle, bass and drums, with no one who was really a lead singer, wasn't viable. It was a matter of changing direction. We had a year of trying different approaches.

I invited Roger Hill, who'd been in The Uglys and The Exception with me, to join. We tried that out for a while but while he's a great singer and guitarist, Fairport's music didn't really suit his style. By this point DM was sick of the whole thing and he left.

We became an all-Brum band for a while, because Tom Farnell joined us on drums. That line-up toured America, playing a lot of dates with The Kinks. The Kinks and Fairport were both Muswell Hill bands originally of course, but we'd lost all our North London connections by then.

I'll say this now, for the record. That version of Fairport gelled perfectly personality wise, we got on as mates and musicians. We were the worst line up of Fairport, ever, however. We weren't the right four people to play Fairport music.

We still had a great time. We went to Finland and toured with Steve Tilston and Mott the Hoople. We were the headline act: it was before Mott became well-known and had hits; Steve was still establishing himself as a singer-songwriter and guitarist. You got Steve with his solo stuff which was exceptional even back then. Then Mott who've always been a great rock band and know how to win over a crowd. Then the main act

– which was us, four Brummies pretending to be Fairport Convention. You know how you get tribute acts where people who have nothing to do with the band try to sound as much like them as possible? We were the opposite – two people who did have something to do with the band but in a group that played their music and sounded nothing like them – an insult act, if you like. Not that we meant to be: we weren't disrespectful.

Roger and Tom and of course Swarb are all great players. I'm not saying anything negative about the musicianship. It's just it wasn't Fairport, as we all knew in our heart of hearts.

We still went down well – because we played stuff people knew because they were Fairport fans coming to a Fairport gig.

We all travelled together in a big coach and we had an interpreter who travelled with us. It was quite a big thing. We got written up in national magazines and wherever we played the local newspaper would publish a review. One of the intepreter's jobs each day was to get the paper and translate the reviews for us. The Fairports came out of it with flying colours – clearly, we knew we were getting away with it. Steve would be commended either for his songs or his playing. But Mott always got slagged off. The Scandinavians just didn't get them at all. We all got on well and it was one of those occasions when everyone on the tour all hung out together.

Eventually the tour arrived in Helsinki. They'd arranged for us to have a night off. The whole crowd of us went down to a local rock club, explained who we were and asked if we could get up on stage and have a play. They let us and so the Fairports, Mott and Steve got up there en masse and ran through old Chuck Berry songs, a bit of Elvis, probably some Beatles. You know, the simple stuff everyone knows.

We had a great time. Then we went back to our hotel. They'd booked us into quite a posh hotel. The bar was on the eighteenth floor – which is a great way of stopping somebody casually wandering in off the street.

We decided to go up to the bar for a drink and they wouldn't let us in. They had a rule for the bar and the dining room that you had to wear a tie. To be honest, even in 1972 that seemed a bit archaic, but that was the rule and no amount of explaining that we were famous rock stars on the road, bringing music to their country etc. was going to make a blind bit of difference. Rules is rules, as they say. "More than my job's worth, mate" sounds pretty much the same in any language.

Nobody had a tie... either on them or even in their room. It was late so we couldn't go out and do a bit of panic shopping. I decided to get creative and come up with a solution. Muggins, in an over-refreshed state, I thought I could sort it out. I chopped up the curtains in my room into what I considered to be roughly tie lengths and I gave them out to all the chaps... a dozen ties for the members of Mott, Steve and Fairport.

Hey presto, we were all wearing ties, which meant we could go into the bar. Interestingly we were all wearing matching ties, which was a bit unusual. Moreover, when we got into the bar, it was obvious our ties also matched the curtains, which was bizarre. The curtains were standard throughout the hotel. At the time, I thought this was fantastic, a move for mankind, some sort of surreal artistic statement.

That lasted until the next day, when we were given the bill which included £300 to cover the cost of damage to the curtains. Turned out to be the most expensive round of drinks I was ever responsible for.

We had great times, but in our heart of hearts we knew that as Fairport the four of us didn't really work out. Roger and Tom decided to quit before it all went pear-shaped and both went back to playing with bands in Birmingham.

That left me and Swarb – fiddle and bass – there are very few situations where that's a bookable combo.

There are certain bands that seem quintessentially English: two of them began life in London's Muswell Hill. There's those preservers of village greens and Waterloo sunsets, The Kinks and there's the fathers of folk-rock Fairport Convention. There was a curious feeling among Fairport fans, and more obviously rock critics, that Fairport had some unspoken duty to preserve this crucial "Englishness".

Karl Dallas, whose four LP box set would in a couple of years chart the complex history of the musical genre Fairport invented, even complained that Fairport's traditional repertoire drew too much on Celtic rather than English traditions.

## Living in a world you didn't make

With the erosion of yet another line-up, Fairport seemed to have reached an impasse. Yet there was a feeling that the band ought to exist. Folk-rock had gained a foothold. B&C Records focused on releasing prime examples of the new genre – early Steeleye, *No Roses*, Marc Ellington, Shelagh MacDonald, Keith Christmas, Andy Roberts, Spirogyra. Peggy found welcome remuneration as a session bass player on several of those LPs. The label also put out budget priced compilations including the classic *Clogs*: among them was a set by Martin Carthy and Dave Swarbrick called *Selections* which drew tracks from *Prince Heathen*, *But Two Came By* and significantly the instrumental EP, *No Songs*. That and the recent reissue of his definitive collection of fiddle tunes *Rags Reels and Airs* led Swarb to consider the notion of releasing a solo album. It was heavily reported in the music press at the time and where his views were sought, Swarb emphasised that this in no way signalled the end of Fairport.

Poor old Swarb, every time he came up with the idea of making a solo LP, he'd get diverted and the material he was planning for it would be channelled into the next Fairport album. *Rags Reels and Airs* is like the fiddle players' bible: both Ric and Chris learned their first tunes playing along with it. A lot of other folk fiddlers will tell you the same. It's a hugely important record and a big part of Swarb's legacy. It was produced by Joe Boyd, who'd heard Swarb with The Campbell Group. Because they'd worked together, when Fairport wanted to include fiddle on *A Sailor's Life*, Joe was able to ask Swarb, who might not otherwise have considered doing a session for a rock group he'd barely heard of. That's one of those ripple effect moments – if Swarb hadn't joined Fairport maybe they wouldn't have taken such a folkie route or at least it would have remained a one-off experiment; if he hadn't been in the band, maybe I wouldn't have joined Fairport when Ashley left. You can go on, parallel universes, alternative realities.

Fairport's Englishness was reflected in its personnel. It came as something of a surprise, therefore, when their next recruits were from what we once described as The Colonies. Things had reached something of a crisis point.

You make it sound like a wartime report: in times of crisis we call on our overseas allies, and all that. It's not like that obviously. When someone leaves the band, you have to decide whether to replace them. Sometimes you know you can't... a year after I joined Richard left and that was the decision we took as a group. Sometimes you look around for someone to come in to the band. Because of the kind of group Fairport is – very social, wanting to enjoy ourselves, all those things we've talked about – you want someone who will work within that dynamic, as well as being a great player. Whatever else you say about Fairport, it can't be denied that the people in it were always great players.

We tend to recruit people we know and whom we know we get on with. Look at the current line-up: Ric was a session player on *Gladys*, he came in because Swarb didn't want to be on the album and I knew him because my dad and his worked in the same school, while Simon and DM knew him from The Albion Band; Gerry joined after DM left to move to America, we'd known him for years even before he was in Fotheringay and I think most of us had played with him on sessions or when he guested at Cropredy; Chris had been around Fairport since we first made our base in Oxfordshire in the late seventies, he played with us and even stood in for Ric after an accident meant he couldn't play at Cropredy; Chris replaced Maart who was someone who'd been mates with the band since the early seventies – he used to come to gigs when he was still a kid. I should make it clear, though, none of those people became part of Fairport because they are our mates: they became part of Fairport because they are great players and they are our mates.

It's fair to say the non-British players in Fairport joined when there was a crisis on three occasions in the seventies. Each time the band was reduced basically to Swarb and myself. A fiddler and a bass player: we couldn't even have gone out as duo.

The band had had all those comings and goings and at this stage Fairport Convention consisted essentially of "the two Daves", myself and Swarb, plus Tom Farnell on drums. Tom was on the point of leaving: Dave Mattacks wasn't sure whether he wanted to continue with the band. The way things were, no one could blame him as he was a very in-demand session player with lots of more certain options available to him. He was The Albion Band's drummer around this time and he'd played on the (first) Steeleye Span LP.

We desperately needed another person. That person had to be a guitarist with enough range to cover the very different kinds of thing we were now playing; ideally, he'd be a good singer; it would be a bonus if he was also a songwriter. As we were The Three Daves we thought we might as well go for the full set of four.

## Settle down and listen to the band

David Rea was an American guitar player. He was Swarb's suggestion. He'd written some stuff for Mountain; they were one of the first American heavy rock bands: Mountain were a four piece who included Leslie West and Felix Pappalardi, who's probably better known for producing albums by Cream. David wrote *Mississippi Queen*, one of their best known songs: Ozzie had a hit with a cover version yers later.

Mountain were a respected rock group. But David and Felix were known on the UK folk-circuit to people like The Campbells as the guys who's come over as the backing band for Ian & Sylvia Tyson, when they toured here in the late sixties. Sometimes the Campbells were on the same bill, and that's where Dave Swarbrick got to know David Rea. He was a great guitar player: if he played acoustic, it was kind of a country / Americana style; when he played electric, it tended to be more heavy rock. Both styles suited me, of course. How much they suited Fairport at the time wasn't an immediate consideration.

Swarb suggested we give Dave Rea a try – and there really is no truth in the rumour that having the first name David meant it was easier to get into the band. He flew over. As it happened, The Manor was just starting up.

The Manor was, as its name suggests, a grand country house, converted by "record shop entrepreneur" Richard Branson into a state of the art, residential recording facility, the first of its kind in this country. Equally importantly, it had no ties to a major record company – Virgin Records at this stage was still no more than the name of a chain of London-based record shops with a quasi-hippy ethos and a tendency towards rock and underground music. If you went into a Virgin store in the early seventies you passed under a sub Beardesly logo of two nude pubescent girls (how seventies does that seem?); the air was always smokey – a combination of joss sticks and "interesting" cigarettes; there were no audition booths of the kind you found in Boots and Smiths – instead you took a set of headphones and dumped yourself among the other listeners on the many cushions on the floor. Bootlegs were prominently displayed and readily available – I've left clutching The Beatles' *Yellow Matter Custard* and *Cum Bak*, Dylan's *Great White Wonder*, *Zimmerman* and *In 1966 There Was* and The Stones' *Get Your Leeds Lungs Out* (March 13, 1971, the finest record they never made). The Manor Studio was where Mike Oldfield would record his album-length ambient prog experiment *Tubular Bells* and thereby launch Virgin Records, created when no other company wanted to take the risk of putting it out.

In was very much in its infancy as a facility. They were still fine-tuning elements of it. Mike Oldfield had been there the month before we arrived, working on what would eventually become *Tubular Bells*. He was working totally solo of course. In fact what he was doing was totally innovative and so didn't reflect the reality of how the studio would be used.

Various ex-Fairports had put the studio through its paces recording that LP of old rock'n'roll songs which they released as The Bunch. We were being offered the studio at a lower rate than it would demand once everything was bedded in. It was great for us because, being in Oxfordshire, it was quite handy. We didn't have to go to London to record and we could go home every night – I think in any case the accommodation part of The Manor was still being put together.

The four of us went there and, working without a producer, we recorded the first version of what eventually became the *Rosie* album. Andy Wheeler, who was our roadie at the time, was there to help with the instruments and so forth but ended up tape-oping because The Manor didn't have any in-house staff as such.

Financially we got a great deal and access to an amazing facility. The problem was we didn't really know what to do with it. Previously, we had Joe Boyd and John Wood around: they understood how to get the best out of a studio and the best out of the band in the studio. I think one of the staff who was overseeing installations in other parts of the building had given Andy a crash course in how to get things on to tape and then basically left us to it.

The band hadn't played together. We'd never played live. I think Dave Rea arrived a couple of days before the sessions started. We were seriously unprepared, which doesn't necessarily matter when you know each other and are used to playing together. Look at when someone like Richard joins us at Cropredy – we don't need to spend hours rehearsing because we already have that bond. We gel. You know it's going to be good and if it pushes the boundaries, goes on a knife edge, all the better. It needs confidence in each other to do that. No disrespect to David but we didn't really know him... and he was American.

As a result, it didn't turn out too well. I'm not blaming Andy or David for that. We were all a bit at a loss, in need of direction. There were some great songs on it, some of which were re-recorded and released on *Rosie... things like My Girl, Matthew Mark*

*Luke and John* and *Rosie* itself of course, which has become a Fairport classic. There were several instrumentals: *Rattletrap*, which David Rea wrote, springs to mind.

We recorded it all and mixed it. Then when we listened to it back, it didn't stand up. It just didn't hang together the way it should. You can partly put that down to the fact that Fairport has always been, above everything else, a live band. That line up went straight into the studio and tried to make a record and it didn't work. The good thing is, we had the sense to realise that and not release it.

The so-called Manor Sessions circulated for years as a much-prized Fairport bootleg. A couple of tracks sneaked out on rarities and archivist compilations. At the time Peggy and I were holding the conversations that make up the majority of this book, a new Island Records Fairport box set had made the majority of these recordings available for the first time officially – ten tracks that included a version of *Rosie* with Dave Rea on lead vocal and an early version of Swarb's setting of *To Althea from Prison*.

It wasn't great. No: I'll be honest, we thought it was awful. Listening to it now, it's not as bad as it seemed but at best, it's interesting. The stuff we did again later is not as good as the released version; nothing else from those sessions could be classed as 'essential Fairport'. We didn't like it. We didn't want to put it out as a Fairport record. We didn't want it to be released at all. There were urgent discussions about what we could do about it. We tried to think what we could do to improve it. I suspect Island were keen to put it out to recoup something. All we could suggest to improve it was to scrap the whole thing.

Meantime, Dave Rea went back to America and Tom Farnell decided he'd had enough. They both left, leaving once more just Swarb and myself to pick up the pieces. We didn't want Island getting wind of a completed album and putting pressure on us to release something we really weren't happy with. Swarb and myself decided, rather than try to make a silk purse out of a sow's ear, we'd be better starting from scratch.

Island were hassling us for a new album – this was back in the days when they still wanted to put out new Fairport albums! In fact, this was around the time they put together that *History of Fairport Convention* double album, which I still think is a good account of the story of the band thus far. It was a great selection and a really lavish package. It ended with an early version of *Hen's March* with the new Fairport line up, which I think is the first thing we recorded.

We decided to re-record the material that we were happy with – not Dave Rea's songs, obviously, now he was no longer part of the band – and we'd ask Trevor Lucas to produce it. We also decided that obviously we couldn't do it all ourselves, so we invited in various friends, people we felt comfortable with, to play on the album. We got Richard to play; Ralph McTell's on a track; Sandy and Linda did some backing vocals; DM agreed to play on the sessions.

We went back to Sound Techniques and had John Wood supervise the mixes. It was what you'd call going back to the old school approach if you were describing the process now. As Trevor was producing, he suggested we get in Jerry Donahue, who'd also been part of Sandy's band Fotheringay.

The cover showed the band that emerged from those sessions, but if you look at the credits the sleeve doesn't reflect who's actually on it. The same thing would happen a couple of years later when *Gottle o'Geer* came out with a photo of the line up with Dan

Ar Braz, who's not on the record at all. At least the five guys on the cover of *Rosie* played on most of the tracks.

The cover showed five individual photos in a rustic frame with the word Rosie hanging like a carved house name. Some were put in mind of the house name outside Fairport in Fortis Green. Later visitors to Woodworm Studios might have felt the sleeve recalled in the elegant carved woodwork. The frame is on a wall covered in pastel wall-paper with roses on it. One critic, seemingly at a loss about what should be said regarding the music, compared the sleeve to that of *Liege & Lief* with its similar individual photos – "Fairport have exchanged gritty daguerreotype Victorian realism for twee faux-rural Metroland suburbia."

The album credits three drummers – Dave Mattacks (who appears on the sleeve as a member of Fairport, which he again was by the time the album came out), Timi Donald and Gerry Conway.

I know that makes Gerry look like he was part of Fairport long before he was... though in a way he's been an honorary Fairport since way back then. The reason he's credited on *Rosie* is because he plays on the two songs Trevor wrote. They were songs from the second Fotheringay album which was abandoned when the band broke up. Trevor reckoned a couple of the songs would work for Fairport, so I replaced Pat Donaldson's bass part and Swarb added a fiddle and we both did some new backing vocals – on *Knights of the Road*. Gerry plays on *Rosie* itself: that was the first track we recorded; the group was me, Swarb, who was singing the vocal now, Richard, Gerry and Sandy & Linda on backing vocals: it's one of those songs which is essential Fairport, recorded by a version of the band that never existed beyond that one studio session. The song stayed in the repertoire, which is not the case with anything else on that album, so we were still playing it on the Farewell tour and Swarb played it most years at Cropredy, until his health made it impossible for him to sing and he asked Chris Leslie, who'd done it with him in Whippersnapper, to sing while he played. It was one of the most requested back catalogue songs that people asked for when we did *By Popular Request* a few years back.

*Rosie* was the first thing we did. Then we brought in Ralph McTell to re-record Swarb's 20's ditty *Me With You* on which he features as The Swarbrick Brothers – David Cyril and Eric. It was still not exactly a Fairport album. It wasn't a Swarb album either. It was the two Daves. I think it was around then Swarb suggested I should try writing some things for the album, so it wasn't all his songs. Trevor suggested we bring in Jerry to play lead guitar – he was currently on tour in France with Sylvie Vartan, whose name will mean a lot more to any of my Breton friends reading this than it will to most people in England or the States. Dave Mattacks agreed to rejoin too, because he sensed that Fairport had once more found a sense of direction.

Fairport Convention now consisted of 3/5s of the *Full House* line up, but instead of Richard and Simon, they had an Australian and an American. Both were of course known to Fairport fans because they had been in Sandy's band Fotheringay. Jerry came from a showbiz background: his father was a well-known jazz saxophonist and his mother was an actress who'd featured in TV shows like Bonanza. Trevor had a definite folk pedigree, having worked with the likes of Bert Lloyd and Martyn Wyndham-Read on LPs of Australian traditional songs for Topic: the latest was *The Great Australian Legend* released at the end of 1971 on which both Swarb and Peggy play. Two tracks into the new Fairport album, the next line up of Fairport had started to come together. Significantly, though, this is always referred to as the *Nine* line up, not the *Rosie* line up.

Right after Jerry joined the sessions and Trevor started playing with us as well as producing, we did a couple of instrumentals including my first original composition for Fairport, *Peggy's Pub*. Swarb brought in a new song, *Furs and Feathers* which is the strongest song on the album after *Rosie*. We weren't a band again as yet, but we were close and getting closer through playing together.

In the process, *Rosie* became a much better album. The song *Rosie* itself is understandably a favourite of many Fairport fans and the whole album has a real charm about it. It's a gentle album in a way and quite informal, funny in places too, which was important because we'd started to take ourselves a bit seriously with Babbacombe Lee.

It's still a record I really like and enjoy listening to, because I tend to forget all the stuff leading up to it and remember how much we enjoyed recording that second attempt at it and of course how Fairport came together as a band as a result of that recording process. From that point of view it was a very important record in Fairport's history.

*Rosie* was released in March 1973, fifteen months after their previous album *Babbacombe Lee*. In that period, Fairport Convention had had eight different members and seven guest members. Their next album came out at the start of October and featured the five-man line up that had come together during the making of *Rosie*. *Nine* remains one of the most highly regarded Fairport albums: so much so that when they marked their half century they used the design of its front sleeve as the model for *50:50@50*. The reverse of its sleeve held its true visual significance – not because of the cryptic message "Sorry dear 'Rabelais' off" but because it showed the new Fairport (left to right – Peggy, Swarb, DM, Jerry and Trevor) in front of The Brasenose the pub at the heart of the tiny Oxfordshire village that would forever be associated with Fairport Convention, Cropredy.

Cropredy became our home, though no one outside the band had heard of it unless they happened to be students of the English Civil War or the development of the Canal System. I doubt anyone who bought *Nine* could have said where the pub was or where we'd taken the photos of the band playing together. The fact that the photomontage in the gatefold included the logo of *La Vache Qui Rit* made a lot of people assume it was in France – wildly inaccurate but intriguing given what was to happen to me a few years later.

Lots of Fairport fans, coming to Cropredy for the first time for one of the Festivals, have remarked to me how startled they were to see the cover of *Nine* "in the flesh", so to speak. That sleeve made The Brasenose as iconic for Fairport fans as the Abbey Road zebra crossing or Heddon Street in Soho where they took the cover of *Ziggy Stardust*.

Aside from our drummers, who as ever like to be the exception that proves the rule in rock bands, most Fairport members since the mid-eighties have lived in or near what you once described as "The Folk Rock Triangle". Swarb and I were in Cropredy itself. Simon and later Fairport's offices were in Chipping Norton. Before that the offices and studio were at my house in Barford, just the other side of Banbury. Sandy lived in Byfield. Chris is from Adderbury. Ric lives in Bloxham.

Quite a lot of our songs relate to the area too. annA rydeR and PJ Wright have both written songs about the Cropredy Festival. Ralph wrote *Red and Gold* about the battle in the village. Then there's *The Happy Man* and *The Eynsham Poacher*. Even *Fotheringay* which is just up the road in Northamptonshire. Chris Leslie is very much a local lad and so has written several songs that relate to Oxfordshire and its history like *Banbury Fair* or *I'm Already There*.

None of us lives in the village now, though the fact our festival has taken place there for forty years makes it very much our spiritual home. Chris's song *Festival Bell*, which was the title track of an album a few years back, commemorates the fact that a few years ago the village decided to dedicate a new church bell to Fairport. It really touched me when they told us that.

And every time they've tolled it since.

It's a unique honour for a rock band. Since its installation, the Cropredy Convention always starts with the ringing of the Fairport bell in the old church tower less than a mile from the festival site. It's an emotional moment, one of those things that makes you tearful. Those bells will still peel centuries after we're all gone. Future guidebooks to the village will have to explain who Fairport Convention were in the same way as they now give the background to the Battle of Cropredy Bridge or the legend of St Fremund.

I'm from Birmingham which proudly lays claim to being the home of heavy metal music – a list of Brum Bands proves the point: Black Sabbath, half of Led Zeppelin, Judas Priest, The Move, even Slade. But when it comes down to it, none of them has a church bell dedicated to them.

That's several tons of cast iron.

That's proper heavy metal.

Eat your heart out, Ozzie!

# Chapter 7

# As the verses unfold
*singer songwriters*

With both Sandy Denny and Richard Thompson as ex-members of the band, Fairport had an astonishing legacy of songs on which they could, if they wished, draw. Although Dave Swarbrick wrote some fine songs for the band, no one would primarily think of him as a songwriter. The arrival of Chris Leslie in 1997 meant Fairport once more had an in-house songwriter. In the gap between, some of the Britain's greatest singer songwriters were happy to provide songs for them.

Each time Fairport moved on or changed line up, we seemed to feel a need to ditch the old repertoire. These days of course we play lots of songs from right across our fifty year history, but, even at Cropredy, it was a slow job introducing them. We were respectful of the material; we tended to think of them as 'a Richard song' or 'a Sandy song' rather than a Fairport song: of course, a lot had painful memories associated with them.

Looking back now, it seems odd to think that for that first decade I was in the band we didn't play things like *Genesis Hall, Crazy Man Michael, Fotheringay* or even *Meet On The Ledge*. Some of Sandy's songs were reintroduced when she rejoined: when she left we put them back on the shelf. *Who Knows Where The Time Goes*, for example, was voted the nation's favourite folk song by Radio 2 listeners. Yet, aside from the times when Sandy sang it or a Cropredy guest wanted to do it, Fairport didn't play it until 1997. Lots of other people did, of course.

All those years when we had this untouched treasure trove of great material, and when did we first start to make use of it?

When we finally had a songwriter back in the band again.

A lot of the people who wrote songs for Fairport, or passed on songs they already had, were people we worked with separately. Support acts on tour, people we'd done sessions for, people we just knew socially, people like annA who recorded at Woodworm. The two people outside the band whose songs we've recorded most – and I think here we need to separate studio recordings from live performances, particularly those at Cropredy which is very much a law unto itself – are definitely Ralph McTell and Steve Tilston. So let's start with them.

Ralph's a great mate from way back. He's always been a friend of the band and I played on quite a few of his albums. He's so easy going, a true pleasure to work with, absolutely solid and open to ideas. Just so it doesn't get forgotten, I ought to say that we did one of Ralph's songs on *Bonny Bunch of Roses*: nearly everything on that and the next album was traditional, but we included a version of Ralph's *Run Johnny Run*, a great song.

I worked a lot with Ralph in the late seventies and early eighties. He used Woodworm for some recordings and demos: this was around the time he was doing a lot of songs for kids' TV programmes as well as his more serious singer-songwriter recordings. I played on half a dozen or so of his albums, starting with *Streets* I think. I wasn't on the hit single, but I played on the rest of that LP.

I was living in Birmingham at the time and Ralph picked me up from the train. We drove to his new house, which I think was so new to him that he was still in the process of buying it. It was an unadopted road in Barnes; that meant the road was not maintained by the council and wasn't in the best of condition. It turned out his neighbour was Brian Rix who was famous for appearing in Whitehall Farces. At one point, he stuck his head over the fence to say hello. I recognised him straight away, because he used to be on TV so much in the early sixties. I actually wondered if I looked over the fence, if he'd have lost his trousers. Which of course will only mean something to people of a certain age.

Several other Fairports were involved in Ralph's recording from time to time – Richard, Jerry, Swarb, Maart, Jerry, DM. So there was a definite bond both personally and with the band.

In 1985, Simon, DM and myself decided the time was right to make a proper new Fairport album. We'd put out a number of recordings from Cropredy on Woodworm Records (and tapes), but that was all old material plus it was all very much live, of course. There wasn't any post production or sweetening on those recordings: what happened on the night was what you got.

We'd reached a point where we either had to carry on literally repeating ourselves, in effect becoming our own tribute band, or we had to move on. Swarb said he wasn't interested in being involved. He didn't live in Cropredy anymore and he'd lots of other irons in the fire. To be fair, there was also the issue of the risk to his hearing. Getting together for an annual Fairport reunion was one thing; anything beyond that was something he wasn't prepared to consider.

Of course, not being a working band in the normal sense, we didn't have a set that we wanted to record. None of us was a songwriter. So we began looking round for things to record. We invited Cathy Le Surf, who was either in or had just been in The Albion Band, to sing *My Feet Are Set For Dancing*; I had an unreleased Richard Thompson song that he'd demo'd at my old Woodworm Studios in Cropredy. I put together a medley of three tunes which we called *Instrumental Medley '85* – see what we did there?

We had the idea of asking Ralph whether he had anything he thought might be suitable. He gave us three songs which make up most of the album's playing time. *Wat Tyler* was an epic historical ballad that he co-wrote specially with Simon. *Bird from the Mountain* was a celebration of poaching with the positive message "he helps them that helps themselves"; a friend of ours, Harold Wells, spoke some of the words – he's from Williamscot which is the next village to Cropredy. Both those song had obvious Fairport connections.

The real jewel in the crown was a song that Ralph himself didn't record for a couple of years. *The Hiring Fair* was co-written with Dave Mattacks. It's gone on to become a Fairport classic, not least because, despite being a sort of Hardyesque narrative, it seems perfectly to evoke the spirit of Cropredy. It's a very romantic song and so untypical of what Fairport normally do, but it became a fan favourite straight away. Whenever we do it at Cropredy – which is most years – a kind of hush comes over the crowd and it feels very focused. It's one of those moments you look forward to each year. Of course, I also like it because it's a long song, about six minutes, and I don't play in the first part of it, so it's great if I need to pop off for a tiddle.

*Hiring Fair* was one of the tracks on the album where Ric appeared as a guest player. I think because people are so used to there being a fiddle on Fairport albums they assume he's on the whole LP but in fact he only played on three tracks. *The Hiring Fair* was the first track he ever played on.

Like Dave Swabrick, Ric Sanders was hired by Fairport to play on three tracks for their next album. He enjoyed the experience; he got on well with the band; they asked him to join; he took a lead role on shaping the next album. 16 years on exactly from the spring of 1969, fiddle history was repeating itself.

Ric is the son of the English teacher at the school where Peggy's dad was the caretaker. Peggy was rehearsing with his first band around the time Ric was taking his first violin lessons. Inspired equally by the jazz of Joe Venuti & Stephane Grappelli, Swarb's folk fiddle, the classical/rock fusions of Stomu Yamast'ta and rock violin pioneers like Jean Luc Ponty and David LaFlamme, he developed a distinctive style that often made inventive use of effects pedals. By the time he came to make his first Fairport recordings he'd been part of Soft Machine and The Albion Band (appearing on *Rise Up Like The Sun*, one of the essential folk rock albums), and worked with Gordon Giltrap, Martin Simpson, June Tabor, Andrew Cronshaw and his own band Second Vision, for whom he wrote August 4, a commemoration of the Fairport farewell gig at Cropredy in 1979. In 1985, when *Gladys' Leap* was released just in time for Cropredy festival, he was unable to attend because he was appearing at Edinburgh Festival with Julian Clary.

In 2012, to coincide with our 45th anniversary of the band, we asked our fans to vote for which tracks from our back catalogue they'd like to hear the new line up record. We knew that would probably rule out the songs we'd recorded since Chris joined, unless we'd radically revised them in some way. We could guess the final list would include things we'd done live with that line up but never recorded, like *Rosie* and *Hexamshire Lass*. The list, when it was finally drawn up, was surprisingly long. Lots of things that got only one or two votes.

Ever hopeful, my list included *Hungarian Rhapsody* and *Wizard of the Worldly Game*.

Some votes were, I hope, not meant seriously – instrumentals from the first album, things like *Quasi B Goode* where the Fairports had been a backing band, even a couple of votes for *All Around My Hat*. There were things you knew were going to be there – *Meet on The Ledge, Matty, Walk Awhile*. There were some real surprises that challenged us a bit, but which have as a result of that vote ended up being part of our regular set – *Fotheringay, Farewell*. There were three post-reformation (if that's the right term... it sounds a bit like English religious history!) – two were by Ralph. One was *The Hiring Fair*, which probably belongs in that list of certainties – things we more or less knew people would ask for. The other was the title track of our next studio album of new songs, and that was a bit of a surprise.

### It did not occur to me that little Cropredy would be witness...

Ralph was visiting me one day and we went for a walk to the festival site, over Cropredy Bridge. I told him the story of the Civil War battle and it obviously caught his imagination. A few days later, he presented Fairport with *Red and Gold*. It's a typical

Ralph song, with a strong narrative and clear direct lyrics that have much deeper meanings. It describes the battle, but from the point of view of an accidental onlooker, a sort of everyman. I suppose that was me telling the story to Ralph, immediate and second hand at the same time. It's a song about a battle that was fought in 1644, but also about all wars, about nature, about social class. It's another that's special whenever we do it at Cropredy – or when Ralph sings it himself as he had a couple of times – because the very field people are standing on is the one we are singing about, that Ralph wrote about.

*Red and Gold* came out in December 1988 and marked the end of an era because it was our last vinyl album. Except, if being in Fairport has taught me anything, it's never to assume that anything is truly the last. Vinyl's had a revival and we now plan a vinyl edition as part of new studio releases: they sell out quickly too. Talk about "it all comes round again"!

## 1987

The gap between *Gladys* and *Red and Gold* was a busy period for the Fairports and quite a strange one in many ways. At first it was the three old hands, Simon, DM and me, a rhythm-heavy trio with a brand new LP. Ric joined. We recruited Maart Allcock, which is a story in itself, that I must tell you later. That meant by 1986, 32 years ago amazingly, we had a new five-piece fully-functional Fairport. Over those three decades there have only been two changes in the line up. Because we didn't have a songwriter, we decided to make an entirely instrumental album. That was *Expletive Delighted*. I don't think it's an album which anyone would put in their top five all-time favourite Fairport LPs, but it did have *Portmeirion* on it. It also has new versions of a couple of my tunes. Everyone should have a copy: I need the royalties.

The next recording project was an odd one. Island records were celebrating their 25th anniversary. They reissued lots of classic albums and put out compilations and retrospectives. Despite all those great acts who've recorded for the label – big chart successes, major album artists – for some reason they decided to ask Fairport to make the new recordings that would mark the anniversary. That's right, the band they had dumped a decade earlier because we were no longer a viable proposition. Still, forget and forgive, eh? They were offering good money and at the time that came in pretty handy. We re-recorded *Meet On The Ledge* which they put out as a single on 7" and 12". It's quite humbling in a way. The label had all those massive hits – Free, Roxy Music, Steve Winwood and so on. Yet the song they think best represents them is one that never made it anywhere near the charts... Fairport's anthem, written by an eighteen year old Richard Thompson... very much a sixties song but also absolutely timeless.

They also, for some reason, wanted to put out a live Fairport album. We didn't have the opportunity to record in front of an audience in the timeframe they gave us, so we went into the studio – the Mill at Farnham – and recorded highlights from our current set live in the studio. They added applause afterwards: it was take from a John Martyn concert in Leeds. Again, probably not one of the LPs people put on their essential Fairport lists.

This was in 1987, which turned out to be an expensive year for Fairport fans. The year began with the first major Winter Tour to be advertised as such; other tours took them overseas – Europe, America, Australia. There was a second shorter tour later in the year.

People think of us touring the UK annually. We do tour every year – The Winter Tour, travelling round the UK for the best part of two months in the worst weather conditions Britain has to offer. There's also an acoustic tour in May: I forget how that first started – I think it was because DM wasn't available and so we decided to go out drummerless. Without needing a drumkit, you needed less equipment: you didn't need a PA capable of matching the sound of the drums which are so much louder than people realise. Then we realised we could use acoustic instruments. The knock-on effect was that we needed fewer crew and we could manage in a smaller vehicle. That meant we could play smaller venues because costs had been kept down. That also allowed for some far more intimate gigs which all of us enjoyed.

One year I wasn't able to do the acoustic tour – we've never called it Fairport Unplugged by the way, though others have used that expression. We were doing it long before MTV came up with the idea. That year, Gerry did the tour, taking a bongo and some small percussion items. That worked because Gerry's a percussionist rather than just being a drummer – which are very different things: most people are one or the other – Ray Cooper's a percussionist; Ringo's a drummer – but very few people are both. These days Gerry also has a small drumpad, about the size of a laptop keyboard that gives him even more flexibility. So what began as a tour for a stripped back four-man Fairport, now features the whole band.

We always start Cropredy with a short acoustic set too – sometimes we bring on a guest even in a short twenty-minute set. Around four you hear the bells of Cropredy church start up – time to ring some changes, as someone once wrote – and then we come on. One of the bells you hear is the Fairport Bell, so the acoustic set can include Chris Leslie's *Festival Bell* in context. Being the first act on at a festival is a pretty bad slot. People are still arriving, settling down, getting to know their neighbours, buying in beer and food etc. It's a hard crowd. As a festival organiser, you know you're going to use it for some lesser known act: you do end up feeling like you're throwing them to the lions. I remember once trying to reassure someone by saying "No, you were OK but the crowd was awful" which, trust me, is no reassurance at all. So a few years ago – I'm sure you can check back to find out exactly when [it was 2011] – we hit on the idea of starting the whole festival with Fairport Acoustic. It was good for several reasons. At the time, the acoustic version of Fairport played shorter tours so not all our fans had chance to see us in that context and now they could. It was good to be able to welcome people: it always felt odd appearing after three days – though we may have been on stage individually playing with other artists – and saying "Hello (at last), hope you've had a nice time". Someone told me once that they were people who thought we only turned up for the Fairport set – which is nonsense as most of us are wandering round the field all the time. Personally, if you want to find me, head either for the bar or somewhere on the edge of the mosh pit.

Back in the early days of the reformed Fairport – there isn't a right word is there? Have any of us become reformed characters? I know I haven't! Anyhow, back then, the second tour was really down to whether there was a slot when we were all free. I had commitments to Tull, for example: Simon did some work with Ashley and they formed the Albion Acoustic Band (I'm not saying they nicked the idea but they did it after Fairport). I think we both worked with Richard from time to time. Everyone in the band, particularly Dave Mattacks, could get as much session work as they wanted... and don't forget that with Fairport in effect dormant for five years building up the contacts to be able to do that was very important.

There were many albums on which Fairport members, or ex-members, appeared as guests or session musicians. There were at least as many on which their contributions went uncredited. 1987 was an expensive time for Fairport completists and there were, and are, a good number of those around. Even for the less obsessive fan, there was a surprising number of releases by Fairport in their own right. One album fell into both camps: it was one on which Peggy, DM, Ric and Maart all appeared – Simon Nicol's first solo album *Before Your Time*.

Simon is many things – great guitarist (one of the best rhythm guitarists in the world), great singer, fine frontman and so on. One thing he's never been is a solo artist. Occasionally he might do a song solo in a set as part of a duo with Swarb, probably to give Swarb chance of a tiddle break or to collect the money or blag a drink or something. Some Fairport songs, like *Hiring Fair* have sections where he's totally in the spotlight on his own. But he's never, as Sandy put it, "gone solo". Making your solo album is a sort of right of passage for any rock musician, ever since George, Ringo, John and Paul (in that order) did it. I'd done one, for heaven's sake.

I had a studio. I had a record label. I had loads of mates inside and out of Fairport that I knew would be happy to come and play. So I started trying to persuade Simon to make a solo record. I suppose I was wearing my "record company boss" hat which usually has no other function than to hide my bald head.

Simon produced the album and I am really proud to have played on it. It includes the first released recording of *From A Distance* which has gone on to become a classic (even Sir Cliff sings it and you can't say that about many Fairport-related songs). There's *The Deserter* by John Richards which eventually became part of Fairport's set – awkward when the band already has a song in its back catalogue with the same title. There's a great instrumental of the title track and *Merry Sherwood Rangers* with Simon, me, Ric, DM and Peter Vettese from Tull on keyboards. The real joy, though, was a track I was delighted to be able to play on, when Simon managed to persuade Linda Thompson literally to break her silence and record *I Live Not Where I Love*. Since the trauma of her break up with Richard, which was messy and affected us all in one way or another because we were friends with both of them, she'd had a problem which meant she physically wasn't able to sing. Simon somehow coaxed a really amazing performance out of her. If you've never heard it, track down the album for that one recording alone.

In May 1987, Woodworm put out another double cassette official bootleg from Cropredy, *The Other Boot*. It featured some (but by no means all) of the marathon set from the previous year. If you were hoping to hear again Robert Plant's surprise guest appearance, you'd be disappointed. This had been a first Cropredy outing for songs from *Gladys' Leap* and tunes from *Expletive Delighted*, some of which made it onto the cassette. There were also some oldies from way back (*Sloth, Time Goes, Lark medley, Mr Lacey*). The first side of the first cassette was dominated by songs that Fairport never officially released, covers of songs by American singer-songwriters that had come out on an earlier Fairport official bootleg *Heyday* in the mid seventies. In September that cassette release came out on LP for the first time.

The *Heyday* release – again it was mixed emotions, like when Island released the *Live at The Troubador* LP. There's some great stuff on it and it's good to have, but it focused attention on Fairport's past when we were really trying to build for the future. As the person who ran the record company that released current Fairport material, it was hard not to resent anything that might cut into those sales. Remember this was also the year when Island first began to release the Fairport back catalogue on CD, as well. It was Joe Boyd who put out *Heyday* on his Hannibal Records label. All the recordings had been made for the BBC and I know Joe did some groundbreaking work in making it possible for that stuff to be released. The Beeb was famous for hanging on possessively to its own recordings. Lots of artists have released *Live at the BBC* albums since – The Beatles, The Stones, The Who, Hendrix, June Tabor – but it was Joe negotiating for the Fairport material that made that possible.

I wasn't involved in any way, of course, either with the release (though because it was a Fairport release and I ran Woodworm Records lots of people asked me about it) or the original recordings. It was before my time, to borrow a phrase from Simon. My BBC recordings with Fairport – the ones for radio anyway – came out in a four CD complete box years later.

Finally before we move from the pocket emptying delights of 31 years ago, we should remember that two Fairport VHS Home Videos became available. The first was *In Real Time* confusingly nothing to do with the LP of the same name, but footage from Cropredy, which was reused as part of *It All Comes Round Again* which added interviews and remarkable archive footage to tell the complete history of Fairport to date. Speaking of the history of the band...

A lot of Ralph's songs that we did seem to relate wholly or partly to Fairport's own story. I don't mean they were necessarily about Fairport. *The Hiring Fair*'s a good example. It's not about Fairport; it's not even about Cropredy. But it fits perfectly. I suppose it's part of the mark of a great writer, to create something that isn't vague but isn't tied down to specifics either.

I've known Ralph since before I was in Fairport. We met when I was in The Campbells and he was a young songwriter establishing his name in a world where singers were expected to perform songs from the tradition, unless they were American. He was booked to play at their club The Jug O'Punch. They always had great guests there, both traditional players and younger musicians: every Thursday night was a treat – Bert and John, Paul Simon, Joni Mitchell, Carthy and Swarbrick.

Both Ralph and The Campbells recorded for Transatlantic which was the British label for folk musicians with an approach that stretched beyond doing straight folksongs – Pentangle, Mr Fox, and a lot of great guitarists. Island, aside from folk-rock bands was cherry-picking the cream of the singer-songwriters, Nick Drake, John Martyn and so on. Right from that first meeting Ralph and I got on really well, so we had a connection from that point. We've remained great friends and Ralph is one of those people I know I can ring if ever I have a problem: he's great to talk to, a real calming influence, chilled and logical, but never cold. I think that comes over to everyone when they see him on stage. It's certainly part of his songs which have a warmth I would say is unique.

Anyhow, Ralph has been around Fairport more or less for its entire life and has been a good friend to most everyone in it. He's been on the sidelines to witness our ups and downs, our triumphs and tragedy. There are a few people who deserve the title "honorary Fairport" even if they've not been a band member – or at least not joined yet. When The Fairport toured America with Traffic, he same to see us because he happened to be in New York at the same time: after the gig we all went out to Nobody's Bar: that was the night we discovered Long Island Iced Tea and another drink called The Zombie In 2014, he presented us with a song which he'd written as a kind of allegorical history of the band. It's written as if it's the life at sea – a sailor's life, if you like – "few would believe it if we said all we'd seen".

It's a great song and it's on *Myths and Heroes*, an album we began after the Wintour and finished in November I think. It saw us back recording at Woodworm, so it felt like old times. Apart from one thing – I couldn't play on the first sessions. I'd had an accident reaching for a glass and had cut my tendon on a broken one that I didn't notice. It was a very deep wound and quite a serious injury. Matt, my son, stepped in for me. It was a like a return favour from when he couldn't play – except, of course, I got The Drifters and he got the Fairports.

He played on the last dates of the tour and then on the first tracks we recorded. I could have replaced his bass parts when I recovered, of course, but what he did was as good as anything I could have done. Another honorary Fairport, then.

I should say, it was a bad time for me. It wasn't just that the injury was painful, inconvenient and uncomfortable. It wasn't that I felt a fool – and the butt of quite a few jokes – because of how it happened. I seriously thought I might never be able to play again. That was a thought I found it very hard to deal with. I have to thank the many doctors and nurses that meant I was fit to play on most of the album and at Cropredy. Still find the mandolin more difficult than it ever was – which I'll keep saying because it's a good excuse.

Of all the Fairport albums since 1980, a couple stand head and shoulders about the rest. One is *Myths and Heroes*, the other is *Jewel In The Crown*.

The title track from that is by Julie Matthews. It was the third of the more recent songs that fans requested a new version of on *By Popular Request*. Simon had learned it while he was in The Albion Band with Julie, Chris While and Ashley, of course. There was something about making that album. We knew it was going to be a good one. It was 1995 and the year had something about it for Fairport. We were getting renewed attention in the press – there was even a big article in Mojo. It was a significant year for me, because it was the year I decided to leave Jethro Tull and put all my eggs in one basket. *Jewel in the Crown* is an important album in Fairport's history for a lot of reasons. We put special care into tracking down the songs that would go on it.

Fairport discreetly put out the word that, still being a songwriterless band, they were on the lookout for songs. Aside from the title track, they got *The Islands* which Ralph McTell had written as part of the soundtrack to Billy Connolly's Tour of Scotland TV series. Beryl Marriott passed on *Red Tide* which had been sent to her by journalist Rob Beattie, for her opinion. The band renewed a long-severed connection with Leonard Cohen and recorded a total reinvention of his song *Closing Time*. I dispatched a couple of songs from the album *Of Moor and Mesa* by Steve Tilston and Maggie Boyle – they were *Slipjigs and Reels* and *The Naked Highwayman*.

That was the start of a long and fruitful relationship with Steve. He's written lots of songs for us and given us first refusal on lots more. He and Maggie made their next album at Woodworm and I think we all played on it, apart from Simon. A second guitarist is a bit surplus to requirements when you're dealing with Steve. He's a man who can put more notes in an accompaniment and more words in a lyric than anyone I know.

*Slipjigs* became a standard, of course, one of those songs a lot of people assume is traditional – despite the wild Mescaleros. A couple of years back, Simon decided he'd re-learn *Naked Highwayman*, which is a mad decision because it's got so many words and goes at such a pace. You can't even singalong with the chorus, it's so fast. Speaking of singing along, when he revived it at Cropredy in 2016, we did it like karaoke on the screen, with all the words and a highlight to show when to sing them. Of course it was impossible. People were keeling over through not having chance to breathe. It was an elaborate gag, but hilarious. We put the new version – without the screen cues – on *50:50@50* as one of the new recordings of old songs which made up half the content.

We've done a lot of Steve's songs and it's a rare Fairport setlist that doesn't have at least one Tilston song in it. Is he another honorary Fairport? Let's say he renewed a lapsed membership from that European tour with us and Mott in 1972.

Like Ralph, Steve felt moved to write a song about Fairport. In the end it became the title track of our CD in 2004, *Over the Next Hill* which was the last we recorded at Woodworm, until *Myths and Heroes*.

It's a song that evokes the spirit of Fairport, based around the various tales we – mainly me – had told him when he was touring as the opening act. Listen to the song again when you've read this book and some of the lines will make even more sense.

Whenever we're on tour, we like to join the support act for their last number, and then stay on to do the first half of our set. It's something we've done for as far back as the early seventies when we did something called *Elizabethan Pop* with Allan Taylor. Usually, whoever we're touring with will pick a song from their repertoire that benefits from being Fairportised. Steve went in another direction and suggested we do *It's Now Or Never* which we all enjoyed because it was a good joke that never wore thin.

We did the Old Songs Festival in New York State with Steve, as I'm sure you recall. It's a proper traditional festival, quite purist and a lot of the regulars found us rather loud, musically and in other ways. They take it all very seriously. Hardly any drinks. There was a little bar, basically a couple of taps and a table: in the UK that would be woefully inadequate, but most times we were the only ones there: you never had to wait to be served unless you were behind another Fairport. We did some workshops with you, I recall. Gerry had a good time looking at native American percussion instruments. Ric and Chris sat in on a fiddle session who were playing the *Liege and Lief* medley as they walked past.

In the evenings, they had a concert on the main stage, which basically everyone attended because that was the only thing happening. I think normally, each of the main acts played a short set, so you got to see five or six acts do twenty minutes or half an hour apiece. Fairport needed longer than that – if we'd done *Sloth*, we'd have need that long for one song! So they gave us a concert length set. Not everyone approved of such preferential treatment. We were told to take off our shorts and put on long trousers: this wasn't a dress code, or hatred of knees, because we were also told to spray ourselves thoroughly with anti-mosquito spray. I'm glad we did because the little blighters were out in force. Not so little either. You could hear them buzzing past above the music: now and then there'd be a pop when one flew into a light. It was hell. I swear at one point I played a wrong note because a bug landed on one of my bass strings and held it down.

Every act on the main stage – and at a lot of other events – had a signer. This was before such things were commonplace in the UK for people with hearing difficulties. *Walk Awhile* was our opening number: it's fairly easy to sign, even if the verses are a bit nonsensical. But we'd come on to absolute silence – no applause, no cheer, you could hear people whisper "that's the guy that was smoking". It's an easy song to join in with, audiences sing along wherever we do it. Except at Old Songs, where the only people apart from the Fairports doing the chorus was probably you, and the signer who was joining in silently. "The more we walk together…": they were having none of it.

We did a couple of things, including an instrumental which gave the lady who was signing a break: she sat at the side of the stage tapping her feet, which felt under the circumstances a bit like getting a standing ovation.

Then we did *Naked Highwayman*, which has loads and words and goes really fast. She tried to keep up, but it was impossible. The only person moving his arms faster was a guy in the audience who'd forgotten to put on bug spray and was fending off multiple aerial attacks. In the end, she just did an exaggerated shrug to the audience, smiled at us and sat that one out. Who could blame her? I never did get to find out what sign language for *Highwayman* is; or *Naked* for that matter which might have been even more interesting.

One thing which did prompt a response – other than the bugs – was a line in Chris' *My Love is in America,* where he mentions New York State by name – people did that strange thing of applauding the mention of their own home.

Another great memory from that festival was an outdoor workshop in the middle of a race track. Nigel was leading it with Steve and, as originally planned, Simon, but we decided to give them the full Fairport instead. It was all quite surreal – it was an odd place to play: being America, there was a lot of tutting when Gerry lit a cigarette behind the stage before we went on – bear in mind he wasn't standing near anyone and was in effect in the middle of a field. We'd decided to do it acoustic… two guitars, hand percussion, bass, two fiddles. That obviously appealed because a huge crowd gathered: they brought extra chairs and it was still standing room only.

It was all very informal and unprepared. At one point you interviewed us and Steve about *Slipjigs* and then asked to play it together, except Steve lost the thread and went straight into *The Naked Highwayman*. At the end, without explaining why or warning us, you led us into *It's Now or Never*. Us lot playing Elvis to die-hard folkies was a risk to say the least, but you'd obviously got the measure of that particular crowd. There were cries of delight when we started and before we'd got through the first verse, there were couples up at the back dancing. It was a strange festival, but that is one great memory to take away – the summer sunshine of New York State, Steve and The Fairports letting *It's Now Or Never* roll on, Chris's mandolin making it more and more Italian (*O Soli Mio*), as everyone smiled and pairs of dancers rotated silhouetted against a perfect blue sky.

**Aside from being in a studio houseband for Ralph and Steve, Peggy, along with other Fairports, regularly appeared on what are now regarded as essential classic albums by the truly great singer-songwriters.**

The list would be endless – some are well known, some less so. We put some of them on one CD of my box set we did together. Trying to put together a list would be impossible, because I keep remembering – "oh, yeah, I did some tracks with so and so".

Of course, there's the various people who've been in Fairport and our mates – Steve Ashley, for example, who I've worked with throughout his career and is a lovely man, if a bit intense at times. There was Marc Ellington, who was a friend of Richard's: that was an interesting session because it involved loads of Fairport people and various members of the Flying Burrito Brothers. There was an album with Murray Head. A couple of tracks on the solo LP by Mike Heron of The Incredible String Band.

I'm particularly proud that I was involved in Nick Drake's recordings. He made three albums and did hardly any gigs. His records didn't sell, though they had huge critical acclaim as soon as they came out. The two things don't go together. You must end up thinking, 'if they're so good, why is nobody buying them?' I suspect that contributed to his depression. The same applied to Sandy, of course: she won awards as Britain's best female singer; everybody knew she was great, but her albums didn't sell well. They've both been rediscovered by later generations, of course, and years after their deaths their records now sell in sensible quantities.

I don't want to compare Sandy and Nick, but I would make a key contrast – Sandy filled her albums with great backing musicians, friends from Fairport and beyond – Diz, Winwood, even Acker Bilk. The credits for albums are still a bit messy – there are things I know I played on that are credited to someone else; there are things that say "Bass: Dave Pegg" that I'm almost certain aren't me. Despite that, it's worth looking through Sandy's album credits just to see exactly who's playing. She was also the only person to share a lead credit on a Zeppelin album as well of course.

Nick was exactly the opposite. There's Robert Kirby's famous string arrangements, of course, but he kept the sound spare – or at least Joe Boyd who produced the albums did. *Bryter Later* is one of my favourite albums. I'm genuinely proud of the fact that I played bass on all but one track on it.

Richard played on the first album. For the follow up, Nick wanted more of a band sound. Joe Boyd sent him to stay at The Angel with the Fairports for a couple of days. Nick was shy. You know when they say someone is painfully shy? I've always thought it was just an expression but with Nick it felt literally true. He found it hard a lot of the time being with other people; crowds were a nightmare for him; when it came to being on stage – you've heard the stories about him not facing the audience or walking off half way through his second song. They are all true. He wasn't being strange or a prima donna: he literally couldn't do it. When the moment came, it was like it was physically impossible for him.

Nick played a couple of gigs with Fairport, as the opening act. I remember he played at Bristol. Roger Ruskin Spear was the other opening act, as he was on the rest of the tour. There's a contrast to start with. Nick was billed as special guest at the gig or something like that. He clearly found it an ordeal. Luckily it was a supportive audience who were prepared to listen

He wasn't easy to get to know. I don't think anyone got really close. But he was a lovely bloke, a genuinely sensitive poetic soul. Just not made for the times and the world he found himself in.

Over a couple days, Dave Mattacks and I worked on the songs with him. We came up with parts he was happy with. Then we went to Sound Techniques and recorded it. We did it more or less live and in most cases, what came out was exactly that with perhaps one other player putting down a lead line – Richard, John Cale or whoever. They generally dubbed their parts on afterwards.

The problem with Nick was that you'd no idea whether he liked what you were doing or not. He could have thought it was the best thing he'd ever heard; it could have been exactly what he wanted; he might have hated it. I had no way of knowing. I didn't know then. I don't know now. I can only say I am really happy with what I did on *Bryter Later* and I was really happy to have been involved in the making of it.

It's a perfect album in many ways. I know Joe Boyd and John Wood have gone on record as saying it's probably the best thing they ever did. It's not every day you get chance to be part of something like that.

These days I get young kids coming up to speak to me because I was the guy who played bass on *Bryter Later*. Fairport, Tull, all the sessions don't matter to them, but that does. They want to know what Nick was like. I suppose if I could think quickly enough I'd say he was like his songs, beautiful, poetic, mysterious, fragile, frustrating... and of course not enough of them.

Unless they are very poppy, Britain isn't good at taking singer-singwriters to its heart. I know there are lots of people who sing and write songs – Elton, Bowie, George Michael – but I think when you use the phrase singer-songwriter you mean something different from that. In many ways, Nick was the perfect singer-songwriter, except he found it difficult to deal with people and, unlike lots of others who have that problem, he never came up with a technique that allowed him to do that. Those three albums, and some of the unreleased material that has come out since, are important records. He may not have been as successful as James Taylor or Leonard Cohen: that doesn't mean he wasn't every bit as good as they were.

It's good that people have finally started to do covers of his songs. For a time they were treated with too much reverence. If you think about the people we're talking about here, it's the fact that other people do their songs that makes them great. The songs are brilliant. I know the tracks on *Bryter Later* are some of the best playing I ever did – not because I was particularly good, but because the songs worked so well: they left space and they brought out the best in you.

I knew Nick through working with him, though that was brief and the sessions were quick, maybe two or three takes for each song and then move on. He was much closer to people like Richard and John Martyn.

John Martyn was somebody else I played with but didn't get to know well. There was a whole group of people, part of the London scene, usually connected to Island Records, usually songwriters, who were a kind of clique and in terms of Fairport history were before I became part of it. I was always aware of that. Not because they were ever nasty about it or made a point – quite the opposite in fact – but because I was always aware there was something there that I have never been part of.

John Martyn was a very different kind of person. You knew pretty quickly if he wasn't happy with something. Nick's music was suited to a gentle, melodic, understated style of playing. John required something much more funky, more jazz. Although John was a folkie and came up through that same scene as other singer songwriters, Billy Connolly, The Incredible String Band and so on, he was also into reggae (which meant he fitted well into Island Records), jazz and rock. John was great to work with. One of the tracks I'm proudest of is *Dancing*: I have the single on the jukebox; the B side is an instrumental version where you can really hear the bass part coming through. He'd booked DM and myself to record this track, Chris Blackwell, the boss of Island records, was producing and, I think, engineering the session. We did a few tracks of which *Dancing* was one. Unlike a lot of John's songs, the chord sequence was simple, four chords – G, Eminor, C, D – it was a kind of dance thing, not reggae exactly. As it turned out, I could only come up with one bass part for it that I was happy with. John didn't like it... at all... and, as I said, when John didn't like something he left you in no doubt about the fact. I just explained that was the way I'd do it. The truth is, I'm not able to change my style of playing in the way a lot of people who do sessions are. If someone books me for a session, it's because they want some who plays bass the way I do, not me playing bass the way someone else does. Luckily my style is quite distinctive and unusual.

I'm honest about it. If someone doesn't like what I do, I just explain they're got the wrong guy and I won't waste their time. I gathered John wanted me and DM to be a kind of Jamaican rhythm section. I wondered why he'd booked us when there must have been twenty bass and drum players who could easily have done that. John was absolutely determined he wanted us. We pressed on. He was right in the end because that track in particular turned out really well. When he mixed it. Chris Blackwell put the bass right up front – I've never figured out whether that was out of spite. Still it works and that's always the main thing.

There's a great story about John Martyn and Swarb, who had been mates for years. When Swarb was seriously ill – this was after the famous incident when The Daily Telegraph prematurely printed his obituary – John Martyn was also taken sick. The situation, to say the least, was not good for him. John, who always had a wicked sense of humour, told a story about finding out that he might have to lose his leg. He went to see his Harley Street specialist who told him not to worry because "prosthetology is coming on leaps and bounds".

John told everyone the story – in a way it was therapeutic for him, not least because it clearly made some of the people he told it to quite uncomfortable.

Of course, he couldn't tell it to Swarb who at the time was on life-support in hospital. I used to visit him and thought, as John was his mate, he ought to know about the situation. I went to see him in hospital in Coventry. He was in a terrible state, hooked up to lots of machine, unable to speak or move easily. To steal one of his jokes, he was at death's door but being a folk fiddler he couldn't find the right key.

I was there for about an hour: I thought perhaps I could cheer him up, tell him a few funny stories and so on. From time to time he'd give a little smile but I could see it was tiring him out. So I said, "You're tired aren't you? Are you ready for me to go?" and he nodded. I said, "Before I go, I should tell you about John Martyn".

I repeated the Harley Street story and explained John would have to lose a leg: Swarb clearly got it because he smiled at the story, a real beam, his face lit up. When I explained the consequences,  he signalled me to come closer. I leaned into his mouth and he whispered, "Get me his pedals."

I was even able to tell John Martyn that story years later when he played Cropredy for the last time. Even he thought it was really funny. Being John, he accused me of pulling his leg!

We were speaking about people writing songs for Fairport: as we've already mentioned Steve and Ralph, I should mention annA rydeR and P J Wright. We've done a few songs by each of them. In annA's case, we were planning the album for our thirty-fifth year as a band, which we called XXXV and we asked annA if she had anything she thought would fit on it. She came up with The Crowd which is a great song about Cropredy that really epitomises that lovely spirit of the Festival. We actually did two versions on the album: the studio recording and another version where we invited the crowd at Cropredy to join in with their song.

The Festival programme included the lyrics of the song and typically off beat instructions from annA as to what she wanted. These included the fact we'd need "a torch if it's dark by the time we sing it, unless you're clever and have learned the words by heart." The recording happened at 9.00pm. annA rehearsed us and did three takes of the crowd singing, "to be on the safe side". As Fairport continued in the more normal manner with the set, Peggy told us it would be on the next album, "but don't all put in claims for royalties... I couldn't handle the maths",

It's one of the many special moments that sticks in the minds of Cropredeers and crops up in those "were you there when...?" conversations. What made it all the more magical, though, was the end of the evening, when Fairport breached their 'no music after midnight' regulation.

### "This next one must be a favourite of Mr Pegg, since he asks for it every time I play with him" – *Ian Anderson*

Ian Anderson, until fairly recently Peggy's other boss, came on as a surprise guest. With Fairport, he played *Life's A Long Song* (which Fairport had covered on *Who Knows Where The Time Goes*), *Portmeirion* (for which Ian joined them on *XXXV*), *John Barleycorn* (the version Peggy included on *Box of Pegg's*), *Someday the Sun won't Shine for You* (from Tull's first album *This Was*), *Serenade to a Cuckoo* (the Roland Kirk tune that was also on Tull's debut and which Peggy included on *Box* in a version from Cropredy 1987 when Ian and Martin Barre had joined Fairport on stage, the song Ian identified as "one of Dave's Desert Island Discs") and *Locomotive Breath*.

A new arrangement of *The Hiring Fair*, featuring Chris Leslie's mandolin led into *Matty Groves*. Matty struck no more; it all came round again; floodlights above the stage lit the audience; fireworks sparked into the dark clear Oxfordshire sky. We made our way, content and Cropredied, towards the exits. Then from the speakers....more music. Everyone turned. Surely not? The stage was empty and dark, but across the field came the sound of the song we'd all heard for the first time and sung on three hours earlier. The man next to me was so startled that he dropped the entire contents of the hog roast sandwich he'd just bought.

That's one of the great things about Cropredy. It's full of individual moments shared by a lot of people. When you talk to people about Cropredy, and, as you can imagine, that happens a lot with me, they all have particular memories or highlights or vivid recollections. Some are to do with great performances but by no means all. annA's song picks up on that.

That was Fairport's 35th birthday. For our 50th PJ Wright gave us another Cropredy inspired song – *Summer by The Cherwell*. It's one of those songs, like *Walk Awhile* or *Rocky Road* where everyone gets a verse to song.

It's a real anthem with a singalong chorus, a celebration of the sense of happiness and togetherness that happens in that field every August.

That was one of the new songs on *50:50@50*. Another is *Our Bus Rolls On* which Chris Leslie wrote about touring, though the bus is a symbol, like Ralph's ship. Each verse describes a different member of Fairport – a thumbnail sketch. So it belongs in a sort of Fairport tradition of songs that namecheck the band, from within the band – which starts with Sandy's *Come All Ye* and includes *Angel Delight*. Only Simon was in them all – "the original mover and shaker", as Chris describes him.

On the other hand, Pegg on the bass likes the Breton way, sea air, a couple of kippers and a glass of cider!

There's been quite a lot of Fairport-inspired Fairport songs. It would make an interesting collection. Swarb did a song called *Our Band* which was on *Gottle o'Geer* and got forgotten about. There's *Rosie* of course and my *Hungarian Rhapsody*. Ashley

Hutchings has written two or three things about the early days and a couple about Cropredy to the tune of *Million Dollar Bash*. There's even the odd Richard Thompson song based on events from his days in the Fairports. Sandy's *Rising For The Moon* is about being back on the road with the band; actually, like so many of Sandy's songs, it's not precisely about that – it draws on that experience; sometimes Solo sounds as if it's about all those people who went off on their own from Faiport, but another time it seems to be about something entirely different. That's one of the great things about Sandy as a songwriter.

*Solo* was one of those songs I played on when Sandy was putting together the album. Not long after that, she was back in Fairport and it became one of the songs she did with the band.

# Chapter 8

# Hazards are Risks and Risks are Chances
*the return of the lady*

In 1973, Peggy was living in Cropredy on the other side of the street from Dave Swarbrick. When they wanted to rehearse, for a tour or a new album the rest of the band stayed at The Brasenose in the village – hence its appearance on the iconic shot on the cover of *Nine*.

The Fairports were working on the songs that became *Fairport Nine*. We worked on the songs in our houses – Swarb's or mine. We'd sit round with acoustic instruments, getting used to the songs, making changes, coming up with ideas.

The time came when we needed a more formal rehearsal space, somewhere where everything could be set up properly, DM's full kit, electric guitars, amps, effects pedals and so on. In those days, you were expected to arrive at recording studios with everything pretty much prepared: a lot of producers would expect you to play things through at the start of the session. I don't mean we recorded everything live in the studio – before you played a song you might say something like "This will have a double tracked fiddle from Swarb" or "This will have a piano part" or whatever. As I've said before, Fairport Convention has always been essentially a live band: with very few exceptions, what we did on record tended to be something we could do on stage. Some of our albums have been studio recordings of things we've been playing live for a while.

The approach suited us. Groups like The Beatles or The Stones or Pink Floyd might be allowed to take over a studio and experiment, develop songs and arrangements there, but studio time is expensive and for a band like Fairport, the less time you had to spend in the studio the better, financially.

With *Nine*, it was a bit different because we were still a pretty new version of the band. We didn't have songs that we'd played on tour. We wanted the new LP to be strong, because I think we were all aware that even though *Rosie* had some great stuff on it, it felt a bit slung together. We knew we had to rehearse to have the songs we wanted studio ready. Ironically, what most people regard as the essential Fairport albums have come about like that, which I would say is the exact opposite of how Fairport operates. I'm talking about albums like *Liege & Lief*, *Nine*, *Jewel in the Crown*, possibly *Babbacombe Lee*, all which were taken into the studio and recorded before they were taken out on the road.

We were based in Cropredy. The most obvious place to rehearse properly with a five-piece band was the Village Hall. It was roomy, had a stage if we wanted to use it and was reasonable acoustically. Even more to the point, it was convenient, less than five minutes' walk from The Brasenose and literally at the other end of the street from where Swarb and I had houses, at the end of Chapel Lane.

This was in June 1973, which I remember as being a particularly fine summer. No doubt someone will check meteorological data and tell be I'm wrong, but that's how I remember it.

Dorothy was the Hall caretaker and lived next door. Because she knew me from living just down the other end of the street, she trusted me to pick up the keys in the morning and to sweep the place and lock up in the evening. She owned a mynah bird and as it was nice weather she used to put its cage outside in the garden, next to the Village Hall.

## Songs in a mynah key I

We had two roadies at the time – Phil Benton and Roger Proctor – and they were around in case anything needed setting up or fixing or moving. So, while myself, Swarb, Jerry, Trevor and DM were working on the big numbers, they were outside sitting in the sunshine, enjoying a cigarette or whatever.

One of the songs we had to work on was an arrangement of *The Hexamshire Lass*, a song we'd got from Bob Davenport, a traditional love song from the north-east, as you would gather from the title. Dave Mattacks had done an arrangement – DM arranged a lot of things for Fairport and I don't think a lot of our fans are aware of that. The song has a lot of words and in our version it's very fast. So that was one of the 'big numbers' we'd earmarked to nail during those Village Hall rehearsals. That was the first thing we tackled, proper folk rock.

The first day as I was locking up I heard some whistling... just two notes.
Not a wolf whistle but that kind of thing. It was the mynah bird, and as I thought it was cute I whistled the same notes back... and it repeated them. I had a chuckle and remember thinking at the time that it was pretty cute. Took my mind off the fact that the rest of the band were already down the pub enjoying a pint! I made a mental note to see if it did the same tomorrow.

If it had been a parrot, the song we did next day would have been very appropriate.

The other traditional song on *Nine* was *Polly on the Shore*. I'd written a tune for it. The idea was Trevor would sing the song, which really suited his voice, and then there was a long instrumental section which included a bass solo and some startling fiddle work from Swarb. It demanded a lot of rehearsal. The first part was easy, and then we worked all day on the second part. When the rest of the band went off to the pub, I worked on the bass part on my own till I was happy with the solo.

That was the second day. I was pleased with how things had gone. I'd a sense that we were working towards a really good album. So I was in a good mood at the end of the day as I locked up. I remembered the mynah bird: before I left I paused and whistled the two notes to see whether it would repeat them again.

Not only did it repeat them, but it added two more.

I thought "Wow: that's amazing"; I almost wanted to applaud! What a clever bird!

Next day, we worked on the heavier rock songs on side two of the album. Again it went well. I was pleased because after a traumatic year or so with aborted sessions, lots of coming and going and an album that was a bit of a hotch-potch, it really felt like we'd got Fairport back. Everyone went off to the pub, as usual. I think DM and possibly Jerry were staying there. I stayed, tidied things, swept, made sure the Hall was OK if it was needed for anything in the evening.

Then the same thing happened, everyone else had gone and I was on my own locking up and again I heard the whistling... but this time with a couple of extra notes. It had somehow expanded the piece, so it wasn't notes, it was a tune and it started to sound familiar.

I didn't tell anyone about this. I didn't dash off to the pub and inform the chaps about it. I didn't suggest they hung around to hear it. I didn't ask Phil and Roger if they'd heard it, as they sat outside whiling away their time, waiting to be summoned. I suspected to them one bird whistling sounded very much like another.

So our week of rehearsals was up. We'd worked hard and it had been productive. We felt ready to go into the studio to record an album that the fans would like and we could be proud of. It had the music created in the Village Hall in the grooves and the band outside the pub on the sleeve. No mynah bird, though, which is a shame because he became very much part of that album for me. I looked forward to hearing him every day. The sleeve of *Nine* is full of in-jokes that most people don't get or understand... or even spot in some cases. My end-of-the-day whistling feathered friend could have made a little appearance.

For our final day, as I locked up the hall for the last time, he serenaded me with two more notes. What a clever bird, I thought.

I didn't need to go to the Village Hall next day. Roger and Phil went along and collected all our equipment and loaded it into the van, ready to transport it on Monday from Chapel Row in Cropredy to Old Church Street, Chelsea.

We moved from local rehearsal to recording at Sound Techniques, which happened in July and early August. We moved on to a different phase and the delight of my nightly mynah bird evensong slipped right out of my mind.

The album that came out of those rehearsals and recordings, *Nine,* is still highly regarded. One side felt deeply rooted in the trad arr / folk-rock that we associate with Fairport. The other, with original, rocky songs, hinted at the direction they were about to take. It remains a favourite among Fairport fans. Its sleeve was the one the band chose to reference for their 50th anniversary CD packaging – though they resisted recreating its classic band-in-front-of-the-pub shot – a pose much imitated by visitors to the village during and outside Cropredy Festival. Fortunately the appearance of The Brasenose has not changed much over the years. While most of the songs on the album slipped almost permanently from the repertoire with Trevor Lucas's departure, its two traditional songs did reappear years later.

*Fairport Nine* has always been one of my favourite Fairport albums – if pushed, I'd say it's joint top with *Unhalfbricking*. It's a very eclectic album but it fits together so well that you don't realise you're covering such a range of musical styles.

Over nine tracks (a neat titular coincidence for the band's ninth LP), the album covers very traditional folk, country picking, contemporary rock and Swarb's setting of a seventeenth century poem.

In a way, it was like starting over. It was a solid line up: we'd been working together for something like a year. There were lots of influences coming in to the music. Trevor was writing some really great stuff – things like *Bring 'em Down* which is a really clever song. We had such a lot of fun rehearsing and arranging the album. Dave Mattacks did an awful lot of work on arrangements – something that he's never really had due credit for. *Bring 'em Down* and *The Hexamshire Lass* in particular, a lot of the structure of those two songs is entirely down to Dave Mattacks.

Despite the range of music, it hangs together really well as an album – even on CD where you hear both sides straight through. More to the point, it sounds like a Fairport record. I can't really explain what that means, of course. If you made a list of all the albums that sound like Fairport albums, you'd find that in almost every way they are really really different.

It's a shame that because of the way things went the songs on *Nine* never really found their true home in the Fairport repertoire. It was great when Trevor and Jerry rejoined the band at Cropredy in 1982 and we could play that great stuff again. We've gone back to some of those songs since: things like *Polly on the Shore* and *The Hexamshire Lass* do still make the occasional appearance in the Fairport touring setlist.

When Sandy rejoined the band and brought her stuff in and then we had the change of direction for *Rising for The Moon*, it felt like we went from playing Sandy's earlier songs and then skipped everything including almost all the *Nine* songs. I hadn't been around what Fairport had abandoned their complete setlists and moved on back in the sixties, so this was the first time I experienced it.

### To change the ways we're bound to go

When Sandy Denny first joined Fairport, the first track on her first album with them was *Fotheringay*, a traditionally structured song about a historical figure who has become almost legendary that she had already been singing for a few years.

When Chris Leslie first joined Fairport, the first track on his first album with them was *John Gaudie*, a traditionally structured song about a historical figure who has become almost legendary that he had already been singing for a few years.

Both were invited to join to replace a departed, established member at the same time as heralding a significant change in direction for the band. Both were already established, and respected, as songwriters, with a bulging songbag which they were, modestly, reluctant to offer up initially to the existing group members.

There's another parallel, too, which perhaps only people within the band fully realise. When Chris joined, the same as when Sandy rejoined, it didn't feel the same as bringing in an entirely new member. Chris had been around Fairport, sometimes playing with us as a guest, sometimes being part of a project, like *The Family Album* by Steve Ashley, that the rest of us were involved in. When Ric had that accident where he cut his arm and couldn't play, it was Chris who stepped in and played the remaining dates on the tour as well as the whole Cropredy set, which he had about two weeks to learn. That was in 1992, five years before he joined Fairport, so he felt like a Fairport already when he neatly slipped into the space on stage left that Maart had vacated.

I joined Fairport days after Sandy decided to leave, so I missed out on her first really productive era with the band. By the time she returned to the fold, I'd already got to know her through working on her solo albums. We also knew her socially of course because she lived in Byfield, only a couple of miles away from Cropredy.

**Sandy is one of the people who have left Fairport and then rejoined later as a full-time member. When Peggy joined, she had ceased to be a member of Fairport only a few days earlier.**

After I joined Fairport, we never considered replacing Sandy. It would have been an impossible challenge. Over the years at Cropredy, some really wonderful singers have sung Sandy's songs with us and they've been great. When Chris While sang the whole of *Liege & Lief* she was amazing, as she always is. We've had many female singers who wanted to be able to do one of Sandy's songs with Fairport, which they regarded as a kind of honour. I can't list them all, but Julianne Reagan is one of many people who did a great version of *Who Knows Where The Time Goes* with us; Beth Nielson Chapman did *Solo* and it was great to be able to play that again. At one of the very early festivals, Cathy Le Surf did a set of Sandy's songs, which was probably the first time we'd ventured into the territory of singing her material. Vikki Clayton did a great job of evoking the spirit of Sandy's singing in the years after that: one year she put together a full set with a Sandy tribute group she called The Nerve. It's a really important thing to get right.

Back in 1970, looking for another female singer when Sandy left was out of the question. She was the best female vocalist, officially, because that's what she was voted in the Melody Maker polls.

I got used to being asked at gigs "Where's Sandy" in that first year. Most people don't follow the ins and outs of bands as closely as their fans, or indeed some band members, might imagine. Some band members might change and no one really notices, but change a front line person and everyone is aware of it. I think some people asking where she was weren't even aware she'd left and started her own band. They probably assumed she was just having a night off. After about a year, I'd got used to it, just in time for people to start asking "Where's Richard?"

Sandy was a very special person. Some years after her death, I heard a song of hers, quite by accident, on the radio and it inspired me to write *Song for Sandy* which is on my solo LP; I re-recorded it with PJ Wright for the CD we did together.

Even though, in terms of the band's history, she was only in Fairport, in total, for a very short space of time, we'll always be associated with her. Her songs, both the ones she wrote and the ones she sang, are a crucial part of the band's history and we still play many of them today nearly fifty years after they were first recorded.

One question I've been asked a lot of times is when, and whether, Sandy appeared at Cropredy. You and I both know that never happened, because Sandy died a couple of years before the first Cropredy Festival, which seems strange because she is still very much a presence around Fairport and the Festival she never had the chance to attend. I was lucky enough to interview Sandy on three occasions. On one of them, she summed up her membership of Fairport very neatly:

> *"I left Fairport to be able to spend more time with Trevor. Five years later I rejoined for exactly the same reason."*

In fact, it was slightly less time than that and probably much less of a conscious decision.

What's always known as The Fairport Nine line-up took off quite quickly. We were very good and word spread quickly. With Trevor in the line-up, we once more had a great singer; we had a great guitarist in Jerry. Unlike a lot of other people who had been in the band since Simon quit, they were both known to Fairport fans because they had been in Sandy's band Fotheringay: they were also both featured on The Bunch album of rock'n'roll songs, which I know a lot of Fairport fans bought.

We got gigs in Britain and Europe, Australia (partly because of the connection with Trevor) and America, where we worked with Sandy who was starting to record her next album in LA.

The following year, 1974, we had a World Tour, which began in London, went to the Far East, then Australia (where we were the first rock act ever to play in the main hall of the Opera House: my old mates from Brum The Spencer Davis Group pipped us to the post at being the first rock act to play the venue) and then America, Britain and gigs throughout Europe. That takes a long time, as you can imagine. Sandy didn't want to be separated from Trevor for that long and so decided to come with us.

I think the release of her album had been delayed and so she was at something of a loose end in terms of her career.

Just imagine the situation. Fairport Convention are on stage. Sandy Denny, probably our most high profile member ever (though Swarb might contest that), is sitting in the wings, doing her knitting or whatever. It doesn't make sense.

Sandy didn't join Fairport Convention again in any simple sense. It began with her coming out as a surprise guest for the encores. Then we'd ask her out during the set. We'd also give her chance to do some solo stuff.

By this point, we were in Sydney, where the tracks with Sandy on *Fairport Live Convention* were recorded. John Wood was out there with us, and the Opera House had an eight-track studio which we were able to use, under the stage. He did a fantastic job of capturing those performances. At that point, Sandy hadn't decided whether she was going to join. It was on the cards, but I suppose she had to know it wasn't a retrograde step. She's formed Fotheringay who made a really great album, but the band didn't last. I think it packed up after a year. Then she made solo albums, each of which was terrific. She was asked to sing with Led Zeppelin. Yet somehow her career didn't take off in the way it should. Rejoining Fairport could have looked like admitting defeat. She loved singing with us: we loved playing behind her. Yet really she was a surprise guest at the Opera House gig, even though that isn't made clear anywhere on the album.

I took some photos on the steps of the Opera House and there is no doubt that Sandy is clearly one of the boys. Once a Fairport, always a Fairport, eh?

By the time we got to LA and a residency at the Troubadour, she was a full time Fairport again.

It changed the dynamics of the band. A lot of gigs during that year were recorded so you can hear how it developed both in terms of the songs in the setlist and how Sandy re-integrated into the band. We became more like her backing band. That's kind of inevitable when you're working with someone who sings and writes songs as well as she always did. It was natural that we started to play some of the songs that were associated with her time in the band – *Who Knows Where The Time Goes, She Moves Through The Fair* and so on – as well as quite a lot of songs from her solo albums. Naturally, to put so much stuff in, something had to go. Not everyone in the band was pleased with that. The *Come All Ye* box set, released around the time Peggy and I had this conversation demonstrates this. A gig at London's Fairfield Hall, right at the start of the tour, in December 1973 features most of *Nine*, a couple of songs from *Rosie*, some instrumentals and some one-offs that showed Trevor's influence: Sandy comes on for the encore – *Down In The Flood* and *Something You Got*. Both those songs featured on the *Live* album which also included *John The Gun* and the reappearance of *Matty Groves*, who no doubt had been given some time off for bad behaviour. By February at The Troubadour, the set is dominated by Sandy: aside from some Fairport oldies, they played *John The Gun, Crazy Lady Blues, It'll Take A Long Time, Solo* and *Like An Old Fashioned Waltz* from her solo recordings; with that, and Trevor bringing in Dylan and Fotheringay songs, Swarb, who had in effect become the band's lead vocalist prior to the recent changes, is left with *Hexamshire Lass* as his only featured vocal.

The *Live* album was rushed out, I think, Sandy rejoining Fairport was big news and Island Records were keen to have product which would capitalise on the publicity. Through no fault of our own, the band's finances were in a dangerous state. It was an expensive tour and that was compounded by errors like sending equipment halfway round the world as excess baggage rather then freight. The Troubadour recordings are much better, as people have finally been able to hear. Sandy had settled in to being part of the band. We were all more certain about the setlist. As I've already pointed out, at this stage I was Fairport's bass player and had no role in its managerial matters: however, I gather that despite the quality of those American recordings we simply couldn't afford, at the time, to pay for them so we could release them.

It's a shame because we've always been, crucially, a live band. This was our first live release. It documented one of our best line ups instrumentally as well as the return of someone that our fans have always regarded as being at the very heart of the band – Sandy. We were playing classic as well as current material. There could have been a much better album, much more representative, than the one that came out. Listening to all the stuff that's become available in recent years, it's easy to see that taking all the recordings from the Fairfield Halls to the Troubadour, a really stunning live double album could have been put together – Croydon to California, eh, there's a title to conjure with!

**What a wonderful way to live, travelling all over the world**

1974 and 1975 were hectic years for Fairport. We seemed hardly ever to be at home. We did gigs in the South of England in December 1973. As soon as the new year started we were off to Tokyo: then it was New Zealand, Melbourne and Sydney and a week at The Troubadour in LA. That took us through to sometime in February. Then at the end of March we toured Scandinavia, Straight after that we went back to America where we gigged from mid-April till over halfway through May. There was a UK tour after that which took care of June. We went back to America again in October, ending gigs right across the country by appearing at the legendary Winterland Ballroom in San Francisco. Four days after that we began a five week UK tour which ended up, almost surreally, where we began a year earlier to the day, at Fairfield Hall in Croydon.

On top of that there were radio sessions and the filming of the *Babbacombe Lee* TV special for the BBC. It was only a couple of years since that LP was out but it was a while since we played the songs – and of course half the band had never played them.

Out of that time on the road, Sandy created *Rising For The Moon*, in my opinion one of the best songs about what it's like being in a band on the road. Certainly it stands up beside the things Jackson Browne wrote for *Running On Empty*.

It really captures that feeling of not really knowing where you are – living your life upside down: working at night, either sleeping or travelling during the day – both if you're lucky. "Many ears to please" is a really good phrase, because Fairport has always had a close relationship with its fans. We recognise them, know them personally. When we go to play a particular town, there are people we expect to see. Once you're into the big touring, music industry machine, it starts to depersonalise everything – all the places start to look the same; bits between them are a blur; you don't really have time to spend with anyone except other people in the band. If two of them happen to be a married couple who are just going through a rough patch, the quarters can seem too close.

Rising for the Moon would be Fairport's next album: despite the band's heavy touring commitment, Island records were keen to have a studio release from the new line up with Sandy. Nine had been a great album, really well received by both fans and critics. Like most Fairport albums it hadn't sold in great quantities, but there was hope the next one might.

We took time out to rehearse in summer, July and August. Sandy had written a lot of new songs. Because most of us lived in the area, I did another deal with Cropredy Village Hall to use it as a rehearsal space. Again we spent out summer putting together an album in rural England. This time the material seemed less at home there.

In the hopes of making Fairport more commercially viable, Island were looking for an album with a smoother, more radio-friendly sound. In America, FM rock was the dominant market; AOR was the buzz acronym. Fairport have often displayed an ability to turn their hand to almost anything. That very year they turned up as a kind of redneck country backing group for wrestler turned singer Brian Maxine. Sure they could create that smooth sound.

It was an all-out effort by Island Records to break the band in America. Among people who knew us, we were very respected. Those people included some really top notch performers. We had fans who were a lot more successful than we were. Unlike every other British band that went over to the States, including a lot of the bands on the Island label with us, we couldn't seem to crack America. It was the next level if you like. Up to The Beatles, it was supposed to be impossible for British pop acts to be successful in the States; after what they were still calling The British Invasion, it was considered the natural thing to do. Cliff has never made it in The States, of course; neither have The Shadows, though every American guitarist knows and admires their stuff and can probably play *Apache*. So we were in good company, but that wasn't really any comfort.

This was the music business and businesses are supposed to make money. For a record company, that means selling records. You only need to look up Fairport Convention in one of those books that list all the top forty albums for it to be obvious we didn't do that. I checked. The Billboard list of Top Forty Albums skips from Donald Fagen to Percy Faith. Its UK equivalent lists five Fairport albums up to 1985: Angel Delight is the only one to make the Top Ten. Rising for the Moon is the last: it peaked at 52.

Chris Blackwell, who was a big Fairport fan, was the boss of Island Records. He put everything he could behind that album. Despite everything that had happened in the eight years that Fairport had existed he still believed in us – which is wonderful display of faith over reality. He even brought in Glyn Johns to produce it. Glyn was one of our heroes: he'd made classic recordings with the biggest acts in the world – The Stones, The Beatles, The Eagles, The Who, Clapton... and he was being engaged to produce us.

For the record, prior to working with Fairport on RFTM, Glyn had worked in a key production role (producing, engineering or mixing) on over eighty albums. They included many of the greatest LPs of all time – *Beggar's Banquet, Sticky Fingers, Desperado, Harvest, Who's Next, Mad Dogs and Englishmen, Quadrophenia, Pentangle, Led Zeppelin, Abbey Road, Stage Fright, On The Border, Let It Bleed* and *Exile on Main Street*.

He was, so far as rock goes, the man with the magic touch. We recorded at Olympic Studios in Barnes and found out he was a real taskmaster. He was clear in his own head what he wanted... and given his track record (no pun intended) who were we to argue? We'd made albums that we were really pleased with and our fans liked, He'd made albums that changed the face of music. Of course, with *Liege & Lief*, so had Fairport though we didn't know that at the time. He was sure what he wanted and also what he didn't want.

The old sound of Fairport was dispensed with. Sandy was clearly the lead singer, despite the fact that the previous studio album had featured Swarb and Trevor on vocals. There was to be, for the first time since Swarb had joined, no virtuoso instrumental track. Gone too were the traditional songs.

We played him the songs we wanted to do. He rejected some out of hand. We were left without enough songs for an album, he sent us away to write new ones... and come back with them next day. As a result, you end up with things like *Night Time Girl* which don't stand up alongside the other songs on the album but at least sound like they're coming from the same place. You're not suddenly confronted with a tale of a 19th century sea battle or a mediæval murder. What you do get are amazing songs like *One More Chance*: that's one of Sandy's greatest recordings and it was her second take. Glyn would not allow endless takes. His attitude was 'If you can't do it, don't do it. If you haven't done it after a couple of takes, you can't do it.' A harsh taskmaster, as I said, but he got results.

Fleetwood Mac, a band almost precisely contemporary with Fairport (FM were formed in April 1967, FC in May the same year), had abandoned their British Blues roots and developed a smooth, harmonised West Coast sound full of confessional songs about the personal dynamics and sexual politics within the band. A rock solid rhythm section, volatile virtuosos, dysfunctional duos, bruised egos – could be either band, right?

Sandy wrote most of the album. There's only one Swarb song and Sandy sings it. The other two songs Swarb had a hand in were co-written with me. They were pretty throwaway at the time and I find it hard to remember anything about them now. There was a lot on the album that never existed beyond the studio. We've never played them live before or since.

There were some great songs and it's those you remember.

The songs on *Rising For The Moon* were rehearsed in the summer of 1974, Many were 'played out' to audiences in Britain and America during the tours in the last three months of the year. The album swas recorded in December and February. Straight after that, the Fairports were off to Perth for the start of another Australian tour, on which they unveiled their new music to their steadily growing legion of fans down under.

Some journalist came up with the phrase Fotheringport Confusion which fans, particularly in Britain, picked up on. You could sense some antipathy in the audience when we strayed out of what they regarded as Fairport territory, like when Trevor did *Ned Kelly* or Sandy sang one of her solo songs. Because the songs for *Rising for the Moon* were something of a new direction for the Fairports, I don't think they were as well received as they should have been by audiences. There was a distrust, I suppose, which is not at all part of the relationship I think of when I consider Fairport and its fans.

It's wrong to make too much of the divide, but it is true that half the band were the Fairport survivors, what was left of the *Full House* line up, while the other half were newcomers from Fotheringay. As a couple, Trevor and Sandy were pretty volatile; as a bunch of people we were forced to be together far too much of the time. We lived in each other's pockets. You can hear that in some of the songs on the album. It got pretty rough at times. Dave Mattacks, who has always been a man who likes a quiet life – he's very civilised in everything he does – was the first to say he'd had enough. He handed in his resignation – I use the phrase deliberately because he didn't just quit. He formally gave us a date when he would no longer be available as a member of Fairport Convention. He worked his notice. This was at the end of 1974, halfway through recording the album, with a very busy tour schedule in the new year.

I was really upset when Dave left because he and I were a great rhythm section. That's not being big headed: it's an objective statement of fact. We always were, every time he was in Fairport or whenever we did sessions together. We still are, as I was reminded at Cropredy this year when we played together both in Fairport and in Richard Thompson's band. Both were an absolute joy.

We had to find another drummer, because Dave gave us a date when he was going. The album wouldn't be finished. There was a tour schedule. He had had enough and that was it. End of, as they say.

We auditioned about forty drummers. Gerry, who would have been an obvious choice, wasn't available and so wasn't one of them. Auditioning drummers can be pretty soul destroying. Auditioning forty becomes a kind of percussive hell. Add to that an increasing sense of urgency and you can tell we were getting desperate. As the other half of the rhythm section, I was pulling my hair out: this was when I still had hair and so that action was a luxury I could afford!

It was an absolute nightmare.

The next set of dates – a two-week tour with a couple of TV appearances in Scandinavia – were looming closer. In the end, Paul Warren, who had been Dave Mattacks' drum technician, asked if he could have a go. We all said "But you don't play the drums, do you?" He said, "Yeah. 'Course I do." We wanted to be gentle with him. After all, we thought he was just being kind, trying to help out. We asked what he'd like to play, by way of audition.

He said, "Just play the set. I've heard it often enough. I'll count you in."

He did and off we went. We played our current set right the way through. He knew it perfectly. He wasn't in the same league as DM, but all those months sitting at the side, watching as we gigged night after night, learning from someone he genuinely admired, had paid off. He knew it all and he knew how to do it all.

He wasn't a professional musician, of course. He got the job and off we went to Scandinavia with him on the drum stool.

One member of the band, naming no names but he was the shortest person in the group, decided to take exception and accused Paul of having wasted our time doing all those auditions when "You could have said you could do it in the first place, you little shit". I think that was the precise phraseology. You can tell the person who said it was a songwriter and had a way with words.

I think Paul would have been fine to continue with the band when we came back and recorded the rest of the album. All the songs were new to us so we'd all have had to learn them, which he was certainly up to doing.

Trevor thought otherwise. That meant Sandy agreed with him. Swarb continued to have a chip on his shoulder, which is very uncomfortable for a fiddle player.

It was Glyn Johns, though, who made the final decision. He explained he needed an experienced drummer in the studio: it was a different thing to sounding fine live: he had to have someone he could rely on. He told us that, if we wanted to carry on using Paul on gigs, that was our decision, but in the studio he needed an experienced, professional drummer. It reminded me of when The Beatles took Pete Best down to Abbey Road and George Martin had a quiet word along the same lines with Brian Epstein. A couple of days later, Pete was called into the office and given his marching orders. Enter Ringo and even he wasn't deemed good enough to play on *Love Me Do*!

Glyn knew Bruce Rowland and called him in to drum on the sessions. He'd worked with Bruce when he'd been in Joe Cocker's band. I think he was working with Ronnie Lane in Slim Chance at the time.

Actually it worked out really well for us, because Bruce fitted in perfectly and was available because Ronnie had had to call it a day with his band. So, like Swarb, Trevor and Jerry before him and Ric a decade later, Bruce joined us in the studio as a session player and left as a fully-fledged Fairport.

He was a fantastic drummer with a totally different style and approach to DM. Sometimes he gets a bit forgotten when people talk about Fairport but he brought a lot to the band. When we did *Tipplers Tales* and *Bonny Bunch of Roses*, the two very folky albums we did for Vertigo, he had a big input, particularly in the way we tackled the songs, not the arrangements but the whole approach. If you look at the songs on both those albums, they had a long life in Fairport in terms of the number of years the band continued to play them. Things like *Eynsham Poachers, Reynard The Fox, Widow of Westmoreland... Ye Mariners All* and the instrumental medley is something we've revived in the last few years after letting it have a rest: it's a great opening number. It's on *50:50@50*.

He stayed with us right into the early eighties when, for personal reasons, he decided to retire from music. He still dusted off his drumsticks to come back and play at Cropredy from time to time though and would occasionally play with mates like Steve Ashley, who wrote a wonderful song in tribute to him after he died a couple of years ago.

So Bruce was brought in and became part of the band very quickly and surprisingly easily, given some of the tensions that had built up. He had an ability to rise above all the personal politics which was something else I admired about him.

*Rising for the Moon* has been compared to *Rumours* by Fleetwood Mac, the recording of which began almost exactly a year after Fairport finished recording their album. Both albums are the second releases by a new line up of a British band formed in the spring of 1967. Both saw the band aiming at the lucrative FM market. Both featured bands whose British roots were entangled with influences from other countries. Both obliquely documented internal conflicts within the groups. Both contained songs that were thinly veiled attacks on other band members. *Rumours* of course became one of the biggest selling albums of all time: overall sales in the States meant that every home should have two copies at least. Fairport's new direction served them less well.

It was supposed to bring us a bigger audience. I think it did the opposite. Fans of the old Fairport found it too smooth, not folky enough, lacking rough edges. New fans we might attract already had a sense of what to expect from Fairport and no way of knowing we were offering something totally different. *Rising for the Moon* didn't get endless airplay or have a string of chart hits supporting it,

### You know you are the master of your art

It's still a very good album, beautifully produced with some great playing. That doesn't alter the fact that it's the most un-Fairport Fairport album. Even at Cropredy, there's very few of the songs on it we've gone back to. Apart from the title track, of course... We recorded a new version of *Rising for the Moon* on the *Festival Bell* CD. I think we'd already been doing it for a year or so. Even though it came from that period when we sounded so different, as a song it suited the current line up perfectly. The words, of course, still apply.

We finished the album and then went off to America for a long tour. Everyone imagines all those documentaries about bands on tour in the seventies whenever you mention things like that – you know, the personalised aeroplanes, every band member having their own limo, ELP having three huge trucks with an initial on each. Fairport were never big enough for that. Touring for us meant driving around in a hired station wagon, really long journeys sometimes. If we flew, because sometimes the distances were so great you had to, it was always economy. We never stayed in posh hotels. We'd find somewhere cheap, sometimes a basic motel because you don't have any extras that you pay for but never use. Because Fairport Convention was a name a lot of people had heard of, people assumed we lived the rock-star lifestyle but, until I joined Tull, I never did... unless I had some more successful mates playing in town.

Of course, all that travelling time, and the fact you have to make allowances for delays or needing a rest after a long and sometimes uncomfortable journey, meant there was a lot of the touring time when you weren't making money. We only earned when we played a gig. Sandy was really good about all that. She was one of the boys and didn't expect any special allowances or whatever. It was often hard on her. She'd received so many accolades and was so well respected but never got the rewards people expected to go with that.

When we arrived in America, we flew straight to Los Angeles. We had two weeks with no gigs when we were expected to do work to promote *Rising for the Moon*. Not a lot had been organised so we more or less had a fortnight to kill. As a result most people spent the time getting drunk or stoned. There were billboards up advertising the band. There was a lot of the usual hype that American record companies are so good at. The trouble was it was all front with no real substance. There was even a huge three dimensionsal billboard on Sunset Strip advertising the album. We did loads of radio spots, often with people who'd never really heard of us and hadn't listened to the album, so they didn't talk about the change of direction and so on. Just another band from the UK, if I may misquote Mr Zappa.

We wanted to be able to say "Look, we've made an album: we think it's great: it's not what you might expect from us: give it a listen: give it a spin on the radio if you can: mention we're on tour." When we started doing our own publicity, through Woodworm, in the eighties, that's exactly the approach I took, And it worked. It was hard work, but it did what we needed it to.

When eventually we started the tour, the dates weren't that well received and we didn't get great audiences. The tour hadn't been well publicised. We toured with Renaissance for a week or so in Ohio, sharing the billing, though most places advertised it as Fairport Convention with Sandy Denny and Renaissance, which was pretty confusing. A lovely bunch of people that I got on well with.

**Then one fine morning…**

The tour – though it was more of an Odyssey, if I'm honest – eventually got to New York. We were booked into some downtown Holiday Inn. We had a night off to begin with. I went out to buy a Village Voice because it had the best gig guide for the sort of things we'd enjoy. I wanted to find out if there was anything on that night off that we might like to go to. I opened it up and there was a full page advert for Renaissance with a full symphony orchestra; the promoter of the gig would be playing the piano and conducting. Right at the bottom of this ad, in tiny writing, were the words "and Fairport Convention". This was at The Beacon Theatre, a famous venue, somewhere we were looking forward to playing. I just hoped no one else in the band had seen it, because I could imagine their reactions. Sandy would be upset; Trevor would be demanding blood; Swarb would go off on one and turn the air blue. Jerry and Bruce, being more chilled, might handle it better: "At least we got a mention" or something like that.

Then I realised that if they'd taken out such a big ad in The Voice, there were probably posters of a similar design all over the place.

I rang up David Denny, Sandy's brother, who was our tour manager and told him to get The Village Voice and take a look at whatever page it was on. He was as shocked as I had been. Obviously no one had told him about it either. Much as we liked Renaissance, we couldn't help feeling our gig had been hijacked.

It was getting on for six o'clock. The sun was over the yard arm. I went down to the bar. There would a couple of the guys from Renaissance, along with some of their road crew. They were dressed up and clearly about to leave. They were a little sheepish about it, but explained they had to go to the theatre for a soundcheck and a run through with the orchestra. So far as they knew, this was the first time I'd heard anything about an orchestra. They explained how the promoter had set it all up. They'd be rehearsing all evening and all day tomorrow. "You know, because of the orchestra."

"Yeah, I get it. You've got an orchestra. What time will our soundcheck be. You know, Fairport Convention. Your 'support act'."

"I'm not sure you'll get one. There's a lot for us to do. But I suppose around 4.30 tomorrow, because we'll need a break and time to eat and get changed."

Oh, I really felt for them.

It was left to me, muggins as usual, to explain all this to the band. There were at the time, certain people in Fairport who had never heard the expression, 'don't shoot the messenger'. None of this was my fault but guess who ended up getting all the flack?

Still, pouring oil on troubled Swarbricks, I managed to calm the situation down. Next day we all gathered to get our cab to the Beacon Theatre. "Bet fuckin' Renai-fucking-sance got a limo sent for them," observed the small voice of one who shall be nameless.

The Beacon was around ten blocks away. We were there as requested at 4.30. We hung around for an hour or so, while the orchestra did various things. It was like having the start of *Sgt. Pepper* on a repeating loop in the background. Then someone started tuning the grand piano. That's never easy on the ear, and we were waiting to tune our instruments: Trevor had eight Ovation guitars that he needed to sort out, for a start. As for getting anywhere near the stage... forget it.

Everyone was getting very restive, including Sandy. I knew those moments well – everyone iritated, frustrated, anxious. You know the moment's going to come when someone says "Fuck it, let's have a drink." That way disaster lies.

Fate intervened and as six o'clock drew close we were told we could get on stage, set up and do our soundcheck. You can imagine the sigh of relief. Then came the second part of the message – "You've got half an hour." And Trevor still had eight Ovation guitars that needed to be in tune.

We were due on at eight. Doors probably opened at 7.15. Before that they'd need to sort out the auditorium: we'd be doing our soundcheck with an army of cleaners hovering to do the final spit and polish. We had, literally, half an hour.

On top of this, we'd expected our soundcheck would have been finished long before six. We were all still in jeans and our everyday shirts. Sandy had left her stage dress hanging in the wardrobe in her room so it didn't get creased. None of us had showered. We hadn't eaten since lunchtime.

We'd need to dash back to The Holiday Inn as soon as we could. We'd have liked longer to soundcheck but not at this stage in the proceedings. We did what we could and then stepped out into the chill November air of New York. It was rush hour. Mayhem. And misnamed – rather than rushing the roads were at a standstill. There wasn't a taxi to be had for love or money. The pavements were absolutely packed with people heading home or heading out for the evening or going for a meal: they were certainly heading somewhere with a strong sense of purpose and when a New Yorker does that you do not get in the way.

Sandy's on the brink of tears, but also getting angry. Trevor's being very projective. Swarb looks like he'll blow a gasket and walk out on the whole thing. Jerry, a chilled native New Yorker, was taking it all in his very cool stride, which at that point in time didn't exactly help.

The only thing to do was leg it. We ran the ten blocks as fast as we could. At the hotel we had about ten minutes to shower, change and whatever else we needed to do before dashing back to the theatre – which we knew we'd probably have to do on foot. Given the state of the traffic, that was probably quicker, even if we could have flagged down a cab.

Sandy's decided to bring her dress and change at the theatre. We get back at 7.15. We know there's still instruments to tune and whatever. Then the security guy blocked our way at the stage door. New York is not like London, where the stage door will have some nice doorman sitting in a little office checking everyone in and out. This was a huge black guy who looked like it was his night off from being a linebacker for the Jets or the Giants. He was big and made a very effective human door.

He tells us we can't get in because we haven't got the right passes. The normal tour pass won't do on this occasion. Because of all the attention Renaissance have been getting, nobody's thought to issue us with the passes for The Beacon, We tell him we're the support band (much as those words stick in our respective throats); we say we're on in three quarters of an hour; Trevor is about to explain with Australian clarity just how long it takes to tune eight Ovation guitars. We even say "Listen to us – we're obviously English. Look at us – we're obviously a band." Sandy waves her dress in his face to emphasise the point. He's still having none of it.

That's when Sandy lost it. A stream of abuse that he probably never expected to her from a small English lady hurled in his direction. Her language was colourful and graphic. She started to hit him with her handbag. This was about a year after *The Exorcist* came out and Sandy certainly gave a good impression of being able to take the lead in some future stage version.

He backs down and lets her through. Just her. She tells us to hang on and she'll go get the passes. I pity the guy who should have given them to us, when she tracked him down. We stood outside, in a terrible state. Everything had conspired to wind us up. The clock was ticking. We could see people going into the theatre. Never mind a day off before the gig, I needed one right then.

At this point, the promoter, who was been watching the 3,000 plus audience go in to fill the theatre, walks past us – with his pass of course. I swear you could see the $ signs in his eyes!

He turns to tell us we're on in 35 minutes. "We know."

"You should be in there getting set now." "We know."

"By the way, Renaissance's set is precisely timed and the orchestra have to set up. You've got sixty minutes flat from when you should go on. 8 till 9, That includes your encore, if you get one. If you overrun by so much as a minute, I'll pull the plug on you."

In Richard's words, the big guys were all spoiling for a fight. It was a powder keg situation and this guy was lighting matches by the fuse.

Sandy arrived with our passes. We pushed our way in, got our selves ready. Sandy was in a totally vile mood, understandably. We walked on stage to a huge roar. Fairport had a lot of fans in New York which we'd been visiting regularly for the past five years. It felt like they'd all turned up that night. As I plugged in my bass, I remember thinking "Up yours, Renaissance". In a nice way, of course.

Then Sandy started to sing. She was superb. All that rage, energy, frustration was channelled into her vocals. The only way I can described it is English soul music. *One More Chance, Stranger to Himself, John the Gun*... she meant every word, searing performances hitting every nuance. There are lots of live recordings of the *Rising for the Moon* line up, but that was one night which wasn't recorded. It didn't need to be. I can still hear it in my head, the night we came through adversity and Sandy gave some of the most powerful performances of her life.

We did our sixty minutes. The encore was a blazing version of *Matty Groves* which Sandy turned into the audio equivalent of a Tarantino movie. One great thing about *Matty*, as we know from the way we do it at Cropredy, is that the instrumental at the end can expand or contract to suit the time available. We played and hit the final note at sixty minutes on the dot. Chuck Berry would have been proud of us.

We came off, buzzing from a great gig, despite all that had gone before. Playing on stage is one of the most therapeutic activities I know of.

The crowd was going mad, shouting "More", clapping, stamping their feet. We could still hear them in the dressing room, where there was a knock on the door and a very sheepish promoter came in and said, "You'll have to go back and do another or they're going to rip the place apart."

It was tempting to take him at his word. "You said sixty minutes and you'd pull the plug. We retain the right to the same privilege." We went back on, did *That'll Be The Day*, and left Renaissance and their orchestra to deal with the aftermath.

It was that kind of tour. When we were on stage it was great. Otherwise it was pretty awful. Rifts were starting to appear within the band. I found myself having to act as a combination of peace negotiator and ombudsman a lot of the time. Jerry was growing increasingly sick of the frustrations and backbiting.

We came back to Britain and we hadn't made any money from the tour. It had been expensive, because it was a big band, six of us plus crew. There was a lot of travelling. Lots of hotels to pay for. The album, despite all the hype and promotion, didn't sell at all, so there was no expected income. It felt like we'd put our hearts and souls into it, thrown away a lot of what had made Fairport what it was in the process, and we had literally nothing to show for it. We arrived home and almost straight away we played a short series of gigs promoted by Jo Lustig who was our manager at the time. That ran through October: big cities, university towns.

The tour began in Cardiff and included Birmingham, Bradford, Brunel University, Coventry, Lancaster, Leeds, Leicester Liverpool, , Manchester, Newcastle, Norwich, Nottingham, Oxford, Portsmoth, Sheffield, and York plus Scottish dates in Aberdeen, Edinburgh and Glasgow. London dates were at The Fairfield Hall and The Theatre Royal. Fairport were in fine form, but, like the hecklers on Dylan's 1966 tour, there were those who came intent on being dissatisfied. There were cries of "We want Fairport not Fotheringay", "Sing a folk sing" and "It's not a Sandy Denny gig". Knowing how few of those were left for us to enjoy, whoever shouted it at the Bradford gig must now truly regret that last one. Possibly to save on expense or cut down travelling time, gigs were scheduled unusually close together: I saw the gig in Bradford on October 9: the previous night I could have seen them in Leeds, barely nine miles away; next night, they were forty miles away in Sheffield.

It was a huge contrast from the vast distances we had to travel between gigs in the States. Of course we didn't fly anywhere in the UK. The distances may be short, but in the mid-seventies Britain's road system was still quite basic and a lot of roads were in a bad state of repair (some things don't change, do they?). We still spent a lot of time in the van which can be pretty claustrophobic with a driver, six musicians and some pretty large and fragile egos. We seemed to have been living in each other's pockets for two years solid. A lot of things had gone wrong. We were all exhausted, fractious, argumentative, nit-picky. Nits were regularly being picked.

Jerry cracked first. At the end of the tour, he said "That's it, I'm off home" and flew back to America.

That was all the prompting Sandy needed. She wasn't happy and, in any case, Island had released *Like An Old Fashioned Waltz* and so she wanted to focus on her solo career. She decided it was time for her to go.

She and Trevor were an item so he went with her.

So once more it was down to Swarb and me, this time with Bruce Rowland.

We had a real sense it had been a last chance. Island were never going to get behind us to that extent again. No other label would have done it in the first place. Island dropped us after the next album. Vertigo didn't stick with us even for the albums they contracted for. It felt like the end was in sight.

But that reckons without the radical shake up that punk was about to give the music industry, the radical rethink that Peggy would have about release and management of a band's output, the radical concept of a record and management company literally as a cottage industry. Today no one looks askance at someone who runs a significant business from home; it's a standard way of working. At the start of the eighties, Dave and Christine Pegg would create the business model for that approach. The answer lay in the Woodworm and the wires.

## Songs in a mynah key – part II

We didn't finish the story of Dorothy's mynah bird, did we?

It's 1982, a decade after the rehearsals for Nine. Plans are underway to have a significant reunion at Cropredy (the fourth of Fairport's Festivals) by reassembling for one night only, the *Nine* line up.

It all came together and August 14th, Trevor, Jerry, Swarb, Peggy and DM, augmented by Bruce, Simon, Linda Thompson and Judy Dyble, included songs from both *Rosie* and *Nine* in the set – *Bring 'em Down*, *Hexamshire Lass*, *Iron Lion*, *The Plainsman*, *Polly on the Shore*, *Rosie*, *Tokyo* plus *The Ballad of Ned Kelly*, *Forever Young*, *Here Come the Cowboys*, *The Claw* and, at Peggy's specific request, *Marijuana Australiana*. The line up even created its most notable session work by bringing on wrestler Brian Maxine to sing *Six Days On The Road*, probably the most shambolic performance in a Fairport set ever. We also got an appearance from Dan Ar Braz, Swarb and Simon bringing their folk club duo to a big stage and two of the earliest Fairport songs revived to date (*I'll Keep It With Mine* and *Mr Lacey*).

Up to that point the annual Cropredy Reunion had sought out a new venue each year. The previous year it hadn't even been in Cropredy. The time had come to bring it all back Home. Peggy, who by the now had moved out of the village to Barford St Michael, found himself back at Dorothy's house beside the Village Hall, to negotiate with the new owner of Home Farm... setting up the deal which would allow the festival to move to its new and ultimately permanent home.

She made me very welcome... you know, "Come in, Peggy, sit down, have a cup of tea. Do you want a biscuit?" Not very rock'n'roll, which was fine by me.

She left me with Clifford Lambert, who had recently bought the land where we wanted to hold the next festival. While she was making the tea, I noticed the cage in the corner of the room and so remarked, "Oh, you still have the mynah bird!"

"Yes, Peggy, and he still knows how to whistle."

As I raised the cup to my lips, she raised the cover on the cage and out came that familiar string of whistled notes followed by something I had never heard back in the seventies, just two words.

My tea went everywhere. I could see from the smile on Dorothy's face that she had timed the moment deliberately and perfectly. She'd obviously got used to it and had long since forgiven me and Fairport for her potty-mouthed pet.

Only then did I realise that our bored roadies had been teaching it to whistle two notes at a time, each day.

Their final shot, which I obviously never got to hear, must have been on the day after we finished as they derigged to take the gear over to the recording studio... that's when they added the concluding vulgar instruction.

It took ten years for their little joke
to have its final pay off...
which is a long wait for a punch line!

# CHAPTER 9
# Dingo days down under
## *Australian adventures*

If we're going to talk about Australia – and we should because the land down under and its Fairport fans have been very important in terms of the band's survival – then we must talk about Trevor Lucas first and foremost. Trevor was already established on the British folk scene when he joined Fairport. He'd made albums with Bert Lloyd. He'd released solo albums. He'd been in Eclection with Gerry and then Fotheringay with Sandy. He was also building up a reputation as a producer.

It's the end 1972. Fairport had been around for five years and I'd been a member for the best part of three of them. Fairport was known from its earliest days as a very English band, even when they did cover versions of American songs. Inventing the British version of folk-rock consolidated that. So far as most people were concerned our band members had always been British. David Rea, an American, was in the band such a short time: nothing with him was released, he never gigged with us. Blink and you missed him.

The *History of Fairport* double album came out. There were no surprising rarities, or unreleased tracks, apart from the final track, a taster of the album we were currently working on: *Hen's March and Four Poster Bed.* The family tree by Pete Frame that was on the cover told you who was on the track – Swarb, myself and DM plus Jerry Donahue and Trevor Lucas. Everybody who was a Fairport fan knew who they were because they'd been in Fotheringay and were on *Rock On* by The Bunch. As the family tree told you, that was Fairport 7.

Now Fairport, the Great British Band, was international: we had both an American and an Australian in the band.

The album sleeve listed only those Fairport line ups which had recorded and appeared on record. Strictly speaking this was the twelfth line-up of Fairport in five and half years.

Trevor established a strong reputation on the folk scene during the sixties: his first album was released in Australia in 1963. A move to England a couple of years later saw him working with Swarb on Bert Lloyd's album *Leviathan!* And the soundtrack to the film *Far From The Madding Crowd* (the version where Terry met Julie). He then moved into pioneering folk-rock band Eclection whose line up included Gerry Conway, not to mention future members of Sailor and jazz guitar legend Gary Boyle. Sandy and Trevor became an item, as we used to say. Eclection and Fairport found their paths regularly crossed, including notably the night in Birmingham when Fairport's van left the road on their way home; the fact Sandy chose to travel back with Trevor meant she was not involved in the crash.

Most recently he had joined Sandy in forming Fotheringay, alongside Gerry and Jerry Donahue. In 1971, he recorded *The Great Australian Legend* with A L Lloyd and Martyn

Wyndham-Read; backing musicians included Swarb and Dave Pegg. The following year, he produced *Rock On*, a collection of rock'n'roll classics featuring Sandy, Richard & Linda Thompson, DM, Gerry (years later Fairport would revive the version of *Let There Be Drums* that he created for this set) and Ashley Hutchings. *Rock On* was the second album recorded at Virgin's new Oxfordshire facility The Manor, to which a small number of artists had been granted access to help bed in the equipment: these include The Bonzos, Dave Cousins, Mike Oldfield and Fairport, together with various offshoots of the band. *Rosie* was begun there but effectively remade at Sound Techniques with Trevor producing.

Swarb knew Trevor and, after the failed attempt to record what became the *Rosie* LP at The Manor, suggested we recruit him to produce a second attempt at recording the album. Trevor became part of the band more or less by default and I am sure it was him that suggested bringing in Jerry Donahue on guitar. DM agreed to stay with the band. As a result of that, we ended up with what I still think is one of the very best Fairport line-ups – the one that made the *Nine* album.

I don't think Trevor actually pushed for Fairport to go and perform in Australia, but it was a natural thing to go to his home turf (a silly way to think of it because you forget how huge Australia is).

### So how are you spelling Aussie?

The way Fairport first played in Australia is a bit more complicated. Sandy Denny, who wasn't in Fairport at this point, was booked to play the first ever New Zealand rock music Festival. That was The Great Ngaruawahia Music Festival, which took place in early January, 1973 – their midsummer of course. It was the first ever open-air festival in New Zealand. Black Sabbath were the headline act.

Trevor was in Melbourne with Sandy, visiting his parents over Christmas, before going on to the festival. He knew the promoter and mentioned that it would be great to get the rest of Fairport to come over and play. The obvious problem was the cost, paying four more air return air fares. There was no way to spread the cost, either, as it would a trip just for the one gig. Anyhow, he said he could offer five hundred quid, plus the cost of the flights, if the other four of us were prepared to come and play the festival.

None of us had ever been there. Trevor was there. Sandy was already booked to perform. We thought it would be great. So off we went, departing January 4th, when we found ourselves on the same plane as Ozzie Osborne.

I knew him from the days when we were both playing local gigs in Birmingham, though Sabbath had become a huge band in the meantime.

Formed in 1968, Sabbath had gone through name changes with a regularity comparable to Fairport's early line-up changes. Around Birmingham, Ozzy, Geezer, Bill and Tony billed as The Tony Iommi Band, Earth and The Polka Tulk Blues Band. In 1969, as Peggy was forming his own short lived heavy metal trio The Beast, they finally settled on the Karloffian Black Sabbath. Despite negative critical response, in 1970 (Peggy's first year as Fairport's bass player as he too left the Birmingham music scene behind him) their debut album was a major success with fans of heavy metal and reached the LP chart top ten; later that year, *Paranoid* topped the album chart and the title track went to number 4 in the singles charts. As Peggy and Fairport were consolidating the foundations of folk-rock, Ozzie and co were laying the cornerstones of heavy metal. By the time they boarded the same plane bound for New Zealand as the Fairport four, Black Sabbath were a big deal indeed.

I'm sure Ozzie still remembers that flight. I know all of Fairport did. I suspect many of the passengers and crew on that flight do too. We flew out from Heathrow, an early morning flight. It was misty, and damp, and generally a horrible morning... more like the middle of the night, to be honest, when we set off. An awful English winter day. All we knew was that we were heading for Australia (you know how in Britain we think of Australia and New Zealand as the same thing even though they're a couple of thousand miles apart and very different as countries) where it was SUMMER (we thought of the word in capitals!). We knew the flight lasted thirty-nine and a half hours, but then it was the other end of the world. Trevor was the only person in the band who'd ever travelled that kind of distance.

We were told it was a direct flight to Hong Kong and from there another flight to Sydney. The problem with that is that we didn't know that 'direct' in the airline business means without changing planes not without stopping. We had about a dozen (Jerry Donahue reckons it was six! – Ed) stops en route, where we had to sit in the plane, with everything turned off while some people got off and more people got on. It was tedious and very uncomfortable. There was no aircon, reduced lighting, you couldn't get a drink or go to the loo. It was a nightmare... an absolute nightmare.

I'm getting ahead of myself. Back to Heathrow. There was Swarbrick, Dave Mattacks, Jerry and myself, sitting in economy, not aware of what was ahead of us. This was back in the days when you could smoke on a plane, which was great for Swarbrick who used to smoke perpetually. All the drinks were free in those days too. It was a TWA flight. The stewardesses were very pretty young American girls. Jerry Donahue, who's American of course and much cooler than the rest of us, decided he'd chat up "one of the hostesses". I was sitting next to him and as the flight progressed he got more and more friendly with one of them, a very pretty lady called Pat.

The first stop was Frankfurt. That didn't take long and soon we were airborne again. I can't remember where the next stop was – I think at the time I may have lost interest. I just recall that it hadn't seemed very long from taking off to setting down again: I knew Frankfurt wasn't that far away from London – we'd been there overland in the past; so at this rate I could see our journey to Hong Kong taking forever. It was more like being on a bus or a local train than transglobal travel!

Meantime, Jerry was getting more and more friendly with Pat. By this point, he'd already told her we were a band, he was the lead guitarist and we were on our way to play a festival in New Zealand. I think he also told her it was our first time going to New Zealand. Then she said, "Gee, that's a coincidence. There's another group on the plane. They're through in First Class." Fellow musicians aboard: that was enough to grab my attention. Then I overheard her say they were Black Sabbath.

I told her I knew them. They were from Birmingham, and so was I. I asked if there was any chance that I could go through and say hello. She explained there were strict rules: passengers from economy were not allowed into first class. However, she kindly offered to go tell them we were here and ask if any of them would like to come back and see us. Basically, she was going to go ask Black Sabbath if they fancied slumming it among the hoi poloi.

I told her to ask for Ozzie, tell him Peggy was down the back and ask if he'd like to come and have a drink with us. About half an hour later, Ozzie turns up. You couldn't miss him... long hair, arms waving, distinctive Brummie accent: "Hey-ah, Peg-gy, you awright moit? Howya doin', loik?"

We shuffle around and he gets the seat next to me. We start drinking and rabbiting about the old days. Of course, even back then, Ozzie was quite famous and very loud, and people were beginning to notice his presence. The plane stops again....somewhere; who knows where: we're still rabbiting away ("you remember when..? Whatever happened to..? Was it you that..?" and so on); one lot of people get off; some more get on; we take off again and start to wonder when they serve the next lot of drinks. That's when they decide to bring the food round.

We'd already had a skinful because we'd been drinking non-stop for quite a while.

The stewardess tells Ozzie he has "a first class meal", which we find funny because it sounds like a compliment. She asks whether he'd like to transfer back to the front of the plane to eat. In thick Brummy accent so slurred by drink that he probably needed subtitles he says, "nah thiziz mimate Peggy. Oi'll ave worrevver heeze avin."

Our food arrives. You remember those aeroplane meals? Little plastic tray with everything on it, all in individual containers with foil lids you peel off. Probably not what Ozzie would have got in First Class, of course. The waitress / stewardess / hostess / whatever hands us the trays and we pass them along. I take one for Ozzie and put in front of him. He takes one look and "parks the tiger". He vomits. There's a panic, because no one wants to get it on them. We've still got a long flight ahead of us. Jerry in particular was very into white Levis at the time – look at any photo of him from that era – that and a black leather waistcoat – very smooth: so he moves quicker than anybody. Amazingly we all seem to have avoided contamination. We check out Ozzie and discover he has literally passed out: the booze has got the better of him and he's gone.

The stewardesses are there, helping to clean up the mess and apologising to other passengers. It's times like that when you realise that their job is not as glamorous as it's made out to be! I'm standing in the aisle because my seat was right next to Ozzie's and he has rendered it temporarily out of service. That's when I spotted Pat, the stewardess: I apologise to her (not that it was my fault exactly) and suggest the best thing is to leave Ozzie where he is and let him sleep it off. He's been cleaned up now so far as is possible. So Pat goes off and gets a blanket and covers him up. Since I can't really use my seat in economy, next to Ozzie, and as he's clearly in no fit state to go back to his seat in First, I ask whether there'd be any chance of my using his seat for a while. Pat's very understanding and says she can't see that being a problem.

So I make way forward, through the curtain that divides Us from Them, and there's the rest of Black Sabbath, with a conspicuously empty seat. Tony says hello and asks what's going on and where Ozzie is. I relate the story and am welcomed into his seat... which is where I stay until Hong Kong, as Ozzie never reappears. Free champagne, cigars, really good food. I had a great trip. Swarb, Jerry and DM remained in economy with Ozzie. I joined them when we changed planes in Hong Kong.

Eventually after thirty-nine hours or whatever we got to Sydney. We'd arranged to stay there in a hotel and get some sleep before flying on to the festival, which was, on this occasion, the only gig we had. Dave Mattacks and I were sharing a room, so we decided to find out what was on that night to see if there was anywhere to go.

*The Adventures of Barry McKenzie* was on at the cinema: it was the first week of release.

**Based on a comic strip, the Barry McKenzie film was the saga of an archetypal uncouth Aussie**

bloke, all beer and barbies and chundering in the old Pacific sea. Barry McKenzie (played in the film by Barry Crocker) was the invention of Barry Humphries, who appeared in several cameo roles in the film including a psychiatrist, a hippie and Aunt Edna Everage.

We were both big fans of the Private Eye series and we knew we had to go. We only had one night in Sydney and what better place could there be to see that film? No one else in the band wanted to go, but myself and DM get a taxi to the movie theatre where it's playing. We take our seats and notice the cinema is almost full. Naturally, we assume Barry McKenzie is as much a cult figure here as he is at home. The film starts and DM and I are literally the only people in the entire cinema who are laughing. And we really laughed.

I immediately got a sense that everyone else was offended, because of course it takes the piss out of Australia and Australian men. So I whisper to DM, "Try not to laugh: I know it's hilarious but try not to laugh". Of course, that only makes it worse because now we're not only wanting to laugh at the film but also at each other trying really hard not to laugh and making strangulated noises.

We managed to avoid any Pommie bashing at the end of the evening. Those people who weren't studiously avoiding looking at us clearly had an expression that showed they regarded us as mentally deficient in some way.

When we got back to the hotel we told the rest of the band about the whole experience. They were all Barry McKenzie fans, including Trevor despite (or maybe because of) being Australian himself. Alcohol had been taken at this stage inevitably. So we decided to recreate a classic Barry moment by walking across Sydney Harbour Bridge and chundering into the sea below. We were lucky we didn't get arrested for defiling a national monument or something.

The next day we caught the flight to New Zealand for the festival. We travelled to Ngaruawahia, played the Festival, stayed an extra day and then caught the flight all the way back. A long way for one gig, but that was the very start of a long relationship between Fairport and 'down under'. We went down well, but when you're playing the first ever festival to people who at the time were relatively starved of music, you'd have to be pretty dire not to... and at the time with that line-up Fairport was at one of its genuine peaks.

We met up with Sabbath again and when we were leaving, Ozzie, bless him, came to see us off. Sabbath were staying on to play some more gigs, which is the sensible thing to do after you'd travelled half way round the world. He was literally in tears, trying to persuade us to stay. He even presented Phil Sterling-Wall, our manager at the time, with an expensive watch that he'd bought for him.

### Definitely top banana

So that was our first time in Australia, even though all we did was go see a film that nobody else was enjoying. Because of that trip, we made some important contacts. Festival Records did a deal to release our albums over there. Some big Australian promoters approached us to arrange a proper tour. The fact Trevor was in the band helped to establish a bond between Fairport and Australia.

In my early days with Fairport we used to go to Australia a lot and spend a few weeks touring. In fact, we were the second English band to play Sydney Opera House – the first were the Spencer Davis Group. They were my mates from way back, of course.

Fairport played on the main stage, usually the preserve of serious classical musicians.

We ended up going there every year or every couple of years until Fairport broke up in 1979: then when we started playing live again after 1985, we were lucky to be asked back and we became aware of how loyal and supportive our fans were there.

Six weeks after the release of the *Rosie* album, they returned to Australia, one leg of a world tour. Confusingly, posters featured a drawing of Sandy who had not been a member of Fairport for over three years. She didn't even accompany them on this tour, though they had worked with her a couple of weeks earlier in LA where she was recording the *Old Fashioned Waltz* album.

That was with what's usually referred to as the Fairport Nine line up: we did a tour of Australia and when we were in Melbourne we ended up staying at the Old Court Hotel. It was quite luxi-plush, a bit out of town, beside a golf course.

We'd just got to reception – this would be about 1 o'clock in the afternoon – with our bags and guitars which we'd brought with us from the airport, having just got off the flight from wherever we'd played the night before.

May 19, 1973. They'd arrived in Australia three days earlier – flying from LA – and had already played Perth and Adelaide They played at Dallas Brooks Hall. Despite official ads claiming that Sandy Denny would be appearing, she was travelling with the band, not part of it at this stage.

One thing you couldn't miss was a silver-framed photo stand with a picture of Warren Mitchell as 'celebrity guest of the week'. We were checking in, getting our rooms sorted and so on, when Warren walks into the lobby. He looked a million dollars, wearing a blue tracksuit and carrying a tennis racket. He was healthy and tanned, unlike us who had recently flown out from an English winter. He walked up to the desk to collect his key.

Warren Mitchell was a respected actor whose entire career was overshadowed by his iconic creation, right-wing, racist, East-End bigot Alf Garnet in Johnny Speight's brilliant *Till Death Do Us Part*. Hugely controversial and extremely popular (if misunderstood and misinterpreted by many), the series was responsible for adding new terms to the dictionary, challenging the blinkered approach of a UK that was far from Swinging and inspiring one of the Monkees' greatest songs. Worth noting in passing that the butt of most of the awful Alf's domestic rants was played by the father of the wife of future New Labour PM, Tony Blair.

This was the first of several interesting encounters that Peggy had with Warren Mitchell.

He took a quick look at us and said "Ah, pop group."

At which point, Sandy, who was never backward at coming forward, shouted "Warren, it's you."

"Oh, Pommy pop group", he observed.

So, Swarbrick steps in with the hard sell "Yeah, we're Fairport Convention. We're playing at Dallas Brooks Hall tonight. It's my birthday tonight, you've got to come along. Come to the show" (Swarb's birthday was actually April 5).

Warren was obviously a big deal, he'd been starring in a production locally and was enjoying the exclusivity of the hotel. It was obvious the last thing he wanted was to be highjacked to some scruffy rock musician's birthday bash... and he obviously didn't know us from Adam. Warren was tactful, though, and said "I'll have to ask my little lady about that." I told him there were two shows and I'd put his name on the guest list for both with a 'plus 1'. He left us saying, "Great. Nice to meet you. Good luck for the show. Might see you later. Depends on the missus."

He was very much the gentleman, very polite and patient.

We go over to the Hall. Both shows have sold out. We played the first show and then had something like an hour's gap. Swarb came over to find out whether Warren had turned up. I hadn't had chance to check but I assured him that Warren's name was on the guestlist for both shows.

Setlist for the show: *Dirty Linen, Rosie, Matthew Mark Luke & John, Hens march/Four-poster Bed, Six Days on the Road, Cell Song, George Jackson, The Claw, Sloth, Fur & Feathers, Ned Kelly, Brilliancy Medley/Cherokee Shuffle.*

We do the second show, which goes down really well. After the show we gather a bunch of people, several of whom are Australian hippies, and head back to the hotel for a party. Still no sign of Warren, of course.

We get back to the hotel. There's about twenty of us, including the hippies who've inevitably brought something to smoke. We're all up in Swarbrick's room – Jerry, Sandy, Trevor, Swarb, DM and myself with the people we met at the gig. Swarb asks if Warren turned up and I have to tell him that, so far as I know he didn't.

Meanwhile, because Australians like a smoke, some of the people with us have started spliffing up. The room's getting quite funky. We've all bought cheap, sparkling champagne-style wine.

Then Swarb says, "Peggy, can you give Warren Mitchell's room a ring and see whether he wants to come up for the party."

It's about half past twelve. Is the hotel reception going to put some British bass guitarist through to the room of their celebrity resident? I don't think so! Swarb is insistent, as we know he could be.

So, I rang reception and said "We're the pommy pop group that Warren Mitchell was talking to earlier. Could you give him a message and tell him he's invited to a party in room 418?"

Swarb, meanwhile, is prompting me "Tell him it's a champagne party." So I did that.

Ten minutes later, there's a knock on the door. It's Warren, carrying a tray with three bottles of proper French champagne – the expensive stuff, not the fizzy plonk we'd been drinking. It was probably about sixty quid a bottle in Australia. He walks into this room full of sweaty musicians, Australian hippies and 'cigarette' smoke and sits down between Swarb and myself. Then he turns to Swarb, hands him the tray with the three bottles of champagne and says "Happy Birthday, mate, these are for you."

Swarb's in the middle of rolling this huge spliff and I'm thinking, 'I hope he has the sense to set it off in the other direction'.

This joint was about six inches long. So Swarb lights it, takes a couple of tokes, and hands it to Warren with the words, "Here you go, Warren, get some of this down you."

Warren looks him in the eye and says, "Swarbrick, one of my best friends is David Kossoff and his son died because of stuff like this." We all knew about Paul of course, lead guitarist with Free. "The grief and the pain and the distress caused by people who got him into this." By now, of course, the room's gone quiet; the party atmosphere's been shattered; everybody's looking at their shoes. Then, Warren says, "Go on: give us a go on it: I'll let you know what I think." He'd just wound us all up totally.

Jerry Donahue came from a showbiz background. His mum was on *Bonanza* most weeks; his dad was a musician, a respected jazz saxophonist. He's from LA. All of which makes him a cool dude. He tried to engage Warren in conversation – something like "Gee, Warren, what're you doin' over here?"

Warren told him "I'm just being myself really. I travel around with a mate from Scotland who's a great piano player. I never do Alf Garnett – I'd have to be really pushed and have run out of things to say. I do comedy theatres and after dinner things: they pay me a small fortune. It's summer here, but it's freezing back in Yorkshire. I just rabbit and people listen to whatever I have to say. I can say whatever I like and people believe me." Jerry asked how long he'd been doing that for.

"Oh, about ten minutes."

He was kind of non-stop and could be a real wind-up merchant... nothing vicious or unkind... just a great sense of humour. We had a great time.

For various reasons, the *Nine* line-up truly re-established Fairport as a force to be reckoned with. Just as they had with Rosie, they embarked on a world tour... but with several key differences. Most obviously it was in the opposite direction – UK, Europe, Far East, Australasia, America (west to east). Unlike the previous tour, the band were now playing music they had created together for their new album. The biggest difference, though, was because of the person travelling with the band.

We ended up doing that World Tour that took us to Japan, Australia and the USA. Sandy was with us: she wanted to be with Trevor; there were delays in releasing her new album. She was at a loose end. You really couldn't have Fairport on stage with Sandy in the wings and not bring her on. Originally, she came on for a couple of encores: by the end of the tour she'd rejoined the band. We recorded several shows in London, Sydney and the Troubadour in LA. The Sydney recordings made up most of the *Live Convention* LP, which is odd in a way, because Sandy was still pretty much playing as a guest, even though she was on stage for a lot of the set.

A live album of the tour was beset by problems which typified Fairport – the London recordings were untypical by the time it came out because they didn't include Sandy; the recordings in LA were not available because the budget didn't allow the band to pay for them. So, *Fairport Live Convention* was by and large a recording of their performance at the newly opened Sydney Opera House. The link to the venue was consolidated by an iconic shot of the group on the steps of the futuristic building that was printed on the inner sleeve.

That's one of mine. I took a set of photos of us there. Some of my best, if I say so myself. It's surprising really when you consider they were taken on a half-frame Rollei – that's a camera designed to put 72 shots onto the 36 frames of 35mm roll of film. In these days of digital photography and capacity to store incredible numbers of images that forty years ago such economies were what state-of-the art is all about.

It's odd really, the first time we played there, Sandy hadn't formally joined the band (we'd only played a few gigs with her back singing with us) and it ended up being our first released live LP. The Opera House had only recently opened.

Australia because part of our normal tour itinerary for a couple of years.

We went back to Australia later on the *Rising for the Moon* tour.

Then we went back after *Bonnie Bunch of Roses* came out.

Five years on from the last Warren Mitchell encounter, there's been a big change in the band. Sandy's joined and left; Trevor's gone with her; DM's quit and so has Jerry Donahue. Simon's come back into the fold. The band is Simon, Swarb, Bruce Rowland and myself. We're in Australia again.

This was a tour lasting almost a month, lasting much longer and taking in more of the country than any previous tour. They started in Perth and ended by playing three different venues in Sydney on successive days.

148

The setlist: *Eynsham Poacher, Sir Patrick Spens, Sir B. McKenzie, Dirty Linen, Country Pie, Limey's Lament, Hexhamshire Lass, Flowers of the Forest, Run Johnny Run, Hens March / Four Poster Bed, Poor Ditching Boy, Bonny Bunch of Roses, Brilliancy Medley / Cherokee Shuffle.*

We were in Adelaide. There was a banjo player there, called Mike Smith, whom I knew because he used to do a floorspot at the Jug O'Punch Folk Club when I was in The Campbells, whose club it was. He'd been a designer at a car factory in Coventry and had moved out to Australia to do the same job there.

He came to our gig and invited us back for a drink. Simon and myself went back and stayed drinking till about seven in the morning. Our flight (to Melbourne, where they again played the Dallas Brookes Hall) was something like 9 am. We made it to the airport, both of us completely blotto: somehow we were allowed on the plane, where we ordered champagne, which the stewardess brought us.

After a couple of hours, we got off in Melbourne and were waiting, rather worse for wear, by the carousel, when who should we spot, but Warren Mitchell again. Simon, who'd heard the story from a few years earlier, asks me to go over and introduce him.

I thought, you've got to be kidding: neither of us is in a fit state and in any case it's an occasion Warren would rather not be reminded about – "Hey remember me and the night you smoked that huge joint in the hotel room?" That's not going to go down well, is it? In any case, I was sure he wouldn't remember me.

Anyhow, Simon insists and we shamble over to Warren who's kind of trapped because he's waiting for his stuff to come off the carousel. I go up him – we were both dishevelled (I had hair in those days) – and say "Hello, Warren, you won't remember me, but…"

He says "Old Court Hotel. Five years ago. Swarbrick's birthday…"

I'm amazed that he remembers and wonder how…

"I don't believe you remember me... How?"

And Warren says "Your breath!"

## Chug-a-lug in Collamundra

Bruce and Swarb smoked excessively: in Australia, you were never short of something to smoke. Simon and myself didn't really smoke, but we were complete lushes. During the tour we took on Festival Records (the Australian rather than the British company), in a drinking competition. Being Australia, it was all "G'day, mate. Have a drink. Chug-a-lug". They fancied themselves as drinkers, but we knew we could beat them. You took it in turns and could choose your own drink. There were four people involved, two on each team: so, you'd start with halves of Fosters and have four lines with six halves of Fosters; then it was our turn to choose – we selected Guinness but had asked the barman to take them out of the fridge beforehand, because we knew Australians can't handle warm drink and it would slow them down; then it was on to Jameson's or whatever. Eventually one of the Aussies collapsed; I collapsed as well; but we were declared the winners because Simon was the last man standing. Or should that be "th'lasht man shtanin"?

Somehow after that we ended up in an apartment with two women. I can't remember what happened next at all.

Many years later we were in Sydney again and Simon found the apartment: he's got a great sense of direction and can always find anywhere he's ever been. It's uncanny. We found the place, but we had no success in finding the ladies again. That night remains, like so much of Australia, forever a mystery.

In 1975, John Penhallow had emigrated to Australia: he had been part of Fairport's close circle in the early days. He'd helped with shifting equipment, organising publicity and ultimately band management up to the arrival of Joe Boyd and his Witchseason organisation. He'd put Fairport behind him along with everything else he had left in the UK. It was in 1986, he met up with the recently reactivated Fairport when they toured Australia. Two years later, he oversaw the release of the first of a series of privately available cassettes of recordings by Sandy and Trevor, both with and separate from Fairport. These were available at Cropredy Festival and also through The Ledge (the UK Fairport fanzine) and Fiddlestix, the magazine of the Australian Friends of Fairport. The Australian Friends of Fairport has remained one of its most supportive fan-groups.

In the early eighties, we did short tours of the UK, a few gigs in Europe and Cropredy, of course. Long-haul tours like Australia and America were out of the question. After *Gladys' Leap*, the next Fairport line up came together, and we toured Australia within the year.

We were playing at Sydney Town Hall: Billy Connolly was doing four nights at the Opera House. All sold out, of course – him, not us. I thought if we could get Billy to give us a plug, we might, on his recommendation, attract some of the anglophile audience. Put a few more bums on seats.

The place where all the bands stop in Sydney is The Seble Town House. I'd stayed there when I was with Jethro Tull because they were quite well off and we'd always stay in nice hotels. The Fairports weren't there, but I figured Billy would be. I phoned up and got put through to him. I explained the situation and asked if he'd give us a plug. He said of course he would and suggested we meet up for lunch next day. We arranged a time to meet at Doyle's in Watson Bay, which was a really good place to eat. By this time it was quite posh... a seafood restaurant... though we'd been going for years: we started when it was still a BYO [Bring Your Own wine] place.

I told the chaps in the band and tried to convince them how it would be a pleasure and an honour to go out for lunch with Billy. As per normal with group arrangements, come half-past-twelve I'm the only one in the lobby – not a sign of anyone else. I waited a bit and it was clear no-one else was coming; knowing I'd be late I set off for the restaurant by myself.

The place is packed inside and out. No sign of Billy. I'm worried that I'm so late he's already gone. So I asked one of the waitresses, explaining I was supposed to meet Billy Connolly. She said they'd put him in a private room at the back so he wouldn't get hassled when he was eating. She checked it was OK and showed me through.

There's Billy... with his back to the wall. I'm about to apologise for being late and being on my own... but it's Billy... I don't get a word in. He grabs me and drags me over... "Come on, Peggy, join us: do you know Michael and Mary?"

It's the Parkinsons!

Anyhow, I admit I don't know them and take a place at the table. We talk a bit and then Billy says, "Come over to the Seble Town House after the show... have a drink (Billy doesn't drink himself of course). Michael and Mary are coming. Invite the rest of Fairport. It'll be good."

We do our gig at the Town Hall. Then we head over to the Seble: all the Fairports – this was the time when Maartin Allcock was in the band. So there's us, Billy Connolly,

Michael and Mary Parkinson and then The McGarrigles arrive, Kate and Anna, who'd been playing somewhere else in Sydney; their band – Pat Donaldson and Gerry Conway were with them.

In the end there's around twenty of us, socialising, catching up because we haven't seen each other for some time. I'm sitting next to Maart, who's sitting next to Michael Parkinson. There's a real hubbub with everyone talking. You know, how sometimes, in situations like that, it suddenly goes quiet... and there's one voice, but it's louder than normal because the general volume has been going up. That's what happened. Sudden quiet. All you could hear was Maartin Allcock talking about being there with Michael Parkinson, "If my grandma could see me now, she'd cream her jeans".

Australia has a great musical heritage, documented in some detail by A L Loyd when he worked out there as a young man. Along with Trevor Lucas and Martyn Wyndham-Read, he brought that unique material to a British audience via a series of albums for Topic Records. Through Trevor's original compositions and the remarkable *Marijuana Australiana* recorded at Cropredy, the music of the antipodes had some impact on Fairport's repertoire. They contributed to the Free Reed re-recording of Peter Bellamy's *Transports*, recording their version of *The Convict's Wedding Dance* at Peggy's Woodworm Studios. Best of all, on the SwarbAid EP, put together by Dave and his then wife Chris, they join Swarb on a version of his gorgeous evocation of his adopted country *My Heart's In New South Wales*.

Swarb eventually moved out there – in 1992. He lived in the Blue Mountains in a lovely little village near Katumba.

We met up when we toured Australia: we went as Fairport Acoustic – that was when we toured without a drummer and electric instruments – years before it became fashionable, incidentally. Swarb was living out there at the time, so we'd meet up: he opened a couple of shows for us and joined us for the occasional number. *My Heart's In New South Wales* is a lovely tune, though – unlike some of Swarb's post Fairport things – it never made it into Fairport's repertoire. One that did was *Close to the Wind*, which he used to do with Simon and brought in the *Full House* line up when he recorded it. Another was a Chris Leslie song that was the first track on his first Fairport album and a track on the first Whippersnapper album, years before that – *John Gaudie*.

## Under Sgt. Nicol's eye

There's a famous April Fool's stunt that was a bonus track on one of the Cropredy CDs: after Fairport called it a day, Swarb decided to move to a remote part of Scotland. We spent March 31 with Swarb and his wife, Simon and Ian Campbell and several bottles of rather fine whisky in Cropredy. Next morning, we were at my house. We knew Swarb liked a lie-in: just before noon next day, knowing he would still be abed, Simon rang Swarb from my house and pretended to be a Scottish policeman telling him that part of the house he was about to move to in Aberdeenshire had been destroyed by an American aeroplane. It's brilliantly done and absolutely hilarious. The problem was, every year after that, I lived in dread of Swarb doing something to get his own back.

One year we happened to be in Australia, in the Blue Mountains, on March 31st. We were staying in Katumba: Swarb lived two miles away. I went to visit him and he told me about this wonderful walk, really beautiful, into the mountains. He said if I stayed over we could do it next day. It seemed like a good idea. It wasn't till I went to bed that I realised what date it was and I began to panic. I literally stuffed the gap around the door with socks and hankies, anything I could find. I was convinced he'd release one of the dozens of poison spiders they had round there or a snake or something... then come bounding into the room, crying "April Fool, Peggy". I went to sleep with fearsome dreams of funnel-webs.

## Two miles down the road....running for his life

Of course, he didn't do anything. I realised I was stupid to think he'd be so unkind as to play a prank that would endanger life... except for the way things turned out when we went for the picturesque ramble Swarb had recommended. There's a mountain trail near the village that Swarb lived in. That's an understatement, by the way, but given the Australian attitude to such things they probably signposted it 'Woodland Walk' or something.

You followed a path down a short incline, quite easy walking, and then made your way along a valley, where the cliffs rose every quickly on either side of you. It was spectacular, really beautiful. The path wasn't steep at first, but steadily became more arduous as you made your way along. There was that beautiful light that's unique to that park of the world; the air was full of exotic bird song and the buzzing of insects; there were fragrancies from hundreds of amazing brightly coloured flowers. I tried to put from my mind all thoughts of dozens of varieties of venomous snakes, poisonous spiders and murderous marsupials. I'm a town person who loves the countryside. This was outside my comfort zone, even if it was beautiful. It was tantamount to jungle. You know, I'm from Cropredy, get me out of here. Except there was no handy Ant & Dec, just Swarb, shuffling beside me like he was auditioning for when they made the Hobbit films in New Zealand.

Swarb wasn't the fittest of individuals and had, in fact, moved to Australia because the purer air would be good for his lungs. The Blue Mountains get their name from the haze that come off all the eucalyptus trees. As you know, eucalyptus is very good for breathing. It can get a bit heady after a while, especially if you're breathing deeply.

Swarb had had a premature obituary printed in The Daily Telegraph. For years after he referred to it as The Daily Epitaph and used to sell signed photocopies of his own obit. For that to happen, of course, people have to think your health is pretty much at risk. We used to worry about Swarb and he knew how to make the most of his anxieties. I could see the path starting to get steeper. Swarb was starting to breathe heavily and look a bit pale. There was just the two of us and we hadn't seen another living being all the time we'd been walking. It's obvious he's starting to find it difficult. We'd already come quite a way, but I thought turning back made sense, and would at least be down-hill.

Swarb was a dogged little soul. He was determined. He said it was a long way back and we should press on. There'd be a way out of the valley soon and that would put us back on the main road. He wouldn't give up. He was like the chap who says, "I'd give up smoking but I'm no quitter."

He was obviously using the advantage of his local knowledge. I should say, his supposed local knowledge, or the local knowledge I wrongly assumed he had.

We press on and eventually pause for a drink of water... and probably a cigarette, back in those days. I was anxious to get a measure of what lay ahead... how steep? How far? How full of creatures intent on ending my life?

Then Swarb said, "This is great. I've always wanted to do this walk."

"You mean, you've never done this before?"

"No but I wanted to. Nobody would do it with me."

This is turning into the worst April Fool's ever. Except I know no one is suddenly going to appear and say "April Fool. Here's your lift home."

"How do you know it's not far? How do you know where the road is?"

"I looked on the map."

Swarb's map reading skills were legendary. He could get lost following a floorplan of his own bathroom.

Kevin Dempsey tells a story of Swarb giving him directions when they were gigging in Germany. Swarb directed them perfectly to the gig, never missing a turn and ended by saying "We'll pass the club on the left. On the right there's a car park." Which indeed there was. This, however, was a demonstration of Swarb's good luck and ability to land on his feet, rather than any cartographical skill. When Kevin looked at the map he had been following, he discovered it was a street plan of the wrong city, and it was upside down.

By now I was really worried. We'd been out ages – much longer than I imagined our short walk would last. I started to calculate how much water we had. We hadn't brought much food and rationing, since it requires moderation, has never been one of my skills. Swarb is determined to press on. I've said before I'm convinced some guardian angel watched over him, He always came out smelling of roses... or whatever flowers were blooming sweetly in this antipodean wilderness.

We went a little way and then, lo and behold, a signpost indicating the way out. We turned right. It was a steep climb, and Swarb really began to struggle, wheezing, signalling for us to stop every a few minutes. I began to become convinced he might collapse. This was long before mobile phones in places like that. I couldn't summon help. Could I carry him if he couldn't go on? He was small, but solidly built. It was a steep climb. I continued my jungle stroll in a state of increasing anxiety.

Somehow, eventually, we reached the top. It was a plateau, really flat, grassed over. As Swarb said, there was a highway. No chance of a bus service, but maybe we could flag down a car. Swarb was something of a local celebrity already, so surely someone would recognise him. If the worst came to the worst, at least it would be a downhill walk on a road.

Swarb wanted to sit on the grass for a few minutes. Who could blame him? The climb was hard. Here there was a nice cool breeze and the sense of falling night created by the high valley sides had disappeared.

As we sat, I saw a car coming in the distance. It was heading the wrong way for us. No point in getting up to ask for a lift. As it got nearer, it slowed down, flashed its lights. I began to get worried again. I'd seen *Deliverance* and *Walkabout* and *Mad Max*. Nice city folks tend to have a hard time in the wild.

As the car drew near, it was clearly pulling to a halt. Trevor's *Ballad of Ned Kelly* was playing in my head.

The car stopped. Out leapt Simon, Ric and Maart.

"Where the hell have you been? We got really worried."

Swarb did his usual thing, and made it clear he knew exactly what he was doing. Apparently I'd needed a break before we walked back to the village.

"Do you know what time it is? You've been gone ages."

"Well, you get a different attitude to such things when you live out here."

They drove us back, It was nothing like as far as I had imagined. Swarb maintained the pretence all the way, regularly checking that I was ok. I was fine: my only problem had been worrying about him. I knew that. So did the other Fairports. The only person Swarb was fooling, that April Fool's Day, was himself.

From our first visits with Trevor, playing huge venues across the country, through the *Rising for the Moon* gigs, the tour with the *Tipplers Tales* line up to the Fairport Acoustic tours in the nineties, we really maintained a bond with Australia. We still have a very supportive fan base, even though it's not really viable for us to tour there anymore, which is a shame.

Quite a lot has been documented on record – the *Live* album; a semi-official bootleg from the *Bonny Bunch of Roses* tour that Swarb put out; a couple of Australian compilations, including those that focus on Sandy and Trevor.

There have even been some live albums that were recorded at concerts organised by Australian Friends of Fairport... *Acoustically Live Down Under* is particularly good. It was recorded at a concert where Swarb turned up and played with us.

It was available as a fan-circulated tape for many years before finally being released on CD twenty years after it was recorded.

Recorded at two concerts in March and April 1996 (the fact the Fairports could spend almost two months touring there is a measure of their success in Australia), the fifteen track collection features Simon, Peggy, Ric and Maart. Swarb appears on the final track, a fine version of *Rosie*.

*"Living in a world you didn't make"*, eh?

# CHAPTER 10

# Myths and Heroes
*Let this be our piece of sky*

*Myths and Heroes* was Fairport's 27th studio album. Its release pattern tells us a lot about how the music industry had changed since Peggy joined the band in 1970. It was not released, reviewed and racked in record shops, primarily. It was available through online orders via their website from January 1, 2015: review copies had been sent out just before Christmas; fans became aware of the album through online posts rather than reviews in the steadily dwindling number of music magazines. It was available during their winter tour which began on January 29, in Tewkesbury. It became available through other outlets in March. In addition to the CD, there was also a limited edition on vinyl. Almost to emphasise the time span, the sleeve was a visual reminder.

Chris Leslie's song *Myths and Heroes* was something we'd been playing for a while. It's a very strong song and one which would be familiar to our audience who had seen us at gigs. To tie in with the idea, Simon and I came up with a concept for the sleeve which looked like *Full House*. That was the first album I made with the band. It was at a time when we were heroes – aside from the stories in this book about 1970 when it came out, it was the year we featured twice as pin-ups in Jackie, the magazine aimed at teenage girls. There we were in full-page colour alongside the likes of Marc Bolan and The Jackson Five. And that's not a myth.

We returned to Woodworm Studios, which I no longer owned, to record the album. Early on we had a sense it was going to be a good one and so, as we had with *Jewel In The Crown*, we let it be known we were on the look out for really strong songs. Some of our mates came up with the goods – the ever-reliable Ralph McTell, the wonderful annA rydeR and my musical sparring partner and fellow Dylan Project member PJ Wright. *Weightless* was a song by a friend from Brittany, James Wood, who was heavily involved in *Excalibur*: he asked me, Chris and Gerry to play on his solo album; as soon as we heard the song we said "We're having that one."

Unlike *Jewel*, when we made *Myths*, we had a songwriter in the band, Chris with four songs for the album. He and I wrote two tunes that went together as a tribute to Roger Bucknell, the man behind the Fylde Guitar company who is very much a real-life hero.

Chris's songs picked up on the theme of his title track and celebrated an itinerant clocksmith from the first half of the 20th century, who became a local legend in Oxfordshire, and Grace Darling who famously rescued nine sailors wrecked off the North East coast in a storm in 1838.

It's not a concept album, but several of the tracks do pick up on theme. *John Condon* is a song about the youngest soldier to be killed in the First World War. When we were recording the album, in 2014, there were lots of events commemorating the centenary of the outbreak of the war. Even though Fairport have recorded a lot of songs over the years that deal with important historical events, the only thing we'd ever done that related to the First World War was an instrumental called *Battle of the Somme*, which was on the *Troubadour* LP. Simon found that song and it's a gem – in fact we included a live version on our next album.

The album ends with a lovely tune from Ric called *Jonah's Oak*. It's inspired by a tree on the left hand side of the Cropredy field, as seen from the stage. The track, and the tree, are dedicated to Johnny Jones, another hero who used to compere and stage manage Cropredy. People might also know him from the Half Moon at Putney. He was quite a character and definitely a hero. The tree was a place he used to go and sit when he needed a few minutes away from it all during the Festival. Over the years, it's become a living memorial to various friends we've lost, like Geoff Hughes and Rob Braviner. The tree had a number of plaques in honour of regular visitors to Cropredy and it's a mark of the festival spirit that it's treated with great respect. It reminds us that heroes are ordinary people. If you look at the songs Fairport have done down the years, a lot have celebrated ordinary people who did something that made them extraordinary. John Condon is one example, John Lee would be another. Chris Leslie has written a whole sequence of songs about people connected to the story of Lord Franklyn, though oddly we've never recorded the ballad itself. There's also *The Fossil Hunter* which is about Mary Anning who was a key figure in the development of palaeontology.

One of the first songs I recorded with Fairport was one that they'd done with Sandy for *Liege & Lief* but didn't make it on to the album. *Sir Patrick Spens* is a ballad about a historical event, but over the years the story has become confused and no one really knows precisely what it refers to. It's one of the great folk songs; lots of people have recorded it; it's in poetry anthologies; people used to be taught it in school. The odd thing is, although the song made Sir Patrick famous, a hero and a myth (the song's got mermaids in it, after all), it's the only record we have of him. No one knows who he was. He was written out of history but survived in a folk song. It's something we still sing regularly on stage, forty-eight years on from Fairport first releasing it on *Full House*.

The sleeve of *Full House* had drawings of the band that looked like tarot cards. For *Myths and Heroes* we updated it with five portraits in which we represented one of our personal heroes. I don't think we explained that on the sleeve and people were a bit confused by it. Perhaps our heroes were not as iconic as we had assumed.
Simon's da Vinci code was fairly easy to crack. Ric's Kung Fu pose meant it wasn't too had to figure out he was Bruce Lee. Gerry chose to pay tribute to a famous Goon, but many fans assumed he was dressed up as a 19th century explorer: Dr Milligan, I presume? Chris's choice was even more baffling because people tended to go "Who?" even when he explained: he was master mandolin maker and Gibson guy, Lloyd Loar... See what I mean? For his hero Chris had a guy in Kalamazoo.

I chose the bass player I admire the most, Rick Danko of The Band, and carefully recreated a famous photo of him, the lighting, the pose, the waistcoat, the hat. Even then some people assumed I hadn't bothered and was just being me. I would like to state formally I Am Not My Own Hero! In the book for *Box of Pegg's*, there's a photo of me with Rick and Allan Taylor.

I've been lucky because in my career I've met and in a lot of cases worked with so many of my heroes. A lot of that was through Cropredy, of course, and we'll talk about that in a moment. People might be surprised that to me people like Sandy, Steve Gibbons and Dan Ar Braz are heroes: just because you work closely with someone, it doesn't mean they lose that quality. I'll admit that the thought of playing in Richard's band again at Cropredy was something that made me nervous: not the actual playing, that was just a marvellous experience, as it always it; it was the build up because after all he is Richard bloody Thompson.

Another real hero is Billy Connolly, whom I've already talked about. In fact, Billy's everybody's hero!

This is the story of how I first met him.

When I was bass player with The Campbells, there was a folk club in Codsall near Wolverhampton, run by some people called The Crown Folk. Geoff Boddenham was their guitarist: he'd formed the group. They'd been commissioned by the BBC to record a religious album. They asked me if I would play double bass on it. You never turn down a session, you never know where it might lead – ask Ric Sanders!

The album was about twenty songs designed to appeal to young people, a spin off from Religious Eductional broadcasting. I think the idea was that it could be used in assemblies. The BBC were recording the album in London. The recording session was all day Saturday, starting around ten in the morning and finishing around five o'clock. There were rehearsals and maybe even some recording on the Friday. So obviously I needed to be in London and have somewhere to stay. Ian suggested Bill Leader. As most people know, Bill was a record producer and hugely important on the folk scene recording all kinds of people for various labels including Topic and Transatlantic and eventually his own labels Leader and Trailer. The list of albums he produced is just astonishing, some of the most influential folk records ever made.

To give an idea of Bill's significance, here's a short list of just some of his productions: ¾ AD (by Alexis Korner and Davey Graham, the record that gave the world *Angi*), Bert Jansch's first album, The Watersons, Young Tradition, The Humblebums (and the albums by its individual members), Mr Fox, Pentangle, Dick Gaughan, Mike Harding, Nic Jones, Christy Moore (*Prosperous*, the album whose players then formed Planxty) and *Bright Phoebus* (on which Mike & Lal Waterson were accompanied by Ashley Hutchings, Richard Thompson, Dave Mattacks, Tim Hart & Maddy Prior and Martin Carthy).

Bill was – and still is – a really helpful bloke and if you needed somewhere to stay in London and turned up at his place with a sleeping bag, he would always find somewhere for you to kip down. Ian offered to ring Bill Leader and ask if he'd mind putting me up.

I went straight to the session, when I got to London. I think it was one of the BBC studios near Oxford Street, pretty central. We got to know each other – not socially, it wasn't that kind of gig – and ran through the songs I was going to play on. It was pretty standard fare and they weren't looking for anything spectacular in the bass department. That was good because I wasn't a particularly good double bass player: I'd heard Danny Thompson and a man has to know when he's beaten!

After the session was over, I got in the taxi with my double bass and went over to Bill's place in Camden Town. He welcomed me, gave me a cup of tea and said, "You're in there: there's already three Scots people in there, but they're very friendly chaps and you'll be fine."

In I went... this would be maybe ten o'clock at night... and there were just these three heads sticking out of sleeping bags, which turned out to belong to Gerry Rafferty and Billy Connolly (who were a group called The Humblebums at the time) and Hamish Imlach. Trust me, that is a pretty awesome trio, even back then. Hang on, do I mean awesome or fearsome?

I know that night nearly killed me. You know the expression 'to die laughing'? That night it seemed like a real possibility.

As soon as I went in, there was a little table lamp on creating a small pool of light. Out of the darkness, a voice said "Well, what have we got here?" A strong Scottish accent in the gloom.

I said "Hello, I'm Dave a bass player from Birmingham".

"Nobody's perfect."

"But you've obviously worked on it."

It just took off from there.

"I knew a bass player once..."

Gerry Rafferty didn't say more than a couple of words, but Billy and Hamish didn't stop telling stories for the next three or four hours. My rib cage hurt from laughing.

At the time, Hamish was the biggest name in this Hibernian triumvirate. He was in the habit of bringing his discoveries down to London whenever he got gigs in what he liked to call "Great Britain's second capital city." It was he who introduced Joe Boyd, despatched by Elektra Records to find interesting British acts, to The Incredible String Band. Though they had just joined forces as The New Humblebums, both Gerry and Billy had been working solo. Billy had yet to discover his true forte and was trying to establish himself as a banjo-playing singer-songwriter. However, anyone who spent time with him off stage knew of his talent as a weaver of hilarious tales. That night, Dave Pegg ("I met him was when he was nae more than a brummy bass basher, ye ken") discovered that talent for himself.

Next morning, I was bleary-eyed and sore. My sides still really hurt. I knew standing playing a double bass all day was not going to help the situation. Bill's wife served up one of those breakfasts which became legendary. A full English. That was the first time I met any of them. I've done sessions with Gerry since and I've met Billy several times since, all of them memorable.

Then Bill called a cab and I went off to my session. I think Billy and Gerry were recording with Bill, who used his front room as a studio. That would have been their first Humblebums record.

The album *Folk in Worship* was released on BBC Records in 1969. Peggy had his own photo credit in the bottom right hand corner of the sleeve. The notes told us he was "twenty-one and has been a professional musician for four years". Most of the album was religious and included almost inevitable versions of songs like *Lord of the Dance* and *Kum BaYah*: surprisingly it also included protest in the form of *Blowing In The Wind, Where Have All The Flowers Gone* and *There But For Fortune*.

About five years ago, at Oxford Apollo, the old New Theatre, there was a week of concerts for someone who'd been a road manager for Status Quo and who'd worked for Billy Connolly and loads of other people. He'd died at an early age. Billy did two free shows as part of the fundraising they did. I didn't know about this as I'd been out of the country: in fact, I missed the first show because I was away, but somebody I knew in Banbury told me about it and said there was another show on the Friday. I rang up about tickets, because they'd asked if I could get any. Obviously, as it was a charity show, there were no freebies, but I could have four tickets and they'd be thirty quid each.

I said that was great and told them to do it. At the time, I'd nobody to go with, having recently split with my wife Chris. I rang round various friends and it seemed none was available. Then Ben Bennion from Freeway Jam rang to say he was free and was keen to take up the offer. Around five o'clock on the day, the phone went: it was my old friend Paul Mitchell, who was passing through and wondered if I fancied meeting up for a drink.

I said, "I can do better than that. Do you want to go see Billy Connolly?" He jumped at the opportunity.

We all go to see Billy. As I know the people who are looking after Billy, I ask if there's any chance of seeing him afterwards. She says "No problem; some of the organisers are meeting in the top bar afterwards. Billy's going to join them. Just go up there."

So after the show, up we went and there must have been around two hundred people there, all hoping to meet Billy. To be honest I thought "no chance!"

Anyhow, in he comes, typical Billy, immediate focus of the room. He clocks me and makes a beeline for where I am, flings his arm round me and so on. Then he says, "Peggy, can you help me out. There's all these people. I just can't go round saying hello to everyone. Can you talk to me, keep me here?"

So I say ok. It's the four of us and Billy in conversation in a corner. Then Paul says, "Billy, I saw you at Shepherd's Bush Empire in 19-whatever... and I've got a story for you."

I could see the look in Billy's eye... "Oh, God, he's going to tell me a joke". Basically out of the frying pan into the fire.

Anyhow Paul just asked how he'd got from one story into another. Billy remembered exactly. And they just – well – solidified. For half an hour they discussed in detail this routine that Billy had done years ago, as if it was yesterday. If was as if there was no one else in the room. Billy appreciated that Paul had analysed what he'd been doing... not just listening to what he said, or laughing at the jokes but appreciating how he did it.

It was as if Billy himself had never thought of things in that way.

**My favourite Martin**

That reminds me of another story which involves the Oxford Theatre. Martin Carthy was staying at our house in Barford St. Michael. I really can't remember why. Maybe he'd had a gig locally; perhaps he'd been doing something in the studio. Whatever the reason, it's always good to see Martin. He was in the section of the cottage that linked to the room where our office was, the part we called The Ledge, playing his guitar. I was in the next room, allegedly working: the playing was fabulous. If you think Martin is great on stage or on record, you should hear him play when he thinks no one is listening. I realised that I'd stopped working and was just sitting listening – spellbound would not be too strong a word to use at this juncture.

As you know, I am really a guitarist not a bass player. The bass thing is just a clever ruse I've maintained for fifty-odd years to keep me in work. To listen to any great guitarist playing just for their own pleasure is a delight almost beyond compare. I don't mean rehearsing or composing, just playing for pleasure. I've had the pleasure of being able to do that with some of the greatest – Richard, Roger, Jerry, Dan, Albert Lee a couple of times and on this occasion, Martin. I wish I could say you can find the recording on track whatever of CD so-and-so of my box set, but of course you can't. It was of the moment, briefly there and gone forever, which was partly what makes such moments wonderful, of course. I remarked once at one of your fabulous parties, Nigel – there was a gathering of great players and I was lucky enough to be able to play along with them – and I said "You should be recording this." You replied, "I never do. It wouldn't be the same." I thought that was absolutely right and very wise.

Anyhow, back to Martin playing in The Ledge...

What interrupted the flow was the house phone ringing. I wasn't in the room so Martin picked it up. That was the time he ended up chatting to Lonnie Donegan. After I'd had my chat and effectively signed Lonnie up for Cropredy, Martin and I started chatting. We'd both been broken off. I probably made us a coffee or something. In the course of conversation, he mentioned it was his sixtieth birthday coming up soon. I asked him what he was doing for it. He said, "Nothing really." Knowing Martin, he'd probably have been quite happy to spend it sitting on a train travelling to or from some folk club.

I'd had a bit of a do for my fiftieth and it had been great fun to get all my mates together to play. We put it out on CD, in fact.

The album was *Birthday Party* by Dave Pegg and Friends. In the year when Fairport marked their first thirty years with a two night retrospective at Cropredy, Peggy gathered friends and colleagues from across his career to celebrate his first fifty years. "Half a century, not out. But I may be by the end of the evening". The gig took place at Dudley Town Hall on November 2, 1997, twenty-eight years to the day since he first saw Fairport. The current Fairport line up were effectively the house band, augmented by past and future members – Swarb, Jerry Donahue and Chris Leslie. There were mates from the Brumbeat days (Roger Hill, John Carter) and Ian Campbell's folk group. A couple of songs from the gig appeared on the first CD of *Box of Pegg's*.

I said, "You've got to have a bash." He was pretty firm that he wasn't planning anything. Christine, my wife, had joined the conversation and said, "Peggy's right. You've got to have a party. We'll organise something for you. You won't have to do anything but turn up." We decided we'd put it in Oxford, which was convenient for us, and we'd invite everyone he'd ever played with. You know how these things work, if you ask enough people, you end up with those who are available and willing to do it. As it turned out, that was everyone – a real who's who of folk. We're talking about heroes and that night Oxford Apollo was full of them.

Martin's box that Nigel did – *The Carthy Chronicles* – was just out and so we had a good source for knowing who to ask. We worked our way down the family tree that came with it. In the end, we covered his entire career – him and Swarb; Leon Rosselson and Roy Bailey; Ashley Hutchings who wrote a parody of *Million Dollar Bash* as a tribute; John Kirkpatrick. There were people who were admirers of Martin like Ralph, Tom Robinson and Gabriel Yacoub from France. The Fairports played, and we represented the various bands he'd been in like The Albion Band, Brass Monkey and Waterson:Carthy. He'd been in Steeleye Span twice and they agreed to appear playing some of the stuff from Martin's time in the band.

The gig was a Saturday night and we arranged rehearsals for a couple of days before. We also arranged for people to stay either in Deddington or at our place in Barford St Michael which had accommodation for when people were using the studio. Maddy

Nigel bids for the Festeno catering

With Ralph at Cropredy

My folks: Albert and Beatty, Cropredy 1981

Christine and Steph June 4th 2006

On tour with Tull/Procols, September 1993 [*photo by Mark Colman*]

Tammy and Matt on our boat Phantom

Austin

Ava

Three great girls, Steph, Ava, Christine

Cropredy drawing by Ava Pegg-Davies

My 50th birthday bash (credit goes to Christine Pegg for organizing it).
*Clockwise from top left:* *1* All aboard the charabanc; *2* John Pegg, Dave and Paul Mitchell backstage at Dudley Town Hall; *3* On the way (L to R: Mick Bullard, Spencer, Steph, Paul Mitchell, Tammy Littlejohn, Simon Hart, Matt)

Harold Wells
and Percy Turley

Fairport/Mott/Tilston in Scandinavia

Paul Warren saves the day! [*photo by Jan Vaes*]

All cossied-up courtesy of Jules for the *Broadsword* tour [*photo by Joe Astro*]

In Estonia: Leningrad Cowboys with Mattacks, Giddings, Pegg, Anderson and Barre.

Pegg, Barre and Perry: 'The Sunshine Boys' in Maui [*thanks to Elayne Barre for the pic*]

A Cropredy warm-up

Danko, Taylor and Pegg; the night I was hospitalised in Denmark

Bass players at Cropredy: Lee Sklar, Alan Thompson, Rob Beattie, muggins

I also play the mando

Pegg and Anthony John Clarke

Our favourite landlord Neil Cutts

Jack Westwood, Jack Snr and Peggy in
Penthièvre – before he lost his 'wallies'

Ellen with Brian O'Malley
September 21st 2004 Chicago

My dear friend AJ (Einstein!)

Rob Braviner, Linc Materna, me, a lady, Chuck Hill. Somewhere in the USA

John Carter and I play at a Breton bar; Maurice and Ann Borgnic look on

Peggy's house and the village [*photo by Stephane Le Goff*]

Ric, Martin Barre and Johnny Logan doing Excalibur at Cropredy

Les Bretles

Pat O'May and annA rydeR rehearse for Festeno

Peggy and Ellen 2013, hand knitted gloves by la belle Julia Clark

Dan and Clarisse at Cropredy 2015

Ava, Emily and Sam at the Pounceys, 2013

Prior had to come direct from Buckingham Palace where she'd been to collect her MBE. After the rehearsals, I took a bunch of people, mainly those staying with us, including Maddy, out for a meal at a local pub. Rehearsals had gone really well. People were delighted to see each other – and in some cases meet their own heroes for the first time. It was Martin's birthday so the mood was celebratory. People got quite refreshed. Not me, on this occasion, because I was designated driver, charged with ferrying people back to where they were staying. I suppose things must have wound up around 11.30 because those were the days when pubs had closing time ("and the Johnny Walker wisdom's running high").

I get people in the car and we set off when Maddy shouts "Stop!" When Maddy shouts you can't miss it, believe me, especially inside a car. I brake. Everybody lurches forward. Nice emergency stop. "What's up, Maddy?" I ask.

"I've left my handbag in the pub... and it's got my [expletive deleted] MBE in it."
The concert – one of those absolute, had-to-be-there, one-offs – went absolutely smoothly and amazingly well. The opening moments were both unexpected and powerful. The house lights dimmed. The stage lights came up. The stage was empty, The audience fell silent. Out of the air came the sound of Martin singing the only recording he wouldn't permit me to include on *Carthy Chronicles*, the first track he ever released as a solo artist, a version of the Cockney song later made famous by Cream, A mother's lament. "Oh your baby has gorn dahn the plug-'ole" sang the disembodied voice of Mr Carthy. Then another voice, an American accent, Paul Simon paying tribute to the man from whom he had famously stolen *Scarborough Fair*. Martin walked on. We all spontaneously sang an appreciative *Happy Birthday to You* and the show began. No CD or DVD was ever released, which made the event even more special.

I'm asked quite often whether concerts are going to be released on CD or DVD, particularly after Cropredy. People assume because I ran Woodworm for all those years that I am still the person who makes those decisions. I'm not because such decisions are made by Fairport Convention Ltd of which I am part. Even then, it's not a simple decision because other artists are involved: they may have existing contracts that prevent them appearing on other labels, though that's not as common as it once was.

Getting permission before the event, to release recordings, just adds to the complications and may create restrictions. When you're performing and you know it is being preserved for posterity, it can effect how you play: sometimes it makes people more cautious, less willing to take the kind of risks musically that makes live performance so exciting.

If you decide to release something after the event, as we are thinking of doing with the 2017 Cropredy performances, it needs a lot of effort and determination and everyone has to agree. For example, the year Fairport did *Liege & Lief* and then Swarb played with us on the Saturday night was a really great Cropredy. It was great to have the whole *Full House* line up to playing together. We decided we wanted to make some of those performances available to people, partly in response to the number of requests we had. Everyone was fine about it, except Swarb said "No", because it hadn't been agreed beforehand. That put the kibosh on the whole thing.

If it's a guest who says no, then you can simply leave off the songs they did. When it's somebody who's part of Fairport that night, it's much more difficult.

Some people would like to have a CD of Cropredy every year. People assume that we could release a DVD because the whole thing is on the big screens. There's a quality issue so far as releasing the screen material and having it viewed on HD TV. If a Cropredy CD was available every year, it would have less impact and we'd be faced with diminishing returns. In any case, it's not just a case of having the recordings and putting them out: you have to select from a three-hour set; tracks have got to be mixed and mastered; there's sleeve design and sleevenotes; even the task of coming up with a title. It's a long and quite expensive process even before you get to the stage of manufacturing and marketing the actual CDs,

So, bearing in mind the topic of this chapter, to those people to whom Fairport are heroes, apologies you can't have everything. As George Harrison once remarked – "we've got a lot of great fans: some are really committed – and some should be."

Speaking of things that fans want to get their hands on... I should qualify this, because among dedicated fans rarities and oddities do circulate. Once upon a time, there were bootlegs, which you bought by mail order or under the counter in certain shops. These weren't pirate copies of existing discs, but albums of unreleased material. It was the really big names first – Dylan, The Stones, The Beatles and so on – then a lot of rock acts. Fairport were in that league. There was a bootleg of early recordings (*A Chronicle of Sorts*) and the original *Heyday* stuff. One of the fan groups did an annual CD of unreleased recordings, mainly live things and broadcasts, that was sent out to members of the group at cost. We didn't mind because the only people getting it would be people buying our albums anyway.

Being bootlegged in a way is a kind of complement. Dylan took it on board by calling his albums of unreleased archive material *The Bootleg Series* and picking up on names like *The Basement Tapes* for official releases. Richard has released semi-official live albums in parallel with his studio releases for years. The whole culture of bonus tracks and archivist releases and things like The Beatles' *Anthology* exist because of the attitude created by the existance of the bootleg culture.

Very often fans are aware of a track and may have it illicitly but are keen that is somehow made legitimate. The April Fools' tape is a good example. That had circulated a lot before we finally put it on an album. There is one track which we'll never release though and I'll talk about it here because Martin Carthy was heavily involved.

It was back in September 1971. We were recording *Babbacombe Lee* which Simon was producing. Mainly the album is songs the band wrote inspired by the story of John Lee. To represent his years at sea, though, we decided to use a set of tunes, like sailor's hornpipes and a traditional song called *Sailor's Alphabet*. The song is from a very respected source singer called Sam Larner. It's a blooming difficult song because you have to sing every letter of the alphabet in order and each stands for something associated with sailors. "A's for the Anchor" and so on.

I think everyone involved had a different version of what happened to this song. Like a folksong, the details have changed in the telling over the years, but this is how I remember it. Simon was getting quite strung out over the whole thing. It was Swarb's pet project and he was putting a fair bit of pressure on us all. It was all new material, written for the project, We'd never played it live. Simon, as producer, would be faced with putting all the tracks together and he'd have no choice in the matter because it told a story. He'd couldn't leave something off because it hadn't worked or put a weaker track at the end of a side, as people often did in those days.

One night, myself, Swarb and Martin decided to have a relaxing night off. We bought in some beer, wine and spirits. Loads of fags because we smoked quite heavily. Martin probably asked how the LP was going and somehow *Sailor's Alphabet* was mentioned. Maybe he asked if we'd stopped doing traditional songs: Martin was in Steeleye at the time, our rival "trad arr" band!!

Somehow we ended up making up new lines and creating what fans know as *The Naughty Sailor's Alphabet*. I'm sure Martin knew the song and we'd just recorded it. The result was extremely rude. We were probably messing around to start with. "A is for Arsehole" and so on. Soon the three of us were trying to outdo each other in vulgarity, but we still were professional enough to make the words scan and rhyme properly.

Like so many trivial things that are destined to go nowhere, it became very focused: we just had to have a rude word for every letter. Try it yourself: it's not easy. C, F, W, B, P and so on are obvious: in some cases you're spoiled for choice. Think of something rude for X, for example. As I recall Y is for Y fronts.

Some time and a lot of booze later, we had a complete set of working lyrics, the whole song. It would have been a shame to waste all that effort so we sneaked into the studio and using the backing track we'd already recorded for the LP, we cut a whole new, disgusting version.

We all fell about when we played it back. We thought it was the funniest thing we'd ever heard.

Then someone (wonder who?) had the idea of taking the master tape for the album out of its box, hiding it and replacing with our raunchy remix. When Simon came to put the album together, he'd be faced with something undeniably naughty rather than essentially nautical.

This was a cruel practical joke. We ended up heading off for our American tour and leaving Simon to finish the album and then join us ahead of the first dates. We weren't there to witness his reaction, but I gather he didn't appreciate the joke... or the anguish as he tracked down the proper recording.

He left the band a couple of weeks later. I don't know if the two things are connected. "J's for the joke that rather backfired."

Every time, there's a Fairport compilation or a reissue of the album, we are asked if we'd changed our minds about releasing it. The answer is "No we haven't" and it always will be.

## Unwelcome here, kind stranger

Martin's birthday bash reminds me of another gig on my doorstep and it's another Warren Mitchell story. You've read the Australian tales, this is closer to home... in Chipping Norton, where Simon used to live and where Fairport's offices have been since they moved from Barford St Michael. The theatre there, which used to be an old Salvation Army citadel, was started up by this frightfully hooray lady called Tamara who simply loved it. She put so much care into developing in and got a lottery grant for improvements and so on. They put on all kinds of good things including one of the best pantomimes in the country: lots of concerts, as well – Fairport have played there. It's only a small theatre, but it's beautiful.

To celebrate getting the grant, she put on two gala nights with lots of special guests who came just for the occasion. One of them was Warren Mitchell. They all donated their services as it was a fundraiser. Simon and I both bought tickets and went along with our then-wives to the first of the two nights.

When Tamara said she'd got Warren, I told her we knew him, or at least he knew who the Fairports are. We had a new album out and I said I'd love to give him a copy of it. She said she'd try to fix it up.

Warren was on first: he began the show by explaining that because he was Jewish, he hated performing for nothing and was doing it only because he'd known Tamara for years. She's done such a great thing here, he wanted to be part of celebrating it: 'It put me in a charitable frame of mind and as I was driving here through Finchley and Golders Green, I passed an old folks home and I thought it would be good to give something back to the community, maybe give a short performance at tea time. So I was invited in to meet some of the older residents. There was one lady who clearly didn't recognise me. I said "Hello, my dear, do you know who I am?" She said, "No but if you ask matron over there, she'll tell you!"'

Anyhow, Warren did his opening act, pretty much in that vein. It was fantastic. No doubt it was the sort of stuff he'd been doing when we last bumped into him in Australia.

Afterwards, he was in the bar talking to Ronnie Barker who ran an antique shop in Chipping Norton. It was his hobby and he loved doing it. People used to wander in to look at antiques and do a double take when they saw Ronnie behind the counter. He wasn't open all hours, however. I always wanted to go in and ask for four candles but I never summoned up the courage. If ever he bought an old violin, Ric would do it up for him, to make sure it was playable.

I'd got the CD to give to Warren. As I started to walk towards them, he spotted me. There was no mistaking the look on his face – complete alarm and panic. He could have been holding up a sign that said "Oh God, it's him!" He's a lovely chap and I just felt I couldn't do that to him. So I swerved sideways and found Tamara and asked whether she would pass on the new Fairport CD to her old friend Warren Mitchell.

While we're on the subject of local events, I have a trilogy of stories... all to do with Cropredy... and things not quite going to plan.

The first happens just after Chris and I moved to the village – Swarb was already living there. We realised it was a great place to live and property, in those days, was very very cheap.

We lived in a little cottage by the Methodist Church. Our next door neighbour, Pamela Keegan, was very keen on the history of the village. She wanted everyone in the village to have chance to become aware of how it was formed and its development and so on. It was something that fascinated me too.

She invited a famous architect who lived locally to give a talk on the background to its buildings in the Village Hall. There are buildings that go back to mediæval times and so the history of Cropredy is literally set in stone. He was going to explain all that with an illustrated lecture. I forget his name – but for these purposes let's call him Mr Forsythe-Lawson.

I'd been living in the village for maybe six months. I was still keen to make a good impression. I didn't want to be thought of as the long-haired hippy musician (you can discuss among yourselves which, if any, of those terms apply to me today).

Pam invited us along and asked whether I might have a slide projector. I think she'd found out already I was interested in photography.

As it happened, I had quite a cosmic projector, which had actually two projectors and a device for intermingling and fading between the slides. A Zeiss projector. In those days, it was a very impressive piece of kit and the results had a definite wow-factor for anyone used to watching slides using an old style projector. I said she could borrow it and if she let me have the slides, I'd make sure they were all properly loaded and working.

Come the day, she phones me up and asks if I was still coming in the evening. I said we were and we'd already bought tickets. We'd be there at six to help set up. She said "Good. Because we can't get the projector to work."

I went straight down Chapel Street – it's a couple of minutes' walk from my house to the Village Hall. I tried everything I could think of – checked the fuses, checked the switches, checked the cable was in properly, checked the bulbs, check the controls that made it operate. Nothing. It was dead.

Pam said it was odd because she'd tried it the night before and everything had worked perfectly.

Pam started to get worried and asked what we were going to do. I said I was sure someone in the village would have a projector, even if it wasn't quite as high-tech as mine. By now it was about six o'clock so I knew the pubs would be open, so I rang the Brasenose and the Red Lion to find out if anyone there had a projector. "Hello, it's Mr Pegg here – the long haired git who's just moved in to Chapel Row. I want to ask a favour on behalf of the Village Hall..." No joy whatsoever.

Then I realised that Cropredy Village School, that my kids attended, must have some kind of projector. I rang up and they said I could borrow it. It was by now about quarter to seven. I got in the car drove to the school, where someone – the caretaker probably – lent me an ancient Aldis slide projector that they must have had for years. Pretty basic but at least it would do the job.

I hurry back. So now I have what feels like the world's most ancient slide projector and four boxes of slides which Pam has carefully arranged so they'll alternate and merge to illustrate the talk.

I get the projector working – it's not great but it's all we've got. Pam's standing beside me holding four trays of slides and she says "Mr Pegg, what do I do?"

She explains she can't do it and asks whether I would. I wanted to say "I'm just a bass player: I just go bumbum bum de dum. I don't do multimedia productions." I should have… but desperate times and all that. She really was stuck.

I say I'll do my best, but I know this involves loading each slide and changing them manually.

7.30 comes round. The hall fills up nicely. Lots of people interested in finding our more about the village and its history, looking forward to a fascinating evening. Well, it was fascinating but perhaps not in the way they planned.

Pam does a really nice introduction, which includes a thank you to me for operating the projector to show the slides the speaker has taken. So now everyone knows who to blame... it's that long-haired bloke who's just arrived in the village.

Mr Forsythe-Lawson begins his talk, starting with something everyone will recognise (and which Fairport fans know because it was on the sleeve of our album *Nine* not long afterwards). "Here's a picture of The Brasenose in 1896", he says – my cue. I push the slide across in front of the beam and on the screen appears... a picture of a sheep... upside down.

If looks could kill. Mr Forsythe-Lawson clearly has me down as incompetent, if not a complete idiot. We've barely started and already the evening is turning into a disaster. So the evening progresses. Transferring the slides from four trays and projecting them not from a self-loading, automated, multi-projector machine but from an antique where you have to load each slide individually by hand clearly has gone seriously wrong. None of the slides fit with what he's actually saying, or if they do it's pure coincidence and probably merited a round of applause. Some are projected back to front or upside down. It's getting worse as the evening goes along. I get more embarrassed and fumbly because there's nothing I can do about it. Pam's beside herself. I'm the laughing-stock of the village. Mr Forsythe-Lawson is fuming but is from that class of person who knows how to contain his emotions, but every time the wrong slide appears, he gives me a look which says "What is this creature who has just ruined my carefully prepared talk... again."

I know it's not my fault. I didn't volunteer. I was just trying to help. I'm the guy who lent them his expensive, flash and (as it turned out on the night) useless projector. They're not going to blame the projector... or Pam who looks close to tears... or Mr Forsythe-Lawson who carries on despite circumstances. He's a hero. I, meanwhile, am just some idiotic hippy musician.

It was embarrassing to say the least.

Roll on a few years....

**On Peggy's solo album there is a track dedicated to Pipe Major Jock Laidlaw of The Banbury Pipe band. It's a tune Peggy wrote for them to play. He is the central character in part II of Peggy's trilogy of Cropredy catastrophe. (It's track 17 on CD 4 of *Box of Pegg's*).**

I'd moved from Cropredy to Barford St Michael on the other side of Banbury. Instead of the mixing desk and tape machine in the shed, I now had a studio in the converted chapel next door, where Fairport and a lot of other artists made their albums. It was pretty much state of the art. My solo album was recorded there.

Jock Laidlaw, to whom *Pipe Major Jock Laidlaw's Fancy* on that LP, is dedicated, is, as you mght guess from his name, a Scot. He runs the pipe band to encourage young people to make music using the pipes and drums.

It's a great thing to do. I love the pipes and drums – being a bit of a folkie at heart.

Jock collars me one day and says, "Dave, you've got a studio. Is there any chance you could record our band?" Now Woodworm Studios was hardly Abbey Road: there wasn't space to fit in a pipe band – it was quite snug with just The Fairports in there. But I don't like to refuse. So I say, yes but I'll need to bring a tape recorder and record where you play. I had some time and, as long as I wasn't working, I was happy to give it a shot. Anything to help.

He said "That's great because we march up and down when we're playing. It'll be easier for them if they can do that."

Anyone who's done any recording knows that it's hard enough to record someone who's standing still. If you get someone who tends to move around and go off mic it's much more difficult. If people are marching around en masse, it's a nightmare. You need an array of mics and multiple channels. It's an expensive and complicated business. You need a BBC outside broadcast unit or the Rolling Stones mobile or something like. Which of course I, as the sole proprietor of Woodworm Studios, did not have.

Which is why I set off one day for the hall where they used to rehearse with a Revox tape recorder, a new reel of tape and a couple of Sennheiser microphones. I'd get what I could. I'd do my best. After all, the people who made all those field recordings like Alan Lomax worked with equipment a lot more basic than I had. My father in law, Percy Turley, happened to be staying with us, so he came with me to Aston le Walls Village Hall.

The recording session is a nightmare. The drums are deafening, even when they are at the far end of the room. The bagpipes... well they're bagpipes, enough said, you know what I mean. On top of which the whole band – and the sound it makes – is moving up and down and back and forth. The sound of their feet also becomes part of the general cacophony. You know that amazing record *Tusk* by Fleetwood Mac with the marching band and Mick Fleetwood banging away on percussion moving across your stereo? It was nothing like that!

I'm in the little kitchen at the end of the hall, using it as a kind of control booth. The sound coming through my ears is unbelievable – and not in a good way. I know whatever is going on to the tape is not going to be listenable.

Percy, my father in law, is meanwhile having a great time with Jock because Jock's brought along a bottle of whisky. They've been discussing the band and getting more and more relaxed.

I go back to the studio and listen carefully to what I've got on tape. As I suspected, it's not sufficient. No amount of post production is going to turn it into something people would ever want to listen to. This was not the band's fault. They were fine. I realised I had volunteered myself onto a very steep learning curve as a recording engineer.

I'd need to do it all again. I spend two more evenings, going to different village halls, hoping somehow things will work so I can get something we can use. I try different settings, different mics, different mic positions. This is all before digital and I was recording through twinned mics so it was basic stereo – decent quality in terms of the actual recording: I was running the Revox at 15ips which is plenty good enough to record music. With care, patience and experimentation, it comes together and ultimately I realise I am recording a sound which properly reflects how good the band is.

I end up with a whole tape which I feel is a good representation of what the band do. I am actually proud of it. I play it to Pipe Major Jock and he's pleased with it too. He thinks it's great. He asks what I think we should do with the recording and I say I could arrange for it to be duplicated on cassette very reasonably. I wasn't going to charge for any of the work I'd done. So they'd be able to sell the tape at a sensible price to parents of the children in the band or people who attended performances they gave and maybe make a decent amount for the band's funds. That could go towards buying more instruments or whatever. On top of which they now had a decent permanent record of how the band sounds.

He liked that idea and asked me to fix it up for him. One of my mates, Simon Stable, who happened to be Judy Dyble's husband, ran a tape duplicating service and he agreed to run off copies for next to nothing because of the circumstances. It was, as they say, all in a good cause. He's the chap who did those Fairport at Cropredy cassettes in the early eighties as well as various other bits and pieces I'd been involved with. I knew we'd end up with a high-quality product.

So I tell Jock and he gives the go ahead and the master tape goes off to Simon's duplicating company.

So far so good. Very good in fact – it's going smoothly and things are turning out, if anything, better than I might have expected. Before too long the pipe band would have 300 cassettes they could sell.

About two months later, I get an invitation from Jock to attend the pipe band's annual dinner. It's quite a big posh event. Chris and I are going to be guests of honour, as a gesture of appreciation for making the tape.

I checked my diary and I wasn't working so I said we'd be delighted to attend.

The night before the dinner, Jock rings up. He checks that we realise we're on the top table. Then he says, you know that recording, I thought it would be good to play a bit of it on the night, to show people what you've achieved and maybe encourage sales when the finished cassette becomes available.

There are several problems with this. First of all, I don't have a finished copy of the tape or the master which is still with the tape company: all I have is a rough working copy on cassette. Secondly, there's no system to play it back at the dinner and all I have is one of those massive portable cassette players – what they used to call a ghetto blaster, though Dave Mattacks called it a Spadio which is very politically incorrect these days. It's loud, loud enough for the room where the dinner was being held in Banbury, but that's really the best thing you could say about it.

On the night, off we went to the venue. We were dressed in our best and looked the business: if I say so myself. The only problem was that I was lugging this huge cassette player which felt like a small plank.

Anyhow everything goes well. We come to the speeches and Jock introduces me, saying something like,

"We're really honoured tonight to have with a us a really famous musician and his wife, Dave Pegg, who's a member of Fairport Convention and Jethro Tull. He also owns a recording studio and has been kind enough to give up his time to make a recording of the band which will be available soon. He's agreed tonight to give us a sneak preview of the tape which I know you're all going to want a copy of."

I bring out this massive beast of a tape player, right on cue, press PLAY and it eats the tape. Huge embarrassment. I tell them it was only a rough copy but whereas this was meant to be an explanation but it just sounds like a feeble excuse or apology. I don't often go red with embarrassment, but I did that night there at the high table with everyone looking at me.

I had my back to the audience to play the tape but I had to turn around to explain all this. Double embarrassment. Then I look to my left and who should I see but Mrs Forsythe-Lawson, who clearly knows all about the previous disaster and has a look on her face that says "Oh Lord, it's him again, the disastrous long haired hippy musician that ruined my husband's fascinating lecture."

Here endeth part two of my trilogy.

## I'll have to give up on the iron Lions

It's a couple of years later and my accountant, a chap called Richard George, who worked for a company called Grant Thornton who are a very respected accountancy firm, was in the Rotary Club. They do some wonderful work, as do the Lions Club (and I admit I do get the Lions and the Rotary confused: I have rotating lions, or as Elton put it The Circle of Life).

He told me how they had dinners with guest speakers every three months or so. I knew what he was leading up to. He explained how my job was so different to his (I knew that because I was paying his firm £25,000 a year to do it) or that of most other people who attended the Rotary Club. He reckoned me giving a talk would be fascinating.

Well, he's obviously never heard me talk. I tried to put him off by saying I didn't do talking: I mean I'm a bass player, "dumdum de dum" and all that. But he was insistent and said how it was all in good cause and so on. He assured me they'd love it. He suggested it didn't need to be all talking: for example, I could play some musical illustrations which would also help to make it, in his words, "a different and memorable evening."

I'd just brought out *Box of Pegg's* and there, thanks to Nigel's help, was a simple source of lots of suitable illustrative material that covered my entire career.

So I agreed to do it, if I could bring along samples of that on cassette to play. Lots of music, less need for me to talk apart from introducing the samples and putting them in context with the occasional funny story. It would mean the hour, which is how long the talk was supposed to last, would pass quickly, for me and, hopefully for the audience.

As I worked on it, I began to realise I could make it interesting by using the musical illustrations to provide something that people would relate to. For example, I'd say something like "I went to Yardley Grammar School. When I was there, I loved The Shadows. You remember The Shadows? Hank Marvin with his horn rimmed glasses" and then play "Dang-ger-dang ger dang-ger-dang". They'd all be nodding and doing "Yeah, we remember that" and they'd all be on my side.

I had it all worked out. I've got all the examples in order on a cassette. I have the feeling it's going to be great. I'm confident. I'm actually looking forward to it. Remembering the old ghetto blaster, I've made sure I've got a reliable cassette player, a decent amp and extension speakers about ten feet apart. As it's a very posh do, held in the old cattle market in Banbury, I've invested in a suit and all that.

I'm the guest of honour, celebrity speaker, looking the business etc etc.

On the day, I arrive in plenty of time, get set up, make sure I look presentable (or at least as presentable as I can manage). It's soon time for the paying guests to arrive. I do a final check and nothing works. I go around checking everything – plugs, fuses, extensions, connections, switches. It's all totally dead. It's too late to do anything about it. No chance of replacement, even.

By now I am getting quite stressed, which isn't helping. I'm also desperate for a drink, as you can imagine.

So the guests arrive and the time comes round for me to give my talk and I think I'd better explain the situation. I tell them what I had planned... the music and everything. Then I apologise and say, "but unfortunately the equipment has failed and I won't be able to play you anything."

I don't know if there was an audible moan, but in my memory I sense one. Suddenly they knew they were faced not with an entertaining and amusing hour with music, funny tales, nostalgia and so on but with an hour of me, droning on in a monotonous Birmingham accent trying to fill sixty minutes most of which I hadn't planned on talking for.

That was the moment I looked across at one of the front tables – I don't think they were 'the expensive seats' but it felt like they were: who should I see but Mr Forsythe-Lawton and his wife, both of whom had a look on their faces that said, "Oh no: it's him again."

Needless to say the evening I'd planned so well and been looking forward to had turned into a disaster.

I've not seen Mr Forsythe-Lawton or his wife since, something I am sure we are both pleased about. If he does happen to read this, can I take the opportunity to give him my sincere apologies?

That's me as anti-hero, I suppose. Banbury's answer to Norman Wisdom. Let's get back to someone who is not just my hero, but until his recent death, genuinely one of the biggest heroes on the planet and probably the only person in this book to be the subject of an Oscar nominated movie.

There's loads of stories that don't really go anywhere but it's nice to share them anyway. Ellen and I were in a restaurant once, having lunch. This was in Liege in Belgium. It would be 2004, something like that.

## A brief history of where the time goes

A guy brought in Stephen Hawking, guided his wheelchair to the table next to ours to have his lunch and then left him there. The place obviously knew him and were geared up for his arrival and everything. It just happened his table was next to ours. We were chatting away and he was obviously listening to what we were saying while he waited for his food to arrive. He was as close as we are now.

Ellen said, "You should say hello; be polite."

I thought – 'As if' ...I mean, what was I going to say? "Hello Stephen. Nice to meet you. I'm Peggy, the bass player with the Fairport Convention. A group you've probably never heard of." A missed opportunity, I suppose... and a bit surreal. Sitting next to one of the greatest, most intellectual men in the world and not knowing what to say.

This was on one of Fairport's little raids. We'd do raids to Germany and Belgium, a few small gigs, all low key, because the band had never been big over there, but as in a lot of places, we a had a small group of loyal fans who wanted to see us and would always turn up when we played. It's nice to pop over there once in a while to see them and let them see us.

We used to go over there with Rob Braviner driving his Toyota Previa and schlep all over Germany for next to nothing. Rob's no longer with us, sadly, and the cost of doing that has increased a lot in the last few years so we haven't really been able to do it for a while. We still play in Europe, of course – Italy, Scandinavia and so on. We'll do a couple of weeks of gigs. I know some bands would call that a European tour, but really it's a case of making our way to a gig, sometimes together, often separately, setting up and playing. One of the reasons we can do that, is that in Denmark particularly, small venues are very well subsidised. It'll be a nice venue, with its own decent PA and a restaurant so the band get fed. All we need to do is turn up with our instruments: I don't even need a bass amp and Gerry takes his cajon instead of a drumkit. It means we can travel relatively light and don't need a crew and trucks with equipment and so on.

Luckily we have Simon Yorath who does a fantastic job on sound as well as driving us round from venue to venue.

Of course, it's much more difficult to do this for fans in America or Australia, because of cost and distances. It's a bigger commitment. The distances between gigs are enormous, so you have to do sizable venues to make it viable. The last time we did the States, you could be driving six hours between gigs and then you'd have to set up and play; it's an exhausting experience regardless of whether you're making money or not. Very taxing in more than one sense.

It's a shame because although the venues we played in the States were quite small, maybe 150 people, Fairport fans would always turn up and be really pleased to see us. They were great. There's the matter of time as well. If you're going to travel that kind of distance, you've got to do a tour to make it worthwhile and you have to carve out a block of time for that.

The Fairports are already committed to the annual winter tour, which is six or seven weeks, the acoustic tour that's now an annual event that people expect, plus Cropredy of course. Then there's various odd festival things we do – like the Butlin's gig in winter. We've also got dates, sometimes a tour in Europe. That's a lot of Fairport stuff, plus we might be working on a new album which of course takes time.

Then we've all got other commitments – I play with Anthony John Clarke and The Dylan Project; Simon and Chris are both involved in different Christmas Shows; Ric's got his trio; Gerry's in the Dylans, Jacqui's Pentangle and other things. Calendars can fill up quickly.

We couldn't end this chapter without a serious nod in the direction of some genuine and literally unsung heroes without whom we wouldn't be telling this story. On more than one occasion, Fairport have needed the intense help of health care professionals, to "see them through and make them good as new". There was the accident on the M1 in 1969. There was the time Ric fell through a plate glass window and nearly lost the use of his arm. There was Peggy's manual mishap with a broken wineglass in 2014. There were years of care, sometimes intense, which kept Swarb alive.

As we worked on this book, there were times when the discomfort in Peggy's hip made him ask for a break and a short rest – "a bit of a lie down". He doesn't succumb to pain easily but the Winter Tour at the start of 2018 saw a high bar stool added to the stage equipment. Peggy literally couldn't stand for the whole set night after night. The stool allowed him the semblance of standing while supported. On his return to Brittany, he put himself in the much-needed care of French health professionals.

The hospitals are so good in Brittany. I needed to have my left hip replaced and spent two nights in the Clinique Mutualiste in Lorient. I went in Thursday morning. The operation was at 12.30. I was back in the ward at 17.00.

Dr Cantin, the surgeon who did the operation, looked incredibly young, which tells you more about me than him. There was a great team of nurses, with the unique skill of being efficient without being impersonal.

Those people are real heroes, because they save lives and improve lives as part of their day to day job. If most of us could do as much for someone in our lives as doctors and nurses do every day, we'd be really proud – and rightly so. They ask for no praise or recognition. Even so, in my very bad French, I wrote a little song for them while I was there:

*Clinique Mutualiste, grande merci a vous*
*M'Hanche a gauche maintenant C'est nouvelle*
*A Docteur Cantin et tous les equipes*
*Rosenn et Anne et aussi Edith.*

*Loic et Clement parle très bons Anglais*
*Mava et tous maintenant je restais*
*A Clinique Mutualiste grande merci a vous*
*11/10 doc bisoux bisoux.*

OK, it's no *Hungarian Rhapsody* so don't expect to see it on the next Fairport CD.

I had to stay in overnight, to be monitored and so on. Word had spread that I was in the hospital and I had an endless stream of visitors, who were all English speakers, keen to use some of their free time to practice their English on me. They really cheered me up. There is something charming about foreigners who make mistakes speaking English. I do that, of course, but that's because I'm from Birmingham. For me it's a case of second nature rather than second language.

We needed to find a doctor when we first moved to Brittany. I think it should be one of the first things anybody does when they set up home somewhere. Our local doctor was Henri-Pierre Evenno. He was perfect because he spoke both German (which is Ellen's native language) because his wife is German and incredibly good English (which is supposedly the language I speak). He's our GP. On my second day in hospital, he came to visit. I thought that was fantastic and thanked him profusely. He explained he did that for all his patients if they were unfortunate enough to find themselves in hospital. That is an amazing service. It's also great that he works within a system that gives him time to do that.

I had Friday in hospital with no chance to get bored as I had more people calling round whenever I didn't have a visitor, all wanting to speak English with me. On Saturday I was discharged (don't you wish they had a more pleasant word? Especially when you think how that term is used in hospitals?). Because our house has the bedroom with en suite bathroom on the ground floor, being at home didn't present any logistical problems. As soon as I felt up to it, I would be able to move around the house and eventually go outside and enjoy the fresh air and birdsong.

Henri-Pierre came along on the Sunday to make sure I had everything I needed, to confirm my accommodation was suitable and to "check my wound" – a strange term, but it makes you feel heroic.

Our neighbour Liliane, who lives two doors down, comes every morning to administer my injections. She changes my dressing every two days. It's so useful having friends who are medically qualified.

Everything has gone really smoothly. Within a few days I was up and mobile, moving around the house using a stick and trying not to get bored.

I need to say a big thank you to Brittany for its medical provision and for great friends and neighbours and for the wonderful looking-after after-care follow-on system. [Nigel, can you put that last bit into English?]

The whole thing cost around € 8,300, which is a lot cheaper than it would have been privately in England. It was a tight squeeze because it had to fit between the end of the Winter Tour which was at the end of February and May 11 when we start the Spring Tour with the acoustic line up. By then I hope to be moving around a lot more easily and with a lot less pain than last time we were on the road.

On tour Fairport always attract some old hippies: this time we'll find out how they cope with a brand-new hippy.

We started these tales of myths and heroes with Billy Connolly. I reckon that's as good a place as any to round them off.

He came to Cropredy a couple of times – not booked, just to enjoy it, the way people do. The first time, he came two consecutive weekends because the first time he got the date wrong. In fact, he went into the Cropredy village shop which had just been taken over by a Chinese lady, who knew nothing about Fairport or the Festival and was suddenly confronted by a huge Scotsman with lots of purple hair trying to buy nail extensions so he could play the banjo.

Anyway. Billy discovered his mistake and came back the following week to enjoy the Festival. He was backstage and this was in the days when we used to have a teabreak at six o'clock so people could go back to their tents or cars or whatever and have something to eat without missing any of the music. People had kept saying I should ask Billy to go on stage and say a few words, but I thought he was such a star already it would be a real insult to ask him.

Then the teabreak was announced. He came over to me and said "Are you not going to ask me to go up and do something?" I explained I didn't want to offend him and he said he'd be offended if I didn't ask. On he went, unannounced and as soon as people realised, it was like the whole field turned round, forgot about their dinners and came back to their places.

Then we heard a police siren. I immediately thought "Oh God, what's happened?" But it turned out to be the chief inspector of Cherwell Valley Police, who everyone knew as Jock. Nothing was wrong – as soon as he saw Billy was on stage, he put his lights and siren on so he could get back to Banbury to collect his LPs and get them signed.

He needn't have rushed. If you put a natural comedian on stage, with no set time to come off, they'll keep going. It's happened with Jasper Carrott, Frank Skinner, Mike Harding (who has some great tales about the years when Maart was in his band) and Billy. Billy got up on stage and there was a mighty roar. He lapped it up, strutting around the stage, stretching out his arms. People were falling about and he hadn't said a word. His first lines were "My people! My people!" which you couldn't script, yet those two words were hilarious. Then he went off on one of his long tales that snaked away in dozens of directions before finally coming back to the punch line. His timing was perfect, because the punchline arrived at exactly the time for the concert to resume. People had missed their allocated refreshment time – and in fact we stopped bothering to include it after that – and probably didn't realise they'd just had a bonus performance, gratis and for free, from the funniest man in the world. If there's an audience, from a couple of people to a crowd of thousands, Billy can't help himself. He loves making people laugh. Thank heavens he does.

That was an unscheduled Cropredy performance that everyone who was lucky enough to be there remembers.

I reckon it's time we bite the bullet and talk about Cropredy.

# CHAPTER 11

# Cropredy Capers

*Well we still walk awhile*
*And it's thanks to the Peggs*
*Matty's still getting caught*
*With his pants down his legs*
*If you gotta go,*
*Partir pour un slash*
*We'll still have a ball*
*At the Million Dollar Bash*
Ashley Hutchings, after Bob Dylan,
Cropredy 1997

You can't talk about Fairport without talking about Cropredy. The two words are eternally connected. It began as an annual reunion, as much for people in the band as for fans. We certainly weren't aiming for a wider audience. It was also much more of a folk/folk-rock festival, mainly because that's what we played and it was the kind of music that the people we knew played.

As the audiences increased and the festival expanded from one to three days, we wanted to expand with it.

We never thought of making the Festival bigger in terms of more stages and other events, the Glastonbury route, if you like.

The fact it's all on one stage in one field is part of its appeal.

Peggy's first couple of years as a member of Fairport included an impressive array of now-legendary festivals. By the end of the decade, the (first) festival era was over. Festivals that had been destroyed by torrential rain and other disasters had put the majority of rock fans off the concept of 'rough gigging' in a remote field. The old guard preferred football stadia or the huge arena venues that were starting to appear. For younger fans, disco had created a new non-live genre of communal music experience, while punk had generated a whole new generation of small clubs much like those in which Peggy and Fairport started their careers. Having decided, for various reasons, that it was time to call it a day, Fairport did a final round of the remaining old-school venues – Victorian concert halls, Town Halls and student auditoria – before playing at one of the few remaining rock festivals, Knebworth. It was then ninety miles from the vast space where they opened to an audience that would peak at 100,000 to a small field where they were the headline act.

Their last UK gig was on home turf at Cropredy, their home village through most of the seventies. We thought we were saying Farewell Fairport, but we were wrong: it was the end of an era and the start of another.

I wouldn't call that Farewell gig at Cropredy a festival, though everyone counts it as the first Cropredy Festival. We'd played the local village fête for the past three years – the first was in Anne Crossman's garden. Although word got round and some fans turned up to see us in this unusual setting, we were only part of what went on. As a farewell, we decided to hire a field from a local farmer and put on a goodbye event ourselves. It was an outdoor concert, so it fits in with people's broad definition of a festival, but in every respect it was nothing like what it has become. I liked it because I could call it a day and walk home afterwards.

The stage was makeshift and very small. There was no backstage. On site facilities were, to put it mildly, limited. Aside from a couple of outstanding bookings in Europe, that was it. Or so we thought.

We decided to have a reunion a year later because people clearly enjoyed it and so did we.

To Fairport fans it became Cropredy Festival: we later rebranded it as Fairport's Cropredy Convention, though it had a few different names along the way, like A Weekend In The Country and the annual Reunion. The village has always been very involved and continues to be, I'm glad to say. To anyone living in the village, it's simply known as Fairport.

The early Cropredy fêtes should have been a clue: on each of the three years attendance had grown until it was too big an event to hold in a private garden. In the same way, Cropredy Festival quickly developed from an annual Fairport reunion to one of the most important festivals in the UK. Within a decade it had become more than a yearly pilgrimage for Fairport fans and was an event with an international reputation and audience too. Fans came from across Britain and Europe. Parties and individuals arrived annually from America. There were visitors from Australia, Russia and the Far East.

That quote from The Guardian sums it up – "As much a part of an English summer as Wimbledon". We had people coming from every continent except Antarctica.

Of course, this was before the internet and email had taken off. To keep in touch with people you relied on the post. We put out two newsletters a year which told everyone about the next to Cropredy and what Fairport were up to generally.

By the nineties, we had 23,000 names on our mailing list. That's far too many for a couple of people to deal with. For Christine, it was a full-time job in effect, but I was essentially a part-timer on that side of the business. Commitments with Tull and eventually Fairport themselves kept me away from home a lot.

If you want to know how this all started, you have to go back to when Chris and myself, and our two kids Matt and Steph moved into the village. We'd been living in Sutton Coldfield. Swarb was already there, having found a place when we all had to leave The Angel at short notice. I knew Cropredy from coming down to see him for rehearsals or to give him a lift somewhere. I thought it would be a great place for the family. What's more, property there was relatively cheap.

We got to know everyone in the village really quickly, much more so than Swarb in fact, because both our kids went to Cropredy village school so we attended lots of events and met loads of other parents. There were also two pubs. I used to enjoy the occasional pint, and that way I met the people we didn't get to know while picking the kids up on the school run. In those days, it wasn't a matter of lots of parents blocking the road as they sat in Range Rovers: there used to be this thing called walking. Kids went to schools that were local. Even in big towns the streets between your school and your home were normally safe places. So parents and kids walked to and from school. Even when it rained. Hard to believe isn't it?

If you're all standing around waiting for your kids, conversations start up. You see the same people every day. You get to know them.

We weren't typical of people living in Cropredy. We weren't local, obviously, like a lot of people. They became aware I was a musician and that I was friends with that other chap who'd been there a while. Eventually, they ask if we'd mind playing a gig for the church or a fundraiser for the school. We'd get various other Fairports to come and play or someone like Maddy Prior would come and do a gig, We had Richard Thompson, Bob Davenport, Ralph McTell, a who's who of the folk scene. I suppose it counts as a best-kept-secret because audiences would travel miles and pay top whack to see some of these people in plush venues. We had them in the school hall or the village hall for people from the village, real intimate little gigs.

We did a couple of these a year. Fairport still try to fit in a gig for the school when they want one if it coincides with one of our tours. As a result, there was rapidly a bond between Cropredy and Fairport.

## We are the Village Hall Preservation Society

It was as a direct result of those benefit gigs that we were asked to play the village fête in Anne Crossman's garden. It was organised by the Village Hall committee as a fundraising event, The money raised would be put towards urgent improvements that were needed. As I've said already, Fairport made use of the Village Hall as a convenient rehearsal space. Of course, we paid for it, but we knew what rehearsal spaces really cost and it was nothing like the small amount charged by a small village hall.

To them, the room was empty and earning nothing, so whatever it could make was an advantage, whereas a rehearsal space, say in London, would be at a premium and might need advance booking. That aside, it was better for the Fairports because it was literally about three minutes' walk from where we lived.

There was a thing before that which I don't think has really ever been written about. The year before we played in the Crossman garden, the committee had asked us to do a gig in the village hall. We'd pointed out it only held about sixty people and the stage was tiny. We managed to track down a farm in Aston le Walls, which is not far away, and they agreed to let us use it for a day. We put on something called "Fairport's Musical Get-together" or something like that. Big local audience, though not particularly to see us. It was more about supporting the village hall and having a nice day out at which there happened to be a group playing some tunes. That would have been 1975, the time of the *Rising for the Moon* line up. Then we were at Anne Crossman's for three consecutive years. The first year was just people from the village, maybe 250 or so. The year after it was over twice that. This was a bit silly, because it wasn't an event equipped to deal with a lot of people, it was a sort of homespun barbecue and stalls; Anne used to let people use her downstairs loo, which didn't really matter when people were local and could pop home if they needed a tiddle.

By 1978, word had spread. People were thinking of it as a Fairport gig, which it really wasn't. Everyone from the village did their bit towards what went on. Fairport lived in the village – at least two of us did – and we made our contribution to the proceedings.

Anyhow that year, 1800 people turned up. The roads were busy – not like the festival these days, but bear in mind we organise for the influx now, direct traffic and most importantly have somewhere for them to park when they get there.

I got really worried. We'd built up a good relationship with the village. I thought if they blamed us for this invasion it could undo all that. As it turned out our fans were really respectful and well-behaved... as they still are every year at Cropredy. The next year was the Farewell concert which we organised on the fringes of the village, so it was less disruptive.

The village has taken the Festival to its heart. I know some places resent the annual festivals which take place there. Some can be quite unwelcoming. At Cropredy, every-body pulls together. It's a real community spirit.

There's so many places doing breakfasts, all run by volunteers, all fund-raising, which reminds me of the homespun barbecue at Anne's. The Methodist Chapel does lunches and afternoon teas, with seats out on the green. That's right by where Swarb and I used to live and people sitting there are so close to where it all began: most probably don't even realise. The village has other things like the scarecrow festival this year. There are performances in the church and the village hall. There's music at The Brasenose and The Red Lion. There's even little pop-up stalls on people's walls, selling books and bric-a-brac... what Americans call yard sales.

On Saturday there's the car boot, too, which has become a massive event and quite a big fund-raiser for the cricket club. I talk about all these things as if I go to them all. Most of that is hearsay from what people at the festival or villagers tell me. I'm usually too tied up with things on the field to get into the village.

The good thing is that the festival strengthened our ties with Cropredy, not the other way round.

When we were working on the first Fairport box set, Peggy took me on a walking tour of the village as part of the research for the *Walk Awhile* guide to the village that was one of the freebies in the first run of the set. He'd lived in Barford for almost two decades, yet still it was impossible to go more than a few yards without someone coming up to say hello and have a chat. We must have declined more offers to come in for a cuppa "or something a bit stronger" in the course of that walk than I did in the rest of the year.

One of the aims of our walk was to call in the churchyard to find the grave of William Timms, so it could be photographed and used as an illustration alongside the notes for Red and Gold which quite clearly states "I may find my rest in Cropredy church." In amongst the fascinating and disorderly graves we wandered. The ancient mossy stones have their own tales to tell, chronicling the life (and deaths) of the village. Yet of Will Timms, there was no sign. The Red Lion, just across Red Lion Street, looked increasingly tempting. Time was clicking on. Peggy: "Tell you what, Nigel, I'll call Ralph. See if he remembers." Mr McTell couldn't remember and added, helpfully, that he may have made the name up. "Tell you what, Peggy: let's go do those shots on Cropredy Bridge."

In 2004, Nigel put together his second Fairport box set. This focused on Cropredy, or at least Fairport's part it in. It drew on the unreleased recordings from over the years and featured classic performances, one-offs, special guests and so on. It was planned as a way of documenting the first twenty-five years of the Festival. As it turned out, it was a complete record of the era when Chris, my wife, and I ran it. Personal circumstances meant that the band took it over the following year and have run it ever since. Simon, Gareth Williams and myself are heavily involved with that.

The book that accompanied the set is a really detailed history in which I shared many of my memories. As they say in Parliament, if you want to find out more, I refer the reader to my previous answers.

The upheaval that followed the personal rift in Peggy's homelife left a permanent reminder of how important Cropredy had become to fans. They found it impossible to imagine it not happening. The internet was abuzz with speculation. Rumours about whether there wouldn't be another Cropredy; suggestions about what to do if Fairport decided not to hold it; fears about Fairport not even existing to be part of it (perish the thought, malicious rumour mongers).

I had too much going on in my own life to pay any attention to that. I wasn't really aware of it, because I wasn't taking it in. So far as Fairport were concerned, I was like the walking wounded. They were supportive, more than you can imagine and certainly in ways you perhaps wouldn't think of, because above all we are a bunch of mates who are in a band rather than a band whose members try to get on with each other.

It was a period of deciding what we wanted to happen. Then we considered whether it could happen. Finally we had to decide how to make it happen. It was all too close to home, literally and metaphorically, for me to deal with. Yet I knew Chris and I were the people with the knowledge of how Cropredy worked. We'd been learning for twenty-five years. Chris had invested her working life in that time to Fairport and understandably she wasn't happy just to hand it all over. She was great about it, I have to say, once she'd made her position clear. She still comes to Cropredy every year and has a great time. It's good to see her enjoying herself and not having anything to worry about anything that's going on around her. For those first twenty-five years, she spent eighteen hours a day trapped in the caravan, making sure it all happened, dealing with any crisis that cropped up. She never got to see any of the festival she spent the rest of the year organising.

Because the Festival always ran so smoothly and continued to do so, people are unaware of the minor crises that can happen. Most are avoided because everything is planned in such detail beforehand – everything from setting up the stage and ensuring power and water supplies work to checking the loos and showers regularly and clearing the field. People are only aware of things like that if they go wrong, and we make sure they don't.

Someone who'd been involved even since the pre-Fairport Cropredy events was Ron Marchington, who, together with his wife Jean, ran the local scouts. They volunteered very early on to take on the unenviable task of keeping the place tidy. When you're talking about a village fête, it's not too big a task: you empty bins if they start to get full (having first made sure the bins are out before anyone arrives); after it's over you clear away any rubbish that's been left, which isn't too bad with a small local group, respecting someone's garden and observing the well-positioned 'Take Your Litter Home' signs. For a festival, especially one that lasts three days, the task increases exponentially. People are there for longer. They tend to stay in one place, and that may not be near a bin. When the day is over, it's dark and so collecting your rubbish isn't easy: it's bad enough making sure you've all the things you need to take. Then there's the amount of litter generated by people camping for three days.

Bless them, Ron and his faithful troupe of woggle-wearers have never shrunk from the task. Even as the number of days, the number of visitors and, inevitably, the amount of litter increased, they never suggested giving up. It's not a pleasant job and it's hard back-breaking work. I always hope people appreciate that and are generous when the scouts come round collecting money rather than rubbish on the Saturday.

I have to say that the crowd that comes to Cropredy is much better than most at using bins and not leaving rubbish. I've been told that by people who attend other festivals, both punters and organisers, and also by people who run sports events where crowds seem to be particularly prone to being litter louts. I've heard of places where the amount of litter dropped in towns hosting festivals has led to councils considering pulling the license: I am delighted that that has never happened at Cropredy. Walk from the Festival field into the village – via the main road, the canal towpath or the fields and cricket club and it's amazing that, despite the number of people, you see almost no litter. Pat on the back to Fairport fans for that – which is handy 'cos a lot of them wear back-pats... or is that packs?

Having attended Cropredy Festival with a large number of very different Cropredy virgins over the years – many of them regular attendees at other large scale events from Whitby to Sidmouth, Glastonbury to Donnington – a thing they always remark on is how clean and clear the field is each morning. One said, "You walk out at night and, of course, there's food wrappers, plastic glasses, boxes, even broken chairs. You have to watch your footing. That happens everywhere and it's nothing like as bad as most places. Next day, you get up and glance at the field as you walk past: it's pristine, like it's be built anew. It's Brigadoon." Another seriously conjectured that Fairport's crew used some enormous vacuum cleaner: he said, he'd heard it during the night when he went to the loo. I managed to convince him this was the combined effect of alcohol and the generator, not some gargantuan Dyson.

That is an amazing job and it amazes me every year. The Scouts go through the field and pick up everything that's been dropped, dumped and trampled underfoot by the dazed and confused. It means the field looks great, but it's important in terms of people's safety – there's nothing you can trip over, slip on or jab your foot with. It's not Health and Safety: we were doing it years before all that stuff started to kick in; it's just plain common sense. That was me and Chris you see – I was common and she was sensible – great team.

Litter's only one of the problems that you have to plan for. If you've nothing in place, by the time you realise there's an issue, it's too late.

There's all kinds of other things. The weather. If it rains, you have to try to keep it safe, stop it getting too muddy, have some provision if someone gets stuck, make sure roads and access ways stay clear. If it's hot we have emergency supplies of suncream and drinking water on hand.

There's a steady flow of artists to and from the site through the weekend. Watch any festival documentary and you see acts being shipped in or getting stuck somewhere. We have Martin Driver who drives a luxury minibus that we hire back and forth between the hotel in Banbury and the festival site. With the aid of marshals, the expertise of the police and the support of local people, we're able to keep the roads flowing: I can't think of a time when someone's missed their start time because they've been stuck in traffic.

Some artists just want to be there for their soundcheck and then in sufficient time ahead of their performances. That's fair enough. A lot more want to be around to see other acts. What's great is when some big name appears and then asks if they can come back next day just to enjoy the Festival. That's a real compliment. Bear in mind, that everybody is treated the same. There's no backstage luxury, no artists' enclosure where they can watch without being troubled by other people, no backstage bar. When they know that's the situation, even big name international stars are fine about it. It works the other way too: the crowd accepts if someone, no matter how famous, is out on the field, they are there to enjoy the music just like everyone else and tend not to hassle them. I think it helps that we have clearly defined and well organised signing sessions which almost every artist does.

We also get artists who attend the festival even though they're not appearing. Ralph comes every year, but performs only occasionally. annA rydeR's wacky camper van is usually somewhere in field 6A loaded up with instruments and t-shirts. Robert Plant's a regular visitor as is Joe Brown. Martin and Norma Carthy call in if they're on their way back from Sidmouth. Every time I go out to the bar I'm surprised who I bump into. On one occasion, there was quite a famous rock star (whom I won't name) and I thought 'I don't remember sending him a freebie', which of course I would have done if he'd asked. Turns out he'd bought his ticket just like everyone else. That is an amazing tribute to the festival in its own individual way.

Almost without exception artists get into the spirit of the event and go along with how things are. We don't have luxury dressing rooms, or nicely furnished hang outs. We don't do elaborate riders. Food is provided in a big tent with long wooden tables and plastic seats. You can get tea and coffee. We've never had a backstage bar. If you want a drink, you go to the bar in the field like everyone else. I think only one person ever objected to that arrangement and that was Lulu.

Lulu appeared as part of Jools Holland's show. That was the year we first had the big screen. It was part of what he did with all his shows. We realised that it would look ridiculous to have him on a huge screen and not Fairport. So big screen it was. If you do something that high profile one year, you can't just drop it. We were committed. A couple of years ago we changed it from a single screen at the back of the stage, which only some of the audience can see, to a screen either side, so now everyone can see.

Having screens demands more than people might think. Lots more staff – camera crews; replacement crews because people can't film all day and you can't suddenly have nothing on the screen when an act is on; graphics and messaging; directors; technicians. It's an operation in itself.

Credit for this has to go to Nev Bull who masterminds the whole operation, both in advance and during Fairport's performance. Nev is also the man behind those videos which appear the screen to accompany some songs – most notably *Matty Groves* – on the big screen when people start to get tired of close ups of our ugly mugs. Usually, the big screen projections (which is probably the wrong word, but you know what I mean) are very much of the moment. I'm pleased to say that some of Nev's animations have made it to Fairport DVDs so people who couldn't make it to Cropredy can still enjoy them.

We also took the opportunity to do some one-off things, like the subtitles for *Naked Highwayman* or the documentary for *Festival Bell* – from the silly to the sublime. It's quite multimedia, which is something Fairport could claim to be pioneers of.

OK we're no Pink Floyd, but when we toured *Babbacombe Lee*, the first time, we had speech sections which were played in and programmes that were like contemporary newspapers. We did the same thing for the first Cropredy programme which was a newspaper about Fairport. When we first played *Hiring Fair* on tour, we had a slideshow to accompany it, which was a series of shots I'd taken of my daughter Steph in period costume.

It's easy looking back at photos, posters and attendance figures to see the impressive curve along which the Festival developed. Conversations with regulars often include the question "when did such and such start?" When did it go from two days to three? When did they first start having rowing club breakfasts? When were the first 'Fringe events'? When did the toilets at the bottom of the field first appear?"

They are all milestones on a path of continuous, steady, positive and purposeful development and improvement.

We always listen to suggestions, wherever they come from. If they're good, we see if they are practical – that means a) can it be done, b) can we afford to do it (in terms of manpower as well as money) and c) can we continue to do it? Some ideas just wouldn't work and tend to get forgotten but over the years some of the dafter ideas have been to allow people to camp in their place on the performance field, to stream the performances so people could stay in their tents to watch and to split the field down the middle into smoking and non-smoking, the way cinemas used to be.

When someone asks for your memories of Cropredy or your highlights, you naturally tend to think about performances that were particularly memorable whether they were spectacular like the Australian Pink Floyd and Alice Cooper, or musically stunning such as anytime Richard has played or wacky like the Leningrad Cowboys or of course, just plain disastrous. I won't give an example of the last category. There was one instance when a band from the more recent era of rock music who had recently reformed managed to get a gig: the attraction was obvious and naturally had a kind youth appeal that the Fairports themselves don't necessarily provide. Most acts, certainly in the daytime, are given an hour's stage time. Everything's worked out to allow for turnarounds – you don't put an act with a big set up straight after one that takes a while to derig: before Fairport we always have a solo artist with one instrument, for example. That's all designed so that while there is a break to give people chance to go recharge their glasses, have a tiddle, chat to their old and new-found friends and so on, people won't be sitting around for too long.

Each act knows exactly what time their set starts, what time they should check in on the field and when they should report backstage. This particular group played for about forty minutes including the encore they were sent back to do. When we said they had to do more, they just replied they didn't know anything else and refused. It was very awkward. It meant people were going to be sitting around for what would seem ages.

Support acts were something we didn't really have to worry about in the early days. It was a one day thing, starting in the afternoon and often ending with a very long Fairport set. The people on before us were our mates or people like Richard who always, to this day, tends to have his own set whenever he appears with the Fairports.

When people ask me when the first Cropredy was, I really don't know what to answer. It's a question I've been asked a lot over the years and, to be fair, as part of the very small team who ran it for the first twenty-five years, it's the sort of thing you'd expect me to know. My usual response of "I'm just the bass player: I go dumdum-de-dum-dedum" doesn't work in this case. Most people, sensibly, count from the Farewell Concert in 1979. That was the first festival-type event in Cropredy that the Fairports ran. There had been four years of Cropredy events at which Fairport appeared before that though. At the time, we definitely thought of it as an ending not a beginning of something. So, it's both right and wrong at the same time.

Then in 1980, we had a Reunion Concert. That was organised by Chris, myself and the Village Hall Committee. It was all homespun and small scale: we even sent hand-written postcards to people who'd bought tickets by mail order the previous year asking for suggestions. I still have the poster we produced for that hanging on the wall in my home in Banbury. Luckily, we'd saved two for sentimental reasons, so when Chris and I split up we didn't end up arguing over custody of the poster. Custody of the festival turned out to be a different matter.

It was Fairport Convention and surprise guests. One of those was Ralph McTell. The others were less of a surprise because they'd already appeared in the afternoon – John & Sue Kirkpatrick and Richard & Linda Thompson. I think we were aiming for a divorce rate record there! The opening act was billed as Captain Coco's Country Dance Band. If you look back at lists of who appeared at Cropredy, they seem to be regulars. Just to clear things up, it wasn't a real band. In those days, we'd start Cropredy by inviting people to come and dance in front of the stage... not festival rock dancing, proper English country dances with a caller. Captain Coco was a band with me, Simon and anyone who knew the tunes who wanted to join us. Dave Langston played bass: I was on either guitar or drums. Sheena Powell was our caller. Chris Leslie was one of the band members. We disguised ourselves by wearing red noses and the sort of bald wigs that clowns wear: I liked mine so much I grew one permanently.

Speaking of Chris, he's someone who's been around Cropredy since it first started. That applies whatever start year you pick. He's appeared with his brother John. I think he did it two or three times with Steve Ashley – he was on Steve's *Family Album* with the Fairports (except Swarb who tended not to go in for the doing-your-mate-a-favour kind of sessions we did at Woodworm): that album was the second release on Woodworm Records. Chris also played with Beryl Marriott's group: he was on her *Weave The Mirror* CD – another Woodworm release. He was a guest during Fairport's set on occasions, including the time he stood in for Ric for the whole set. Eventually, not having learned his lesson, he joined full-time twenty-one years ago and has been trying to find Maart's map to the escape tunnel ever since. Only joking, of course, he's really happy in the Fairports and the current line-up is the longest lasting the band has ever had by far. Twenty-one years – almost half the lifetime of the band – yet we still think of him as the new boy!

We had the Reunion gig, the four members in the final line up plus Richard, DM and guests, in 1980. Simon invented his Cropredy catchphrase "same time next year". The crowd shouted yes. We were committed.

In '81, it wasn't possible to hold the Festival at Cropredy. The guy who owned the fields had passed away and there was no one who could give definite permission for the Festival to take place there. He'd died intestate. (As Swarb said, "I don't care what state he's in, can we have the reunion there?"). That year Cropredy was at Broughton Castle. It's the home of Lord and Lady Saye and Sele and is a for-real castle with a moat, just the other side of Banbury.

It was an unusual festival in other ways too – we screened the *In One End And Out The Other* film (another Chris Leslie / Cropredy Connection): it was also one of the few appearances of The GPs, a sort of fun pub band with Ralph, RT, me and DM doing stuff we just enjoyed playing – rock'n'roll, country, Dylan.

It also saw Judy Dyble singing with The Fairports for the first time since 1968. Not only did the Festival not have a regular venue yet, a name seemed to be a problem, now extended to a two-day event, they christened it *The Weekend Reunion*.

This was the first time a Festival had been really well documented. We put out an LP, which was Woodworm WR001, the very first release on my own label. It was a proud moment for me, It was called *Moat on the Ledge* (see what we did there?) and had versions of us doing some Fairport classics like *Walk Awhile*, *Rosie* and *Matty*. I've never counted up how many versions of *Matty Groves* we've released, never mind how many times we must have played it. If all our versions of *Matty Grove* were laid end to end... Lord Barnard would probably come in and kill them.

Of course, a couple of decades after this, when the demise of Woodworm Records was one result of my marriage breakup, Fairport started our own label which we called Matty Grooves. The name came to us courtesy of Graham Post who printed our Cropredy programmes at the time. There were also some things on *Moat on the Ledge* which fans wouldn't have, stuff we used to do around the time of *Full House* because that was the band that was reunioning (!) that year – *Poor Will*, *Country Pie*, *High School Confidential*. There was also an unreleased Richard Thompson song which is always good for sales.

Aside from the LP, there was also a video. We're talking commercially released VHS tape. It has a certain charm and obvious archive value. I've been involved in some impressive video productions: this definitely wasn't one of them. Changing the subject...

Years later, we unearthed the tape of The GPs, which we'd made just so we had a souvenir of the four of us playing together. It still sounded OK. We put it out as a CD on Woodworm. It was our first CD release, I think.

Johnny Jones – Jonah to his mates – was our compere in those early days. He was a great fan and supporter of the band and came every year until his tragically early death. The tree where he used to go when he needed a few minutes' peace and quiet is known as Jonah's Oak: we recorded a tune by Ric dedicated to it and to him.

There's loads of great Jonah stories. Thanks to Paul Mitchell who funded it, he made a double CD of them. As well as Jonah's dulcet tones, it had music by Fairport and various other people. I suspect it's long deleted now, but if you know someone who has a copy it's worth giving it a listen.

We couldn't include *Jonah's Oak* this year at Cropredy. Because we were marking fifty years of Fairport there was a lot to squeeze in. Inevitably, some things had to go. When Richard decides he wants to play *Sloth*, you're not going to say no, but you also know that three or four songs are going to get squeezed off the list. Inevitably what we cut was the newer material because we're there every year and can play them anytime. Who knows when we'll next have Judy or Iain or Ashley or DM or Richard. They'll probably all be back. I certainly hope so. But probably not all in the same year, on stage together. We restrict ourselves to a three hour set, though we did start early this year because we had so much to get through. Our longest set at Cropredy was over four and a half hours and had forty-six songs. That's hard work, believe me. There have been quite a few times when we've played both Friday and Saturday and of course you quite often see one or more Fairports cropping up in other people's sets as guests or part of their band.

There's quite a sad story behind the 1981 Festival. We didn't think we could get the Castle, basically because they thought we were a bunch of long haired folkies. They are proper aristocracy, beyond posh. And what were we? Struggling folk rock musicians...

the nouveau poor! However, Bruce Rowland knew a chap who worked at a building society in Banbury and was also in the Banbury Rotary Club. Let's call him Geoff. Geoff was aware that Fairport were looking for somewhere to hold our reunion. He said we should do it at the Castle. We thought this was impossible but he explained that he knew his Lordship and if we were prepared to do the gig and make a donation to charity from the proceeds, then there was a good chance he would give his permission. He did. There was, however a big problem with security.

There were two ways into the Castle which meant we had to man two gates all the time. I know we do that now, but it's a bigger, smoother operation these days. Back then we were learning and no one had written the handbook on how to run an outdoor festival so we could refer to it.

**Some years later both Kate Collins and Chris Pegg did exactly that. With the exception of recent updates on Health and Safety and Security, they remain the standard works, based very much on what was learned developing Cropredy into what has been described "as the most crowd-friendly, welcoming, hassle-free, efficient and enjoyable festivals in the world."**

We asked the Rotarians or the Round Table to man one gate. We explained our system which Ron Marchington and his team of senior boy scouts would be operating on the other gate. Essentially, you take the person's ticket – or direct them to the sales point if they haven't got one – you tear their ticket in half, give them half as proof they're paid and keep the other for accounting purposes. At the end of the day, you count the stubs and you know how many people have been let it. You can then match this against takings. The numbers should tally. I don't know if we put wristbands on people in those days: I suspect that came later.

You have to remember this was in the days before debit cards and buying on line and such. If you wanted a ticket in advance, you'd have to send a cheque: once it had cleared, Chris, from our office, or front room as we tried to think of it, would post you a ticket from the post office next door. These days people buy tickets up front because they know that the Festival has sold out several times. Back then people turned up, cash in hand, and paid on the door. There was a lot of money floating around and you had to have a way of keeping tabs on it, especially as some of it as going to charity.

PayPal in those days was your mate who's decided to treat you. A mobile phone was having a particularly long cord so you could take it into the next room. I think Cropredy telephone exchange, because it still had its own, was run manually with an operator you spoke to and a load of jacks and sockets.

The festival office was a small mobile caravan, which is where you'd find Christine and myself along with our good friend, Ray Mayo, and his wife Geraldine. They'd count and check the money as it came in. Then Ray would go off and deposit it in the night safe at Barclays Bank in Banbury.

If all this sounds like it belongs to another era, it's because it was.

Ray was brilliant at this accounting. The most the gate takings were ever out was ten quid one year and he sweated blood trying to track down where the error happened. They were meticulous.

To digress slightly, I should tell you they were both in the police force. When they got married, they asked me to be their best man. I got up to do my best man's speech and did my Dixon of Dock Green impression – "evenin' all". I had the whole thing worked out. It was going to be hilarious. Except the moment I said those two words,

I knew I'd got it wrong. Two words in and I wasn't going down well. I felt the mood change. The crowd turned against me. I dropped all the jokes about taking down my particulars and using my bass to accompany them to the station. I made a very short, dull speech. It didn't go down well, but it went down a lot better than the one I nearly made.

Time came to go on stage. I knew a lot of people had come in, around 4,000 as it turned out. It didn't look to me like there was enough money. I went up on stage. It was still light enough to see the crowd. There was obviously a lot of them. Looking at a crowd from a stage you can judge numbers much better than from any other perspective. I glanced to the side and there was Ray counting the money. I was worried. If the amount was short I didn't want anyone thinking we'd ripped off the charity. Christine and I were the promoters and therefore ultimately responsible. This wasn't a matter of being mercenary. It was down to wanting to know if the system was working properly and if not, why not? Once you knew that, you could do something about putting it right.

We finished the concert. I was still worried. Ray had paid the money in and he was concerned.

Chris and I went back to our house. I was really worried. I was convinced the takings were light. Not ten quid out, thousands of pounds light. I had no idea how it could have happened. I knew I was going to have a sleepless night with worry.

Next day, we had to deal with the load out at Broughton Castle and see people off. I watched the last tent come down and the last car leave the car park: I remember it clearly, a deux-cheveaux. The whole weekend had gone smoothly. The drug squad had been there both nights. I was introduced to them by Ray at the bar, but I'd had advance warning.

I can say this now because Ray, bless his soul, is no longer with us. He rang me on the Thursday to say "I've got some good news and some bad news for you".

"What's the bad news?"

"There'll be seven guys there all weekend, plain clothes, from the drug squad. If you see someone with a spliff or something, tell them to cool it and be careful."

"OK. Thanks for the tip off. What's the good news?"

"I made them buy tickets."

I had a word with them on the Saturday to see how it had gone. They said, Great, they'd really enjoyed it. I told them I meant in terms of their constabulary duty. They said it had been fine, they'd had to have a quiet word with a couple of people but there'd been no need to arrest anybody: clean bill of health.

That was great but my other worry hung over me like the sword of whats-his-name.

Sunday night, when I got home, I couldn't rest easy. I had to do something. It was around eight o'clock. The phone rang. It was Ray again.

He said "I've got some bad news and some good news."

"What? Again? What's the bad news?"

"The drugs squad have just arrested four people at Broughton Castle."

"When was this?"

"In the last hour. And it's class A drugs."

"That's ridiculous. I saw the last of the punters leave. All the musicians have long gone. What's the good news?"

"They raided the Castle. They're arrested a relative of his lordship up from London."

That was a relief and made me smile. It didn't get rid of my money worries though

I decided I'd call Ray, and Ron from the scouts, and Geoff from the Round Table, to an emergency meeting in the morning and try to get to the bottom of what had happened. No excuses. Everyone was going to have to be there. I was going to get to the bottom of it. I went round to the bank first thing on Monday and discovered we were several thousand pounds light.

Chris and I had moved in to the house in Barford about a month before. Even back then, when the Cropredy Reunion was a much smaller event, this was particularly bad timing. Now here I was gathering people for this heavy meeting. It wasn't the kind of house-warming you want. Ray was in a real state: he'd just bought a new car and was convinced suspicion would fall on him. Compared to buying a new house, which I had to say represented quite a step up in the world, that was a small expenditure to account for.

I didn't think there was any dishonesty involved anywhere, but clearly the money must be somewhere... unless a lot of people had been let in for free, which I doubted. Everyone knew it was all raising money in a good cause, several good causes in fact. We all gathered in our dining room, around, ironically, a big round table I'd just bought. Everyone looked worried. Everyone had that face when you know you're not guilty and are trying to look not guilty but failing as a result. It was like a convention of the world's worst poker players.

I knew it could get heated so I deliberately took steps to keep things calm. First I asked Ron if he had his ticket stubs. He produced a big plastic bag: he knew how many tickets were in there. That meant we knew how many people had come through his gate and we could work out who had paid in advance and therefore how much money would have been taken on the day. Ray, being efficient, had kept clear records of which amounts came from which gate. Ron then gave us the receipts from the cash which had been taken over to the caravan for money counted and countersigned by Ray. It was a nice clear system, which clearly worked. What do they call it these days? Transparency. Ron, after a couple of years, was used to the system.

Then I turned to Geoff and asked for the stubs from the Round Table gate. He didn't have them. The guy had forgotten to tear them in half. I started to get cross. I explained he only had one thing to do. How could he not do it? How could we check the money was right. Geoff was really apologetic and said the guy in question was really sorry. He said a lot of people didn't want their tickets tearing. They wanted them as souvenirs. He just stopped doing it. I don't know whether that was a decision or just the fact he didn't get in the habit.

The simple fact was our system hadn't been put into operation. We now had no record of how many people had come in. That was it. The end of the trail. I was left trying to decide what to do next.

I didn't even get any comfort when the Banbury Guardian came out on Thursday. There was not a word about the drugs bust of his lordship's relatives (surprise, surprise); there wasn't any detailed coverage of all the performances at the Festival which was disappointing. There was, however, on the front page, a photo of topless girl taken at the Festival and an article about how we should take steps to stop people stripping off at outdoor events.

Then, as I was checking the list of court prosecutions again, I came across the name of the guy who had, supposedly, been tearing the tickets on the gate at Broughton. He worked in a shop in Banbury and had just been done for embezzlement. He'd been sent down for two years, so it must have been a major sum. I don't know why the Round Table thought he was a suitable chap to have in charge of takings on the gate at a Festival.

Perhaps someone said he was good with money. Which he was, but not in a good way. Obviously, that was the way the money went. Pop goes the weekend!

Allegedly (as my lawyers have advised me to say).

It was terrible for us. It was terrible for Lord and Lady Saye and Sele, who were trying to raise money for a minibus with a lift fitted that they would give to a local disabled charity. It would make a big difference to the lives of a lot of people. A genuinely good cause. As the promoter, I'd offered him 25% of the profit, which from the previous year and obvious increased interest, I was sure would be plenty to take him over his target. Without the money, from the gate, which was run by a charity heavily involved in the fund-raising, we weren't even going to be in profit. There'd be no money to hand over. Woodworm, who ran the Festival, and were a pretty new company, stood to make a loss on its main activity.

It still grieves me to think about it. So many people giving their time, energies and talents, such a well-thought out system, and yet so many people lost out because of the fraud and greed of one man. No matter how many selfless people there are, it just takes one selfish one to screw the whole thing up.

It's thirty-five years ago. Thinking about it makes me both angry and tearful still. How could he do that? I'll never understand.

Peggy has clearly become emotional. We're sitting at the small metal table outside his house in Brittany. The sky is blue. The birds are singing. Passing neighbours, seeing us outside, have been stopping their cars. "Bonjour, Pegg-ee, comment ça va?" Playing back the recording, the scene recreates itself... Peggy's voice, usually suppressing laughter, the birdsong, the sunshine, the occasional clink of a wine glass, the sound of tyres on the gravel, a car door closing, a Breton voice, my greeting in faltering French, then the tape pauses. Memories preserved over the couple of months it's taken to get to this point in transcription, still fresh, rich and vivid. As Peggy has related the last story, the tone of his voice has been audibly darker as his mind went back and vivid memories returned, as clear down the long tunnel of time as my more recent recollections. I suggest perhaps we should pause as the recollection had upset him.

Yes probably a good idea. Let's just round the story off.

We'd no way of getting the money back. We were all sure what had happened but couldn't prove it. No point in playing the blame game. Ultimately the buck stopped with me. The one positive thing – apart from the obvious fact that everyone had a great time and pretty good live album or two came out of it – was that we learned from what had gone wrong. We never made a similar mistake again. It is a good little mantra – 'See what was great and keep it: learn from your mistake and don't repeat it.' Have I just made that up? Probably not.

The following year we returned to Cropredy. They welcomed us back and the disappearing gate money was forgotten about. I had that productive cup of tea at the home of Dorothy King, the lady with the mynah bird that learned to swear courtesy of Fairport roadies. That got us permission to use the field where the Festival takes place to this day. You almost couldn't design a more ideal spot: it's a natural amphitheatre;

the only access is through other fields which means it's easy to keep secure; there's land all around for parking and camping; there's plenty of room for backstage and backstage camping too; the field drains into the river.

When Christine and I started the festival we had great help from two electricians. Wayne Averill and Mick Peters. Mick has been with us ever since: he tour manages our winter tour, and site manages the Cropredy festival. He is named by the band "Sir Mick". And quite rightly so – as without him we would be lost, in more ways than one! When we were working on the *Box of Pegg's* set, I spent the week leading up to Cropredy at Peggy's house in Banbury. There had been heavy rain that summer and lots of flooding. On the Monday a report from the field told us that at last it was dry enough to continue putting up the stage, but the whole of field 6A, behind the stage, was under about a foot of water. It's used for artists and close friends of the band to camp. That seemed out of the question. By Wednesday, when I went to pitch my tent, it was totally dry. Yet again the weather gods had smiled down on Cropredy.

That was the other year the Festival nearly wasn't at Cropredy. We couldn't be sure of the weather. So, Gareth Williams made contingency plans. If it hadn't cleared up, or the field was too wet to use, we'd identified a disused airfield we could hire with a huge hanger and plenty of space for parking and camping, all linked by the runways. It didn't come to that.

We discovered the flooding was the result of barriers on the Thames being closed which stopped the Cherwell emptying. I suppose they were worried about London getting flooded. I can't say who, but someone had a word with someone who knew the right person to speak to so the barriers were opened. I imagine someone saying "You've got to let the water through because there's this really nice folk-rock festival that can't happen unless you do."

There's thousands of Cropredy stories. Dozens from every year. And that's just my perspective. Enough for a book in their own right, which is a thought. As you said, best to knock off for a bit.

Peggy heads inside, his empty glass magnetically attracted to a suitable bottle. I glance across the Breton-paved yard to the open sided barn. On one of the wooden support pillars, the breezes catches a piece of paper – the setlist for that year's debut appearance of The Bretles. I imagine a similar makeshift setup forty years earlier in Anne Crossman's garden. Old habits die hard and Peggy is now directly involved in two annual festivals.

Each year we hold a get together with music. There's a barbecue and the whole village attends. It's in our garden, so it does mirror those early Cropredys at Anne Crossman's. I usually invite over some mates from the UK – annA rydeR's been and John Watterson – and local musicians like Dan Ar Braz and James Wood. The little community where I live in Brittany is called Lesténo so we've called the event Festéno. Thanks to local farmer Claude le Goff for the name.

I always said Cropredy was like a hobby that got out of hand. Some people have a train set and end up building a layout that is amazingly detailed and fills the attic. Some people have massive collections of every recording released by their favourite artist. I started a little local festival where the members of a band that thought it had its day could get together; I thought it would be an event for us to have fun and a few fans and local people to enjoy it. It was never more than that. I was wrong. Fairport become a successful full-time band again, with solid line-ups and perhaps more success than we'd ever had. Cropredy became an internationally celebrated event that regularly sells out and attracts an audience from right across the world. A village that almost no-one had heard of is now famous, entirely because of what Fairport do there once a year. We get bands from Australia, Europe, America, Russia, the Far East who've heard of it and want to come play.

Rather more than a nice little hobby.

I've learned how to do that. Which means, I suppose, I also know how to avoid it.

Festéno is something for our friends in the village, a few more who know us in other parts of Brittany and some mates from England. The last two groups are very much the guests of the first, who are the people who run it.

It's very much a local event for local people!

# Chapter 12

# Songs from the Woodworm
*You take stock of the new day*

Following 1979's moratorium on matters Fairport (outside the annual reunion), Peggy accepted an unexpected offer to join Jethro Tull, initially for a seven week US tour as stand-in bass player. Having worked amidst Fairport's failing fortunes, membership of the hugely successful Tull was a new day indeed.

Tull were such a huge band, especially in the States. There's a poster on the wall in the other room of three nights Fairport did supporting Tull at the Fillmore in 1970. So we had met the band, or at least an earlier incarnation of it, but we hadn't actually bonded in any real way.

Jethro Tull were formed in 1967, the same year as Fairport. In the course of that year, they'd tried out a number of band names (among them Bag o' Blues and Navy Blue, before settling on one which paid tribute to an obscure 18th agriculturalist; if, some early interviews suggest, the choice was to draw attention to the father of modern farming and inventor of the seed drill, the ploy failed: mention Jethro Tull and most people think of the band or its lead singer. In TV and radio interviews, it was often clear that the interviewer clearly thought Ian Anderson was Jethro Tull! It's a far from unique problem – vide Alice Cooper, Lynyrd Skynyrd, Belle and Sebastian, Franz Ferdinand, Principle Edward's Magic Theatre: file under "By the way, which one's Pink".

Initially, they were a blues band – their time line appears in the 1967 Blues Boom section of Pete Frame's Rock Family Trees. They rapidly moved into a unique prog-fusion of jazz and folk, consolidating their reputation with a string of hits and some memorable if intimidating Top of the Pops appearances. John Glascock, the band's bass player for the past three years, was taken seriously ill. With a major US tour about to begin, Ian Anderson approached Peggy to ask him if he'd stand in on bass. But that crucial stage in his career almost didn't happen.

I was busy setting up Woodworm Studios. Fairport Convention had effectively ceased to function beyond the annual reunion (and at the time we had no idea how long that would go on for.) I kept getting phonecalls from Ian Anderson – messages left for me. The only Ian Anderson I knew was the musician who edited Southern Rag, which became Folk Roots: I knew he had a group called The English Country Blues Band because he'd sent me a copy of their LP. I presumed he was ringing to get a gig at Cropredy. At the time, the only people who played Cropredy were people we knew personally, often with a close connection to Fairport because in those days it was still a fairly small-scale Fairport event. So I put off returning his call. I may even have told Christine to say I was out if he rang.

One day, Christine had gone to the shops. The phone rang. I answered it. It was Ian Anderson, but the other Ian Anderson, the one from Jethro Tull. He began by asking if something was wrong because normally if he asked someone to ring back they did so straight away. I'd not responded for a couple of weeks.

I apologised and asked what it was about. He said he'd like me to come and audition to be his bass player, because Barry Barlow his drummer and Richard Digance who was one of his mates had recommended me. He knew about Fairport's packing in and everything.

His usual bass player John Glascock was ill and couldn't do the next tour with them. They were going to America in two weeks and needed a bass player. It was seven weeks in the States. Obviously that was too good an opportunity to miss – though I nearly had by not returning his calls. I went down to Radnage where Ian lived: he, Martin Barre and Barry Barlow were there – they played a few chord sequences and got me to play along with them. Then he asked "Do you have any tax problems?" I said I hadn't because I'd seldom earned enough to have to pay tax. So he asked whether I could learn the material in time and if so, did I want the job for seven weeks.

I said that'd be no problem. The album that was current at the time was *Stormwatch*: Ian had played most of the bass on it because John was ill. It was complicated stuff.

So that's how I became a member of Jethro Tull for seven weeks... and ended up staying for sixteen years.

After I accepted their invitation to join the band, I had two weeks to learn the set for a huge American tour. We already had a holiday planned for myself, Christine and the kids, Steph and Matt – Ralph McTell who has a cottage in Cornwall had invited us down there – I didn't want to disappoint them so agreed I would get on with my Tull initiation while they relaxed and enjoyed their break. I was swotting away: it was very different from the sort of thing I'd been doing with The Fairports, sometimes incredibly complex stuff. It was really hard work, but I shut myself away and got on with it. After a week or so, I was confident that I had a grasp on most of the songs. It was *Heavy Horses*, *Songs from the Wood* and the *Stormwatch* album. However, there was still some stuff I still couldn't get. Martin Barre, who's a fellow Brummie though he comes from a posher part of the city than me, invited me to his place in Henley-on-Thames to go through the stuff with him. I went down there for a kind of crash course in the things that were still causing me problems. I was there for a couple of nights which was fantastic because he was really helpful, particularly with the stuff with really complex time signatures. You've got to remember that if you were a non-musician, or a rock musician, like myself or Martin or Ian at the time, you'd no formal way of writing that stuff down: everybody had their own system, but only you understood it. Everybody would count stuff differently: if you look at Martin Barre's foot, even today, when he's playing it seems to have no relation to the tempo or the rhythm of what he's actually playing at the time. It's weird but it's what works for him. He plays it perfectly.

As I said, some of it was very complex music but I got my head around it all with his help and a lot of hard graft.

When we turned up for the production rehearsals, a lot of the really complex stuff wasn't in the set anyway.

Unlike Fairport, who've always been a bunch of mates who play music together and like to have a good time, the Tull crowd, including the huge crew, aren't party animals and tend to keep themselves to themselves. It was very generous of Martin to be so supportive and he's remained a good friend right up to the present day.

After Ian confirmed I'd got the gig and I'd be off to America in a rapidly decreasing number of days (I was really starting to wish I'd returned his call sooner and given myself more time), he suggested I come down to his house, Pophleys, and he'd explain how things worked within the band. Basically, he said he was always busy, arranging details, doing publicity, giving interviews and so on, so I probably wouldn't see much of him on tour apart from on stage (which did indeed turn out to be the case), and he added that the rest of the band would have a lot to say about him – "So, to save time, I'll tell you what they think of me, right now". Which is exactly what he did, and it wasn't exactly flattering, and, do you know what, he was exactly right. It was perfect: over the next seven weeks, various band members would start in: "You know Ian... he's [this that or the other]" and every time I knew exactly what was coming.

I noticed that there were always two limos at the airport to pick us up: there was always mass avoidance of getting in the limo with Ian – and not just because he was a pipe smoker. David Palmer would join him: he's from the Black Country and a fellow pipe smoker.

Tull itself was like an army operation – again totally different from Fairport – they had two crews so that while one did the gig, the other would be on the road with an identical load of equipment, maybe four big trucks, heading to set up the next night ready for the band's arrival, which normally was by plane. In total, Tull on Tour in the States involved about sixty people working for the band, quite aside from all the staff at the huge venues we played. The fact that, aside from the band itself obviously, you'd be working with a different set of people every other night made it even harder for a new boy like myself to get to know who's who.

It was very professional. And Ian ran the whole thing himself: the band didn't even have a manager. There was Kenny Wylie, the production manager, who was astonishing: he'd reccy venues, check the get in, decide where lights would go and so on. He had a huge amount of responsibility. It was like an army operation. At the time, it was one of the biggest productions touring the states.

So off we went: the first gig was in Canada at a venue that holds something like sixteen thousand people. That's a much bigger crowd than I was used to playing to in recent years. I was also aware how dedicated and passionate Tull's fans were so there was a lot of pressure.

Peggy made his debut with Tull on October 5 1979 at the Maple Leaf Gardens, Toronto.
The set list that night was: *Dark Ages, Home, Orion, Flying Dutchman, Old Ghosts, Elegy, Dun Ringill, Something's On The Move, Aqualung, King Henry's Madrigal* (which included a drum solo), *Heavy Horses, No Lullaby* (whose extended flute solo, included *God Rest Ye Merry Gentlemen, Kelpie, Bourée), Bach's *The Well-Tempered Clavier, Songs From The Wood, Jams O'Donnell's Jigs, Thick As A Brick, Too Old To Rock'N'Roll, Cross-Eyed Mary, Minstrel In The Gallery/Locomotive Breath/Dambusters March*. *Warm Sporran* was played from tape as part of the intro. The orchestral version of *Warchild* was played as the audience left.
To give a sense of perspective this was exactly two months and one day since Fairport's farewell concert at Cropredy. However the lassez-faire, come-as-you-are approach of Fairport on stage was clearly going to be a thing of the past.

The night before the first gig, at Maple Leaf Gardens, we were all in some posh hotel – again quite a contrast from those final weeks on the road with Fairport. It felt like *Help!* where The Beatles all live in one long terrace house, each with his own front door. We were all in adjacent hotel rooms, occupying one corridor.

It's about 11.00 the night before the gig. I haven't gone out because I'm nervous. I've got my bass and my Walkman on, desperately trying to remember the arrangements. That was another change from Fairport – the complexity of the music... and the fact you knew you wouldn't get away with getting it wrong.

There's a knock on the door. It's a big box being delivered with my name on it. So I open it up and inside were two yellow towelling outfits painted with green stripes. I honestly thought it was some kind of joke: you know, maybe some arcane Tull initiation ceremony or something. Then I found the note:

"Dear Peggy,

This the outfit for tomorrow night. Put it on and come out into the corridor at midnight and we'll all have a look."

By now I was convinced it was a wind up – make the new boy put on a ridiculous outfit and we'll all have a laugh before we go to bed. I decided it was best to go along with it. So, come midnight, I put this stupid thing on and, with some trepidation, prepared to step out into the corridor of this hotel. I expected flashing cameras and the rest of Tull having a good laugh at my expense. I opened the door and stepped out.  As did the rest of  the band, all very sheepishly. Four of them, myself included, looked absolutely ridiculous. All the outfits were indescribably bad. Barry Barlow, the drummer, came out last, and we all went "You lucky bastard". He looked great. He'd got a netted light blue vest and shorts with matching blue running shoes.

He just said, "It's cool when I stand up. But try sitting down in this thing." It was so tight, and when he sat down – which is how as a drummer he spent the entire set – it pulled against him and he looked about eighteen stone. Unflattering doesn't enter into it.

We wore them, as instructed, on the first night. I made myself feel better because I wore the big brown boots I'd found in a second-hand shop in Exeter – the ones I'm wearing on *Nine*, the famous shot outside the Brasenose. They are now owned by Tristan Bryant and still very much in use. (I include that fact as a testament to the skill of British shoemakers – though you might think they're a load of cobblers.)

I was very aware that Maureen, one of Sylvia Nicol's best mates who'd been a bridesmaid at her wedding to Simon, was in the audience. It was so embarrassing... and obviously word of how ridiculous I looked would make it back to England long before I did.

When Peggy joined Tull, the excellence of his bass playing was beyond question and the track record of artists he played with live and on disc was immediately impressive. However, it is fair to say his skills as a composer tended to slip below the wire... there's that peerless classic *Hungarian Rhapsody*, some sections of *Babbacombe Lee* (where the ambiguity of the labelling hid the extent of his contribution), the remarkable setting for *Polly on the Shore* and a handful of tunes. Yet these latter did not escape Ian Anderson's notice...

I haven't written that many. But there were those things I'd written for Fairport: I think we did *Jams O'Donnell's Jigs* and *Peggy's Pub*. Tull had always done some instrumentals – things Ian had written and classical stuff like *Bourree*. Mine were a lot more folkie... and simpler to play.

It came about because, like the other members of Tull, he gave me my own little feature slot. As a bass player you don't have a lot of scope as to what to do with that. *Jams* works well as a fairly heavy rock number, different from the way Fairport does it. *Peggy's*

*Pub* is a jolly little tune – dah-da dup, dah-da dap, dah dah deedle deedle dup dup – that suited the flute well. It was nice: it gave me a number where I could step forward and that allowed the fans to find out who I was. Although in many ways Tull and the Fairports seem alike, the audiences they attract are different: so as far as most people at a Tull gig were concerned, the fact I'd been in Fairport for a decade meant absolutely nothing. I don't mean that in a bad way: it's just the kind of fans that rock acts, like Tull and Fairport, tend to attract can be very loyal but also very focused. Someone, for example, who could recite all the line-up changes of Tull and name all the tracks on each album in order might be hard pushed even to name more than a couple of Fairport albums. So, as far as they were concerned, I was just some guy who'd joined the band to play bass. I suppose you could say I had to earn my place in their eyes.

Anyhow, at some point in the set, Ian would introduce me and I'd mumble some kind of intro to whatever we were going to play. I was careful not to say "This is from *Rosie*" or "Here's a tune I wrote for *Bonny Bunch of Roses*" because they're not generally well-known Fairport albums.

It's not like when Richard plays an old Fairport song and says "I used to be in a band... " There's always a sort of cross between a laugh and a roar. That's because Richard's fans are very aware of what he did in his early career: most will be fans of that early period of Fairport. That's not to say they've kept up with what we did since Richard left of course.

It was a very generous thing of Ian to do... to give me that moment in the spotlight each night. It was a live thing, but my tunes were recorded and the story behind that is rather odd. When Richard Digance had his show on Capitol Radio in London, he was very supportive of Fairport. We were struggling and Richard, like one or two other DJs up and down the country – including yourself – was very supportive. It wasn't an easy pitch. Radio 1 was out of the question, we were seen as rock dinosaurs... and in those days we were probably too rocky for Radio 2: so it was down to commercial radio, which was still pretty new in the UK in the late seventies. Mostly the commercial stations played it safe and stuck to familiar chart stuff – and there we were, Fairport, whose pitch basically was "We had one very small hit years ago. The band has effectively broken up. We haven't had a new record out for a few years. But we do get together each year for a festival. Could you give it a plug?" Some did – and we're grateful to them to this day – but most probably hurled the letter at the nearest bin. Anyhow, Richard Digance was one of those who did. He'd have us on quite regularly to play and he'd do interviews to promote Cropredy and so on.

Sometimes, if someone had cancelled or he hadn't got a guest, he's invite me in to just sit and rabbit. As you know, I can go on a bit about things to do with music; I've worked with a lot of different people; I listen to a lot of music and like to keep in touch with what's going on. We could always fill a few minutes.

One day he asked "What's the chances of getting Jethro Tull in to do a set?"

My reaction was obvious. I just said "There's no way." While I had a lot of influence in decisions about Fairport, it was a very different situation with Tull, on top of which I was still pretty much the new boy in the band.

I still mentioned it to them and to my amazement they all agreed, So the entire band did the whole Richard Digance Capital Radio show live from the foyer of the radio station. It was a great set and a very special thing to be involved in. As you'd expect the set was more folkie than usual, though that was one of the great things about Tull – the music they played covered such a wide spectrum: there was something there for heavy rock fans, the hits for pop fans, a huge folk influence, jazz definitely and of course Ian's classical things like *Bouree*. Because of the circumstances in which we were playing and the programme it was being broadcast on, I'd say that set was Tull at its most folkie – but then you must consider things like the Christmas album which also lean very much in that direction.

I think we did *Peggy's Pub*, with Ian on flute and myself and Martin Barre playing mandolins.

Martin Barre, it goes without saying, is a brilliant guitarist but he hated playing the mandolin – even though he's a really good mandolin player: he used to call it "the little scheisse". His friend Paul Hamer, a great Chicago guitar-maker, had made him a black mandolin. [Hamer Guitars, now part of the Fender group, were founded in 1973 in Wilmette, Illinois.] It was a Les Paul shaped electric mandolin with built-in pick-ups. Ian would insist that he played it.

I should add that Ian Anderson's a very good mandolin player himself. Take a listen to something like *Fat Man*. [*Fat Man* is on Tull's second album *Stand Up*, the first to include Martin Barre. It was recorded on April 21, 1969, a few days after Fairport completed work on *Unhalfbricking*.]

There is a lot of Jethro Tull stuff that was ahead of its time, and that's particularly true of acoustic things, like *Heavy Horses* or *One Brown Mouse*, the song that comes before it on the *Heavy Horses* album or earlier things on their second album. *Heavy Horses* is a genuinely great song, as good as it gets in my opinion – a wonderful overall sound and stunning lyrics. *One Brown Mouse* too – you know "Smile your little smile…" and so on. Great songs and great to play. *Jack in the Green*, too, from *Songs from the Wood*. More intimate in a way than the big venue material that Tull are perhaps most associated with.

Tull played an amazing range of material that you only discover if you really listen to their albums. They were experimenting with their version of folk-rock at the same time as Fairport started playing it, though they approached it from different directions. So that set on Richard Digance's show might have been, as I said, folkier, but it was still very much classic Tull.

There's a great story about *Jack In The Green*. Tull did The Prince Charles' Trust, the big concert that's put on each year to raise money for his charities. Robert Plant was on it, and Kate Bush. The fretless bass player from the band Japan, Mick Karn, was in the house band. Jethro Tull were somewhere further down the bill. We didn't have a drummer at the time – the drum stool was vacant, as they say. Phil Collins was in the house band and so he offered to play with us. Ian sent him the four songs we'd decided to play, one of which was *Jack In The Green* which has some really difficult time changes – not difficult for Phil Collins, of course, but it's one of those songs you can't busk: you have to learn it, no matter how good a drummer you are. The other songs were quite difficult, too, (they also played *Pussy Willow* on the night with Ian on mandolin for the first part of the song) but Phil Collins was going to do it, no problem.

Our soundcheck was Wednesday afternoon. We ran through four numbers. Phil was totally on top of them. No problem whatsoever. The only thing was Phil's kit was about ten yards away from us because it was set up for him to play with the house band. We didn't have a keyboard player either at that point. There's just Ian, Martin and myself at the front of the stage with Phil somewhere in the distance behind us. We needn't have worried. By the end of the rehearsal, everything had gone smoothly. It had been brilliant. We knew, thanks to Phil, that we'd be great on the night.

The gig was on Saturday night. It was The Dominion Theatre in London: our slot began at 8.30. I have to say, we were announced not in a great way – kind of "welcome the old has-beens, Jethro Tull" – not in so many words, but you sort of got that feeling. Not that we minded because it gave us a "right-we'll-show-them" approach before we even started. And we had Phil Collins on drums!

So, we get up there. The monitors aren't working properly. I can hear Ian's vocals but not his acoustic guitar and the whole thing hangs on his guitar. Martin Barre has similar problems. I've no idea what Ian was hearing. Ten yards behind us, Phil Collins has got nothing at all. I had to nod to show where beat one [1] was. I have to say he coped incredibly well and we got away with it, even *Jack in the Green*.

I bumped into Phil a few years later. Fairport were playing in Los Angeles somewhere and Dave Mattacks was playing drums with us. We went with our wives, DM and myself, to Benny Hana's Japanese Restaurant in Beverley Hills. It was Friday night, quite crowded. We look around the room and about three tables away from us is Phil Collins, who's there with his daughter. DM is quite excited about this, so I tell him the story about him playing with us at the Princes' Trust concert. DM said, "I'd love to meet him". So I said, "Come on, we'll say hello". Phil's a lovely bloke and I knew it would be fine.

DM's very polite and didn't think we should disturb him when he was having his dinner.

I waited till they finished eating and then went over to speak to him. I wasn't sure whether he'd remember me so I went over and said "Don't know if you remember me: I'm Peggy from Jethro Tull" (even though technically I was Fairport Convention that night!). Phil said, "Yeah, course I remember. The Dim Onion [sic]. What a gig. I'm really sorry. I couldn't hear a thing you know. It was all guesswork. I had no monitors. It wasn't my fault." I had to stop him because it was a bit embarrassing: so I said "Don't worry, you played great." Then I explained I was in town to do a gig with Fairport and I was at the table over the way with Dave Mattacks. Phil had never met DM but knew of him because, he said, he had a lot of the records DM had played on and he really admired his work. So now I had Phil Collins wanting to meet Dave Mattacks, as well as the other way round. So Phil paid his bill and came over to sit chatting with us, talking drumkits with DM or whatever, until it was time to go. Lovely bloke and one of those people who proves that no matter how famous you get you can still be a nice person – and a better person for it. It doesn't apply to everyone, but nice to mention someone that it does, very much so.

In fact, the same thing happened with every drummer's favourite drummer, Steve Gadd. This was around the time of *A Little Light Music* when DM was briefly a member of Jethro Tull in 1992. Tull were playing at some jazz festival. Steve Gadd was playing with some jazz outfit. [Steve returning to his first musical love just ahead of celebrated work with Eric Clapton, Paul Simon et (you can call me) al.] We spotted him backstage and again I insisted on introducing a reluctant DM to one of his heroes. Just like with Phil, Steve knew and admired DM's work and a mutual appreciation society was formed on the spot. DM is a modest chap by nature and never seems to realise how highly he is thought of by fellow musicians, particularly drummers. I'm lucky to have worked with him in Fairport on three different occasions, as well as in Richard Thompson's bands. It's always great when he comes over to Cropredy: being part of a rhythm section with him and Gerry Conway on drums is truly and always amazing.

[Though they hadn't met, DM and Steve both played drums on Paul McCartney's *Pipes of Peace* album, as indeed did Ringo Starr.] Although Peggy was brought in as a temporary bass player, by the end of the tour he had become very much part of Jethro Tull.

After Fairport broke up, I didn't really have a definite idea about what I was going to do, unlike the other three members of the band. There was Woodworm Studios, which I wanted to develop. I knew I could always get session work. Straight after the Cropredy Farewell gig, we started talking about a reunion in a year's time: a festival takes a lot of organising and, for various reasons, it was obvious that it would be my wife Christine and myself doing that.

Playing live, in a band, though, has always been my first love. Ian's call came at exactly the right time for me.

The so-called Fairport Confusion (again, we have Pete Frame to thank for the succinct phrase) is legendary. Through the seventies, the music press regularly carried stories of the band's disintegration and reformation. One wondered if typesetters kept the phrase Phoenix Fairport on a permanent block. Often the band you saw on stage was not the one who made Fairport's most recent album. The Fairports seldom released two albums in succession with the same line up. If Peggy thought things might be different in Tull, he was in for a rude awakening.

Things changed almost immediately after I joined. Ian parted company with everyone in the band apart from Martin Barre and myself. Everyone else saw that coming, apparently. This is all Jethro Tull politics which I obviously can't go into.

Ian was – and still is, though Jethro Tull is a very different thing these days – brilliant at the business of running a band. It goes without saying that he is a great musician and composer, but I suspect most people don't know about the other side of his involvement in the music business.

Tull had had managers and so on before and there had been some disasters – tours of America that cost them money to do: they'd had albums and tours that had made them a lot of money, of course. But it's when money's been spent unwisely that a band will start to whinge about it. As I understand it, Ian took it all upon himself because that's what the band at the time wanted him to do. Of course, it's a huge amount of work that somebody in a band wouldn't normally have to think about and a terrific responsibility – there are so many things to get right and so many things that can go wrong. That was one of the reasons we had that conversation before I joined, when he told me what everyone in the band thought of him.

He did a brilliant job. I learned a lot from him – partly because it was so very different from Fairport's approach. I was able to bring some of that knowledge to the table when as a band we decided to manage our own affairs.

Before we move on from my early days in Tull, let me update you on those ludicrous early costumes. They weren't consigned to the bin or charity shop: they didn't disintegrate from the amount of on-stage sweat they had to absorb. When I celebrated my sixtieth with a concert of a lot of the friends I'd played with over the years, Tull did a set and the costume, modelled by Tristan Bryant made a surprise guest appearance, to great applause: I'd have worn it myself but it seems to have shrunk in the wardrobe as it's now a bit tight for me. I no longer own it: recently I put it up for auction to raise money to support Jerry Donahue; it raised an amazing £600, so thanks to the person who was so generous (I hope you and the costume will be very happy).

The first album I made with Tull was *A* which, apart from Ian and Martin, had two other great musicians Eddie Jobson on violin and Mark Craney on drums. That was done over ten days at Ian's house using Jethro Tull's mobile studio, Maison Rouge. It's a fabulous album, but it was a one-off and the line-up didn't last.

The Tull story does get complicated…

The next Tull line up introduced Peter Vettese on keyboards and Gerry Conway on drums. Gerry's story weaves across Peggy's. He was a member of Sandy Denny's band Fotheringay and played, as did Peggy, on her solo albums. Because a couple of tracks that would have been on Fotheringay's second album instead were released on the next Fairport LP, he is credited on that record as drummer with Fairport, whom he eventually joined full time in 1999. Peggy and Gerry are not the only members to span the Fairport-Tull axis – Maartin Allcock went from Fairport to Tull in 1988; Dave Mattacks had a brief stint with the band in 1992.

Tull made a huge difference to my life. When we made the album *Rock Island* Ian gave me a £55,000 advance which I used to buy the cottage in Brittany that I called *Rock Island*. I never had any arguments with Ian and he was always very generous towards me. He could predict with amazing accuracy what a tour or an album would cost and how much we'd make from it. He's an incredibly shrewd and honest businessman. I know some ex-members of Tull have whinged or claimed he ripped them off or whatever; personally, I can't understand that; it certainly never happened in my case.

Of course, since we're talking about Ian as a businessman, let's acknowledge all the other things he did. He had the farm at Radnage when I joined the band; he was a serious farmer, not just a landowner who let others do the work and lived off their expertise: he knew all about it himself. It was a successful working farm, 850 acres in the end.

He also had his place on Skye with a smoke-house for fish. In the end that factory counted for 10% of the Scottish output. It wasn't just the salmon from Ian's Strathaird enterprise, but from other salmon farms across Scotland. That started out because one of the roadies – this was before my time but I have it on good authority – had got married and decided with a family he no longer wanted to be on the road away from home for a long time. He was from that neck of the woods.

For me those years with Tull were always exciting times and I was playing with such monster musicians. Ian has very high standards and always recruited not only the best but also the right people for whatever project he had in mind. Ian had already bought the house and the estate with a loch: he wanted to do something with the property – it had a few highland cattle and so on, but he wanted a proper enterprise, which is how he hit on the notion of raising salmon. So he sent the guy to college to learn about aquaculture. He was then qualified to oversee the project which developed into a huge enterprise. In the end there were over a hundred people working for him at the factory in Inverness.

He got out of that just before the blight which devastated the industry. Lots of people in the rock world had invested in salmon farms and some of them lost a lot of money. Ian didn't. Clever guy!

After the shock of the costume arrival before his first gig at Maple Leaf Gardens, Peggy must have been relieved when Tull's dress code relaxed somewhat. But theatricality is deep within Ian Anderson's being...

A couple of tours later – The *Broadsword and The Beast* tour – everyone was wearing their own clobber. I had a Breton outfit – striped hat and t-shirt. So that was OK. Then one night, Ian told us that he'd been in touch with a chap called Jules who was the costume designer for The Royal Shakespeare Company in Canada. He'd been to see the show and had ideas about what we should be wearing.

You could sense the apprehension!

Apparently, he'd formed ideas about our individual identities and come up with concepts about what we each should wear.

As you can tell, it was all getting a bit Spinal Tap.

Ian had arranged for him to meet up with us at the hotel after gig. There we all were, in the bar, hot and sweaty and a bit exhausted as one tends to be after a gig, when Jules flounces in. He was a lovely chap but he tended to form a very fixed view of your personality in terms of how he saw you on stage. He turned to me and said "Dave, I see you in flowing purple and silver silk. With a really big hat, with a wide brim."

Let me just explain that I've often had ideas about how I should look... and that was certainly never one of them.

To be polite, I just say, "That's great". He needs no further encouragement. Out comes the tape measure and he'd inviting me to come with him to be measured up.

To be fair, he did design outfits for each of us and they were great. We had two matching outfits. You had to, because you sweat so much on stage. You'd come off totally saturated. On tour, there wasn't time to get laundry done, so literally, you'd come off stage, wash your costume through in the sink in your dressing room, stick it in a plastic bag and take it back to your hotel room. Before you got something to eat, went to the bar or anything, you'd wash it through with whatever kind of travel-wash you were using, rinse it in the sink or the shower, wring it out by hand then hang it in front of the air conditioning sytem and hope it would be dry by the time you had to leave next morning.

Only then could you relax and go down to the bar.

When I was in Jethro Tull, we had a friend who lived in Boston whose name was Ron Lovely – he was a magician, children's entertainer and semi-pro singer... not a bad singer either.

When Tull played America, our soundcheck was always at 4.00. Then after sound-check, around 5.30 there'd be catering for the crew and the band. In the early days, Ian would bring his own cook out and we'd have our own kitchen units and utensils and so forth that travelled with us. In the later years, we brought in outside caterers wherever we were. But the band and most of the crew would sit down together to eat. There'd be about 20 of us in the catering area. Whenever we were in the Boston area, Ron would turn up and entertain us with magic tricks and so on. It wasn't just Tull, he knew lots of people and would provide entertainment – Led Zeppelin, Pink Floyd, Clapton and so on. Sometimes you think someone's spinning you a yarn, but I once asked Robert Plant if he knew Ron and he said " 'Course I know Ron" and went on to describe exactly the kind of thing he'd put on for us.

As an aside, I was reminded this during the 2018 Winter Tour, when Chris Leslie started doing bits of magic at the soundcheck. Leger de main as we call it in France. Slight of Hand, which is a great title for a tune or an album – or a somewhat insulting Steve Knightley tribute act!

Ric's already built up his occasional joke into a short stand-up routine within the set. If Chris starts doing a bit of the old Paul Daniels, we could soon have a nicely rounded variety package to take on the road. What next? Does Simon juggle? How's Gerry on the highwire? Me? I'm just the bass player. I go dum-de-dum dum-dum-de-dum.

We were in Providence, Rhode Island and it was Martin Barre's birthday.

The day before, we'd all been in the Mayor's office because we'd been given the keys to the city. The mayor was called Buddy, and apparently had had a few run-ins with the law but was still elected mayor: he was a big Tull fan and had decided to give the whole band the keys to the city. It probably helped that he was the boyfriend of the sister of my friend, Linc Materna, of whom more shortly. Ron came along next day, for the gig, and did his magic show, but also rented a suite in the hotel, next to Martin Barre's room so he could throw him a surprise party. He decorated the room, laid on drinks, set up a buffet and invited all of the band and anyone from the crew who wasn't working after the show to come along... which we all did.

At about midnight, after we'd all sung *Happy Birthday*, Ron said to me "Do you know the Bee Gees are staying in this hotel, we should ask them if they want to come down and join us." I thought that was ridiculous, even if they were they'd never come to a party – I doubted they'd heard of Jethro Tull. Ron found out their room number and I found myself outside as he knocked on their door. Maurice Gibb answered: it turned out he and Robin were doing a promo tour of radio stations. Ron invited them down, and of course they had heard of Tull. Ron explained the situation and invited them down. They replied "yeah great": I thought, as we went back to the party 'There's no way they're going to come down.'

Ten minutes later there's a knock on the door. It's Maurice and Robin with a bag of grass the size of a handbag. They start spliffing up and everyone's a bit on edge because no one in the band really smokes – especially Martin and Ian who says he's never had a joint in his life, and I believe him.

The two Bee Gees had a smoke, sang *Happy Birthday* to Martin and hung around for a few hours. After they left everyone thought it was a bit surreal. Imagine a meeting of Tull and the Bee Gees and it's the Bee Gees who are the far out ones!

Ron Lovely not only managed to get the Bee Gees to sing *Happy Birthday* at Martin Barre's party, he later decided to organise a benefit gig for Scotty Moore. Scotty was Elvis' guitarist in the early days – the Sun recordings and so on – and he'd recently been very ill. He said he was going to get everyone he knew to play on a DVD and it was going to be called *A Tribute to a King*. He had a list – Clapton, Gilmour, Knopfler, Bill Wyman's Rhythm Kings and so on. I thought 'this is never going to happen'. Then he said would you and Simon like to play on it? I'd no idea what he'd want us to do – if you've got Bill Wyman why would you need me to play bass: that's all I do, really.

He'd thought it through. He was going to do a list of twenty Elvis songs and send them through to people to see what they want to do.

Basically, I told him I didn't think there was a chance it would happen. Oh me of little faith!

About a year later – by which time I'd kind of forgotten about the whole thing – Ron gets in touch to say he'd got some German company to support the whole thing, he's booked Abbey Road for two days and Eric, McCartney, Knopfler, Bill Wyman and a bunch of other people were all set to do it. So, which songs had Simon and I picked.

I got in touch with Simon and he hadn't thought about it either. Neither of us really believed it was going to happen.

Next month, another message. It's Ron to tell us it's definitely on the following Monday but he still needed to know what songs we were doing. Simon said he hadn't picked anything, let alone learned the songs: there was no way he could do that by Monday. Knowing the situation, I emailed to explain that singing Elvis wasn't really Simon's style. He's a great singer, don't get me wrong, but that's not what he does. Then I suggested Steve Gibbons, because he'd be great doing Elvis and we'd still be there backing him.

Come the day, we turn up as arranged and it really is happening – everybody's there. There's a German film crew. An invited audience is going to watch it all. Scotty's health has improved, and he's turned up and is going to play. It's a real big deal. Then Bill Wyman sees us and comes over to Steve and says "We've got a bit of a problem. McCartney can't make it. Do you know *Heartbreak Hotel*?" Steve knew it, but not with enough certainty to sing all the words. Bill said there was a teleprompter with all the words loaded... so no problem on that score. "Let's try a run through."

Steve just goes for it – *Heartbreak Hotel* and then *Jailhouse Rock* – gives it his full Elvis. Does the moves as well. Everyone's playing along. When he finishes, everyone in the room, all these legendary rock players burst into spontaneous applause. When the DVD came out, it was that rehearsal performance that they used.

We did a couple of numbers. Bill Wyman was up in the control room for that. So, you know, playing with his band, I was nervous when I went back up. He looked at me and said "Still playing with a plectrum I see." Always have... always will.

If Fairport's Farewell had demonstrated the loyalty of Fairport's fan base, Tull's proved to be if anything even more fanatical.

Tull's audience were so loyal. You can't believe what it was like when you're playing, say, Madison Square Garden or some 15,000 seater venue in Germany: the place is packed; everyone's going bananas for about 15 minutes after you come off; you're soaked in sweat and the band has been incredible. It's unbelievable, the experience, and you honestly never quite get used to it.

Things like the *Broadsword* tour were so good musically: you went out there, everyone played their balls off and every night was as good as it gets. It was an incredible satisfying experience musically.

It was also important as a source of income. It meant I could still put time into Cropredy, Woodworm and Fairport without having to worry about money. Ian was very understanding and generous about it, right up to the point I left, he made sure there was no clash between my Tull commitments and working with Fairport.

## Postscript: In Search of Some Game
Aside from the cross-over of group members, there were other connections between the two bands, as Peggy remained a member of Tull and Fairport's reputation and workload increased. Tull played Cropredy of course; they toured the States with Tull, making for very

work-heavy evenings for the bass player in both bands. Ian had been a guest in Fairport's set at Cropredy and made guest appearances on their albums (both live and studio). Fairport returning the complement by covering the Tull classic *Life's A Long Song*. There is, however, one less well known instance of crossover that sticks in Peggy's mind.

When I was in Jethro Tull, Ian Anderson had a farm at Radnage: he was serious farmer. He had a pheasant shoot there. He employed a gamekeeper. Each October he'd invite people to come and enjoy a day's shooting, which was quite expensive: I think it was about eight hundred pounds for a day.

Sometimes, he'd invite Martin Barre and myself... if he was a couple of guns short. I spent most of the time hoping nothing would fly into my line of fire because I really had no great desire to kill small birds and really just went along for the day out. It was a free afternoon or day, certainly something different, so Martin and I would go.

At the time, this would have been easy to organise. Peggy's main commitment was with Jethro Tull, the three key members of which were engaged on the shoot. Woodworm Studios was a situation where he was literally his own boss and unless he needed to be there as a session player, it could be left to run itself for the odd day. Cropredy Festival had not yet developed into the massive three day event and year round operation it now is. Fairport Convention was effectively dormant.

Aside from Cropredy and the occasional one-off gig or very short tour, Fairport wasn't happening. At the time the band consisted of Simon Nicol, myself, Dave Swarbrick and either Bruce Rowland or Dave Mattacks on drums.

When Swarb moved to Scotland, after Fairport split up, he had this idea of becoming self-sufficient. This including shooting rabbits for food. He had his own twelve-bore and was interested in hunting.

The living off the land idea never worked out, but when he moved back to Coventry he professed to me that he had become quite useful with a gun and said it was one aspect of living in remote Scotland that he'd miss.

I mentioned this to Ian Anderson and he suggested inviting Swarb down for half-a-day's shoot, free of charge. I'd already suggested to him that it would be great to hold a barn dance at the end of the season and invite all the staff – gamekeepers, beaters and so on – as a kind of thank you. I knew I could put a good ceilidh band together from mates and so on. Ian had said, it'd be great but we couldn't do it without including Swarb and he'd want a lot of money. So the two things kind of came together – Swarb gets a day's shooting and in return plays at the barn dance in the evening.

Aside from the beaters, we could invite the people who were paying out eight hundred quid a day. They were all well-off people, local land owners and so on, tending to be a frightfully hoo-ray but all very nice people. I knew I had the contacts to put together a great band, with people like Beryl Marriott.

The way it turned out was typical Swarbrick.

He was really up for it... the whole thing. I told him he'd need to wear the right kind of clobber... hunting green, something like that. I went to pick him up around 7.30 in the morning and he was the worse for wear. He seemed to have forgotten all about it. So I asked him what he had to wear. He produced this bright yellow checked coat. I said, "You can't wear that: you'll stick out like a sore thumb and scare all the birds off." So I fetched some of my gear to lend him, which may not have been the greatest fit but was at least an appropriate colour.

We drove to Stokenchurch and the house that Ian had there, Pophleys – a beautiful old country house.

Ian welcomed us and asked Swarb if he'd brought his gun. Of course, he hadn't. So Ian said to me "Dave, here's the keys, go up into the loft and get Swarb a gun."

The top floor of the house was full of Martin parlour guitars and Purdey shotguns – all very expensive, top-of-the-range stuff: some of the guns were matching pairs which cost thousands and thousands of pounds. So I found a gun and brought it down for Swarb – whose reaction was something like "Fuckin' 'ell, Pegg, it's a fuckin' Purdey." And off we went to join the shoot.

When you go shooting you pick a peg, one of eight positions you shoot from, and you rotate as you go round the estate. There are lots of rules and protocols, shooting etiquette, like letting a bird gain sufficient height before opening fire and limiting your angle so you don't fire across someone else's field of fire and hit something that was really their target.

We start off and I'm at one end, hoping nothing will come over me so I don't have to try to kill it. The next shooter is forty yards away... everyone is separated by that kind of distance. Swarb is way off, at the other end, at the other side of a hill: I can't even see him on the first stand.

No birds come in my direction, but there's an awful lot of activity where I reckon Swarb is.

So it goes on, moving, changing positions, until eventually Swarb ends up shooting in the next position to me. I asked him how it was going and he said "Great! I've used two boxes of cartridges already." That's sixty rounds: and he hadn't hit anything.

Then it was lunch, which was provided at Ian's neighbour Jason Abbott's, who's a gun dealer, in his barn. We go into the barn and tables are laid out with silver cutlery and place names and everything. One reason Swarb was on the shoot was that Ian's father-in-law David Leroyd had been taken ill and couldn't come. His place name had been replaced with one for Swarb, but I noticed it was right in the middle of all the posh shooters. That wasn't going to work, so I rapidly swapped the placenames to make sure he was out of harm's way with Martin Barre and myself at one end of the table.

I was breathing a sigh of relief, when Ian grabbed me and said "Dave, could you have a word with Swarbrick over lunch?" I said Sure and asked why. Apparently, he'd been shooting all over the place and had nearly taken out two of the beaters, one of whom had literally had his hat blown off.

Over lunch, I could hear Swarb was the main topic of conversation among the other guns – "That little geezer... who is he? What's he think he's doing?"

Of course, come the evening, Swarb redeemed himself. We had the barn dance... Beryl and Roger Marriott, Chris Leslie, Simon Nicol, myself, Swarb, about ten of us, plus a caller... a proper full-on ceilidh band with Hugh Crabtree, who now plays with Feast of Fiddles as caller. Swarb was on top form, playing at his best, enjoying playing music he genuinely loved alongside some great musicians. Everyone loved him: all was forgiven: it ended up being a great day... and absolutely hilarious.

Chapter 13

# Hello Land of Plenty
### *Across in a new country*

In 2001, Fairport Convention recorded Chris Leslie's song, *My Love Is In America*, which tells of a promised land across the deep blue. Six years previously, they'd recorded Steve Tilston's *Slip Jigs and Reels*, the tale of a young man who heads across the Atlantic to seek his fortune. Both songs have become folk standards in the intervening years. They are clearly set in an earlier era, and while the United States had lost some of its mystery, it retains its mystique. Unlike many musicians for whom every city is the inside of a concert hall and the very similar four walls of various hotel rooms, Peggy has always liked to take every opportunity on tour to branch out and discover the less familiar parts of the cities he stays in. In this chapter he shares five of his more unusual Transatlantic expeditions, usually into districts you won't find recommended on Trip Advisor.

Let's start with one that's in two parts. The first part comes during a tour we did in 1971. It's the tour when Simon decided to leave the band. We were supporting Traffic which I liked because Steve Winwood had been a mate for years. The tour lasted the whole of October. Then we were due back in England for a tour to promote the *Babbacombe Lee* album.

## Through the Willows and the Pines
> *"I'll be The Man. I'll be the best there is."*
> – Steve McQueen in *The Cincinatti Kid*

1971 had been a traumatic year for Peggy – Richard's departure from Fairport, the crash that terminated their tenure at The Angel, Simon's decision that it was time for him to go, not to mention the heavy work schedule that included two tours of the UK, University and club gigs, tours of Europe and America, a string of festivals (Glastonbury, Crystal Palace Garden Party, Ruisrock in Turku, and Ahoy in Rotterdam), not to mention radio work, recording two albums and even an appearance on Top of the Pops.

That tour with Traffic proved to be very stressful. We finished *Babbacombe Lee* just before we left. Simon mixed it and the finished album was sent out to us. He actually did a brilliant job in difficult circumstances but Swarb in particular was less than kind when he heard the acetates. Simon decided to leave. We knew he'd do the tour when we got back, but the future beyond that was uncertain. Dave Mattacks had also said that he wasn't really happy in the band anymore. In effect, that left just me and Swarb. So I thought once we got back to the UK, we'd need to get together to decide what happened once the year and the *Babbacombe Lee* tour were over. We had something like a week between getting back to the UK: the tour was a big event, in large halls, with the speech bits of the album played in live from tape, a special newspaper-style programme that told you all about the album and one half of the concert devoted to playing the album straight through, like a recital. It was ambitious and in fact quite ahead of its time as a concept. The first gig was on November 11, at Liverpool Philharmonic. Our last gig in the States was in Anaheim, at the Convention Center on October 30.

It would be a long flight but that was never a good time for having serious discussions about the future with Swarb. No matter what pressure we were under, it would need to wait. At least getting together with Swarb once we were back wouldn't be difficult in that short gap: he lived literally over the road from me in Cropredy.

For anyone trying to visualise these events – at the least Cropredy end of them. If you've ever gone to the Methodist Church to eat – excellent soup; tea and cake: perfect on the Thursday lunchtime or before a fringe gig in the Village Hall – a favourite venue for events staged by Fairport's other bass player, Ashley Hutchings. That's where we are talking about.

As they say, what happens on the road stays on the road. After one of the gigs, there was a reception. This wasn't unusual in the States – and the one in Spinal Tap with the little sandwiches is certainly not far from the truth. You get all kinds of people there – local politicians, people connected with the venue, other musicians, friends of the band, record company people, sometimes fans or groupies try to gatecrash: you have to be nice to people, though usually you've no idea who they are; you 'press the flesh' as the Americans used to say – lots of handshaking.

One of the people there was a very beautiful young woman, who was a cheerleader… very athletic, stunning. I didn't know her name at the time and still don't. She was eye-catching and clearly she was very taken with one member of Fairport.

I said to Swarb, "She really fancies you. You're in there." We were refreshed. We'd been away from home a while. He didn't need telling twice.

Let's just say he never turned up at our hotel that night. Let's assume he took the expression "pressing the flesh" pretty literally.

Next morning he arrived back as we were having breakfast. He told us it had been fantastic; as usual, he went into some detail, though whether that was to make us envious or just to demonstrate his prowess I'll never know. He was never good at remembering names and he'd dubbed this girl The Cincinatti Kid.

And now part two: the story shifts on a few years. The time came around for another Australian tour. After the tour, we were due to fly back via Los Angeles. When we landed there, we were told there were only two places left on the British Airways flight. So, some of us would have to stay over and fly back next day. At the end of a tour, I always like to get home as quickly as possible. During the tour I get out and about, visit places, see the sights if there's time. But when it's done, it's done and I like to rule a line and get back to normality – or what passes for normality around me.

I got one of the seats, but Swarb said he wasn't bothered. I asked him what he was going to do and he replied "I'm going to Cincinatti… You remember The Cincinatti Kid?" The idea was that anyone who hadn't got a seat would hang around LA and return on a later flight. Not Swarb.

Instead of hanging around Los Angeles then flying back to Cropredy next day, he headed off to Cincinatti. I told him he was mad: he hadn't seen her for a couple of years: anything could have happened in the meantime… More to the point, what was his wife Birgitta going to say? His reply was "It's the Cincinatti Kid: I've got to go."

So he did.

I meantime flew back overnight to Heathrow, caught the train to Banbury and then a taxi to Cropredy. I kept thinking "What am I going to say to Birgitta?" The Swarbricks lived almost directly opposite us so there was no way she wouldn't know I was home: obviously she'd ask where Swarb was. If he was due back next day, I could simply explain about the lack of seats: I could even make him sound altruistic, giving up his place for other people. That's fine, if he was due back the next day. I knew that was not going to be the case. He wouldn't be back the next day, or, probably, the day after that. In fact, I had no idea when he would be home.

Anyhow, as we drive through Cropredy, I notice a large Danish removal van parked outside the Swarbrick home. I thought it was a strange coincidence with her being Danish and everything. In the cottage was Birgitta: there was a table and chair, a plate, a cup, a knife fork and spoon. Everything else had been loaded into the van.

News of what Swarb was up to – or perhaps, to be more accurate, whom Swarb was up – had clearly travelled fast and beaten me back. I don't know how. Maybe he rang with some flimsy excuse that she saw through easily. Maybe someone let something slip by accident. Maybe someone had dropped him in it.

I had worried about not knowing what to say when I saw her. Now here she was and I didn't know what to say for entirely different reasons. I stood open mouthed. She spoke first.

She said, "I'm going. I'm going. This is what I've left him. I've had enough. I can't cope with it anymore."

I thought I'd got away with it, I wouldn't have to think of some excuse or explanation…but then she asked "Where is he?"

I couldn't say "He's gone to see The Cincinatti Kid." I just mumbled something about there only being two seats and how he'd let me come home on one of them. I knew I wasn't fooling anyone. I then leave and head back to my house, glad that I don't have any explaining to do.

Within the hour, Birgitta with all the furniture goes back to Denmark. I don't hear anything from Swarb for a couple of days, but at least I don't have to invent some preposterous cover story for him! I'd then have to brief him about what I'd said and live with the fear he'd forget and drop me in it as well.

Eventually the phone went. It was Swarb saying that he'd found a flight and would be on his way back, adding "You won't believe what's happened to me."

I thought "You won't believe what's happened to you either."

Of course, I couldn't say anything about it over a transatlantic phonecall.

A couple more days pass and he arrives back. I'm expecting to be regaled with typical tales of carnal success. This time the story is very different.

He got to Cincinatti. He had correctly remembered her address and even recognised the place when he eventually found it. It was after midnight but he still rang the door-bell. A woman answered the door and he didn't recognise her: she didn't recognise him either. But it turned out she was The Cincinatti Kid who, over a couple of years, had gone from being cheerleader shape to being more matronly.

She asked him in, and Swarb who not only had been flying across time zones but hadn't slept for two days was obviously knackered. They went to bed and, despite everything, started to have a romantic episode. But then, in Swarb's own expressive phrase, "I shat myself."

That was it. He left, found a hotel, slept for a couple of days solid and then made his way home.

It's an amazing story. It went on much longer than the version I've just given. Then a thought strikes me and I ask the million dollar question – "Have you been home yet, Swarb?"

"No, I came here first because I wanted to tell you the story. Obviously I won't be able to say anything about it when I get home."

Unless he had a very judgemental dining chair, he could say whatever he wanted, of course. He just didn't know that yet.

## If you ever go to Houston, you better walk right

*Sweet meat, look,*
*Fresh and ready to cook*
*Crawfish* – Elvis Presley

My daughter Stephanie had been in Houston on an exchange to do some work. This was during the summer holidays. She had a good friend there, who was a Fairport fan, a chap called Gary Coover. She'd managed to get a job working in a bar.

Jethro Tull were playing on the next tour in Houston, in a beautiful big old auditorium. The next day was a day off and we were supposed to go on to Denver, ready for the next gig.

Steph suggested that while we were there I should look up Gary and invite him to the concert. So I invited Gary to come to the gig. He brought a friend with him. He kindly offered to give me a lift back to our hotel afterwards. He also offered to take me out for dinner at a restaurant called Atchafalaya.

Located on the North Freeway, and therefore not particularly handy for the gig, Atchafalaya was a highly regarded cajun seafood restaurant. Sadly, it closed down a couple of years after Peggy's visit.

It was exactly the kind of food I love to eat... but I had to explain to Gary that with Tull things worked rather differently to how they were with Fairport. It was usually rather difficult to get away after the soundcheck.

He assured me it was only a ten minute drive away and there'd be no problem if I did the soundcheck and then went to eat: we'd be back in plenty of time for the gig. In fact, he'd already booked a table for six o'clock.

Tull weren't on till 8.30. So I told him that if he was able to pick me up and drop me back, I could probably get away for an hour. He agreed that he'd be waiting outside as soon as I was ready.

I did the soundcheck as quickly as I could and then dashed out, straight into his car, and off we went. The car, by the way was an Austin Sheerline, one of those big old limousines with a split windscreen. Huge great beasts of a car, and in their day pretty high on the comfort scale. I'd been in one before, because Diz Disley used to own one. The Stones used to travel round in one too in the early days: one time after a gig where the band I was in had supported The Spencer Davis Group, the Stones' driver had picked us up in it and taken us to a party.

It is, however, an unusual car to have in Texas, one that's almost guaranteed to get you noticed.

Off we went, and arrived, as promised, at the restaurant after a very short while. Martin Carthy and John Kirkpatrick were also there because they were coming to the Tull gig.

The food was superb and we had loads. The margaritas were also excellent and we had loads of them too. Crawfish was one of the house specialities and we ate lots of it. In fact, it was such a notable feature that all the waiters wore hats with a big crawfish on the front and the name Atchafalaya.

John K calls one of the waitresses and asks if we could have a couple of hats, as a souvenir. She explained they were for staff and only people who worked there could have them. So he explained we were part of the famous English rock band Jethro Tull (which he wasn't, just to be clear) and we were playing the Amphitheatre that night. If she'd get us four hats, we'd wear them on stage.

I knew enough about the way Tull operate and Ian Anderson's attitude towards stage presentation to know this was not a good thing to promise. I try to explain to John, but it's too late. The waitress is talking to the manager and returns with four hats with huge crawfish on the front. We put them on and think it's hilarious. By this point we were over refreshed on margaritas and therefore very likely to find such things funny.

I realise time is moving on and say we need to be getting back. I was very aware that, having had perhaps a couple more margaritas than I should, I would need to be on my very best behaviour when I got backstage. Ian and the other guys would not be impressed by the thought of me going on stage in that state.

I went into the tuning room to get my bass ready and so on. I should explain that so far as Tull were concerned the tuning room was like a shrine: the focus was the tuning device; there was a thermostatically controlled heater, thermometers all over the place, and the instruments maintained at constant optimum temperature. The temperature had to match the temperature on stage, so that when Ian walked on stage with his guitar it remained perfectly in tune. He was meticulous about this and a roadie was given the job of monitoring the exact spot where the guitar was going to be on stage and making sure the tuning room temperature matched.

I'm checking my two basses and Ian comes up to me and asks "Are you all right, Dave? Where've you been?" I explain I met up with a couple of mates and popped round the corner for a bite to eat. I said I'd heard how good the crawfish was and wanted to try it. At this point, I am still wearing the hat, with the name of the restaurant and the big crawfish, because I plan to wear it on stage.

We go on stage. I've kept my part of the bargain: I'm still wearing the hat. The stage itself is very dodgy. The show, as usual, was energetic: Ian was leaping about all over the place. From where I was, I could see the microphone bouncing up and down every time he got to the middle of the stage. Ian's trying to play the flute and it's impossible because the mike is dancing around like it has a mind of its own. Ian, understandably, is not a happy man.

He stops the show. Dead, just like that, and demands to see the promoter instantly.

We all come off, not really sure what's going to happen next.

Ian takes the promoter on stage, shows him how the mike moves about and askes whether he could perform at his best in such conditions. Bear in mind this bizarre sequence of events is taking place in front of a packed audience, who must have been wondering what on earth was going on.

He told the promoter flatly, the show wouldn't continue until everything was fixed.

It's a real ultimatum. He was entirely right, especially with his perfectionist approach to all aspects of Tull's music. It's not, however, something that most rock bands would think of doing.

The show was held up for about fifteen minutes. Among the entourage that travelled with Tull was Ronnie Gilmour, the group's carpenter (I'm not making any of this up, honestly!). It wasn't the group's responsibility but the sooner it could be fixed, the less irate the audience would be. He came in for a bollocking because the whole situation should have been spotted much earlier and put right. He was set to work, trying to brace the stage and make it more stable.

There's some slow hand-clapping that picks up when we finally come back on stage after about a quarter of an hour. I don't think anyone had taken the trouble to inform the audience what was going on. This was in the days before big screens and close-ups so probably only people down the front would have realised.

On we go, and most people are clearly glad and relieved to see us back. We're just putting on our instruments when all the lights go out and out of the darkness comes a voice "You wanker, Anderson!"

It was John Kirkpatrick. I knew it was him because I recognised his voice and I knew the general area it had come from and where he was sitting... which was roughly the same place. It was in the third row back from the stage. Ian knew where it had come from too and obviously an English voice, especially one with a bit of a regional accent, stands out in a Houston audience.

His suspicions were confirmed when, as the lights came back on, light spilled from the stage on the front rows of the audience, where sat three guys wearing red hats with the name Atchafalaya and a large crawfish attached. Just like the hat his bass player was wearing. In that moment, you could see Ian putting two and two together and getting...cross. I got a stern glance, but nothing more. At the end of the gig, things had gone smoothly and, unusually, it was all forgotten about. The expected bollocking never came. I wasn't summoned before the headmaster.

We packed up, and then, with the promised lift, the five of us headed back to my hotel. That's me, Gary Coover, his mate, Carthy and John K. We'd picked up some beers earlier and called in the liquor store on the way back. There was a minibar in my room, but that was rapidly drunk dry as we knew it would be.

It was a luxurious hotel and we were all on the twentieth floor with a wonderful view, overlooking a large swimming pool where I'd spent most of the afternoon. Swimming is a great way to relax when you're on the road, incidentally.

Around 3.30 in the morning, the room phone rings. I go to answer it, assuming it will be someone complaining about the noise. We've started to get rather loud, as you might imagine under the circumstances. In fact it wasn't a complaint: it was our German tour manager, Gerd Burkhardt, calling to tell me that there had been a change of plan – instead of spending time in Houston and then heading to Denver, Ian had decided we would leave early and spend our day off in Denver. The flight would leave at 10.00 am. That was just over six hours hence... and of course, we'd need to be at the airport well before that, plus the time it would take to get from the hotel to the airport. There was I, over refreshed, with four house guests in a similar state and seemingly no plans to move on anytime soon. That wouldn't have mattered if we'd been staying the day in Houston, but plans had changed…

I told Gerd I couldn't do it. Bluntly I said, "I'm not going." He insisted the decision had been made and I had to go like the rest of the band. I continued to refuse.

We returned to our drinking. To be honest, I returned, the other four had carried on without me.

Then comes the knock at the door. It's Gerd. He puts it simply: I have to go; everybody with Tull is going; the seat is booked on the plane. We would all leave at 8:00. I told him I couldn't go; I would stop in Houston as planned. I wanted a day in the sunshine not in Denver where it was -10. Obviously, over my shoulder, he could see into the room to the more practical reason why an 8.00 check out was not going to work for me.

I promised I'd get a flight the day after and be in Denver in plenty of time for the gig. He was shocked and said something like "No one has ever done this. You must come with us. This is Jethro Tull. This is the way it works."

I explained it didn't work for me and I definitely wasn't going. Looking back I feel sorry for Gerd: I was putting him in an impossible position. But I had that determination that only comes with really focused drinking.

At this point, Martin Barre appears behind Gerd at the door.

He's an old hand in Tull, of course, and he tries to reason with me "Dave, you simply have to come. No question. If you don't, you could well get the sack and you don't want that to happen."

My reply was a reflection of my state of mind, in several respects, "Sorry, Martin. I am not going. It's a matter of principle. You can't tell somebody in the middle of the night that arrangements have been changed and expect them just to go along with it."

The next bit of the conversation consisted of Martin saying firmly "You'll regret it" and me saying even more firmly "I'm not going". This dialogue was repeated a few times.

Then Pete Vettese arrives and he tries to persuade me to come. The more people tried, the more I dug in my heels and the more that seemed like exactly the right thing to do. I'm not blaming them in any way, but I think I was by now receiving a certain amount of moral support in my stance from my friends inside the room.

This argument has rather put the dampers on the party, though. Realising they were not getting anywhere ("on your own head be it"), Peter, Martin and Gerd go back to bed; then Carthy, John K, Gary and his mate decide it's time they were heading home. So around 4.30 I roll into bed.

I don't seem to have been asleep for five minutes, when the phone goes. It's my alarm call from Gerd: "Get up; you've got to come." I say I'm not going, slam the phone down and fall back to sleep.

I wake up around mid-day and realise the band will be landing in Denver. My next thought was "Shit! What have I done?"

The room is a complete mess, with empty bottles everywhere. Somehow I have to sort out getting myself to Denver, where in all likelihood I will get the sack and be left stranded in the middle of America with a lot of explaining to do when eventually I get home.

I try to make a futile attempt to tidy up, as I realise the band will all have been checked out together and I've probably gone over check out time. Another problem. At that point I stumble upon a note from Gary Coover. It said something like "Thanks for a great night. Here's my phone number. If you're ever in Houston again and need anything give me a ring."

My first thought was "now's the time to do it". I called Gary and explained what had happened. All I wanted was for him to give me a hand getting to the airport and getting a flight. Instead, he suggested I sort out the room and he'd pick me up and take me for lunch. Lunch became afternoon drinking... then dinner... then out clubbing. It was next morning that I finally made it to Houston airport to try to find a flight to Denver. Luckily I did.

I arrived at the band's hotel just in time to get on the coach to go to the gig for the 4.00pm soundcheck.

Nobody says a word about it.

Except Ian, who eventually very calmly and quietly asked whether I had any friends who were likely to be attending tonight's gig.

These events took place on November 11 1984, when Tull played the Sam Houston Coliseum. The free day was the result of the cancellation of a scheduled concert at The Reunion Arena in Dallas. It perhaps says something for Peggy's state of awareness that the gig he recalls as being in Denver was in fact in Boulder.

That year, as part of Tull, Peggy spent the first part of the year, when the band was drummer-less following the departure of Gerry Conway, recording Under Wraps. In September, after an initial late August gig in Dundee, they played major cities in England, ending with three nights at Hammersmith Odeon. Three days after that, they started a European tour, beginning with a gig at Barcelona's Palacio Municipale Deportes, a massive stadium, on September 12. After three nights in Spain came five nights in France, then Scandinavia, the Low Countries and a dozen gigs across Germany. The final night of the tour was October 7 in Zurich. Five days later they opened their US tour in New Haven: with a four-day detour for Canadian dates from October 21, they remained on the road in the States until a gig on November 22 at Los Angeles Universal amphitheatre. Then it was a flight to Melbourne to play Australia until December 12.

In contrast, Fairport's schedule that year consisted of a short US tour supported by 10,000 Maniacs, Glastonbury, where on June 24 they were second on the bill to Weather Report, and the fifth annual reunion at Cropredy (August 10 & 11).

Cropredy 1984 was the year it might most justly have been called a folk festival. The line-up included The Battlefield Band, Ian Campbell, Bob Davenport, The Oyster Band, Pyewacket, Ragged Heroes, Steeleye Span, Allan Taylor and Whippersnapper. On Saturday night, Fairport (Swarb, Simon, Peggy & Bruce) were joined by Adderbury Theatre Workshop, Ian & Lorna Campbell, Bob Davenport, Matt Pegg, Cathy leSurf, Richard Thompson and Wally Whyton.

In a way that was a nostalgic year, with the Campbells and Wally and RT playing some of his oldies. We did a skiffle set in the middle and I think Richard played *Move It*.

Indeed, he did, curiously in a medley with *Sloth*. The set, which was full of one-off performances, also included Fairport backing Cathy le Surf on folk-rock's greatest 80's hit *Daytrip to Bangor*.

The following year, Cathy was guest vocalist on *Gladys' Leap*, the record that marked the rebirth of Fairport as a full-time working band.

Increasing numbers of attendees at Cropredy and the emergence of Ian Burgess's Friends of Fairport fan group provided a tangible argument for reforming the band yet again. Phoenix Fairport stirred in its ashes. Meanwhile, fans could enjoy a double cassette of the band's complete performance at Cropredy 1983, released by Peggy's Woodworm label as *The Boot*. As that came out, in May, Dave Swarbrick had again requested that the band call it a day.

Fairport played at Cropredy annually, of course. We all did occasional gigs and short tours in the UK and overseas. Swarb's hearing problems had continued: they'd been the reason why he knew continuing to play with Fairport was dangerous to his health and after, what would it be, five years, he decided to put his foot down.

There were other elements too. He'd moved out of what you once described as the folk-rock triangle and was now living in the wilds of Aberdeenshire, where he had several new projects going. One of those was his new acoustic group, Whippersnapper, with Martin Jenkins, Kevin Dempsey and Chris Leslie: they played Cropredy that year, one of their first big gigs – probably the first time *John Gaudie* was played there, but not the last of course, after Chris brought it with him into Fairport's repertoire.

Swarb also had a duo with Simon Nicol and they released their studio album on Woodworm at the start of the year. So he had a lot going on and decisions to make. One of those was that he couldn't continue as a member of Fairport, especially as we were considering working together on a more permanent basic. I suppose the reason he thought Fairport should call it a day was that he couldn't imagine Fairport without him in it. Neither could we, at the time, I suppose; after all, he'd been part of Fairport for as long as I had been in the band – he and I were the only consistents in the band through the seventies.

Fairport did continue, of course. Eventually, the increasing workload with Fairport and running Cropredy and the touring and recording commitments with Tull would become just unmanageable – but that was a good way off in 1984.

You can see from a glimpse at Tull's tour schedule we spent a lot of time together. Not only did we tour the UK, the USA and Europe regularly, we also played South America, behind the old Iron Curtain, the Far East, and Australia. Everywhere except Antarctica, as someone once said.

That's a lot of time together – on stage, backstage, in hotels, in studios, travelling between gigs and so on. You can end up longing for some 'me time'... which is really what the next story is all about.

## Got those St Louis Blues

*There's Technicolour and Cinemascope,*
*A cast out of Hollywood*
*And the popcorn from the candy stand*
*Makes it all seem twice as good* – The Drifters

How did I end playing bass for The Drifters? My son, Matt, is also a bass player. He plays bass with Procol Harum. Like most jobbing musicians, he's happy to take on other work, sessions and so on. One of those was playing bass for The Drifters on a UK tour. There were some gigs he couldn't do and suggested I stand in for him. They weren't the most demanding bass parts to play, because they were economical – they did exactly what was needed of them. Great songs, of course, classic pop – though I did get pulled up later for referring to the classic Motown bass parts. The Drifters were on Atlantic. Which shows how detailed my knowledge is about some areas of music.

I don't think any original members of the group were involved in the line-up I played with: there are several acts around Europe operating as The Drifters, each including a member who has been part of The Drifters at some point.

If you look at the history of the group, it's had more than enough line-up changes to put even Fairport's famously changeable history to shame. Some of its members, like Clyde McPhatter or Ben E King, are famous in their own right. Their first wave of hits came in the fifties; classics like *Save The Last Dance For Me* were in the early sixties; they enjoyed a new wave of success in the mid-seventies. The group has had over sixty members: alongside the more famous names are some unlikely ones – Gerhart & Andrew Thrasher, Charles Baskerville, Beary Hobbs and Dock Green ("evening all").

It seems incongruous that at one point the bass player for this iconic black group was the man known for playing with such quintessentially British bands as Fairport Convention and Jethro Tull.

When Tull toured America, our nights off would usually be a Monday or Tuesday, nights when people don't normally go out to concerts. Tull weren't a social band in the way Fairport were, so on days off, you'd tend not to want to do things together. You spent so much time together – on stage, at soundchecks, eating, travelling between gigs – that you needed a break.

As a result on those days off, you'd often find yourself at something of a loose end.

On this occasion we were in St Louis, staying in a downtown posh hotel. It would have been around 1982, the *Broadsword* tour. I'd taken to wearing English country gentleman's attire – moleskin trousers, tweed jacket, deerstalker hat, brogues. It was a distinctive look, especially in America. I think someone had suggested meeting up in the bar at 7.30 and then trying to find somewhere decent to go out for a meal.

I really didn't fancy that, so I decided to look at what was on at the cinema. I asked at reception and they gave me a paper with all the listings. Of course, this was for the whole of the St Louis area and as a result I had no idea where any of the cinemas were, whether they were local or miles out in some suburb. I noticed one place had a rather odd double feature – the Led Zeppelin film *The Song Remains The Same* and *Blazing Saddles*. As Zeppelin are old mates and I love fart jokes, I decided that was a perfect Monday night off for me. I decided not to tell anyone where I was going, in case they fancied those two films and decided to tag along. I just said, "See you later", grabbed a cab outside the hotel, told him the name of the cinema and let the driver take me there. The driver gave me a funny look, so much as to say "Are you sure?": so I showed him the advert in the paper and off we went. We were travelling for quite a while, and I realised that was probably why he was puzzled that I was taking a cab so far out of town. The meter was ticking over and passed 15 bucks. I'd been in the cab for twenty-five minutes and I'd no idea where I was.

Eventually the cab pulls up. I pay the driver, give him a tip and get out. I'm standing right outside the cinema which is indeed displaying posters for the double bill. I went to the box office where a black lady served me: unusually I wasn't offered senior citizen's discount, which I'd been getting on most of the tour, despite being only 40 – the advantage of early baldness!

It had taken so long to get there, much longer than I had anticipated, that the performance had already started. The cinema was therefore dark when I went in. The cinema was almost empty, only about half a dozen people in there, most of whom seemed to be in the back row. So I got a good seat, about halfway down, right in the middle, and settled down to enjoy the show. The adverts are playing, so I haven't missed much. A few more people come in; no one sits near me; they all seem to be heading for the back of the cinema. It was quite nostalgic. I didn't think anyone still did that.

After the adverts and a trailer, there's a short break and the house lights come on dimly... presumably for anyone who wants to go buy a hot dog or popcorn or use the facilities. I take the opportunity to glance around and realise I am the only white face in the place. This cinema is in an exclusively black neighbourhood, which might account for the poor turn out to watch a white English heavy rock band with a couple of Brummies in it.

That doesn't bother me. I enjoyed the two films, a great double bill, as I knew they would be. I've no idea how many other people were actually watching the screen but there were some very interesting noises and aromas coming from those seats behind me. The films finish. It's quite late. This is when I realise I have somehow to find a way to get from wherever I am – and I had no idea where that was – back to the hotel in downtown St Louis. I was pretty certain there wasn't much chance of being able to flag down a cab outside the movie theatre.

It's around eleven o'clock, very dark. The streets seem to be full of people out partying. Lots of nightclubs and bars have opened up and the joints, as they say, are jumping. I also seem to be the only white person there. Everyone seemed very friendly so the only thing worrying me was how to get back to the hotel which was at least half an hour away, even by a direct taxi.

I am conscious that my white face makes me stand out in this particular crowd. Then I realise I am also wearing deerstalker, tweed, moleskin and brogues. I must have been like a lighthouse.

There are no taxis. I have no idea which direction to go in. Everyone walking past me is doing a double take and saying things like "Hey, man, check out this guy." One kid told me I had cool threads, which I think was a compliment but might have been sarcasm.

At this point, I noticed a fried chicken emporium – not a KFC: the real deal, your actual down-home corn-fried chicken. The place is busy but nothing like as wild as every other place in sight. There must have been about fifty people in there. I realised I was feeling hungry, so I went in to join the queue.

As I walked in, it was like that scene in every Western when the stranger walks into the saloon. Suddenly everything stops; complete silence; you could hear a pin drop. As I join the queue, I hear murmured voices around me, expressing a mixture of mystification and admiration. The clothes and the colour of my skin clearly suggested I was either a total idiot or very brave.

I'm not brave – believe me.

So eventually – and I have to say service was rapid and unusually quiet – I reach the counter and am about to order chicken and fries.

The pretty black girl who's serving at the counter goes "Yeah?"

Suddenly I am aware of the absolute silence around me and a sensation that every eye in the place is fixed on my back. They obviously wanted to hear what this weirdly dress white guy had to say for himself – or maybe even more simply just what he sounded like.

So I said, "Excuse me, could I have a portion of chicken and fries, please?"

To which she replied, "Huh??? Whatdya say, man?"

"Fries, please and a portion of chicken."

"Nah, man. Don' gettit. Watcha wan'?"

I repeat the order, trying to turn down my Birmingham accent as much as possible. This time she gets it.

"Chicknnfries. Why dincha say so?"

The noise of conversation picks up. My food arrives is put on a tray with a cup of coffee. I now have to find somewhere to eat it. Luckily, just by the exit there's a place at a table. An old black guy is sitting there on his own. Being English, I ask permission to use the only available seat.

"Excuse me, but is it OK if I sat here to eat my chicken?"

"Sure, man. No problem. It's what it's for."

Then a long pause and as I am about to take my first mouthful of chicken, he asks the obvious question, which probably everyone else who'd seen me that night wanted to ask.

"Hey, man, what the hell you doin' here?"

Now I am aware there is something of a language barrier, but I also feel I owe him and everyone else in the place some kind of explanation.

I take a breath. "Well….."

Then I explain that I've just been to the cinema, I'd wanted to see the film because some of my mates were in it. I'd taken a cab from downtown. Now I was here, hungry, with no idea how to get back to the hotel. I was gabbling and I suspect it made no kind of sense to the guy. But he was patient. He told me I was cool where I was, just to eat my food and then go out catch the bus from the stop he pointed out through the window. That would take me straight downtown and I'd be fine.

I remember his words which managed to be scary and reassuring at the same time, "You're in the wrong part of town but you'll be ok. Don't worry: most folks here are friendly." Most? MOST? What about the few that aren't? What if they're on the bus which I knew would have a long journey back to St Louis centre.

I eat the chicken, say goodbye and thanks to the guy... then to the restaurant in general to be on the safe side. I cross the road and go stand at the bus-stop. It's gone midnight but buses are still running. I reckon I must have just missed one because I am standing there on my own. I begin to feel conspicuous again – brogues, moleskin pants, tweed jacket, deerstalker hat, white face. After a couple of minutes, a couple turn up to wait for the bus. To be polite, I say hello.

"Man, watcha doin' here?"

"I just want to catch the bus into downtown St Louis. Is this the right stop?"

"Sure. Any bus from here. Where you come from, man?"

I told them the name of the hotel, thinking they might know if the bus stops nearby.

"No, man, your accent. You ain't from round here."

I told them I was from Birmingham. Now, if you're in an exclusively black district of most American towns and you tell people you're from Birmingham, despite the accent the English Midlands is not the first thought that comes into their heads. So I explain I'm from England and though I come from Birmingham, as my accent makes obvious to any Brits who here me, I actually live in Oxfordshire.

They've heard of Oxford and seem to be impressed. I even get a Wow. Then another question – "Why are you wearin' that stoopid hat? And where the heck didya get those weird clothes?"

I explain about the clothes. I may have said something about English country gentle-men or Sherlock Holmes. I tell them how I travelled from downtown to see the movie. I know we've got into a proper conversation which is reassuring, when another black couple turns up. By now, I'm like the long lost friend of the first couple, who introduce me and start explaining what they know about me.

Then comes the question from the second couple: "What's a guy from Oxford-shire doin' in St Louis?"

I explain I'm in a rock band and we're playing in St Louis next evening. Today has been out day off.

"No way, man. Whatdya play?"

I tell them I play bass. I tell them it's with Jethro Tull, whom they clearly have never heard off, and I tell them all the band like to wear unusual and distinctive clothes.

It's now obvious that a bus is due soon as more and more people are turning up at the bus stop to join the queue. My story is shared with any new arrivals – second and third hand because I have no need to speak at all myself now, everyone is doing it for me. It was like being on a surreal version of This Is Your Life.

Passers-by are stopping and pointing. They are immediately told a version of my saga by someone. Most start with the words, "You won't believe it but..."

The bus arrives and about twenty of us get on. The first lady naturally takes it upon herself to tell the driver who I am. I think at one point she's about to ask him to detour to take me to the door of the hotel, but she says the driver will tell me when to get off and where to go from there. Apparently it's only a short walk. It's reassuring that these are people who naturally think of walking rather than doing what other Americans do, leap in the car or call a cab.

I thought it was a white guy driving the bus, but it turns out he's an albino. Yet more surreality, of course: this is Peggy-in-Wonderland down-the-rabbit-hole mad-hatter's-chicken-dinner stuff. I'm the white rabbit checking his pocket watch and starting to panic.

It's a pay-as-you-enter bus. I've no idea what the fare will be, though I am sure it will be a lot less than the taxi.

It turns out to be a dollar fifty. I give the guy the money, He gives me a ticket and directs me to sit in an empty seat, at the front, right by him. It's marked "Reserved for pregnant women or the elderly."

Everyone else behind me in the queue gets on, pays and heads for the seats further back. As the bus fills up I can hear my story being shared again with those people al-ready on it. I feel like I am literally becoming a legend. I catch audio glimpses of garbled versions of the story, which has clearly been the victim of Chinese whispers... well, not Chinese, but you known what I mean. "He's a teacher from Oxford." "He's still in his stage costume." "He plays with a guy call Geoff Rotill."

Every mile or so, the bus stops and more passengers get on. They're all black couples, heading for St Louis to enjoy the nightlife. Each time another couple gets on they do a double take when they see me in the reserved seats and as soon as they find their own seats another version of The Legend of the Oxford Musician is recounted. It's like The Canterbury Tales:

*The carl unto the pics hadde longed to go*
*There to see the metalled ferting shewe.*

*In moleskinne pantes and deerstalker hat*
*The which yon gudden folke did marvel at*
*And one vrai thinge that Pegg the bassman knew is*
*He was in the wrong parte of St Louis*
– The Bass-clerke of Oxenford's Tale

To quote Chris Leslie, 'our bus rolled on'. Looking out of the window I could see we were moving into the more affluent parts of town, business areas, shopping districts, none of which I recalled seeing on my taxi journey out. By the time we hit the outskirts of downtown St Louis and the first of the partygoers after getting ready to disembark there's around forty people on the bus and everyone knows I'm an Englishman called Dave, who's from Oxford-shire (though most have no idea where that is) who plays bass with Jethro Tull (whom none of them have ever heard of).

You can almost see how myths begin. Years later this could become a traditional ballad. As the story spreads further afield, its location changes to somewhere nearby; Dave's instrument and place of origin alter according to local preference; Tull's name is swapped for a more familiar band. This is the oral tradition in operation. Somewhere in America, some senior black lady is recounting the night a white British musician came to the cinema in the wrong part of town "and, lordy, wouldya know it, he was a guitarist from Manchester with The Rolling Stones."

The driver tells me it's the next stop. I happen to spot our hotel a block or so across and instinctively press the STOP bell as I stand up. As I'm getting off, I yell "Night, everybody". The whole bus replies "Night, Dave."

*'It's a great huge game of Chess that's being played... I wouldn't mind being a Pawn, if only I might join'*

I walk into the hotel. It's pretty late now, getting on for one o'clock. The Tull guys after still downstairs after their night out having a meal. They're perched on bar stools having a drink. They call me over – obviously they spot me because my outfit – deerstalker, tweed, moleskin, brogues, beard – still stands out.

It turns out they'd found a good Japanese restaurant and have spent the evening there. They were worried where I was because I hadn't joined them and wasn't in my room. They were even more worried when they got back and there was still no sign of me.

I said I was sorry if I had worried them. Someone, who shall remain nameless, replied "We were more worried about who was going to play bass tomorrow night."

"Where've you been?"

I just told them I'd been to the pictures. Not a word more. When they read this, it'll be the first time they discover what happened that night in St Louis.

*Now it's in St Louis after dark*
*That Dave Pegg took a night off work*
*And he raised many a curious smirk*
*There goes the Tull bass-player*

*He's at the pics but where's he's at*
*There's no one else that looks like that*
*With his moleskin pants and his Sherlock hat*
*That bearded Tull bass-player*

## Peggy, Bourbon St. and the Jack of Hearts

If you've never been to Bourbon Street in New Orleans, you have to go. Especially if you're into music, because it's full of bars, everyone of which has got an incredible band or an amazing soloist. You see people like Dr John, who was playing there the night we went.

You go into a bar and buy a drink or a cocktail, which they always serve in plastic cups. You can check out what's going on – what kind of music it is, how nice the bar is, what the rest of the patrons look like. If you are happy with it, you stay and enjoy your drink (maybe several drinks) and the music. If you're not all that keen you move on, taking your drink with you. You go into the next bar, and they don't mind you going in with a drink you bought somewhere else. The only thing they don't like is someone standing round without a glass in their hand. Or should that be a plastic in their hand? Nobody is actually holding a glass. It's just a chain of bars with different styles of music – even an Irish pub: this was before there was an Irish themed pub in every town you go to. So alongside all this great New Orleans music – blues, jazz, rhythm'n'blues, country, rock'n'roll, boogie woogie, you could still hear the dread *Fields of Athenry*. The very last bar is quite large and has two grand pianos, slotted together facing each other, with two wonderful lady pianists playing duets and singing: it's like having two Janis Joplins who can also play like Jerry Lee, swapping songs, dueting, jamming. They are incredible. As I said, if you're into music, it is the place to be.

It was a night off on a Jethro Tull tour. About a dozen of us, some band, some crew, including myself and my ex-wife Chris, went down to Bourbon Street. Our plan was to work our way down, calling in as many bars as possible, stopping a while in those where the music grabbed us. If you're in large group, it's difficult to all keep together because some of the gang will want to stay in one bar because they like bluegrass; then the next bar's got, say, a trad jazz on and some people want to stop there; or maybe there's an R'n'B band or a soul band. They're all fantastic players, so it's not about finding the place with the best band, it's more a case of hearing music you love played as well as you're likely to hear it played ever. That might sound like an exaggeration, but, trust me, it's not.

Inevitably, we all got separated. There's waifs and strays of the Jethro Tull entourage all up and down Bourbon Street. There's no point in trying to gather people together because, even if you could find them, they might not be ready to leave yet and you'd probably lose some every time you went looking for someone else. By half-past twelve, there's just me and Christine. Even though it's late, Bourbon Street is a pretty safe place, simply because there are so many people there. We go into another bar. There's a black guy playing a Fender Rhodes piano. That's it, just him playing right up beside the counter in a very tiny bar. There's no more than a dozen tables. Basically, the kind of place you might glance in and just move on. When we went in there was just on other couple in the place, right in the far corner, almost out of sight.

We sit down, order some drinks and start to listen to the piano player. He's playing vintage R'n'B stuff, the kind of songs that the Spencer Davis Group used to cover when we were young, songs like *Every Little Bit Hurts*. He was brilliant, playing great versions of the songs. It definitely wasn't just a nostalgia thing – you know, "Great to hear that again". It was like rediscovering all these classics. I'm really knocked out by the guy.

He can tell we're into it because we're singing along with the choruses. It must have surprised him because not many white people from England would even have heard of these songs. Birmingham had a particular affinity with southern R'n'B and soul.

While people think of The Beat Boom of the early sixties as a kind of national movement that sprung from skiffle, different areas of the country had their own particular focus. It's true that most found inspiration in Lonnie Donegan, who himself drew on the music of Leadbelly and Woody Guthrie to create the singularly English, homespun, low budget teen genre known as skiffle. From The Shadows to Led Zeppelin, The Stones to Pink Floyd, The Beatles to Van Morrison, the world of the cheap guitar, the washboard percussion and the tea-chest bass were where it all started. However, as the music developed, different regions became dominated by their own styles, all drawn from what were, at the time, obscure American genres. We knew little of them because even if American records were released in this country, they were unlikely to get airplay thanks to the BBC's control of the airwaves and the power of the Musicians' Union protecting the livelihoods of its British members.

So London favoured Chicago-based R'n'B, Newcastle has a fondness for country blues, Manchester embraced Motown and Liverpool raw rock'n'roll. Each area also had a crucial local influence from folk music: The Troubador and Ballads and Blues were two clubs in London which were a magnet for aspiring folk musicians (and others), Newcastle had the High Level Ranters, Manchester was home to collectors of Industrial song, Liverpool The Spinners. While Birmingham's folk scene was dominated by The Ian Campbell Folk Group, its bands were drawn to raw southern soul and R'n'B (a crucible in which Heavy Metal was first forged); Peggy spent the sixties with a foot in each camp and could just as easily join in with a song by Bessie Banks as a Big Ballad.

We're loving the music, applauding enthusiastically, which is a little odd – and very noticeable when there are only four people in the room. At this point, a drunk staggers in. He's very well dressed, wearing a suit and a tie that obviously aren't cheap. He's loaded. Which he is – both in terms of the amount of cash in his pockets and the amount of spirits in his system.

He staggers over to the bar and orders a really large drink. To pay, he pulls out a money roll, which is pretty obviously all $100 bills. We exchanged glances... myself and Chris, the only other couple in the bar, the pianist and the bar-tender... because it's obvious this guy is a) very rich and b) very out of it and c) putting himself in several kinds of danger. Not from any of us, I suspect, but he was clearly too far gone to listen to reason about some of the less safe places around. I'm not talking about Bourbon Street, so much, but he could have got in a cab and ended up anywhere: trust me, there are parts of New Orleans where you wouldn't want to end up in the middle of the day, totally sober, with nothing much on you – none of which was the case with the chap currently standing at the bar.

I think we kind of knew he was fine for now... and when he decided to move on, we'd better think what to do about it, if anything.

Then the pianist, who had stopped playing (it was like one of these scenes in a western, when the stranger walks into a saloon, and everything freezes... and you could hear a pin drop), began to play a slow blues... something like:

*Oh, I was down in New Orleans one Friday*
*Just playing on my piano.*

I decide it's not a song I know, so I don't pay much attention. When he gets to verse two, I realise he's describing the bar and the handful of people in it. He's improvising an original song about his job and what he has to do for a living, but it's more than that.

He mentions the couple in the shadows in the corner... and two folks from England who know all the songs. It's amazing and I wonder whether it's something he does every night, changing details to suit the occasion.

Then we get to verse three…

*Suddenly, some guy walks in*
*Overdressed and overpaid*
*He orders an expensive drink.*
*On the bar a bill he laid.*

Something like that, anyway. It hits me, he's singing about now. It's like live reporting, cinema vérité. It's a kind of virtual reality. For some reason, it all starts to feel a bit weird. The rich guy finds himself a table, puts his drink on it and the pianist describes what he's doing, as he does it. A couple of girls have wandered in and go over to sit with him. He buys them drinks, of course: that's hardly unusual. They appear in the song, too, which is a bit unusual.

Then the pianist starts verse four... and this is where it really does get weird.

*Suddenly the lights go out*

Which they do. It's totally dark. You can hear a scuffle but you can't see anything. It's a scuffle accompanied by blues piano and words which obviously we are no longer listening to. You can tell the noise is coming from the table where the guy's just sat down... the noise of the scuffle that is... obviously the piano noise is from the piano!

The lights all come back on and he carries on with the song. Nothing's changed, except the rich guy is now lying in a heap on the floor, minus his wallet. He's just been ripped off before our eyes. Well, it would have been before our eyes if we could seen. Though we didn't need to see, because it's all in the song. I can't believe it. Obviously, the pianist knew what was going to happen: he didn't need to see to describe it.

Despite all this, we stayed till the bar closed. The rich guy left, staggered out and obviously we didn't need to worry about him getting robbed anymore. As they were shutting up, I went over to have a word with the singer. I wanted to tell him how good we thought he was and how much we enjoyed hearing those all R'n'B songs. As soon as I told him I was a musician, we bonded and I helped him carry his Fender Rhodes back to his apartment.

No doubt you're as curious as I was about the song. Once we were out of the building, I summoned up courage to ask him. He explained it was pretty much standard New Orleans practice: some guy on his own with too much money and too much drink comes in; as he serves him, the barman presses a button under the bar which alerts people in a room nearby; a couple of hookers respond and start chatting the guy up; he gets comfortable and offers to buy them a drink; this means they've seen where his money is; all prepared, they give the barman the nod; the lights out; they grab his dosh and run off with it. It's all over in a few seconds. The lights come on and the guy finds himself without cash or company, and in this case, simply because he was too drunk to stay on his seat, on the floor.

So why the song?

Apparently, it was for our benefit. It kind of warned us, talked us through what was happening, make it seem like everything's under control. I can only say it was a weird kind of actuality, living through a song that was being sung. With Fairport, we sing a lot of songs about things that have happened, epic detailed narratives, but never one about what's actually happening…or in fact what's about to happen in the next few seconds. As I said, New Orleans is an amazing place. You have to go there.

## Blowing in the windy city

*Peggy, do ya want to go*
*Down to that old Chess studio*
*Back in sweet home Chicago?*

To quote the old blues, we've been 'going to Chicago' for many years. Over the years, I've got to know lots of Chicagoans, some of whom have become great mates. I've been with Fairport, Tull and PJ Wright. The first time I went there was in 1970, when we did three nights at Beavers. Of course, given when and with whom I've played there, I've done quite a range of different size gigs, from almost literally people's front rooms to some of the city's biggest venues.

There's a great place, a rock club, called Martyrs, where I've played with PJ and where Martin Barre's band play when they're in the States: they usually do a couple of nights there. Fairport played places like The Chicago Museum of Folk Music, which sounds impressive and is a fantastic place to play.

Everyone, of course, associates Chicago with The Blues, but it's also full of amazing Irish musicians: for example, Martin Hayes, the violinist used to live there. I think every time Fairport played there, we'd end up some place with Martin and his mate Dennis Cahill, who's a guitar player. Our friend Brian O'Malley seems to know every Irish musician in Chicago and you can guarantee that he'll set up a session somewhere. The Fairports love to play and just making music with great musicians is an absolute joy.

The time I played Martyrs with PJ was quite an informal tour when I planned it so we could spend some time enjoying the places we visited. It gave us time to go to 2120 South Michigan Avenue, which is the home of Chess Records, the great electric blues label. It was the label that brought out most of the records the Birmingham blues bands copied – Muddy Waters, Bo Diddly, Chuck Berry, Little Walter, Otis Span, Honeyboy Edwards. Visiting there was a kind of pilgrimage for me, as it had been for lots of British musicians.

In the sixties, Chess records have proved a magnate for The Stones (Keith spoke to Mick on Dartford Train Station because he spotted the fact young Jagger was carrying a couple of imported Chess LPs), Manfred Mann, Savoy Brown and Fleetwood Mac, who recorded a classic double album there working with some blues greats.

Jeremy Spencer who played slide guitar with Fleetwood Mac disappeared for years after he became involved with some cult in the California desert. No one knew what was happening. Then a few years ago, he turned up in Brittany and I ended up playing with him at one of the more bizarre *Excalibur* live performances.

It as our last day in America. We were due to fly back to England next day. It was a Monday morning. We decided as we were in Chicago with a day free, we had to go to Chess Records, which unfortunately is closed on a Monday. We didn't know that of course. So we arrived to be told it wasn't open to the public. We decided to ignore the sign and keep ringing the bell.

Eventually a lovely black lady came down to see what we wanted. She told us they did open to the public and there were guided tours – but not today. She hoped we'd come back when they were open.

We explained we couldn't come back another day because tomorrow we'd be on a flight to England. "Leaving on a jet plane, don't know when I'll be back again", as the man said.

We put on our best sad and disappointed faces in the hopes of getting some sympathy. By this point, we were almost begging – you know, "Is there any way you could make an exception... bend the rules... just let us in for a quick look?" I think it was PJ who asked if we could just look at the studios because we were musicians and we both had recording studios at home (which was a slight bending of the truth at that point in both our lives).

The fact we were musicians clinched it. She'd let us in and would give us a private tour – but we hadn't to tell anyone. So I'm not telling you now... all right? She took us in, through reception and then down a corridor to the recording studio. On the wall, there was a huge picture that showed Chuck Berry, Jimmy Johnson on piano and on bass Willie Dixon. I immediately remarked it was incredible and because Willie Dixon is one of my heroes, I started talking about the classic songs he wrote – *Little Red Rooster, Hoochie Coochie Man* and so on.

At this point, the lady who'd let us in just said "Oh, that's my dad": not only had we the privilege of being given a private tour of Chess Records and effectively having the place to ourselves, the person showing us round was the daughter of one of the most important bass players of all time – a genuine legend.

I've still got the souvenir t-shirt that I bought
...and which I got her to sign.

## Chapter 14

# All for me Bob

*To be on your own like a rolling stone*

1979 saw Fairport decide to call it a day as a going concern. The four current members went off in totally different directions. For Peggy, this meant focusing on developing his studio and working on what was known as Fairport's Annual Reunion – almost instantly nicknamed Cropredy by fans and Fairport by locals.

Fairport was starting to crumble. We'd been dropped by a major record company and nobody was interested in releasing our records. In fact, we'd been paid by our record company not to make any more albums – which is a bit of a hint, really – and we all felt we were quite well off. You do start to have self-doubt when you discover you earn more by not making music than by recording it. There can't be many acts who've got out of a record deal by threatening to make the records they've been contracted for.

Someone once said "It was like the record company were trying to tell us something." They weren't trying: they were telling us. What they were telling us, was 'shut up and go away.'

Through the 80s lots of the big music acts of the sixties and seventies would find themselves out on a limb, dropped by the record companies with whom they felt secure. As was so often the case, Fairport proved to be unwitting pioneers.

We laugh about it now, but it was quite a knock. After Island dropped us, Vertigo had signed us – a very credible label, the bit of Phonogram that focused on prog rock and folk.

At the time the label's roster included Kraftwerk, Black Sabbath, Nazareth, Gentle Giant, Thin Lizzy, The Sensational Alex Harvey Band, Dire Straits, Graham Parker & The Rumour and Status Quo. On the folk side, they'd released classic recordings by Ian Matthews, Dr Strangely Strange, Magna Carta, Anthony Phillips, Tudor Lodge, Alan Stivell and Rod Stewart's first two solo albums.

We'd changed direction and made two albums which were probably the most folkie of our careers, packed with traditional songs including electric versions of some absolute standards. For some reason, it hadn't worked. The albums hadn't sold – but then Fairport albums never really had. The label was busy signing up new, fashionable post-punk acts. We really didn't fit anymore and they paid us off.

We'd each been given £7,000. My cottage in Cropredy had only cost £10,000 and I was able to pay off the mortgage which makes a big difference when you're thinking in terms of your financial future. For most people, it's what they hope to do around the time they retire. I was just 33 with more than half my working life ahead of me.

I formed a company – Woodworm – with my ex-wife Christine, partly with the intention of making and releasing records by other people.

Christine became a big part of the Fairport story because from that moment when everything could easily have fallen apart for the band, she was the one who held it together in terms of the business.

Fairport weren't planning to record but there was a live album which we made on the Farewell tour had been picked up by Simon's Records. Nothing to do with Mr Nicol, though I know a number of people – you not included – have assumed that over the years: it was another couple from the village who put the album out through one of their mates in London. That didn't really work out and we re-released it on our own label.

Our house in Cropredy had a little outbuilding at the back. I'd converted it into a studio. The main reason for this was that I'd been asked to do the soundtrack for a film about Adnam's Brewery called *In One End and Out the Other*. I'd borrowed an eight-track TEAC recorder and we had a mixing desk and good mikes and so on, so I was able to do the soundtrack. Because we had to call the studio something, so it looked official, I chose Woodworm Studios. It comes from Diz Disley's nickname for a double bass – the Woodworms' Hilton, which is probably an even older jazz joke.

I don't really write music, but I reckoned The Fairports could do it. Then Swarbrick pulled out of the project – to be fair, he'd never really been interested in doing it. So, I asked Chris and John Leslie, who were local musicians from Banbury, if they'd like to get involved. There was another chap called Arthur Conduit, a songwriter, who'd done some demos on my home equipment and he came on board.

It worked out well – songs written by Chris and Arthur – all of us playing various instruments. We showed the film the year the Festival was held at Broughton Castle. Coincidentally, the year that produced the recordings for the first Woodworm LP.

My idea when Fairport was drawing to a close was to develop this small accessible studio that would be able to take on things other studios, for whatever reason, may not want to do. It wasn't originally planned to release Fairport albums

Perhaps, we should differentiate between the series of live albums that came between *Tipplers' Tales* and *Gladys' Leap* and their first studio LP on Woodworm. After the *Farewell Farewell* album which they reissued came the LP *Moat on the Ledge: Live at Broughton Castle* – which had a "here we still are and this is what we're doing" feel to it. Then followed a couple of recordings from Cropredy Festivals ('82 & '83): these were intended more as souvenirs of the event than formal releases: although they subsequently were available as CD reissues, they were originally mail order-only cassette releases.

I was planning to record friends of mine – Steve Ashley's *Family Album* was begun in that little studio in Cropredy: at first it was a studio recording of a stage show that Steve did with myself, Simon, Chris Leslie and Martin Brinsford. We finished it at the Barford St Michael studio after I moved there. I was enjoying the flexibility at the time. I certainly felt freer than I had in a while and it was good to have more time at home. When the journey to work is literally no more than a walk across your garden, the situation has a special appeal. It was absolutely literally a cottage industry.

It's been said that Woodworm Records was set up to release Fairport albums. Of course, we did that – there's more albums by Fairport on the label than any other act. But there'd been several other studio albums before the first one from Fairport, *Gladys' Leap*. My idea was to have a place where people who'd recorded at the studio could release their own stuff. This was the early eighties when a lot of acts who'd been signed to big labels, including Fairport, suddenly found themselves without a contract. A lot of smaller labels who used to sign new or unknown acts had gone out of business. It wasn't a record company in the traditional sense, more along the lines of some of the newer companies that had sprung up in the wake of punk and new wave.

It was a way of getting things out. Our first release, Woodworm 001, was *Moat on the Ledge*, an LP of tracks recorded at Broughton Castle which is where we held the annual reunion in 1981. It was a souvenir of the *Full House* line up playing together again, augmented by Bruce Rowland and a guest appearance from Judy Dyble. We put out similar albums of other years, just on cassette because it was all mail order and they were easier and cheaper to produce and post.

When we moved from Cropredy to Barford St Michael, I was able to create a proper set-up: the studio was state of the art and separately housed in a disused chapel next to our house. The house on the other side we converted into accommodation, using the name Woodworm's Hilton – no one tried to sue us for breach of copyright.

Other facilities, most famously The Manor where Fairport recorded in the early seventies, offered similarly comprehensive facilities, but we were more affordable. As a musician, I knew what musicians wanted from a studio and aimed to provide that. As with organising the festival, I'd learned from experience, both good and bad.

It wasn't just about making records, either. People used it to do demos; we recorded some soundtrack stuff for TV; sometimes it would be used as rehearsal space. Because the chaps in Fairport tended to be quite local, they operated as a house band: if you look at some of the albums recorded there – Steve Ashley, annA rydeR, Bob Fox, Steve Tilston & Maggie Boyle – you can see the backing band is essentially Fairport.

It was also a good facility for individual Fairports to work on solo projects – Simon, Maart, Chris, Ric, Swarb and, I have to say, myself. Mine was the first: while I might have encouraged other people to use the chaps on their recordings, mine was totally solo. Multitracked of course.

*The Cocktail Cowboy Goes It Alone* was released in 1983, Woodworm Records' third album. The eleven track LP includes traditional and original instrumentals, a cover of an obscure Jethro Tull song, songs by friends, songs he's picked up on his travels and a touching tribute to Sandy Denny. The LP also is an unwitting glimpse forward as it introduces a couple of Pegg tunes that would eventually made their way into the Fairport repertoire. Dave, beer glass in hand, appears on the sleeve in a pub, sporting a curious double-necked electric instrument. The credits say "Instruments [all]" – D Pegg: we hear guitars, basses, mandolins, keyboards, percussion and much else along the way. Peggy points out that the LP did contain "a little bit of keyboards played by Mark Powell."

I really enjoyed making the album, even though it was odd working totally alone. I learned a lot about recording and using the studio in the process. It was a situation where I could make mistakes and get things wrong with no one around to see me doing it. The studio and the label ran for twenty-five years and there are a lot of recordings that came out of that little cottage industry – which is what it really was – that I am really proud of.

I should also say, with the studio, visiting musicians, Fairport business meetings, the Fairport office and the organisation of Cropredy, it did put a lot of demands on my home which was right at the hub, metaphorically and physically, of that whole operation. I can never thank Christine, my wife through that time, and my kids Steph and Matt for putting up with that amount of disruption and permanent intrusion on their lives.

As if the various demands of Fairport and Cropredy, the requirements of Jethro Tull and a large amount of session work wasn't enough, in 1998, Peggy accidentally embarked on something which was to become another permanent commitment in his life.

I'd known Steve Gibbons for years. I also knew he was a big Dylan fan. We were talking about it after some gig where he'd come to see us, in Birmingham probably. I said I thought he should do an album of Dylan songs. He said it was something he'd always wanted to do. I told him he was welcome to use Woodworm, very much at 'mate's rates'. I also said I was sure the various members of Fairport would be happy to play on it, because they loved the music and they all knew Steve. Aside from Gerry, they all lived locally too. That's how it came about. Almost by accident.

Or as Steve put it when I interviewed him around the time of the album's release: "I love Dylan. So do Fairport. Peggy had a studio with some free time and a label he could release the album on. Bob's your uncle." That would have made a great CD title, wouldn't it?

We referred to what we were working on as The Dylan Project, because literally that's what it was. The name stuck for the album and the band. All the Fairports were on that first album, as well as Maartin Allcock. PJ Wright was in Steve's regular band and he played lead and slide guitar. That was the start of a great friendship for us and a professional relationship. PJ has played with the Fairports at Cropredy and written songs for us, including *Summer by The Cherwell* which is a great song celebrating the Festival.

He's also played there under a number of guises – him and me as a duo, with Little Johnny England, Morris On, The Dylan Project and Trad Arrr. I loved working with PJ as a duo, doing gigs in all sorts of places not just clubs and concert halls. We made the album *Galileo's Apology* of course, That came out on the label Fairport set up after we wound up Woodworm Records, Matty Grooves.

That's typical of how things tend to develop within the way Fairport works.

When it was my sixtieth, we had a concert at Birmingham Town Hall. In a way it was like a live version of *Box of Peggs*. Lots of the people I'd worked with over the years came, often to do just one song. We had Ian Campbell with Swarb, Dave Peace (I played electric guitar just like I did back in the sixties), Fairport, Tull, annA, me and PJ, Ralph, Dan Ar Braz, Steve Ashley, Steve Tilston and to complete a trio of Steves, Steve Gibbons. I couldn't have celebrated sixty years without a man who's been part of so much of it.

Steve's amazing: in the Dylan Project he's do epic songs like *Sad Eyed Lady of the Lowlands* and word-for-word recreations of intros. He'd decided to do *The Ugly Blues*, harking back to my days in The Uglys, with me on bass and Roger Hill on guitar. It's a song he wrote, but on the night it eluded him, slipped right out of his memory. It was hilarious. He'd keep trying and losing it. He'd ad lib. He'd tell Roger to play a solo. We all got the giggles. Everyone else was panicking because what should have been one short song was stretching on and on. The show was on a tight schedule with so much to squeeze in: people were restricted to one song and asked not to make speeches or do long intros. That spot with Steve went on for something like ten minutes. Backstage Simon Care who had the job of stage managing was pulling his hair out. It's on the CD of the concert, but as a hidden video track because you have to see it to appreciate it. The whole gig went well. The audience loved it. Everyone else gave perfect performances that in other contexts would have been show stoppers. For me, though, the highlight was the three of us getting back together, the way we were in 1966, in the midst of all these legends of rock and folk, and the whole thing falling apart around us. It was priceless. The best birthday present ever.

The Ugly Blues was a humorous talking blues that had been the B side of *Wake My Mind* released in May 1965 a year before Peggy joined the group. The 42-year-old obscurity was, to say the least, a somewhat eccentric choice.

Given that we started out with something that was meant to be a studio project because we all had some free time to work on it, it's great that thirty years on The Dylan Project is still a working band. We don't record much – the last album was a live double and the one before that was ages ago – but we do play festivals and occasional gigs as well as a tour in November or December of each year. That's well timed because it comes before the Fairport Winter Tour but fits in nicely with when we need to get together to plan it. Gerry and myself are touring with The Dylan Project; Simon is on tour with Ashley and The Albion Christmas Show; Chris is part of St Agnes Fountain who also tour just before Christmas; and Ric often does work with his jazz trio. It works out very nicely.

It's ironic in a way, that part of what I do is to work in a respected Dylan covers band, because before I joined Fairport, they were known for their versions of obscure Dylan songs. Those early albums include some of the best Dylan covers you'll ever hear – *Percy's Song*, *I'll Keep It With Mine*. They also had a hit with *Si To Dois Partir* which is *If You Gotta Go, Go Now*. The current Fairport did a cover version of that on *Over The Next Hill*, the last album made at Woodworm Studios before I sold it. That track has something rare on a Fairport recording – sampling. Famously on the original Fairport recording, Martin Lamble didn't have a washboard so played the back of a stack of chairs, which during the recording fell over, exactly on the beat. We couldn't recreate that so we sampled it and built it in alongside Gerry's drum part.

We didn't stop doing Dylan songs, even though they didn't make it on to records at the time. The *Full House* line-up used to do *Country Pie*, which Swarb liked (a version ended up on *Moat on the Ledge*) and *Open the Door, Richard* (a Basement Tapes song that we eventually recorded for *Red and Gold*).

Both Sandy and Trevor were Dylan fans, so in the mid-seventies we'd do things like *Down In The Flood*, *All Along The Watchtower* and *Knocking on Heaven's Door*. *Forever Young...* though that might just be something we did with Trevor at Cropredy. Of course, over the years there's been lots of Dylan songs the Fairports have done at Cropredy, like *Girl from the North Country* with Robert Plant or *You Ain't Going Nowhere* or Sandy's version of *Tomorrow's a Long Time*.

Fairport do Dylan…<br>
now that would make an interesting compilation,<br>
wouldn't it?

Chapter 15

# The Woodworm Swung
*Give me clear water*

Most fans of Fairport will recall the point in 2005 when Peggy was at the centre of a crisis that made them anxious about the future of the band. Rumours of his divorce from Christine had developed into articles in national newspapers. Fan groups and discussions on the Internet speculated, sometimes with a fearsome lack of useful knowledge about the future – which, somewhat selfishly, seemed to focus on whether and how Cropredy Festival could take place. One of the more bizarre suggestions was that if Fairport didn't hold the festival, fans should just hire a field and do it themselves (as if).

The previous year, I'd worked on *Cropredy Capers*, the box set that chronicled the festival's first twenty-five years. Even today it seems bizarre that I was unwittingly documenting the end of an era.

The *Cropredy Capers* set happened just before everything fell apart for me. It had been great going back and looking out all the old photos, programmes and posters. In fact, a few years later, I suggested a design for the Festival t-shirt using posters from every year it took place, which Mick Toole turned into reality with his usual blend of vision and skill: it's still one of my favourite Cropredy t-shirts.

There were recordings of most years. These ranged from modern digital recordings through multichannel mixers right back to the days when the only audio record was reels of tapes made my standing my Revox by the mixing desk with two mikes pointing at the stage. There were released recordings too: LPs, cassettes, CDs, VHS tapes and DVDs. Sometimes an odd track would have been included as a bonus song or on a compilation. But there were dozens of hours on unreleased recordings that in some cases no one had ever listened to.

You and I were already mates of course: we'd known each other for years. Working on the Cropredy stuff, which is such a big part of my life, is when we really became friends. I know you were one of the people I turned to when times got really hard. So you know a lot about the background of this part of the book, even if you're not able to put most of it in print.

With its future uncertain, as Peggy acknowledged in his programme note, Cropredy had been rebranded Cropredy Music Festival in 2004. After Cropredy, Fairport worked pretty non-stop on American and British tour that last right in December. The UK Wintertour of 2005 began at the start of February and ended on March 12 with a gig in Birmingham where they were joined by Swarb, Maart and Kevin Dempsey.

Peggy's programme notes took up the theme from the Cropredy programme, but more positively confirming that the renamed Fairport's Cropredy Convention would take place as usual in August and paying tribute to Christine's 25 years organising the festival with him.

His brave face was somewhat enshadowed by a small ad at the bottom of the page offering for sale his Hymer motorhome, Boston Whaler ski boat and Mercedes 320 coupé with Bose sound system.

Following a couple of festivals, at the start of May they began their UK acoustic tour.

Four days after the UK tour finished, the Fairports were on a tour of America and, to be blunt, I was in a bit of a state: I was drinking a lot, even by my standards, and I was in the process of getting divorced from Christine. My head wasn't in a good place and to say I'd become a bit unpredictable would be an understatement – not so much on stage: I've always been lucky that whatever state I was in, once I stepped on stage and picked up the bass, everything comes into focus; but in other respects, I gather I was a bit of a nightmare to be with. The tour was booked and so we had to do it – it was a Fairport Acoustic tour, so quite stripped back: we started out in Virginia – The Birchmere in Alexandria. The next gig was in Allentown. Things weren't working out for me, which was more obvious to the rest of the chaps. So those were the only two gigs I played.

I don't recall the details, so this is what I've been told by Simon, Ric and Chris. Gerry wasn't with us because in those days the acoustic tours were drummerless. I do remember having a lot to drink, Before the next gig, they decided I wasn't in a fit state to play. Next day we had a meeting and it was decided that I should take a break and do something about getting myself together. I was upset: I knew they were right, but when you've travelled to America to do gigs and then find you can't, it isn't an easy thing to take. I don't like letting people down – myself, other band members or fans. The truth was, whether I went on stage or not, I'd be letting them down one way or the other.

They did exactly what was needed, because I remember thinking, "These are my friends and if they think I'm not in a fit state, they are probably right." That's one of the things about being in a band where you're mates: it's a totally different dynamic to just being with people who play together. Fairport has always been a group of mates who also make music, which fortunately people happen to like.

I knew I had to sort myself out. It was a really bad time – the divorce meant sorting out lots of things – selling houses, various possessions, the whole Woodworm business which included the studio, the record label, Cropredy, management and so on. I was rootless.

My first reaction was resentment – I thought the chaps should have stood by me and been more supportive – but actually they were. The best thing for me was just to stop... take a complete break from everything. Not just playing with Fairport, but the drink, the aggressiveness, all that stuff that happens so easily when you're on the road and disorientated. In short, I'd become too rock'n'roll for Fairport.

Typically, Peggy shrugs off what was in many respects an absolute life crisis for him. The answer was far from simple. A year later, when the UK acoustic tour brought the band to Victoria Hall, Saltaire, he was still going through it. The venue is less than ten minutes' walk from my house, so after the gig, the chaps came round to my place and after they climbed in to the van to head off to the hotel, Peggy stayed to talk.

I remember that night. Your neighbours had made amazing authentic curries with all the trimmings. Ric and Chris had never seen your house before and were open mouthed at all the memorabilia. Gary Boyle turned up out of the blue – he's a respected jazz guitarist now, and quite a hero of Ric's – but he was once the guitarist with Eclection and knew Gerry from there: so they had fun catching up.

Fairport have mates in every place we play – as Sandy said in *Rising For The Moon* – "a heart in every place, a tear in each farewell". It's always great to see them, whether it's a quick hello after the gig or a longer conversation in the pub or wherever. The nature of being on the road means you often don't get chance to spend as much time as you'd like with people.

You're kept busy on tour, travel to the gig, soundcheck, grab a bite to eat perhaps or a pint or so, play the gig, meet people afterwards, then back to the hotel, up in time for breakfast, travel to the next gig, soundcheck etc...

There are people you regard as real friends, people you want to spend more time with. I wanted us to have chance to talk that night... and we did into the small hours. When the time came to leave, Peggy realised he'd forgotten the name of the hotel. It was far too late to ring anyone in the band. So a little detective work and some memory jogging, followed by phonecalls to local night managers, identified the right place... less than fifteen minutes away. Assertively refusing a taxi, Peggy determined to walk because the fresh air would do him good.

It was simple enough, all he had to do was follow the main road. He made it safely there, though next time I saw him he was convinced part of his journey had involved walking beside the canal. Thank goodness he didn't try.

Obviously, this is not the place to repeat what we talked about, but those few hours made a big difference. Men seem to find it hard to talk, but if you're going through a hard time, seriously like the old proverb says "A problem shared...". It probably won't solve it, but it makes it a lot less scary.

When we agreed I shouldn't continue on the US tour, I thought how often I'd been to America and all the people I'd got to know but never really had chance to spend time with, never seen the sights and so on. I had a return flight booked for the end of the tour and so I decided to use this unexpected leave of absence to take a holiday. The flight back was from the West Coast: we were on the East Coast. We had a place to be and a time to be there. I said to Ellen "It's a holiday. I'm going to get in touch with some of these people and see whether I can take them up on their offer." I became that guy you meet on your holidays and say "If ever you're round our way, get in touch", never really expecting he will. I did.

The first person I called was someone who was already a friend Linc Materna. He's a huge Fairport fan, who used to live in Denver, but he's moved east and lived near Providence. He'd also lived in Florida. He'd often told us we should go and stay at his sister's beach house there. I rang him... and the offer was good. She wasn't there; she wouldn't mind; he told us where to get the keys to the beachfront apartment. We were there soaking up sunshine for ten days. We took time out to go down to the Keys. I learned to dive. Ellen is an expert diver and a great instructor and the waters in Florida are a great place to learn. I took to it like a duck to water... well not a duck, they tend to stay on the surface... but aside from the joy of actual diving, a new experience for me, the discipline of training to do it was exactly the right thing to sort myself out.

While we were there, I decided to look up another old friend of ours, Chuck Hill. He has a house in Newport and another in Florida. He's a big Tull fan and also into Fairport. We stayed with him for five days. I also looked up my dear friend, Peter Simonian.

This must have been this week, but twelve years ago, because, as now, it was just coming up to Ellen's birthday... and it was one of those round number birthdays that tend to be special. We had to decide where to go to celebrate it. I suggested a place where we had a lot of friends – Chicago.

For those whose knowledge of America is a bit shaky, that's the other end of the country, heading South – North, certainly not in the direction of the plane home.

In particular I wanted to see Brian O'Malley and all his Irish musician mates. As anyone who loves playing music will tell you, if you stop for even a few days, you really start to miss it. I'm a bass player so for me that means playing with other people. I've never been much of those sit-on-your-own-and-strum types.

As soon as I told him we'd like to come, he decided he was going to throw a party. That wasn't what we'd planned, but he wouldn't be persuaded otherwise.

The day came and we sat out on his back terrace with maybe fifty other people, many of them musicians, talking, drinking and eating. Then a dozen Irish musicians turned up, all playing *Happy Birthday*. It became a fantastic session that went on all night, till about 5 am.

As you can imagine, all this made me feel a lot better. It was an escape, which is what I needed. I realised things had got too much.

I think Fairport cancelled the last dates on the tour, because they weren't happy playing as a three piece. I understand they were pretty pissed off with me, because it was my fault entirely... and shouldn't have happened. But it did – and I know stories have circulated about some of the things that happened in the lead up to them saying "enough's enough" – I honestly can't remember the details though. That's how out of it I had become.

I don't know whether the other Fairports missed me – or at least missed the old me. I know I missed them. I know I missed being part of a band – in fact I missed being part of that band. The break had really helped me. What was meant to be an escape resulted in my facing up to a lot of things: I may not have done that otherwise – at least not until it was too late; I was lucky to be in a position to be able to do so. I made a promise to myself never to allow myself to get in that state again.

I also offered up a silent thank you for having friends who are supportive and know the right thing for you to do, even when you can't see it yourself. Fairport has always been like that – it's a family: like all families, we have disagreements, fallings out, rows but when push comes to shove, they're always there for you. Reliable may not be a very rock'n'roll quality but to the many people who've been in the band, or worked with us, or have become friends or fans over the years, I think it's word they'd use to describe Fairport.

I may have missed that tour with Fairport... and this was not long before new regulations made it ludicrously difficult to go and play over there... but that American trip was important. It took me to the brink. It straightened me out. It was a long way up to get out of the place I'd kind of sunk to, but at least now I could see the footholds.

I was determined to carry on playing. Fairport had already said that I could do Cropredy and then see how I felt about the Winter Tour.

One result of easing back from Fairport was that I teamed up with PJ Wright when I got back to England. He's another great mate. We made an album together and we didn't exactly tour, we did occasional gigs. You came to see us in Hebden Bridge which was a rather odd but memorable event.

PJ's still part of the Fairport family and wrote a song about Cropredy for our fiftieth anniversary album. He's a very busy chap. He was in Little Johnny England and the reformed Fotheringay and a great folk rock band Trad Arrr, who, as their name suggests, play largely traditional material.

Playing with PJ was important, because it was unpressured. The gigs were informal, not the usual venues – we did a house concert you organised in a converted 17th century barn, didn't we? I loved the informality that gigs like that allowed. Everybody was laid back about it. You didn't have to work to a setlist. You could play whatever you felt like playing. Did we do Del Shannon's *Runaway*? With the ladies in the audience singing the high bits PJ couldn't reach! We played all kinds of things – old Shadows numbers, things we'd written ourselves but didn't often get chance to play, favourite songs like Mark Knopfler's tribute to Lonnie Donegan.

I was enjoying playing acoustically and was able to play guitar and mandolin. It didn't matter if we were informal, even a little ragged around the edges. The people who came to see us were always very supportive. The whole thing gave me back my confidence which had taken quite a hit because of what happened with the Fairports.

Because of all the friends in America, many of whom I'd renewed contact with during that time out of Fairport, we were able to organise a short tour there for me and PJ. It was a different experience. I've always been used to being in bands, standing at the back with no need to be particularly entertaining. Certainly, I wasn't expected to do solos or sing lead vocals. Suddenly in a duo I was able to do both those things and really enjoy them.

The highlight was playing two nights on Linc Materna's boat to an audience of about ten people, which I have to say was a capacity audience under the circumstances. We spend two nights cruising around the bay at Newport as a kind of floating concert. We also played Shelter Island on July 4: it's one of those places that's empty apart from summer because most of the houses are summer homes used for holidays. There's an old church there that holds about a hundred people and that's where we did the gig.

My sixtieth was coming up too. I decided to hold a big birthday gig at Birmingham Town Hall, a few steps on from the more local thing we had for my fiftieth. Lots of the people I've played with over the years were on stage for that from the early Brum bands to the current Fairport. Thinking about that, I decided I wanted to do a box set of my musical life. You were the person I wanted to do it... and that became *A Box of Pegg's* which is a set I continue to be really proud exists.

So once more we find a natural bracket around a phase of Peggy's career. At the time, the very worst of times, but nevertheless a strong foundation when the winds of changes shift. Both those brackets involve Peggy, me, boxes of tapes and antique vinyl, albums of photos, books of press clippings, scrapbooks and memories, creating a book and box set.

The soundtrack for the era comes from the album *Over The Next Hill* whose biographical title track reminds us of time spent...

*Wandering on a dusty stage*
*And wondering where the time goes*
*Over the next hill there'll be rainbows.*

The way Woodworm Records started was quite sad really. Fairport still had an audience... and an increasing audience as attendance at Cropredy and the occasional gigs we did showed. Nobody wanted to put our records out. Phonogram who'd signed us up, put us back on track by having us make more folk-centric (is that a word? It is now) records and spent money promoting us, had dropped us after two releases and basically paid us not to make any more.

We had arranged to release a souvenir album of the farewell tour, which would have been great to sell at the farewell gig at Cropredy.

That wasn't possible. It had a very limited release. It was the first Woodworm release, though not on our label. It came out in September. That was a shame, because although it's not a great Fairport album, it's historically significant. On that last tour we dug back into the archives and played things the band hadn't played for years; some of the things I'd never played at all – ever. One of those was *Meet On The Ledge* which today seems a preposterous state of affairs. It might have been a record of Fairport's last gasp but it was also a glimpse of our future where we would regularly go back and revive old material, sometimes reinventing it.

You could only get it via mail order. People who own a copy are in possession of a Fairport rarity.

This was on Simon's Records (not that Simon, in case you were wondering – you wouldn't be the first). Unfortunately the whole thing went tits up. I think. There was even a single – a version of *Rubber Band* by Mike Waterson, done as a sort of joke against ourselves. That was survival from the Vertigo sessions: if they didn't want it, we might as well do something with it. There was nothing on that LP that we'd recorded after *Babbacombe Lee*. The Fairports, aside from the fact the Bruce was now our drummer and not DM, was the one that made that LP.

The *Angel Delight* Fairport was the last line up to maintain unbroken link with the Fairport Convention of 1967. Simon left and so there was no one still in the band who had been there for their first three albums. Simon eventually rejoined full time (and stayed in the band), as did Dave Mattacks (who didn't).

Over Peggy's forty-seven years with Fairport, those severed links with past members have gradually been repaired, until, a month before the interviews that make up the majority of this book, we had the delight at Cropredy, of seeing, for the first time in forty-nine years, the line-up that made the first album.

One track on the album was *Mr Lacey*, which is not only before my time but was written by Ashley Hutchings, whom I replaced as bass player. It's very untypical Fairport in that it's a straight blues, which as you know is a genre of music I've always liked playing.

It's also one of Dan Ar Braz's Fairport favourites!

Confusing this folk-rock stuff, isn't it?

# CHAPTER 16

# Alors, je l'ai fait encore – Brittany
### *The more I learn the Lesténo*

The conversations that make up this book took place over many years, in a huge variety of locations –
clubs and concert halls,
backstage and in the stalls,
in lounges and bars
ferries and cars,
in sun, rain, snow, gales
in Oxfordshire fields and Yorkshire Dales
in Banbury and Barford
Albany and Bradford,
but, with this book firmly in focus, most took place at Peggy's home in Brittany.
Round a couple of bends in a road so out of the way it's not even on Google Earth, stands a collection of houses, homes to the neighbours who are frequent visitors to Peggy's converted long house (a *longére*). He is very much at home there and it's very obviously far more than a holiday home.
It's quite remote – the nearest village (and therefore the nearest boulangerie, tabac and supermarché) is the best part of an hour away on foot. Deer roam the nearby woodland and early morning chasseurs eliminate the roving wild boar who a few weeks earlier devastated a bean crop.
In a month which ranged from glorious sunshine to driving rain, we talked as the recorder rolled across the iron furniture on the decking, across the long wooden kitchen table, in the white mental gazebo near the pond. Eventually we turned to the subject of how we came to be conversing in this beautiful part of Northern France.

Holidays is how it all started, I suppose. It's a simple trip from Oxfordshire on the ferry. We'd be in the car, family holidays, travelling around, finding places to stay. Brittany was full of great campsites: it still is. I fell in love with the place and wanted to have my own house here, a more permanent base, a second home.

Eventually that dream came true...

If you drive down the peninsula to Quiberon on the Côte Sauvage, you pass through a little village called Penthièvre and on the edge of the town is the small house that Christine and I bought. I have Jethro Tull to thank for it. The village is in the northern part of the isthmus that sticks out into the Atlantic in Southern Brittany. It's very narrow, at one point just wide enough for a single road. On one side is the wild Atlantic; on the other, the much calmer Bay of Quiberon. There are sand dunes all around and oyster beds so deep you can walk over them at low tide. The area is known for its food, especially its shellfish. The buildings are fascinating too – a famous chateau, ancient fishing ports, modern spas, man-made catchments build a couple of centuries ago for storing live fish and molluscs and inevitably for this part of the world an array of military buildings that spans centuries.

There's also several fascinating little islands, some of which are nature reserves, just offshore. It's one of those places you can never tire off because it is naturally ever-changing.

Some of the places on the peninsula feel strange because so many of the houses are holiday-homes. A lot of the time the places seem empty and, of course, unless you are on holiday at the same time, you never ever meet your neighbours. Penthièvre is different because it's a place where people live and it's busy, lively because there's always traffic travelling through.

I have Jethro Tull, and Ian Anderson in particular, to thank for that. When the *Rock Island* album came out, he gave me a huge advance – around £55,000 – which I invested in a property I really liked, in a place I really liked.
**The album came out the week after Cropredy 1989, when Ian had been a guest during Fairport's set, along with Martin Barre.**

Having your own place, a second home, somewhere makes a huge difference. It's a way to escape – if it's somewhere like Brittany (not that there are many places like Brittany so far as I am concerned), it can change the whole pace of your life. We named our little haven Rock Island in tribute to where the money came from. The name had nothing to do with Leadbelly or Lonnie, though you're not the first to assume that.

With the hectic life I was leading and the various demands that were being made on me, it helped to keep me sane. Some places make you feel in a way invulnerable. For a while at least.

By 1995, I'd decided that it had become impossible to continue to balance the commitments of working with Tull and Fairport. Ian had always been understanding and helpful: as Fairport became more re-established, he arranged tours to avoid clashes, so I could be part of both bands; there were even occasions when Fairport toured with Tull, which certainly kept me busy all night, every night. He always made sure that Tull had no commitments that clashed with Cropredy, which left him available to make several appearances there as a Fairport guest – versions of him doing *Portmeirion*, *Matty Groves* and *John Barleycorn* with us have been released and they are all brilliant.

By the mid-nineties, though, Tull were as successful and in demand as they had ever; Fairport's workload was growing with two UK tours as well as tours in the US, Europe, Australia and festivals. I think both bands were due to record new albums. I just did the maths. When you look at a diary with over 200 days of the year earmarked for gigs and you add to that time for planning and running Cropredy, rehearsing, recording, doing TV radio and press, you realise it has reached the point where something has to give. It could be your health or your sanity.

I asked Ian for a meeting, nothing formal – we met as mates and I shall always be grateful for his approach. Certainly, if money had been my guiding factor, I would have stayed with Tull and asked Fairport to find a new bass player. As it was I stuck with the band I'd been part of the band I'd been in for quarter of a century. It was all amicable and of course there have been times I've worked with Ian since, like the Christmas album where I played on some tracks.

Christine and I had that house in Penthièvre for about fifteen years and aside from being our house in Brittany, it became a kind of holiday home for anyone in Fairport or other friends who wanted some time away. There was always someone there. We'd invite people to come and stay or people would stay when we weren't. There are so many memories associated with it. Some of course are linked to the inevitable mistakes you make when you first start living in a place that is culturally unfamiliar. You look back later and wonder how on earth you could have got that wrong because the other way of doing things has become so much part of your life. The priorité a droite rule is one example: for anyone who doesn't know, there's a rule in France whereby traffic has to give way to vehicles approaching from the right – no matter how minor the road they're on is. It's a bit nonsensical and apparently the law dates back to rules affecting horses and carts in the middle ages. The thing is, the rule isn't universally applied and where it is in force varies from village to village. That means every place you come to – generally it doesn't apply on the open road – you have to look for signs to tell you how traffic behaves there. The signs are, of course, unfamiliar because we have nothing similar in the UK: that's something else you have to get used to. After a while, it becomes second nature, like driving on the right (or 'driving on the wrong side of the road' as so many British visitors still refer to it).

We made friends with lots of people locally. Wherever I've lived, I've felt it was important to know and get on with the people who live around me. I also want them always to feel welcome in my home. We used to have lots of visitors from Britain too, as I said. Among them were our friends from Glasgow, Jack Westwood and his family. They came over to stay for a week. It was a lovely summer. Great weather forecast for the week they'd be there.

About a week before they arrived, Jack rang to say his parents Jack Snr and Belle had rented a gîte about ten miles from Penthièvre. So I made arrangements for us all to meet up for lunch. This was at the time I had my little catamaran, which I'd leave on the beach, near our house: when it was a nice day, I'd sail out to the little island, La Théviec. I thought that would be a good thing to do with Jack. He asked if his dad could come, because he loved sailing: he used to be in the sailing club in Glasgow.

His dad was in his mid-seventies (which seems a reasonable age to me now, but back then seemed quite old). I was a little worried but I knew the weather was forecast to be calm, and the island is only a short distance from the coast.

The day came. They arrived and off we went for lunch. A typical huge French seafood lunch, at the restaurant just down the road from us. Quite a lot of white wine was drunk in the process.

Then we went back to our little cottage, Rock Island. As forecast, the weather was great – sunny, a perfect wind, hardly a cloud in the blue sky. I asked Jack if he still felt like taking the catamaran out. His Dad leapt at the opportunity and said, "Can I come?" I checked he'd be all right and he assured me he would.

The only problem was, I only had two wetsuits and you do tend to get drenched on a catamaran, even in good weather. You're close to the water with little superstructure by way of protection. Being a good host, I gave them the wetsuits and accepted I was going to get sea-splashed and it wasn't going to run off me as usual.

It took us several attempts to launch the boat. We'd point it at the oncoming waves, with us behind it: every time a wave came, it would flip the boat over. I was thoroughly wet even before we set sail. More to the point, the experienced French boatmen watching us were thoroughly amused. We decided to use Jack senior as ballast, putting him on the boat with his arms and legs wrapped around the mast. It was a mad idea, but it worked, partly because he could see the waves coming and warn us, which was very much to our advantage, and definitely to his.

Like you do, despite experience and the fact I was wet and wearing normal beach wear, I somehow convinced myself that once afloat I would dry out in the warm sun. You don't. Even on calm days, the waves can be significant and you do get drenched: it isn't called the Côte Sauvage for nothing. Secondly, there is usually a wind and once you get any speed at all, there's a cold blast that cuts into you even on the warmest days.

Still we set sail. Three intrepid seaman with a grand tradition of British maritime history behind us. Those of you familiar with Fairport's back catalogue will know that alongside the Drakes and Nelsons, that history includes a great many disaster-prone captains.

Peggy's second session with Fairport had seem him singing harmony on a remake of an old ballad that had failed to make it on to *Liege & Lief*:

> For I was never a very good seaman
> Nor ever do intend to be

Along the way there have been little boats running aground on rocky islands, ships in distress, hard-pressed whalers, Chris Leslie's revisits to the story of Lord Franklyn, sailors who were

> Out on the bar
> And going too far
> With the red tide rising,

and *"mountain waves like avalanches"*. When Ralph McTell wrote an allegorical song about Fairport's long history, his choice of imagery was almost inevitable

> I want clear water from here to the horizon
> I want some calm sea for the journey ahead
> Fair weather as we head to the skyline
> A clear sky in the morning and every sunset red.

Once we were away from the shore, it was perfect sailing conditions: we got some speed up and sailed around the island and along the coast towards the Côte Sauvage itself. We were out for about two hours and, not having a wetsuit, I was starting to get a bit cold. I'd given both mine to the two Jacks. I said I thought we should go back because it's starting to get chilly. I was shivering by this point and I knew it would take a while to get back. And even longer to get warm.

Eventually we made it back, got the boat onto the beach and dashed straight into the house. The house had only one bathroom, though the toilet was separate in its own little area. We all needed showers to warm ourselves up, but obviously we'd have to take turns. We got Jack Snr into the shower first because we thought it was most important to restore his body temperature. It was important to get the salt off his skin too: the older you get, the more seriously it can affect you. Meanwhile Jack Jnr and I opened a bottle of Calvados and started drinking to warm ourselves up. Then Jack Snr came out and I carried on drinking with him while Jack Jnr went and got his shower. I'd got out of my wet clothes, but still felt soaked through and very very cold.

Eventually it was my turn to have a shower. By this point we'd finished the bottle and realised we were starting to feel hungry. While we'd been out, my wife Christine and

Justine Westwood had prepared a buffet. Lots of food and loads of bottles of Muscadet. It would have been great just to come in, sit down and enjoy it. We were in no state to do so and our limited facilties caused a longer delay than any of us would have wished for.

It was around seven o'clock we started to have our tea... Everything was going well. Then Jack Snr disappeared. He'd been gone a while and I said to Jack "Do you think you should check your Dad's all right? He seems to have been gone for a bit." Jack reassured me, saying he was used to drinking and he'd been a sailor: he could take it all in his stride.

I was still worried, but at that moment, the kitchen door opened and in came Jack Snr. He was a ghostly colour, somewhere between green and white. He said something undecipherable to his wife, Belle. Something like "Ivost myvorrez".

I said to Jack, "What's he saying?"

"He says he's lost his wallies."

I was none the wiser. No idea what he was talking about. It turned out "wallies" is a local Glasgow name for false teeth. He'd started to feel the effects of the sea and the booze and had gone to the toilet to be a bit poorly, in the course of which... the inevitable happened. He was holding on to the chain, and flushed the toilet by accident... not realising that his false teeth were in there along with everything else. He was now a gummy landlubber rather than an indentured seaman.

This was his first night in Brittany. They were here for the week. He had no spares with him. He spent the rest of the holiday surviving on fish soup and coffee. Far from the best way to enjoy the excellent cuisine of the region.

Particularly after the intensity and stress of Cropredy, the various members normally allow themselves a month or so off. For Peggy, that means heading for Brittany.

There's obviously a wind-down after Cropredy, post-mortems on what worked well and what wasn't so good. Issues people have raised. The financial side. The return of the field to its rightful owners – the Friesian cows. When my wife Christine and I ran the festival we could be tied up with things for quite a while afterwards, by which point you're already into next year's festival, planning for which starts almost immediately.

Nowadays it's easier. A week or so after the Festival, Ellen and I drive down to Portsmouth where Brittany Ferries operate their service to St Malo. I much prefer it to flying because there's no hanging about in airports, dashing from place to place, queueing to get into the plane and then squashing together for the rest of your journey. You sit in your car, steadily moving forwards until you drive on board and into your parking space. Then we head up to our cabin, drop off our overnight bags and head straight for the restaurant. The food is always really good, with a huge serve-yourself section for salads and so on. It's properly international too, so there's great French, English and Breton food to choose from. As you slip into the Solent and your food arrives, you begin to relax and you can feel the cares and pressures drop away. You pass the Isle of Wight, head out into the Channel, and, as the sun sets, the white cliffs of England's southern coast disappear into the distance.

The other thing that makes it better for me than a plane is the simple fact you can move around. You can go out on deck and enjoy the fresh air or the view: even in the middle of the Channel there's always something to see because it's so busy. On clear nights the stars are wonderful too.

After we eat, we'll head for the bar. There's usually some entertainment – a singer or a magician or whatever. I've seen some surprisingly good acts, though I've yet to offer one a Cropredy gig!

By the time you wake up next morning, you're in that big North Brittany bay, passing the Channel Islands, with the Breton coast in the distance on either side. It's a real sense of arriving and my little Brum/Breton heart beats faster. You watch St Malo come closer; you see all those lovely islands with their beaches and castles and tiny communities as you pull in to the harbour; then it's time to go down the steps and find your car.

Over the years, we've found one or two roadside cafes that we really like, so we tend not to breakfast on the boat: eating in a small local place with people calling in for coffee or a baguette has that sense of confirmation of being in Brittany.

I love Brittany. It's the open space, the huge skies, the glorious summers, the sense of history... actually not just history, something deeper, older even, rooted in the earth, pagan perhaps. There's a section of road up the hill from our house... when we come back from the UK or wherever, we turn off the main road... we're already in the countryside as you know…and then there's a section of road before you hit the hill that leads down to the house; so it's before you see the house for the first time and the fields on either side are open and wide and edged by trees, woodland that has deer in it; the road twists illogically across it; no walls, just open space and a huge dome of sky. That is just wonderful. That's one of the reasons I love it here.

When Christine and I split up, obviously the house was something that had to be divided. Ellen Thomas, my new partner, and I knew that we both wanted to spend a lot of time in Brittany and so we decided to start house hunting. We went round in our camper van, Thomas the Hymer, looking for somewhere that we both liked. We looked at lots of places and you know how it is, nowhere was quite right.

We'd become very good friends with a chap called Maurice Borgnic. He lived in the village of Kerne, which is a little further south down the road from the original house. He said he'd found three longères:  he was sure one of them would be just what we were looking for.

Longères are typical rural houses in Brittany and other parts of France. Low built and often single story with additional rooms in the eaves, they are literally extended buildings. Traditionally they provided shelter for humans and, in adverse weather, animals. To British eyes, they appear somewhat barn-like, solidly built against often fierce weather, usually without windows on sides facing the wind-direction, with a southerly aspect for the door and main windows. They tend to radiate from a central entrance which usually leads directly into the kitchen and general living area.

As the houses were already on the market, we took his advice and came over literally for a couple of days to take a look at them. We found a home, near Merlevenez. It was the third one we looked at. We immediately loved it. It was an instant decision to buy it. As it happened, the house was owned by the local estate agent, so negotiations could flow quickly and smoothly. The deeds were due to be exchanged on November 3, 2005. My birthday is November 2. So I asked the owner if there would be any chance of moving in a bit early to celebrate my birthday there. He gave us the paperwork to let us do that, which was both trusting and generous of him.

Our great friend Martin Driver borrowed Christine Pegg's jeep, and we hired a trailer for it in Banbury. We also had our car. In one trip we were able to get over everything we needed to survive. Luckily there's a great selection of supermarkets and household shops a short drive away. It was 'interesting' to do it so quickly but as people reading this will I'm sure have gathered, once I know what I'm doing, I tend to dive in at the deep end.

We celebrated my birthday here. Then we came back the following January. We didn't know anybody in the immediate village at the time. Ellen's French was good even then; mine was, at best, basic. We knew that local people would be unlikely to speak a lot of English, but we didn't want to be the Brits who descended on their community... maybe even just visited occasionally and left the house empty. There are quite a lot of those in Brittany; some are in little enclaves that can seem like ghost towns part of the time. We wanted to make it clear that we intended to be part of the community.

That's always been my approach whether it was in Sutton where I grew up, or Little Hadham in my first year with Fairport, or Cropredy, or Barford St Michael, or Penthièvre or now in Lesténo. When I joined Fairport, my local paper reported the story with the headline **Sutton man joins Fairport Convention**: it gave me a special feeling of local pride that they phrased it like that.

So, starting a new life in a new place, we wanted to begin as we intended to carry on. After all, all the houses in this community are on the same road. People must have seen us coming and going as we made trips over from England with stuff or went shopping for household essentials or had work done or things delivered. I felt sure they would be getting curious about us. I know I would have been. That's the way rumours start of course: mystery couple move into the empty house and people start to speculate.

We knew the best way to get to know people would be to have an 'open house' and invite them round for "apéro". We were happy with how the house was now looking. When you first move into a place, it takes a while to get things in order. I didn't fancy trying to explain my plans for home improvements in my basic French but we reached a point where you could see where things were heading.

We picked a date – one Saturday in January – and then Emily Pouncey printed about twenty invitations. We went out of the house and went up the hill by our gate – the house is on a left turn at the bottom of a hill – and put an invitation in the mailbox of the first ten houses we came to. Then we came back and did the same thing in the other direction. You've walked along both routes a lot while you've been here and you know you have to walk a fair way before you pass ten houses in either direction. We came back home knowing we'd invited our twenty nearest neighbours. All we could do now was wait and see who turned up on the next Saturday.

The invitation was "de six heures à ??". We'd no idea how many people would turn up, if indeed anyone did. We didn't know what they'd expect. As you've noticed, you don't see many people out and about on the streets in Brittany, so chances are there'd be people we hadn't even seen before, let alone met.

My nephew Richard Pouncey and his family came. Our friend John Carter, who was in Martin Barre's first band, was having quite a stressful time at work and had decided to come over with us for a rest. He didn't get much in the way of calm or rest.

We spent that week planning for Saturday, buying in food and drink, making the house as welcoming as we could, then preparing food and so on. It was quite stressful: it usually is when you have guests round for the first time... that multiplies, believe me, when you've never met them before, and you don't really speak the language yet. Both Ellen and myself were aware that this would be a very important first impression.

Everything was ready in plenty of time on the Saturday. Ellen had made some great food. I had glasses and corkscrew at the ready. I could say "My name is David. I am a musician from England. Welcome to our house" reasonably fluently.

At six o'clock prompt, there was a knock at the door. Unlike the British who regard the time on an invitation as something after which to arrive, the French, and particularly Bretons, are great believers in promptness.

I answered the door, expecting to welcome our first guests. There stood Marie-Therese, who lived in the big house over the road. We knew she was the village's oldest resident, someone held in great respect by everyone. I said hello politely, momentarily forgetting to speak French, and as I ushered her in, I noticed, behind her, in the dark, was a very orderly queue of people, all of whom had arrived, as instructed, at six o'clock precisely.

I really wasn't used to this and for a moment I wondered whether we'd moved into a place where everyone was affected by some kind of OCD. It's the local traits and customs that aren't in the guide books and so on that can catch you out. I soon realised that this was just the way things happen in Brittany: if you arrange a time, then that's the time you mean.

As most of the community filed past me in to the kitchen, I realised this was either going to be a great occasion or else a complete disaster. Certainly, getting to know so many people at once was going to stretch my basic French.

I went to Marie-Therese first, not only because she was the first to arrive but also because she was the oldest person in the village and merited that respect. She was in her eighties. I suspect she hadn't been there first – she was only over the road so didn't need to time her arrival – but had been put to the front out of deference.

"Welcome. What would you like to drink, Madame?" I'd made sure I had some really good wine to serve and had checked carefully what other drinks I should have available.

"S'il vous plait, monsieur, un peu d'eau".

A little water? This was worrying. I then thought, perhaps because she's getting on a bit, she doesn't drink. I'd brought through that big wooden chair, the Rock Island chair, as we call it, and so was able to give her a place of honour to sit right at the head of the table. I placed the glass of water in front of her.

Next was her son, Michael, who still lives over the road. I offered him a drink. He too said, just water. I thought, 'Oh ho, this could be a problem.' It was hardly likely to be a great party if people were drinking water. What if our local community were not only obsessive time-keepers but were also all teetotal.

I didn't have time to worry as more and more people seemed to be arriving, including a couple who would become very close friends Rosen and Nicolas, Bernard and Liliane Schmitt who live next door-but-one ("à côté mais un", as they say over here), the local farmer and his wife Claude and Marie-Renée – we were meeting all the people who would be important in our community life at once – in most cases for the first time. In the end we had thirty-six guests in our kitchen and dining room.

They didn't stick to water. I learned that accepting water on a first visit is a kind of etiquette. Soon my carefully chosen wine was being appreciated. Bottles of Breton cidre were being opened. Someone was asking about English beer. Ellen's buffet was going down well: as you've observed, cooking for French guests is pretty nerve-wracking, because they really know their food; Ellen's a great cook and, as we discovered, when the food is good they really appreciate it.

One thing about Breton people is that serving food as a buffet doesn't work. They don't feel right just helping themselves. You have to go round with plates and offer food. It's all really polite.

Trying to show how I wanted to fit in, I'd found a recipe for a popular concoction, petite punch: basically, it's white rum and sugar cane. I'd followed the recipe very carefully, so I knew it was exactly right. I'd made about half a gallon. I offered it to two or three people who all had the same reaction – "trop fort" – too strong. However, it seems the more you drank the less strong it became: by the end of the night, it had all gone and people were asking if there was any more.

Most of the smokers were women: they congregated in the lounge area.

John Carter and myself got our guitars out and were entertaining people with live music. We did lots of Everly Brothers, Beatles and Buddy Holly. It was a great evening. Everyone relaxed. We made a lot of friends. Everyone had a great time.

As you know, Dan Ar Braz is an old friend dating back to the time when he was briefly a member of Fairport. I've played on some of his albums; he recorded at Woodworm; he's joined Fairport on stage at Cropredy a few times. I thought as we were having a party it would be good to invite him. He's not local: w didn't expect him at the start.

It must have been around eight o'clock. People had eaten, had a couple of drinks, started to relax. Someone told me that it wasn't just a matter of us getting to know them: even though they were neighbours, a lot hadn't ever really spoken to each other before. I learned later that it was the first time a lot of these people had been in the same room together. It had a very positive happy feel. It was a true house warming... or even a heartwarming, you might say.

At that point Dan arrives. No fuss. He can tell that it's busy and Ellen and I are socialising. He just lets himself in and tracks us down. Suddenly everything seemed to go very quiet. Ellen said to me, "I bet that's Dan".

Now I've always known Dan was "Big in Brittany" but I'd never quite realised how big. People couldn't believe it. It was as if a Beatle or Dylan or Jagger or someone like that had walked into the room. He's regarded as a national treasure. Word starts to spread. There's a definite sense of "Is that who I think it is?" Quite honestly, you don't expect to pop to your new neighbours and stumble upon a star. He went round the room talking to everyone and, bless him, built me up as a fantastic rock bass player from England. They had probably never heard of Fairport or Jethro Tull, but they knew Dan. If I came with his recommendation, then I was obviously all right.

Actually, Peggy's bands were not entirely unknown, When Nicolas and his wife visited during my stay (I'd made tapas so it was my turn to be nervous about discerning Bretons sampling my cooking), he'd told me that he'd owned a copy of *Liege & Lief* since 1970. I pointed out that was the album before Peggy joined and received a very French response "Yes, but 'e knows all ze songs."

Eventually, Dan picked up a guitar and played.

"He knows Dan" people whispered, clearly impressed. That wasn't why I had asked him, of course, but the ar Braz connection did my standing in the village no harm at all.

My history with Dan goes back forty years.

At the start of 1976, the current line-up of Fairport broke up. I know that is a line which appears several times in this book, but that's because it kept happening. In fact, at the time it seemed to happen with frightening regularity. This was the *Rising For The Moon* line up of Fairport, a great band that I loved playing with – Jerry, Trevor, Sandy and Bruce Rowland on drums, though we had DM and Paul Warren on the kit before him.

As had happened at the start of 1972, that essentially left myself and Swarb to create a new version of Fairport. We had some bookings coming up. Swarb brought in Roger Burridge, a young fiddle player who I think he'd met at Sidmouth: that was the first time Fairport had a twin fiddle sound, though it turned out (surprise, surprise) that Swarb had an ulterior motive because it left him free to focus on vocals – with both Sandy and Trevor in the band he'd been edged out of that particular limelight. I turned, as I often do, to my mates from Brum and recruited Bob Brady, a keyboard player who'd been in Wizzard with Roy Wood; you might not think of keyboards as part of the Fairport sound but they had become that with Sandy in the band for a couple of years. Bob is also a really good singer. That still left us without a guitarist. This was worse than being without a guitarist when Richard left because we still had Simon: now we'd lost not only Jerry's lead guitar but also the acoustic guitars of both Trevor and Sandy.

It was Swarb who suggested Dan. Alan Stivell, the legendary Breton harpist, had done a tour of Britain – large venues including a gig at the Royal Albert Hall. This was in 1975. He needed a violinist and, of course, Swarb was the person everyone recommended. So he ended up doing the entire tour. Dan was the guitarist in Alan's band and had come over with him. Swarb was really impressed by his playing.

You know Swarb has quite an ear for great guitarists. He worked with Martin Carthy for a few years and continued to do so for the rest of his life. He joined Fairport because he loved Richard's playing when he was hired for the *Unhalfbricking* session. He worked with Diz Disley, Kev Dempsey, David Rea, all great players. He came back from the tour and one of the first things he told me was that if ever we needed a lead guitarist for Fairport, Dan should be our first choice, because he was perfect.

Of course, that requirement cropped up sooner than I think either of us anticipated. Fairport had moved away from its folk-rock route during the time Sandy and Jerry were in the band.

*Rising for the Moon* stands out as one of the few Fairport albums not to include a traditional track. Produced by Glyn Johns, it clearly took the band more in the direction of the FM rock sound that had proved so successful for Fairport contemporaries like Fleetwood Mac.

Bringing in Roger Burridge, who was a traditional fiddler and in some ways Swarb's protégé, and Dan Ar Braz, who was one of the leading figures in Celtic folk rock, showed that Swarb intended to steer Fairport back onto its folk-roots-based tack.

Swarb had been working on a solo album, which Island Records decided should become a Fairport album. It became, in the end *Gottle O'Geer*, which is another of those albums which doesn't really have a proper working band on it. If we were going to release another album, then we'd need a band to promote it. Dan was the name at the top of our list. That six piece version of Fairport appears on a picture on the back of that album, which is ironic really as Swarb, Bruce and myself are the only people from the band on the album.

Dan had been a Fairport fan for years and so was delighted to be asked to join the band. We rented the cottage two doors down from where I lived in Chapel Row in Cropredy and he moved over with his wife Zanu to start rehearsing. He really settled into Cropredy society, became a regular in both pubs and made a determined effort to learn to speak English. For some reason, he selected me as the person to help him with that and as a result everything he says in English, to this day, has a slight Birmingham accent.

I remember one of our neighbours once remarked that it was odd that I spoke English with the same accent as Dan. I didn't enlighten them that actually it was the other way around.

He had a great method of learning English. He always carried a notebook and whenever he heard a word or expression he was unfamiliar with, he'd write it down. The words, so long as he got a reasonable spelling, he could look up later in a dictionary. It's a great way to learn a language. For words he couldn't find and longer expressions – idioms – he used to ask me. I became very aware of how illogical some of our familiar expressions are; we all know what they mean but they are impossible to explain; why does it rain cats and dogs, for example. I expect you know, Nigel, because you had a University education, but I'm a Brummy who went to an ordinary school and left, as they say, with a swimming certificate and a CSE in woodwork.

One night we decided to have a darts game in our kitchen. We hung the dartboard above the boiler, which probably convenes all kinds of safety regulations but was the best place to have a decent distance to throw from.

Swarb was there and Sandy, who was no longer in the band but lived in Byfield, a couple of miles away. There was quite a lot of beer consumed. Dan followed me in the order of play and so each time I'd recovered my arrows, I'd pass them to him and say "Here you are, Dan" and he'd have his three shots, which were normally a lot more accurate than mine in that he was still capable of actually hitting the board with all three.

He was of course still dutifully noting down English expressions to look up later. No doubt he added such useful words as bullseye, diddle and oche to his vocabulary.
Oche is one of those which would have created problems when he tried to look it up since it's pronounced the same as hockey. Heaven knows what he would have made of someone scoring three 1's – otherwise known as a Bag O'Nails, like the sixties rock hangout in Soho where the Jimi Hendrix Experience played one of their first gigs.

Next morning, Dan, who somehow seemed to have a much clearer head than the rest of us after a night's drinking (a skill he retains to this day), called round with the words he hadn't been able to look up and tick off. I was still having breakfast and feeling bleary. Dan pulls out his notebook and asks "Peggy, what is this E.R.? I do not understand the meaning."

E.R. ? I'd no idea what he meant. Emergency Room – we hadn't been near a hospital. Our local post box was old and so said G.R. rather than E.R., so it couldn't be that. We hadn't been talking about exchange rates.

I told him I was sorry but I had no idea what he meant. "Last night when we were playing darts, each time you brought back the darts, you said 'E.R.'. What is it?"

The penny dropped (another phrase I'd tried to explain to him unsuccessfully) and I explained I was actually saying "Here you are." He looked puzzled. Why would I tell him where he was? He couldn't be anywhere else. I did my best to explain, but soon realised that here was another phrase English people understand despite the fact it doesn't make sense.

Dan was really meticulous, keen to learn the language properly. It must have been frustrating for him.

Certainly, since I've been spending more time in Brittany, I have learned my lesson and I know not to be judgemental when some phrase or saying doesn't make literal sense.

Just like English, French has developed hundreds of almost inexplicable idioms such as:

- Aux calends grecques *(On the Greek calends)* – never: when pigs fly
- Avoir le cafard *(To have a cockroach)* – to be depressed or have the blues
- Parler du loup *(To speak of the wolf)* – almost the same as speak of the devil, to talk about bad things and cause them to happen
- Reconter des salads *(To talk salad)* – to invent facts when telling a story or include unnecessary details
- Revenons a nos moutons *(Let's return to our sheep)* – we should get back to the matter in hand.

Dan loved being in the Fairports. He was a fan of the band before he joined of course. That's true of a lot of people who've joined the band since the eighties. Ric's always been a big Swarb fan and I know he came to the farewell gig at Cropredy, because he wrote a tune about it for his band Second Vision. Maart used to come to Fairport gigs when he was young and would offer to help carry instruments and equipment. He's retained that ability, which I think is a common trait of a lot of Fairports, to be both a professional musician and a fan of other musicians. He loves playing when it gets a bit rocky and I can easily visualise the broad smile he has when playing lead guitar behind someone like Robert Plant. Chris was a Fairport and Swarb fan and a local lad too, so he was always around at Cropredy – he's played with all sorts of different people there, starting with his brother and Steve Ashley.

Dan was both a Fairport member and a Fairport fan. Sadly, the line-up he was part of didn't last long for all kinds of reasons. It didn't really gel and always felt a bit unstable. It's been called a stop-gap, which is wrong: it was one of those line ups that simply didn't work out. What recordings exist – live and usually not well recorded – prove that we could be great on stage.

One sad time for Dan when he was with the Fairports was when he heard the news that the Irish songwriter Phil Coulter had died. There's a kind of bond, which I can't begin to explain, that exists between Celtic musicians. It doesn't matter where they're from Ireland, North America, The Scottish Islands, Brittany, Wales, Cornwall, Nothern Spain. There's a definite kinship that shows up in shared legends and mythology. Near Etel in Brittany there's an island called St Cado which has a Welsh chapel that's dedicated to the saint who was Prince of Glamorgan. There's all kinds of connections, including, of course, the stories of King Arthur that came to play quite a big part in my life for a while.

Unfortunately, the news Dan had got had become garbled. Fake news I suppose we'd call it today. Phil was in fact alive and well and living in Derry. In the belief that this giant of music had passed away, Dan decided to use the solo spot he had in Fairport's set each night to pay tribute to him. He played *The Town I Loved So Well*, which is a really beautiful song. At the end, he announced that it was sad to play because the man who wrote it had just died. This was before the days when everyone leapt onto their phones to check, but as no one else had heard about this, we all gave him a look which basically set, "I don't think so, Dan." Still, he did do a beautiful version of the song.

It's a shame the line-up with Dan didn't do many gigs. We did the Rockpalast in Germany and few other European gigs. There is some film of the Rockpalast gig which I think is still up on YouTube. We never recorded, though I know you unearthed a couple of live tapes when you were doing the Fairport boxset.

That drive to Germany was pretty scary. We rented a van from Aynho, which is just down the M40 from Cropredy. Our driver was George Tolley, who still had the nickname Big Slacks from before he lost weight. I think he lost quite a bit of weight when he was on tour with us actually.

Bert Jansch was with us and Ralph McTell's bother Bruce, who was his manager, asked me to keep an eye on Bert, make sure he didn't get into trouble or lose his money. We had about ten gigs booked and Bert was our opening act. I told Bruce that perhaps I wasn't the best choice to be someone's chaperone or minder or whatever he was asking me to be. I like to have a good time when I'm on the road, as I suspect you'll have gathered by now. Bruce said he trusted me and all he wanted was that I made sure Bert got from gig to gig, was on stage when he needed to be, got his money and didn't blow it on stupid things before he got home.

Of course, as a folk guitarist, Bert is quite rightly a legend, so Dan was particularly pleased that he could spend time with him and see him play every night. It would be fair to say that in terms of their approach to doing gigs Bert and Dan were probably polar opposites. Dan is very professional and wanted to make sure everything is right and the gig is the best it could be. Bert famously used to turn up to gigs without a guitar and just borrow one when he got there. That didn't apply on this tour. I made sure his guitar was in its case and back in the van before we moved on from each place we played.

### A wall that so divided us
### Brought down by people's will (Myths and Heroes)

Our first gig was in Berlin. We all got off the ferry and obviously everyone had bought duty free, which you could do in those days. It was a long drive to Berlin and the last section was on some very badly maintained roads, incredibly bumpy. This was still East Germany, of course, and it was obvious that things were not quite as affluent as they were in the west.

Bert was sitting on the back seat of the Transit, where, in the course of the journey, he'd proceeded to drink most of the bottle of duty free brandy he'd bought on the ferry. He scribbled a note, which he asked us to pass to George, who was driving. It was polite, but impossible: it read "Could you please avoid the bumps, George?". It made us smile, and we asked if he was OK because there was no way we could make the road less bumpy and we had to get to the gig. He smiled, raised his nearly empty bottle in a toast and carried on quietly keeping himself happy, occasionally singing a bit of a song. Eventually we reached the town where the first gig was next night. Fairport had a TV show before the gig, so after we'd done that, we went back to the hotel where we were staying and picked up Bert. Bert, left to his own devices, could usually track down a good source of booze. He had obviously taken advantage of his free time to do that. I hoped Bruce May couldn't expect me to keep an eye on Bert when I had to be in a TV studio a few miles away. He was OK and I'd decided part of my job would be, once we'd done our soundcheck, to make sure everything was in place for Bert to go on stage – mikes in position, chair for him to sit on, and so on. I think he was only using one guitar which he carried on, so no need for a stand for that.

Bert took his place in the back of the Transit as we head off to the venue. I notice he's again clutching the bottle of brandy. Except it wasn't the bottle of brandy: it was another bottle of brandy, which he proceeded to work his way through on the relatively short journey to the gig.

I tried to focus on those little jobs to make it easier for Bert when he got on stage. However, my clear sense of purpose kept being sidetracked by three separate, but related points:

• This guy, despite being a hero, clearly has a serious drink problem.
• Given the amount he's putting away, how's he going to play to a hall full of people??
• Bloody hell, he's our opening act!!!

By the time we reached the gig, Bert was swaying in a way that I've rarely seen anyone else do while sitting down. He kind of poured himself out of the van and into the hall, where he stood, with his brandy, while Fairport did their soundcheck. This would have taken longer than usual, because this was a new line-up and there were six of us and we were all keen to make sure our instruments sounded right.

Once we were happy with how we sounded, the chaps went off but I stayed behind and carefully set things up for Bert.

From the darkness of the hall came a recognisable if somewhere slurred voice – "You can take the stool away. I won't need it. I fancy playing standing up."

With the greatest respect to Bert, the state he was in, standing up was in itself a challenge: multitasking that with playing and singing seemed a Herculean ambition. I felt a sense of impending dread. I also thought about Dan who, as a guitarist, held Bert in such esteem.

I was tactful. "Is that a good idea? You still seem a bit wobbly. Maybe you haven't quite found your landlegs yet. You'd probably be better sitting down."

"Don't worry, Dave, I'll be fine. This looks like the kind of gig where you should stand."

That's fine, thought I, it may indeed be that kind of gig but there's quite a distance between what you should do and what, I suspect, you're actually capable of doing. Anyone who knew Bert will know that he wasn't someone you should argue with at the best of times. This most definitely wasn't the best of times.

At least I didn't have time to worry about how we'd go down with the audience – a new line-up of Fairport, with a bunch of faces the audience wouldn't recognise instead of Sandy, Trevor and Jerry, and a setlist which leaned heavily on instrumentals.

The setlist for the tour, and the subsequent UK tour which started at Southend Football Ground on May 1 began with three songs that spanned Peggy's time with Fairport: *When First To This Country* (from *Gottle o'Geer*), *Now Be Thankful* (their single from 1970) and *Hexhamshire Lass* (from *Nine*) after that it was instrumentals concluding with an epic version of *Sloth* (as good as an instrumental really) and Peggy's *Jams O'Donnells Jigs*. This was one of the very few line ups which didn't include *Matty Groves* in its setlist. In total this version of the band played fourteen gigs.

Bert was very wobbly. Sometimes he'd stumble into the mike stand or clunk it with his guitar. Sometimes he'd miss it altogether and wander across the stage, as if in search of it. He was such a great performer that it was really sad to see. What's worse, it continued throughout the tour and there was nothing we could do about it.

We could have taken his booze off him. We tried, which is something only fools or very brave men would attempt. As I've said, I'm not a brave man! Next time you saw him, there'd be another bottle. He could produce brandy like it was a magic trick.

Somehow we made it through the tour. Somehow Bert played a support set every night.

Once the tour was over, we went and caught the ferry home. The Fairports hadn't made much out of it: what we did make had to be divided between six of us and before that we had to pay our driver, the van hire, travel and hotel costs, and all our running expenses like food. Bert, on the other hand, had done well, collecting his gig fee each day and very sensibly squirreling it away safely. I hadn't really needed to watch to see whether he wasted any of it; he didn't. As a result, he very kindly offered to buy dinner for us all on the boat home. It made for a nice ending to the whole experience.

However, we got back to England, the customs decided to make us empty the van completely and then walk through and be checked individually. Our Duty Frees were scrutinised to make sure we hadn't gone over the limit. It was all very thorough and took quite a while. It was a hassle and things were a little fraught. We started to get cross. In its own time, the process concluded, and we were allowed back into our van to continue our journey home to Cropredy. We'd agreed to drop Bert off at home on the way. He was living in Putney at the time. As we left the port there were two hitchhikers, a bloke and his girlfriend. We had space and offered them a ride to London, which suited them perfectly.

We opened the van's back doors, stuffed in their rucksacks. They climbed into the spare seats. Off we went, eventually, thanks to another detour, dropping them off at Victoria Coach Station. They were a nice young couple and they were really grateful. It was effectively a door to door service for them for a journey which might well have taken them hours.

Next we dropped Bert off. Once more he was shaky on his feet. I felt embarrassed to deliver him home in such a state – it didn't occur to me they were probably used to it: I took the coward's way out (as I've said already, I'm not brave). I helped him to his front door and kind of propped him up there. Then I rang the bell and ran back to the van, leaping in as we made our getaway.

We got back to Cropredy and I have to admit we all breathed a huge sigh of relief as we opened the first bottle of duty free.

Next morning, quite early, the phone rang. It was Bruce May. "Peggy, have you any idea what happened to Bert's bag?"

This was the bag with his clothes and bits & pieces and, of course, the wad of money he's accumulated on the tour.

I said I was sure he had it when we dropped him off. We'd dropped him off at his front door. (I didn't mention the running away.)

Bruce explained calmly, "He hasn't got it now. He's no idea where it is. He doesn't know where he might have left it. He doesn't know when he last had it."

My first thought was "Shit! The hitchhikers." You know how it is: they seemed such nice people you don't want to think badly of them. Yet they were the most obvious answer. But surely we'd have noticed. And why would anyone want to nick a bag that, so far as they knew, contained two weeks' worth of folk-musician's dirty laundry?

There was another possibility – the hassle we had at the customs. We'd all been split up and I knew I hadn't checked whether Bert had his bag when he came out or whether he put it in the van. Bruce picked up on this and said he was going to ring Customs at Dover straight away. You can imagine, even though it wasn't my fault, I was starting to feel very responsible.

Bruce had figured out that he must have taken it with him because it had his passport in it.

A few minutes later Bruce rang back, Bert had indeed left his bag at HM Customs. Nothing had been removed. The contents were still intact, including all his money, his credit cards and his passport. They had arranged to courier it back to him at home and he'd have it in a couple of hours.

Another sigh of relief on my part. After all, Bruce had only asked me to take care of Bert in Germany and this had happened in Dover. The people there had, Bruce said, been very helpful.

Now you know why the Fairports always respect ancient British customs!!

I then asked Bruce if Bert was OK healthwise, because he'd seemed so shaky and out of it at times. Bruce told me that in fact he had to go into hospital for an operation. This was information I'd have preferred to have before we went on tour, but never mind. I asked what it was – his liver? his kidneys? because the amount I'd seen him drink was clearly going to do damage at some stage.

Bruce said "No he's got the Rockfords." Rhyming slang, for those who don't know... also known as "the I Can See Fors". Both of which, as you can guess, rhyme with haemorrhoids. That explained why he'd found the bumpy roads so uncomfortable and why he insisted on standing up at gigs: it also explains why he was downing nearly a bottle of brandy a day. These days we'd call it self-medicating.

Let it serve as a warning: next time you're with someone and you think they're a pain in the arse, they might literally be!

For readers unfamiliar with rhyming slang, it involves substituting a phrase that rhymes with the one you want to use. An example would be "apples and pears" instead of "stairs". Sometimes the second half, rhyming, section is lost, making the connection even less obvious – "look" is "butcher's" (a truncated version of "butcher's hook"). Recent times have seen references to contemporary culture provide even more oblique refernces: in this case it's to the 1970s James Garner detective series *The Rockford Files* (or alternatively The Who's hit *I Can See For Miles*).

I really felt for Dan, because he'd been in the middle of all this. He really worshipped Bert – he was a fan and he respected him as a musician. It was one of those feet-of-clay things. They always say it's risky to meet your heroes. When all the pieces came together, the way Dan tells the story these days, it was obviously a case of meeting up with Bert at a really bad time in his life. I won't say seeing him at his worst because that sounds judgemental and most nights his playing was as brilliant as you would expect. It was one of those Wizard of Oz things – amazing on stage but pull back the curtain and it's just a man.

He's still one of Dan's heroes, though, and rightly so.

Which brings us back to our house-warning party, where Dan, who to me, as well as being a brilliant guitarist, was a mate and a member of that large club labelled Ex-Members of Fairport Convention, to all my neighbours in the house that night was an absolute hero, the sort of person they would never expect to meet.

After the Fairport line up with Dan broke up, we went our separate ways. Swarb, Bruce and myself continued with Fairport: Simon, who worked as producer on the *Gottle O'Geer* album, decide the time was right to rejoin and that created what was the "final" Fairport line up, certainly the one that played the Farewell tour before Simon and myself had second thoughts about calling it a day. Dan returned to his native Brittany and his solo career really took off. Eventually he put on a show called *L'Héritage des Celtes*: the live shows had sixty or seventy musicians including Breton Bagads and guest musicians. He made a series of great albums that reawakened Breton consciousness.

During my stay in Brittany, Peggy took us to see the astonishing arrays of standing stones at Carnac. The best way to see all of them – especially on a chill wet day like the one when we visited, is on the little road train that runs around. Between the informative commentaries, the music that played in our headphones was taken from Dan's albums.

His music from the early nineties, especially the Héritage tunes, have become the unofficial national anthems of the Bretons. If you want a measure of his esteem, while Fairport have been celebrated by having real ale named after them, Dan was celebrated with an exclusive and very expensive signature whisky by Eddu, Brittany's top distillery... signed bottles and everything.

Dan kept up his contact with me and the Fairports and he'd often come over to record at my studio in Barford St Michael, which meant I had the privilege of playing on some of his albums. He's one of my best mates in Brittany and certainly the one I've known longest. He was obviously one non-local person who had to be on the guest list of that first party in my new home.

That first time when Ellen and I were 'at home' to our neighbours was a great evening, a proper start to feeling part of the community we'd moved into. The fact that it coincidentally had a role in bringing that community together for the first time was an unexpected bonus. It also had a legacy. Each year since, in June or July, there's been a get together for the people of the village. The last six have been in our garden and garage.

A village fête if you like – which is ironic because even though it's a French word fête doesn't have the same sense as it does in Britain. We have a barbecue and live music – friends come over from England and local musicians come and play.

We put up three big tents. We even have a regular band: Paul Mitchell comes over with Jimmy his drummer; annA rydeR and Noel her husband come and play. John Watterson came over for one of them. He does a Jake Thackeray show and works as Fake Thackeray. One of the songs he does is Jake's version of *Le Gorille*, a song by Georges Brassens that Jake translated into English. Someone there was a Brassens fan and they performed this great bilingual version, which was a unique performance. We've had The Churchfitters doing a set. Dan's played a few times. James Wood's played. Pat O'May, who's a famous French rock guitarist. Inevitably, it ends up as a massive jam session.

I realise that Peggy has just listed three of the artists who have been, like Fairport, members of the *Excalibur* family, another Breton connection.

Dan was responsible for that. When Alan Simon was planning his *Excalibur* concept, the first album, which came out of work he'd been doing with students around the various Arthurian legends, Dan suggested he came over to demo the songs at my Woodworm studios. Alan is a fan of Fairport and when I suggested that we could ask the Fairports to play in the recordings he really liked the idea. This was back when Dave Mattacks was still in the band. So we became the house band first for the recording and then for the live performances which have included stadium gigs and tours in Germany and France.

It's not as outside our comfort zone as you might expect because although it's a French concept, it's bilingual. A lot of the lyrics and some of the music were written by James Wood who's an English musician from Sheffield who lives in Nantes. Fairport became part of the whole *Excalibur* thing. It's three or four years now since we were part of it but we did a lot of work on the project from 1998. There were five albums we played on and a lot of live shows. It's part of Fairport that even some of our most dedicated British fans are pretty much unaware of, yet it's huge in Europe. The shows are massive, often done in costume, broadcast on TV.

The first live performance of *Excalibur, Le Concert Mythique* in Rennes on October 12, 1999 saw Fairport playing alongside The Prague Symphony Orchestra, a Bulgarian choir, Le Bagad Kemper, with guest singers that included Roger Hodgson from Supertramp, Gabriel Yacoub, Nikki Matheson and Jacqui McShee. The show was narrated by the actor Jean Reno.

The Rennes performance was in a huge arena, over five thousand people, a massive cast, great lighting... and less than a day's rehearsal, which even then some of the performers couldn't be at. Didier Lockwood, the famous jazz violinist, could only make it for the gig itself... so when you see him on the DVD he's playing the stuff live for the first time. He's an electric violin legend and you can see the sparkle in Ric's eyes when they get to do a duet.

It's been an exciting thing to be involved with and certainly it's meant we've played with some very famous singers and musicians from genres you wouldn't associate with Fairport. We also played some songs in our own right, as Fairport. Because the whole *Excalibur* thing didn't really take off in the UK, a few years ago we put out a CD called *Fame and Glory* which was a compilation of Fairport tracks from the five albums we'd made as part of the project. We used the original recordings that means, like *Rosie* and *Gottle O'Geer*, it's a Fairport album with an extensive list of guest musicians and singers.

We included an *Excalibur* sequence in our set at Cropredy that year, with a lot of guest musicians from the albums. We played it in the most horrendous storm, relentless rain. Jacqui McShee sang *Morgan le Fey* about the witch who is Arthur's arch enemy in one of the most spectacular lighting storms I've ever seen. It was apocalyptic, to the point where we were checking how dangerous it was for people to be in an open field. The answer was "not very" because of all the natural lightning conductors around. It was as if God had decided to lay on special effects for us. There's this dense black sky, rain like showers of arrows caught in the spotlights, an endless rumble of thunder, and lighting streaking across the sky so bright it dazzled you and all this accompanies Jacqui intensely cursing the knights of the round table...

*Blood fire war and the Devil at my side*
*I shall avenge her tears*
*Falling like rain.*
Eat your heart out, Rick Wakeman.

That's typical of the Fairport/Cropredy symbiosis. We've been able, because we're musicians who run a festival, to persuade people to play who might normally shy away from a gig with an audience of 20,000 in a remote Oxfordshire village. Of course, as the reputation of our Cropredy Convention has grown, we get really big names – including some very surprising ones – asking to do the festival. It's led to some unique performances over the years and it's definitely one of those festivals people don't want to miss because of that.

At Cropredy, especially in the early years, many of the guests would be people the Fairports had played with either on gigs or in recording sessions. It's easy to say, "Look we have this festival. You'd love playing there. Can we do a deal where you'll come?" I sort of used the same approach to ask people to come and play to a much smaller crowd in our garden. It started off as a little get together but it's developed into a mini local Festival, something of an event, which we've now called Festeno.

I'm reminded of the three pre-Cropredy gigs which began as a village fete held in Ann Crossman's garden. As the local group, Fairport were asked to play. Word got round and after a couple of years Fairport fans started turning up. It was the little acorn from which the mighty oak of Fairport's Cropredy Convention grew.

There are similarities, though it's important it stays an event for people in the local community and a few invited guests. It's very much their occasion. Just like those garden parties, the toilet facilties are our downstairs loo. Mind you, the men don't use it. They just wander over to a convenient hedge. It's a French thing, possibly the result of the lack of mains sewage – most of the houses here have septic tanks. Of course, men who do that at Cropredy get shouted at.

Pee on the hedge, one ponders….

On a post of the long, converted barn which serves as a carport and performance area, there was evidence of that year's event – a setlist of Beatles classics (and an aide-memoire complete lyric for *Come Together*) that makes me wish I could have been there to hear it. I remarked to Peggy it was good to see that he is still very much a Beatles' fan.

I'm reading a biography of Paul McCartney at the moment. After all these years, I discovered his first electric guitar was the same model as mine – and he found it a swine to play too. Like me, he moved from guitar to bass, though in his case not because there was a better guitarist – him and George were both really good even early on – but because there was no one else willing to do it. McCartney's still one of my favourite bass players and his style of playing was a huge influence when I changed to bass and joined The Uglys. Being left handed he bought what became known as The Beatle Bass – the Hofner 500 – because, being uniform in shape, he could play it left-handed and it didn't look upside down, which most basses do. They are designed for right-handed playing.

I've owned two Beatle basses in my time. The most recent I bought six months ago, after we decided to create a Beatles tribute band for a one-off gig in our garden. We called ourselves The Bretles – the Breton Beatles – we all had copy Sgt. Pepper outfits and fake 1967 moustaches – even annA rydeR. Mine wasn't fake, I just shaved what I already had into shape. That's my only regret about that event – the tash looked great on the day, but later when everyone else was peeling off their fifty-year old facial hair, I was still stuck with mine.

We had a pig roast, good weather, lots to drink. About a hundred people came.

Some come from England, mates of course, not fans. It's a gathering of friends, not an audience. Alan and Wendy Grant come over most years. He helps with some of the manual preparations. Particularly Alan is responsible for putting up the three big tents we use. He got the job because Wendy told me he was very good at erections. Martin Driver, who is a professional driver and can be spotted ferrying artists between the Cropredy backstage and the Banbury hotel each year, always comes over. Anthony John Clarke who I tour with each November and who's been the compere at Cropredy for the last couple of years always comes with his wife, la belle Julia: last year AJ was one of The Bretles: he and I were in competition as to who should be Bald McCartney. (I had the bass. I won!)

Mike and Lynn Lucas also come. You may remember the Mikron Theatre Group, which was based on canal barges and performed at Cropredy in the early days: they were the people who started it all up. They live about twenty miles away from us in Brittany, quite a coincidence. There's also Tim and Hilary Dieu la Belle-Fontaine, a great name: they are English and play saxophones and other musical instruments. They come and help out, swelling the sound and generally contributing to the atmosphere. The way I know them is because Tim used to run the insurance company that insured my boats.

It was a great gig, a lot of fun. It's something we do every year. So, yes, in a way, it is like the way Cropredy started on a smaller scale. I just won't let it get out of hand this time. It's great to be able to host something that allows people to get together. In our village, there are none of the usual things you might expect to bring people together – no bar or tabac, no shops, no square or a central well. There isn't even a church or chapel, aside from a strange little place about twenty minutes into the woods beyond the old German "holiday homes". People just don't have cause to meet up.

You don't bump into people. The houses are far apart, and most have plenty of ground either attached to them or adjoining them. You can go for a walk on your own land, which is what most people tend to do. You seldom see anyone walking along the road...and when they do, as you and Christine discovered when you wandered beyond the village, they tend to arouse suspicions. It you look as you travel round, there are generally no pavements, except in towns.

It's quite strange to think that the event we held to introduce ourselves became the basis for a sense of village community life which hadn't existed before. Ellen and myself tend to be given the credit for that, but in fact it's everyone, if the whole community hadn't decided to pull together, we wouldn't have made any difference at all.

It's kind of gone full circle. We wanted a house in Brittany and bought the one we have because we liked it. So we were coming because of the house. But we wanted to be part of the community. We didn't realise there wasn't a community, just people living on the same stretch of isolated French road. Then they got together so we could meet them and they became a community. More importantly they became our friends. Now we come to our house to see our friends.

On the ferry over it's always something that's on my mind: what's been happening while we've been away; how everyone is; what's the local news; how soon will we see them. For some, that last one is easy: as soon as they see us pull into the driveway they come round to say "Bonjour" and give us all the latest news.

Barford... Banbury... Brittany... the key places in my life for the last forty odd years, over half my life.

Brittany, though, is very special to me, a lifestyle I love, and it's so peaceful.

## Chapter 17

# Closing Time
*We ain't your Rolling Stones*

### You ain't goin' nowhere

As we reach the end of Peggy's account of the ins & outs and ups & downs of his life…full of incident and accident, we turn our attention from things that happened to things that didn't happen, at least in the way intended.

Let's start with a couple of days after he joined Fairport Convention and the rather bizarre attempt at band communal living at The Angel, Little Hadham.

At the time it didn't seem that wacky really. It was one of those myths about bands that they spent all their time together – like that knocked-through set of terrace houses that The Beatles live in in HELP! There was also the 'getting it together in the country' thing that bands of that era were fond of…

Traffic, Led Zeppelin, The Increds and The Band all famously tried it reasonably successfully. The first two included mates of Peggy from his early Brum days; the last were a Fairport favourite whose members included Rick Danko, Peggy's all-time bass-player hero, whom he chose to represent on the cover of *Myths and Heroes*, which was itself a parody of *Full House*, the album created when Fairport first moved into The Angel. Still with me?

Richard Branson of Virgin Records developed The Manor as a residential recording facility with the same ethos in mind. Famously used to record Mike Oldfield's *Tubular Bells*, it was tried out with recording for *Rock On* by The Bunch, a studio only group that included Fairport members past present and future – though surprisingly not Mr Pegg (who had the mumps at the time). When he came to set up Woodworm Studios, Peggy followed a similar model with cottage accommodation next to a studio in a remote Oxfordshire village.

The small towns and villages of Oxfordshire obviously have a particular appeal for the Fairports – Swarb and I chose Cropredy; then I moved to Barford. After that, when I moved to Banbury it seemed like a metropolis. Where I live in Brittany is even more off the beaten track… in fact the road down the side of the house is a beaten track. Ric chose Bloxham. Chris is in Adderbury. Fairport's offices are in Chipping Norton, where Simon lived for many years. Sandy and Trevor lived in Byfield.

Fairport themselves had first tried the experiment themselves on the album before Peggy joined, the acknowledged classic *Liege & Lief*. Island Records had arranged for them to stay in a Queen Anne manor house at Farley Chamberlayne to recuperate after their M1 accident, rebuild the band following the tragic loss of their drummer Martin Lamble, and develop the concept they had for their new album.

*Liege & Lief* was literally just before my time. As I joined, it had just come out and was being celebrated as one of the most important releases of the year. Anything I could say about its creation would be either hearsay or supposition on my part. I joined the band because Ashley left, apparently because he wanted to continue being totally focused on folk-rock in terms of updating traditional songs and the rest of the band wanted to have a wider focus. Sandy had also left, though she would rejoin the band a few years later, which I was really pleased about because out of that came one of my favourite Fairport albums *Rising For The Moon*, which, as you've said, is about as far away from *Liege & Lief* as the same band could get.

Though we were obliged in many ways to move on and leave *Liege & Lief* behind us – anyone turning up to see the *Full House* Fairport expecting to hear *Liege & Lief* would have been pretty much disappointed, we carried on playing a couple of things: *Matty Groves*, of course, which became the band's anthem in a way, the last song in the set – it even provided the name of our record label, Matty Grooves; I think we also did *Tam Lin* for a while and maybe *The Deserter*.

Of course, we're returned to all the songs on that album in recent years at Cropredy and even in our core touring set. *Crazy Man Michael* is always a great song to play both for us and for the audience and I love the new arrangement which features Chris Leslie's whistle solo. We also did new studio versions of *Tam Lin* and *Farewell Farewell*: at the Cropredy that marked Fairport's fiftieth, Ashley Hutchings put together a set within Fairport's set featuring the music from the time before I joined, including a lot of *Liege & Lief*, but I insisted that the current line-up of the band return to the stage, without any guests, to play our version of *Farewell Farewell*. It was a way of acknowledging that despite all the changes of personnel, musical direction, record labels and whatever, we're still a band that respects its own heritage.

We all moved into The Angel and it worked well. We had some great times. It was convenient. Some amazing music was produced. Even after Richard officially left the band he continued to live there. He was still living there when the accident happened.

The Angel may have had its faults when we first moved in, but after the accident it was totally uninhabitable. We didn't look for another place to share. I think we'd learned our lesson about that. Instead we all found places independently. I went back to Sutton, where I bought a house.

That was in the days when I had hair.

Peggy suffered what seems the common fate of folk-rock bass players – premature baldness. A man with a finely tuned sense of humour, he's normally on top of any joke, but there was one he didn't get.

Maartin Allcock used to keep coming out with the expression "I don't believe it". I'm not a big TV watcher and so I never got the reference to *One Foot In The Grave*.

One night we played St George's Hall in Bradford. That's where you and I would meet up when Fairport were on the road, of course. We loved St George's Hall, a wonderful Victorian concert hall, but huge. A point came when it was too big a venue for Fairport really. Anyhow, it closed down for massive refurbishment, so we had to look for somewhere else to play in West Yorkshire. That's how we ended up playing The City Varieties in Leeds, which is a beautifully preserved music hall, which a lot of people reading this would recognise because it was where the BBC filmed *The Good Old Days*. We still end up visiting Bradford on every tour, of course, but that's so we can go to The Kashmir which is Fairport's favourite curry house. On one occasion, because visiting Bradford tied in with a day off, Maart ended up having four curries there in a day. I don't recall whether it was the same occasion as this incident, though.

The night before that gig I'd happened to see *One Foot In The Grave* on tele and realised immediately how much I looked like Richard Wilson playing Victor Meldrew. I realised at that moment that Maart and the chaps had been taking the piss out of me, whenever they used that expression. I decided not to make anything of it, pretend I knew all along and shared in the joke.

So we went on stage at St George's, where there was enough light shining on the audience to be able to see the first rows quite clearly. I remember being struck by the fact that it was quite a young audience. So as I was putting on my bass, I realised that we must be attracting new people, people who perhaps weren't aware of the history of the band. It's more obvious these days, but that occasion for some reason made an impression on me. It was obvious there were people who had got into Fairport after we reformed and went full time again in the eighties. Some of them would not even have been born when I joined the band.

Because the audience had so much light on them, I spotted, in the third row back, a couple who were obviously students. As I was putting on my bass, the girl nudged what I assumed to be her boyfriend and very clearly said "Look, it's Victor Meldrew."

I'd missed the joke.

I didn't believe it.

## Deserted Island Discs

Island Records did their best for us. Chris Blackwell was really on our side. But if you look back at those early samplers – *Nice Enough To Eat* and *Bumpers* and so on – they're full of people who had hits... Cat Stevens, Free, Jethro Tull, Traffic. That's something the Fairport crowd never did – even before I joined, so for once no one could claim it was "all Peggy's fault". Even though our albums were well received by fans and critics, they never sold in huge quantities. Several of them are regarded as classics today, but the music business is a business and ultimately like every business it's about making money. As far as a record company goes, we're not a money-making concern. If you look at those gold discs in the other room, they're nearly all for things I did with Jethro Tull. The Fairport one is for accumulated sales of all our albums on Island.

There is a photo of Fairport being presented with this disc. It's taken at Swarb's cottage in Cropredy with the *Rising for the Moon* line up and Richard Thompson. Very soon after the photo was taken, Island decided not to renew Fairport's contract.

To be fair, they'd stuck with us for a very long time. If you look back at some of the other acts who were on the label in the late sixties, when I joined, they'd been 'let go' long since. The industry had changed enormously in those ten years that Fairport were with Island. Punk had happened: the label were quick to embrace that – which was quite right because it had always been a label that spotted trends and got in there early. It was formed to bring reggae to a British audience and its faith was rewarded when people like Bob Marley started having hits.

They'd kind of given us a last chance – actually, they gave us several over the years, but without ever putting it in those terms – when they let us do the *Rising for the Moon* LP, which was quite a a change in direction – no traditional songs, and a much more radio-friendly sound. It was closer to the things you heard on FM in the States.

Lots of other bands had reinvented themselves and become part of the FM radio scene – members of Linda Ronstadt and Rick Nelson's country backing bands had regrouped and become The Eagles; Pink Floyd had moved from hard-on-the-ear psychedelia and produced AOR classics; the Bee Gees discovered disco and never looked back at the lights going out in Massachusetts: blues band Fleetwood Mac had emerged from its ashes with *Rumours*.

All of those little independent labels, like Island, that had been started up by people who were really into music, like the bands that were on them, had either vanished or become so successful that they now were the industry that they'd been created specifically not to be part of. They were taken over by suits: the accountants moved in and they were the ones making the decisions.

The staff had changed too. People we'd known, including Chris Blackwell, had moved on from Island. Essentially, if we went into the Island offices, no one had any idea who we were, never mind all the things Fairport had achieved. If they looked us up and saw our revenue stream for the label, they probably wondered why we were still signed to it. So almost inevitably, the day came when we weren't.

I don't blame them. In a way they had no choice. The fact was we weren't selling any albums. We'd reached a peak in terms of sales a while back and the number of our records that people actually bought tailed off. It doesn't matter how much credibility an act has, or how much the music press write about you, or even how many people turn up to see you play live, so far as a record company are concerned, if you're not selling records, they're not interested. In those days, as well, if you didn't have a record deal, you didn't have the support and back up you needed to go out on the road and tour. It was a sort of circular argument.

The last album we did for Island was the *Gottle o'Geer* album. That started out as a Swarbrick solo project. Again, the band was essentially the two Daves, me and Swarb, with Bruce Rowland on drums. It was the same as it had been in the lead up to *Rosie* – we'd had a strong line up, with a couple of great records; then we went through a number of line ups that didn't work out and never made any records. We were recruiting people we knew to play with us – Bob Brady, Roger Burridge and Dan Ar Braz.
Like *Rosie*, *Gottle o'Geer* is an album that doesn't actually feature the band shown on the sleeve. Thirteen other musicians are credited with contributing to the record, among them Martin Carthy, Robert Palmer, Gallagher & Lyle and Simon Nicol.

Simon agreed to produce it. That was the best thing about that album: it led to Simon rejoining Fairport. Perhaps he realized he'd missed us. Perhaps he just had a great time being with us again. Perhaps he was just at a loose end. Anyhow Fairport got him back and he's been with the band ever since, of course. If he hadn't rejoined, I doubt whether Fairport would have continued. He's the link to the past... though we do have an ongoing thing about the longest serving member of Fairport. On paper, it's me, because the time Simon took out from the band, but it feels like it should be him because he was there at the start. I've been a member of Fairport convention for 47 of its fifty years, and Simon still has the ability to make me feel like the new boy!

We were dropped by Island but fortunately Phonogram picked us up. So, we signed what they used to call a 'multi-album deal' with a company that was one of the 'Big Three' players in the record business. We were a quartet – Swarb, Simon, me and Bruce. We'd no idea at the time that we'd be the final Fairport line-up – but then when we knew we were the final line-up, we didn't know that we wouldn't be.

These days all those labels that Fairport recorded for – Polydor, Island and Phonogram – are part of Universal, which wasn't even in the record business back then.

Now you see compilations that pull together that entire early history of the Fairports... the first twelve years. I suppose anyone who's got into the band more recently – and we are picking up new fans all the time, a lot of whom weren't even born when all this stuff we're talking about happened – will not differentiate. But changing labels was a big thing back then. We had been an Island band since the early days of the label: being an Island band had a certain kudos – it was what later became known as an indie label; it had a huge amount of credibility; it was like being featured in serious music papers or being on Whistle Test or being asked to do a Peel session [all of which Fairport did, of course – Ed]. Although we signed to a major record company, we were signed to a label which still tried to give the impression of being indie.

Philippa Clare, who had taken over a managerial role, did a great job for us. She came out on tour with us. She even came to Ireland when we did some dates over there. At the end of one of the gigs on that tour – I won't say where, except it was in the North – all of us were scared to go and get our money off the promoter. Philippa was braver, though she said afterwards that when she went into the backroom afterwards to close the deal, the first thing she noticed was that he had a gun on the table.

Vertigo – famous for its "mind-blowing" op art label – was the consciously prog label of Phonogram records. It was a pioneer in boutique specialist labels that disguised their affiliation to major conglomerates that might alienate fans of a particular genre. Formed in 1969, its roster was deliberately credible, including acts like Colosseum, Black Sabbath, Status Quo, Uriah Heap, Patto, Gentle Giant, Aphrodite's Child (Greek prog giants whose line up included Demis Roussos and Vangelis) and the Sensational Alex Harvey Band. Rod Stewart's early solo albums, too, offered a more acoustic folky approach than his work with the Faces: in fact, the label boasted several acts that might be called as folk-prog: Magna Carta, Fairport-escapee Iain Matthews, Dr Strangely Strange ("The Emerald String Band"), Mike Absalom and Alan Stivell (whose studio band included one future Fairport member Dan Ar Braz).

The two albums we made for Phonogram were very much back in the electric folk mode. I'm not sure you'd call them folk-rock, because they were more about playing folk songs on electric instruments, which is not quite the same thing.

I actually really like them still. The Fairport four-piece was a tight little band [Peggy interrupts himself, catching what he's said and laughs]. We were tight in more ways than one. It was a boozy little band. Hardly surprising that the second album kind of focused on the theme of drinking.

Tipplers Tales (the position of the apostrophe, if used at all, appears arbitrary even on the original vinyl copy which offers Tipplers, Tippler's and Tipplers') is hardly a concept album – though it could easily have become so. Starting with a drinking song (preceded by a tune called Jug O'Punch), it offers the rebirth myth of John Barleycorn, the saga of a three maidens who drink away their maidenheads (and another who had a gynecologically dubious approach to restoring hers) and a pair of Peggy tunes entitled The Hair of the Dogma/As bitme.

I love those two albums. They were heavily influenced by Swarb, of course: very much his choice of material in the main and certainly largely his arrangements. There's a lot on those two LPs that we still play today as part of our regular set. Ye Mariners All, for example, was one of the songs we had a new version of on our last album. They were good songs and great versions of them.

We're lucky because Chris Leslie has got the same vocal range as Swarb and musically it's easy for him to do the songs. He's such a fan of Swarb's and worked with him a lot, particularly in Whippersnapper: there's a lot of Swarb's spirit in his performances of the songs. That's not just a good thing; that's a really important thing.

It's not always easy emotionally, of course – like when he had to do *Rosie* at Cropredy when Swarb was no longer able to sing or after Swarb died. It's like deciding to do one of Sandy's songs or one that Trevor brought to the band, it's a far more complex decision that just saying "can we play it?", because of course we can, we can play most things: it's very important to do it justice. So, the songs from *Bonny Bunch* and *Tipplers* are special to me because that was the bit of the old Fairport (if I can put it that way) that carried over most naturally.

There's great playing throughout both albums, especially Swarb, who knew most of the songs and had recorded some of them in the past with other people. It was stuff we enjoyed playing. Bruce had a lot of input, creating percussion rather than drum parts. There are some pretty complex arrangements too – nothing like the arrangements I was going to have to tackle with Tull very soon but pretty involved nonetheless.

It's a shame they kind of get overlooked. I suppose that's partly because they sat between The Island Years and The Cropredy Years. Also, they were unavailable for quite a long time, whereas the Island stuff and the Woodworm recordings have remained pretty constantly available one way or another. If you look at what we played on the road or at Cropredy from 1978 to when the Fairports reformed, you'll see the core repertoire is pretty much drawn from those two LPs. We toured Australia with both of those albums and some good live recordings came out from those tours.

Each was both recorded at Chipping Norton Studios, where there was a great engineer called Barry Hammond. We made each album, start to finish, over a ten-day period. I don't mean just the recording, but the whole thing from finding the material through arranging and rehearsing, all the recording and mixing, ten days, start to finish. Both albums included an epic set piece that displayed Swarb's fiddle prowess and occupied a sizeable chunk of the playing time, *Tippler's Tales* included *Jack Orion*, an English retelling of the Orpheus legend, in one version of which a virtuoso fiddle player ends up bedding the gorgeous lady of the manor and acquiring a decent pair of socks into the bargain (can't imagine why it appealed so much to Dave Swarbrick!). It's Child Ballad 67 and Swarb had previously recorded it with both Bert Lloyd and Martin Carthy. The epic on the album before that, their first for Vertigo, was the Napoleonic saga that became the title track.

*The Bonnie Bunch of Roses* was a song the Fairports had tried before. It's a bit of Fairport history that almost frames my first decade. We recorded it in 1970, when Richard was still in the band. Although it's on the *Full House* CD, it was recorded after that album was finished. We did it at Gold Star studios in Los Angeles, which is where Phil Spector had made all his classic hits with the Ronettes and the Crystals and so on. It was Joe Boyd's idea. It was an honour and a fantastic experience to go there. Some studios acquire a legendary status not necessarily because they are great studios but because of the great music that was made there. To a musician or a music fan, they are places to visit like great churches or museums – Sun in Memphis, Muscle Shoals, Chess in Chicago (and I told you the story about going there), Abbey Road, of course. To be able to record there is a thrill it's hard to describe: you feel yourself as part of history because of all the things in your head that you know have happened there.

By the time we recorded there, it had become pretty run down, though it still retained some of the old magic. I don't mean in terms of equipment or facilities: it was nothing like as good as the studios we were used to using in London – but it was Gold

Star. It meant we could say we'd recorded where The Crystals did *Da Doo Ron Ron* or Tina Turner belted out *River Deep Mountain High.* There we were ploughing through some 19th century English ballad about Napoleon... Fairport Incongruous might be a good description.

Despite its being a confusing and arcane narrative (it's actually a fragmentary imagined conversation between the Duke of Reichstadt (Napoleon's son, later Napoleon II) and the Empress Mary Louise, his widow), the song proved very poplar in its day. It was written in the 1830s by George Brown. As Bert Lloyd pointed out, the song was one of the Greatest Hits of its day. Its popularity lead to its being found in the repertoires of traditional singers across the British Isles, Ireland, Australia and North America. There are recordings of it by most of the greatest source singers of British folk – Harry Cox, Sam Larner, Phil Tanner, Walter Pardon, Seamus Ennis, Noah Gillette, Louise Holmes, Fred Jordan, Bob Copper, John Galusha and Cyril Poacher – and the biggest names of the Revival followed suit by perpetuating their interpretations: check out recordings by Bert Lloyd, Ewan MacColl, Shirley Collins, Bob Davenport, Louis Killen, Nic Jones, Barry Dransfield, Martyn Wyndham-Read, Paul Clayton, Martin Simpson, Maddy Prior, Pete Coe, Dolores Keane, De Danaan, June Tabor and Sam Lee. What Fairport didn't know was that the old folk song had been recorded by, of all people, Glen Campbell – at Gold Star Studios.

I don't think the song was ever part of our core repertoire back then, though I think we did it on the John Peel radio programme. When we had our restart on a new label, Swarb suggested we go back and give it another shot. That's when we started playing it in public.

It's a good point to end on because it kind of sums the Fairports up. It's an ending that also turns out to be a beginning. That's happened so often and in so many different ways. Hardly surprising our anthem says, "When you really mean it, it all comes round again."

## A tree with roots

There's one place that will always be the spiritual home of Fairport – Cropredy, with their songs about its history, the church bell named in their honour and that field, some special place, where each second week in August it all comes round again. Like the bell which will toll long after everyone in that field is gone, there's a landmark which serves as a good stopping point in our saga.

Jonah's Oak. It's part way up the left hand side of the field... just by the gate that's only open to let people out at the end of the festival. That oak tree has become part of Fairport history. Jonah's ashes were scattered there – Johnny Jones who was the first Cropredy compere and a great friend to the band. It's quite right that Ric named a tune in its honour.

It's become a focus for people who want to remember Cropredy-goers who are no longer with us. Several people have put up memorial plaques. All the names there are people who've worked at Cropredy or are special to people who've played there. It's only a matter of time before all our names are added to it. That, oddly, is quite a comforting thought, being permanently remembered in such a special place.

There's one for my brother. We scattered his ashes there on the Sunday after Cropredy, 2017. It was the last thing we did on that 50th anniversary weekend and it seemed a very suitable moment.

It's a great thing that something memorial like that exists in a place that for a week or so every year changes from being a place to where cows graze to being somewhere to hear great music and see world-famous performers and a certain folk-rock band I joined 48 years ago.

The cows aren't there then, of course.

They always refuse to buy tickets.

POSTSCRIPT
# Bring it all Back Home
### *On the 14th of May, at the dawn of the day*

Where were we?

Ah, yes, dear reader, travelling by train (if not by steam) from Yorkshire to Banbury on Bonny Black Hare Day, 2018.

It's a journey I've made many times since 1980, the year, you'll recall, of my first interview with Mr Pegg. There were journeys from home to University in the seventies, trips to the first Cropredy Festivals in the early eighties (before it extended to three days and a car was needed for the tent and all the necessary stuff for the weekend) and visits to Cropredy, Barford, Chipping Norton et al to work on various Fairport-related releases, books and boxsets.

It's the release day of the latest Fairport album, whose creation exactly runs in parallel with the volume you now hold in your hand.

*What We Did On Our Saturday* is the double CD of the Fairports' performance at Cropredy 2017. Thanks for the title, by the way, Nigel.

It's great to be able to put out these recordings because they brought together a lot of ex-members of the band. Everyone significant who's still around, in fact, with the exception of Jerry Donahue who's still recovering slowly in hospital.

We were talking about the possibility of going through the tapes to see if there was anything good enough to release when we headed off to Brittany to start work on this book, if you recall. They're not tapes any more, of course: that's just me showing my age. I know you said at the time it would be great to have a permanent record of the performance because it was historic, not just because it marked Fairport's fiftieth.

There's many a slip twixt tape and chip, as Peggy's remark reminds us. The various Cropredy releases down the years provide an overview of the development of recording technology and the record industry.

The first Cropredy release was *Moat on the Ledge*, an LP on Fairport's own label Woodworm, owned by Dave and his wife Chris, who handled Fairport's releases until the next century. The potential for small independent labels as an alternative to the music industry corporations had been a spin-off of the "just-do-it" approach of punk.

I don't suppose we thought of Woodworm as an indie label, though of course it was. That and later Matty Grooves were Fairport's own labels really. Lots of big name acts have formed their own labels since – I suppose The Beatles were the first with Apple – often because big record companies want nothing more to do with them. It's a genuine alternative. Island Records had started out as a little independent label, originally leasing its stuff to bigger labels.

[Early Island hits included *My Boy Lollipop* and *Keep on Running*. Both were released through Fontana. The Spencer Davis Group, who had a hit with the second song, were mates of Peggy from Birmingham. The song, however, reflected Island's musical roots, having been a reggae hit in Jamaica for Jackie Edwards.]

Island was a reggae label – reggae, ska, bluebeat or whatever name was being used for it – hence the name Chris Blackwell chose for it. In the late sixties, he got into the folkier side of British rock. Which still works, because Britain's an island too. Fairport were one of the first bands on the label. Free, as well, who were a great band. Plus lots of singer songwriters, most of whose records I was lucky enough to be invited to play on – John Martyn, Nick Drake, Cat Stevens, Richard and Linda, Sandy, The Incredible String band towards the end of their career. Heavier bands too – Traffic, Tull, King Crimson, Renaissance, Mott the Hoople, ELP. Of course, they were the key label for reggae too – Bob Marley, Toots and The Maytals, Sly & Robbie, Jimmy Cliff.

If you've read this book (and not just flicked to the final chapter to find out whodunnit) you will realise how many of those Island names have close links to Peggy's story.

Eventually, they started picking up the more credible glam acts like Roxy Music and Sparks... and even later some punk bands. Loads of successful acts who had hit singles and top selling LPs and huge profitable tours. And then there was the Fairports, who'd been on the label forever, never having a record in top twenty, releasing albums that fans and critics loved but not enough people bought. Eventually someone at Island noticed. We couldn't carry on keeping our heads down.

It was only a couple of years after Island dropped us that we decided to call it a day ourselves. Out of that, of course, grew Cropredy Festival and all that followed... right up to the CD you're holding in your hand. As ever in the Fairport story – and mine too as I hope has become obvious – when one door closes another usually opens.

As technology advanced, so did the various releases that documented Cropredy Festival. The first release from it had been *Moat on the Ledge*, a vinyl album. The next four Cropredy audio releases were cassette only and pretty much 'what-you-heard-is-what-you-get', including in one case the complete Fairport set. At the same time, a series of VHS videos was released: they were out of Fairport's direct control and pretty rough-and-ready; the kindest description today would be to say they are of archivist interest, technically speaking. In 1998, the first Cropredy CD was released: *The Cropredy Box* documented, over three CDs, the epic concert, spread over two days, in which the band told its history over three decades.

We'd recreated earlier line ups of Fairport at Cropredy before but this was the first time we'd reformed in a chronological sequence. Ashley Hutchings wrote a great linking narrative for the whole thing. Because it was such an event, we wanted people to have a permanent record of it, so Cropredy releases moved into the CD era. It still works as an album; it has some great performances by Fairport and others; the excerpts from Ashley's linking monologue work really well too.

Rolling Stone magazine, in an in-depth article about "essential live releases", compared it favourably with The Band's *Last Waltz*, which had similar ambitions.

For last year's concert, we knew we had to squeeze fifty years of Fairport into a three-hour set and as a result we decided not to plug the latest album *50:50@50* at Cropredy. That was quite a bold move: it had happened once before, when we'd just released *Gladys' Leap* and Swarb wanted nothing to do with it.

We also wanted to make the most of having so many ex-members of the band available. As you pointed out, it was the first time the line-up on the first LP had performed together since 1968. Judy Dyble is someone who comes to Cropredy every year, but we seldom see her up on stage.

Just in case anyone is thinking of writing to correct me, I know we have to 'bend the rules', when we reconvene previous Fairports at Cropredy. Because of the various Fairports who've been "blown off the mountain", there's no line-up before 1986 that we can now fully recreate. There's always going to be subs, like DM playing Martin Lamble's part or Chris While singing what Sandy sang on the original recording.

But we had Iain and Judy, Richard and Simon and Ashley playing those very early Fairport songs, including a great version of *Reno Nevada* where Richard heads off into a solo. I put the Cropredy setlist together, but handed over the choice of material for those early years to Ashley Hutchings, who picked all the material that represented the time before I joined the band.

The way Cropredy has been recorded changed too over the years. It started out literally with a Revox standing on the mixing desk and a pair of mikes pointing at the stage. This was the way live bootleg albums often got recorded, of course – someone in the audience sneaking a tape machine into a gig and hoping to get a decent recording of the gig. The big reel-to-reels were transferred to cassette for the purposes of storage. We eventually moved on to DAT and made digital recordings straight from the desk. With only a couple of exceptions, we have recorded Fairport's set at Cropredy every year. Those invaluable tapes became the basis of the second Fairport Convention box-set *Cropedy Capers*, which I put together in 2004, as the follow-up to *Fairport UnConventional*.

I still love that set. It covered so many aspects of the Festival – the various returning band members, the surprise guests, the non-Fairport songs that we play as one-offs, the things that went perfectly and even the odd example of when things don't go quite according to plan.

It was planned to mark the first twenty-five years of Cropredy. As it turned out, it was also a document of the years when Chris and I ran the Festival. It came out the year we split up and as a result the management of Cropredy changed.

It remained within the band's control, of course, but purely by chance that box set documents a very definite era.

Although we record every Cropredy – not just for ourselves, some of the other acts who appear there have released things too, including The Dylan Project and The GPs, of which I'm a member – we never plan to release the recordings. Sometimes, there's something special – like the time we had a sequence of great female singers paying tribute to Sandy or Roy Wood and Richard doing *I Heard It Through The Grapevine* – when we feel the event merits a permanent record (no pun intended). The new CD is very much in response to public pressure. People kept asking whether we were going to put out a CD or even a DVD. Luckily, everyone was up for it and no one put any blocks on using any of the performances, which has happened with Cropredy releases before. Just as they progressed from vinyl and cassette releases to CD, Fairport's official video releases moved from VHS to DVD. Again, releases were occasional. The title of one (*Off The Screen*) reflected a physical change at the Festival.

The big screen came in the year Jools Holland appeared. It was part of his requirement. We couldn't have his band on screen and not Fairport, so we bit the bullet. Obviously, people liked it. It meant everyone in the field could get a better than front row view. Once we'd got the whole thing operating smoothly, we released that DVD which is literally a copy of what people saw, live vision-mixed, on the big screens that night.

People were asking whether we could do it again this year, but it's another of those advancing technology things. The big screen technology is fine for the field and was good enough for DVD. The quality simply doesn't stand up to Blu-Ray and HD requirements.

Documenting fifty years of Fairport is no mean task. Every single fan would have a wish-list of songs they wanted Fairport to perform, songs they think they ought to perform, and a handful they simply have to perform. Partly because of the number of people returning from the early years, when the band's line-up was more volatile, there was a focus on the early material. *Liege & Lief* was performed almost in its entirety, for example – though not perhaps in the way one might expect.

We'd played *Liege & Lief* complete and in sequence as a Friday night set a few years back. There was no point in repeating that. It was important to feature what is the most important album in the band's history. What we tried to do was not to treat it as a sixties archive recreation – Fairport has never been its own tribute act – but rather show why it remains the most important LP in our back catalogue.

Some of the songs featured the band that made the album – with Chris While singing and Chris Leslie playing Swarb's parts.

They did *Come All Ye, Lark In The Morning, The Deserter* and *Tam Lin*.

We wanted to do the version of *Farewell, Farewell* that the current line-up created for *By Popular Request*, though this performance had the benefit of double drummers as DM joined Gerry. As Richard remarked, he left the stage so we could play two songs he wrote. *Crazy Man Michael* is a Fairport perennial: we played the version from our current setlist, as we did with *Fotheringay*.

*Matty Groves* speaks for itself. It's the one song that's never really left the setlist since the band recorded it. Since the early eighties, it's always been the last song in the set.

First performed on stage on September 20, 1969 at Van Dyke's club in Plymouth, Fairport's version of Child Ballad 81 survived the many line-up changes of the seventies and continued beyond their official Farewell, though early Cropredys into the band's continuing story. It has the unique distinction of being the only song Fairport have played twice in the same year at Cropredy. They've released over twenty different versions. A conservative estimate attributes over 5,000 different performances of the song to Fairport.

Like everyone in Fairport, Peggy is very aware of the band's musical legacy.

As I said before, it's an amazing treasure trove of songs: all the great music written by people in the band – Sandy, Richard, Swarb, Chris; all the songs that great songwriters have given us – Ralph, Steve T, PJ, annA, plus songs by Dylan, Leonard Cohen, Joni and so on; all the songs from the folk tradition that the Fairports turned into rock songs. What's great is that we can go back to those songs and we don't have to be like a tribute band faithfully recreating the recordings. That's a pop approach. We reinterpret them and rearrange them to suit the current band, which has always been the way folk music works. Folk songs evolve and continue to develop over time. The version of *Matty* on *What We Did On Our Saturday* is quite Appalachian with Chris' banjo and some almost acapella sections: over the years it's been folk-rock, acoustic, heavy metal, reggae, almost country... I don't think we ever did a disco version, but somebody probably has a tape that proves me wrong. It's not just the amount and quality of material that's available but also its flexibility.

There's a huge range of music on *What We Did On Our Saturday*, but that doesn't just reflect our music from the past fifty years. It's music that's still valid. Fairport – and this sounds odd for a band famous for updating centuries-old songs – have never been about nostalgia. We always look forward with an eye on the past. Of course, as we get older, the future isn't what it used to be.

Speaking of looking forward, it's worth noting that by most systems of reckoning Cropredy 2019 will be the fortieth anniversary Cropredy. Any plans?

We've never really marked Cropredy's own anniversaries – I mean the Festival, not the village which has its own red-letter dates like most places in Britain [should that be Red and Gold letter days?] – though we have used the Festival several times to mark significant band anniversaries, like the 50th, or the 30th, or the anniversary of Sandy's death a few years ago. I don't think we have anything planned to mark Forty Fairport Cropredy Years, but we're always open to suggestions and no doubt we'll receive quite a few in the course of this year.

The Cropredy Mass Conversion to Fairport's half-century began with a short acoustic set, introduced with the distant peeling of the Fairport bell in St Mary's tower: it featured, over four songs, everyone who's been a band member since the great reConvention of 1985. As Peggy says, allowing for the inclusion of the occasional substitute, all the classic line-ups featured during the Saturday set and the CD, bar one.

The *Rising for the Moon* line up. The album we made and the couple of years we gigged are among my favourites. We toured the world and came back to rehearse for the album at Cropredy Village Hall – a contrast that kind of represents Fairport in a nutshell. There can't be many acts whose gig list in a year includes huge halls in Japan, legendary venues in the USA, Sydney Opera House, The Royal Albert Hall and the local village school!

Last May, when we played The Union Chapel in London on the precise anniversary of the very first Fairport gig, Sally Barker joined us to sing *Rising for the Moon*, as she did at Cropredy later in the year. It struck me then, and the thought makes me sad whenever I return to it, that only DM and myself are still playing from that great collection of musicians. Jerry Donahue is very slowly recovering from the stroke he had in 2016: Sandy, Trevor, Bruce and Swarb are all gone. The other song from that LP we did at Cropredy was *White Dress* which Ralph McTell sang.

I'm glad that's on the CD, because Ralph has always been a great friend and supporter of Fairport, which is why I was so pleased he agreed to write the introduction for this book. He's always at Cropredy, even if he seldom comes up on stage.

My journey to Banbury this 14th of May, is almost complete. The land levels as we move from the North, through the Midlands, passing the Cotswolds on the right and Cropredy on the left.

It's a week short of a year since I was on a train heading to London to join Fairport as they celebrated the precise anniversary of their formation fifty years before. It's six months since I made this same journey prior to the trip to Brittany where most of what you have read was written: then as now, a train failure and an enforced change of service at Birmingham New Street delayed my arrival by over an hour.

Oxford countryside yields to urban development.

Fresh rails curve in from the left and parallel ours.

The smell of chocolate drifts from the Nestlé factory.

And now my train approaches Banbury.

Peggy's red Fiat 500 awaits in the car park.

Everyone's happy and things are just fine.

# Now Be Thankful...

Peggy wishes to give a huge thank you to Nigel Schofield for his patience, tolerance and knowledge and fab poems. He has transformed my ramblings into a book which I am incredibly proud of. A labour of love above and beyond.
Thank you Nigel.

Thanks:

To Mick Toole for the layout and for all his great artwork and design for Fairport over the years

To John Garrad at Akcent Media for his printing expertise

To Kevin Smith for fab photography

To any photographers whose work is not attributed

To Christine Schofield for her tolerance and attention to detail

To Ellen Thomas for all her love, help and support

To everyone within these pages... if you've already read it, you will know why

And, finally, to you dear reader for purchasing and hopefully enjoying this book.

Cheers,
Dave Pegg. June 2018.

# INDEX

*'The time has come', the bassman said,*
*'to talk of many things,*
*of picks and strings,*
*and Zeppelins,*
*and waiting in the wings'.*

As the conversations flowed like wine over many hours in Brittany, it was Ellen Thomas who observed that with so many characters in it, this would be a book that really needed an index. She was right, of course: so here it is – an A to Zappa of over 450 individuals mentioned in this book. I've avoided indexing bands (because it soon becomes obvious where to turn if you want to read specifically about Tull, Fairport, The Dylan Project, The Uglys, The Campbells or the GPs), song titles or places. References to Tull, Jethro are to the seed-drill inventor.

There are a couple of fictional characters among the many famous and not-so-familiar names. The chap who has joined Fairport on stage at almost every gig since before Peggy joined the band has, I think, merited his own place in this list.